Checking Theory
and
Grammatical
Functions in
Universal
Grammar

OXFORD STUDIES IN COMPARATIVE SYNTAX
Richard Kayne, General Editor

Principles and Parameters of Syntactic Saturation
Gert Webelhuth

Verb Movement and Expletive Subjects in the Germanic Languages
Sten Vikner

Parameters and Functional Heads: Essays in Comparative Syntax
Edited by Adriana Belletti and Luigi Rizzi

Discourse Configurational Languages
Edited by Katalin É. Kiss

Clause Structure and Language Change
Edited by Adrian Battye and Ian Roberts

Dialect Variation and Parameter Setting:
A Study of Belfast English and Standard English
Alison Henry

Parameters of Slavic Morphosyntax
Steven Franks

Particles: On the Syntax of Verb-Particle, Triadic and Causative Constructions
Marcel den Dikken

The Polysynthesis Parameter
Mark C. Baker

The Role of Inflection in Scandinavian Syntax
Anders Holmberg and Christer Platzack

Clause Structure and Word Order in Hebrew and Arabic:
An Essay in Comparative Semitic Syntax
Ur Shlonsky

Negation and Clausal Structure: A Comparative Study of Romance Languages
Raffaella Zanuttini

Tense and Aspect: From Semantics to Morphosyntax
Alessandra Giorgi and Fabio Pianesi

Coordination
Janne Bondi Johannessen

Adverbs and Functional Heads: A Cross-Linguistic Perspective
Guglielmo Cinque

A Handbook of Slavic Clitics
Steven Franks and Tracy Holloway King

XP-Adjunction in Universal Grammar:
Scrambling and Binding in Hindi-Urdu
Ayesha Kidwai

Checking Theory and Grammatical Functions in Universal Grammar
Hiroyuki Ura

Checking Theory and Grammatical Functions in Universal Grammar

Hiroyuki Ura

New York   Oxford
OXFORD UNIVERSITY PRESS
2000

Oxford University Press

Oxford   New York
Athens   Auckland   Bangkok   Bogotá   Buenos Aires   Calcutta
Cape Town   Chennai   Dar es Salaam   Delhi   Florence   Hong Kong   Istanbul
Karachi   Kuala Lumpur   Madrid   Melbourne   Mexico City   Mumbai
Nairobi   Paris   São Paulo   Singapore   Taipei   Tokyo   Toronto   Warsaw

and associated companies in
Berlin   Ibadan

Copyright © 2000 by Hiroyuki Ura

Published by Oxford University Press, Inc.
198 Madison Avenue, New York, New York 10016

Oxford is a registered trademark of Oxford University Press

All rights reserved. No part of this publication may be reproduced,
stored in a retrieval system, or transmitted, in any form or by any means,
electronic, mechanical, photocopying, recording, or otherwise,
without the prior permission of Oxford University Press.

Library of Congress Cataloging-in-Publication Data
Ura, Hiroyuki.
Checking theory and grammatical functions in universal grammar / Hiroyuki Ura.
p. cm. — (Oxford studied in comparative syntax)
Includes bibliographical references and index.
ISBN 0-19-511838-3; ISBN 0-19-511839-1 (pbk.)
1. Generative grammar.   2. Grammar, Comparative and general.
I. Title.   II. Series.
P158.U7   1999
415–dc21   99-23232

1 3 5 7 9 8 6 4 2
Printed in the United States of America
on acid-free paper

*This book is dedicated to my parents, Sachiko and Atsuo Ura,
and to my wife, Maki,
with all my love.*

Preface

In this book I attempt to investigate some consequences of the theory of formal feature checking under the minimalist framework, developed and elaborated by Chomsky (1992, 1994, 1995a), by studying a wide range of data, some of which are unfamiliar in the Principles-and-Parameters theory, data which are drawn from a variety of languages in the world. More specifically, through analyzing "grammatical function splitting phenomena," in which some of the grammatical functions alleged to be associated with a certain grammatical relation are split up, I explore the significance and implications of the theory of multiple feature checking, which is a possible extension of the Agr-less checking theory proposed in Chomsky (1995a). The main purpose of this book, thus, is to demonstrate that the minimalist program gives a natural explanation to a wide range of data found in a variety of languages, in a very consistent way with a limited set of parameters.

In GB theory, grammatical relations (GRs) were regarded as not absolute but derivative (cf. Chomsky 1981 and Marantz 1984), following, basically, Chomsky's (1965) idea that they should be structurally derived/defined, and the widely held assumption was that an argument with a particular GR assumes particular functions in syntactic respects. According to Chomsky (1981), an argument with the structural relation of [NP, S] is regarded as the "subject of the clause," and, hence, the argument assumes all grammatical functions (GFs) associated with "subject" (such as the abilities to induce subject agreement, to bind a (subject-oriented) reflexive, to control the missing subject in a subordinate clause, in a rationale clause, etc.). It is noteworthy that, because structural relations are uniformly defined in this framework, GRs and GFs ought to be structurally defined in a uniform fashion. (See Ura (to appear c) for some retrospective discussion on the theory of GRs/GFs and their relation to the theory of abstract Case in the GB era.)

From the viewpoint of Chomsky's (1994a, 1995a) minimalism, this structural determination of GRs and GFs is conceptually problematic, because no structural relations can be defined in a uniform and absolute fashion any longer in this framework owing to the abandonment of the "conventional" X-bar theory due to its lack of conceptual necessity. In this framework syntactic structures are not absolute, but relationally defined entities. Then, we lose the conceptual basis of the definition of GRs/GFs. How can we define these relations/functions in the Chomskyan minimalist theory? Moreover, the GB-type approach to GFs encounters empirical problems, too. Many researchers (e.g., Keenan 1987, Comrie 1989, Bhat 1991, and Palmer 1994) have revealed that some GFs that an argument with a particular GR is believed to bear are not absolute and invariant ones, but they vary from language to language or even from construction to construction in a single language. These kinds of phenomena (what I call GF-splitting phenomena) in which GFs are split up can hardly be given any consistent account under the theory that considers GFs to be uniformly defined.

In this book I will try to demonstrate that, by minimally extending Chomsky's (1995a) feature-checking theory, we can establish a cogent theory of GRs/GFs which is free from the conceptual and empirical problems that the GB theory of GRs/GFs bears. The leading idea is that a GF results from a certain feature-checking relation with a particular head. For example, it will be argued that the ability to control a missing subject results from a ϕ-feature checking relation with T (= Infl), and the ability to bind a subject-oriented reflexive results from an EPP-feature checking relation with T. Naturally, other types of feature-checking relation may result in other grammatical functions.

Given the theory of multiple feature checking to be elaborated in this book, under which a checking relation holds not between categories but between individual formal features, this idea can provide a consistent account of various GF-splitting phenomena. This theory may give rise to a situation in which a head H has formal features, each of which differs from the others in terms of the checking relation into which it enters. Now suppose that due to a certain parameter, all formal features of T must be checked by a single element in a language L_1, while they can be checked separately in a language L_2. Then, we can expect that some GF splitting appears in L_2, because the situation is possible in L_2 where DP that has a ϕ-feature checking relation with T does not check T's EPP-feature. If this situation happens, the DP has the ability to control, but does not have the ability to bind a subject-oriented reflexive. In L_1, on the other hand, DP that occupies at Spec of T has both abilities, because that DP checks all of T's nominal features in L_1, and, hence, it has all "subject" properties. In this book I will show that similar situations (i.e., GF-splitting phenomena) can be cross-linguistically found in a variety of constructions (active/inverse voice alternation in Bantu and Apachean, anti-impersonal passive constructions in Lango and Quechua, dative/quirky subject constructions in Japanese/Korean, Tamil, Icelandic and other languages, locative inversion in Bantu and Japanese, etc.). Furthermore, I will present a analysis of ergativity and various phenomena involved in it along the same line, because some kinds of GF-splitting are well attested in languages with ergativity. In this regard this book can be viewed as a minimalist approach to establish a theory of grammatical functions/relations (and ergativity) in Universal Grammar.

This book is a substantially revised version of my disseration, which was submitted to the Department of Linguistics and Philosophy, MIT, in February 1996 (Ura 1996b). Technical details aside, most of the core ideas presented in the original work remain the same in this book, although many minor revisions have been made throughout. The chapter on ergativity has been added, and data and discussions have been added in the other parts. Of the data introduced in this book, most notable are those on Japanese locative-subjects. Chapter 2 and chapter 3 in the original dissertation, which dealt with long-distance raising constructions, were totally omitted from this book. As I argued there, there is a good possibility that these types of constructions involve multiple feature checking; however, the discussions on them were passed over here because of their scarce interaction with grammatical function splitting phenomena (see Ura 1997c for updated analyses of those constructions under the theory of multiple feature checking).

Portions of this book were presented at Tohoku University, Tokyo Metropolitan University, Utrecht University, Osaka University, University of Connecticut, Tokyo Gakugei University, Yokohama National University, MIT, Risshyo University, Kwansei Gakuin University, Kanda University of International Studies, Miyagi Gakuin Women's College, and Nanzan University.

Kawanishi, Japan   H.U.
April 1999

Acknowledgments

It is my greatest pleasure to acknowledge my intellectual debts to Noam Chomsky here. Had it not been for his constant support and warm encouragement, I would not have been able to complete this book. Most of the leading ideas developed here emerged from extensive and constructive discussions with him. I am also much indebted to Ken Hale and Howard Lasnik. Ken, explicitly through discussions and implicitly through his work, gave me the courage never to yield to less-familiar languages with exotic phenomena such as deep ergativity, inverse voice, VOS word order, and so forth, and Howard was always very considerate to prompt me to organize my messy thinking into a theory.

I would especially like to thank Chris Collins, Toshifusa Oka, and Akira Watanabe for many stimulating and rewarding discussions. Many aspects of this book have greatly benefited from their valuable and helpful comments. I wish to thank Richard Kayne for giving me the opportunity to publish this book. Special thanks go to Peter Ohlin and Cynthia L. Garver at Oxford University Press, U.S.A., for their helpful assistance.

Thanks are also due to Jun Abe, Jonathan Bobaljik, Yoshio Endo, Danny Fox, John Frampton, Koji Fujita, Naoki Fukui, Heidi Harley, Dianne Jonas, Masatoshi Koizumi, Martha McGinnis, Hideki Maki, Alec Marantz, Roger Martin, Shigeru Miyagawa, Yoichi Miyamoto, Norvin Richards, Mamoru Saito, Vaijayanthi Sarma, Carson Schütze, Hiroaki Tada, Daiko Takahashi, Yuji Takano, Koichi Takezawa, Chris Tancredi, Wei-tien Dylan Tsai, Ken Wexler, and Mihoko Zushi for their useful comments/suggestions/discussions on materials presented in this book. For their beneficent guidance over the years, I am particularly grateful to Taro Kageyama and Seisaku Kawakami. Special appreciation goes to Michiko Bando, Tomohiro Fujii, Kaori Takamine, Hiroyuki Tanaka, and Maki Ishino-Ura, for their assistance in the editorial process.

Finally, but most important, I wish to express my sincerest thankfulness to my parents, Sachiko and Atsuo Ura, and to my wife, Maki, for their everlasting support, patience, and love.

Contents

Abbreviations	xvii
1. Introduction	3
1.1. Grammatical Function Splitting	5
1.1.1. Grammatical Functions and Grammatical Relations	5
1.1.2. Grammatical Function Splitting Phenomena	6
1.2. A Minimalist Theory of Grammatical Functions	11
1.2.1. Grammatical Relations/Functions in the PP-approach	11
1.2.2. A Theory of GFs in the Minimalist Framework	12
1.3. Theory of Multiple Feature Checking	14
1.3.1. Minimalist Assumptions	14
1.3.2. Theory of Multiple Feature Checking	20
1.3.3. Multiple Feature Checking and GF-Splitting Phenomena	24
1.4. Preview of Major Proposals	25
1.4.1. Strong Features and Violability of Procrastinate	25
1.4.2. Syntactic Mapping of Argument Structure	28
1.4.3. What is SUBJ/OBJ?	30
1.4.4. Multiple Specs, Equidistance, and DP-Movement over DP	31
1.4.5. Optionality	32
1.4.6. Feature Checking as a Syntactic Operation	35
1.4.7. Some Parameters	36
1.4.8. Definition of [±Construable]-Features	38
1.5. Organization	39
2. Active/Inverse Voice Alternation	40
2.1. Bantu Inverse Voice	41
2.1.1. Basic Properties of Bantu Inverse System	41
2.1.2. Mechanism of the Active/Inverse Alternation in Bantu	45
2.1.3. Deriving the Parametric Differences	53

2.1.4. Summary: Bantu Inverse Voice	54
2.2. Apachean Inverse Voice	55
2.2.1. Basic Properties of Apachean Inverse System	55
2.2.2. Mechanism of the Active/Inverse Alternation in Apachean	58
2.2.3. Animacy Hierarchy and the Deletion of Infl's EPP-feature	60
2.2.4. Subjecthood of SUBJ in Navajo Inverse Voice	62
2.3. Summary	63
Appendix A: English Quotative Inversion	64
Appendix B: Inversion and Local Economy	68
3. Anti-Impersonal Passives	**70**
3.1. Anti-Impersonal Passive in Lango	71
3.1.1. Basic Properties of "Long Object Shift" in Lango	71
3.1.2. Wither Does OBJ Go by LOS?	74
3.1.3. Derivation of Anti-Impersonal Passive in Lango	79
3.1.4. Grammatical Function Splitting by LOS	82
3.1.5. Summary for Lango Anti-Impersonal Passive	83
3.2. Anti-Impersonal Passive in Imbabura Quechua	83
3.2.1. Basic Properties of Imbabura Quechua Passive	83
3.2.2. Grammatical Function Splitting	86
3.2.3. Explanation	87
3.2.4. Parametric Variations	91
3.2.5. Summary for Imbabura Quechua Anti-Impersonal Passive	92
3.3. Summary	93
Appendix: A Very Short Note on Impersonal Passives	93
4. Dative Subject Constructions	**95**
4.1. Japanese (and Korean)	96
4.1.1. Basic Facts	96
4.1.2. Proposals	103
4.1.3. Analysis	104
4.1.4. Explanation	105
4.1.5. Supporting Evidence	112
4.1.6. Summary and Problems	116
4.2. Tamil	117
4.2.1. DAT-ACC Pattern	117
4.2.2. DAT-NOM Pattern	120
4.2.3. Analysis	121
4.2.4. Evidence for the Difference between Dat-Acc and Dat-Nom	124
4.2.5. Summary and Dative Subjects in Kannada	125
4.3. Icelandic	126
4.3.1. Data	126

4.3.2. Analysis	129
4.3.3. Passive and Dative Subjects in Germanic	133
4.3.4. Experiencer and Inversion in Dutch	139
4.4. Theoretical Implications of DOC	141
4.4.1. Inversion in Germanic and Local Economy	141
4.4.2. Icelandic and Bantu Inverse	142
4.5. Summary	145
Appendix A: Old English and Historical Change	146
Appendix B: DSCs (QSCs) in Other Languages	149
1. Russian and Polish	149
2. Hindi (and Other Indo-Aryan)	151
3. Italian (and Spanish)	151
4. Accusative Subjects in Quechua	152
5. Georgian	154

5. Locative Inversion — 156

5.1. Bantu Locative Inversion	156
5.1.1. Basic Facts	156
5.1.2. Explanation	160
5.1.3. GF-Splitting by Bantu Locative Inversion	164
5.1.4. Deriving the Parametric Variation	165
5.1.5. Lexical/Syntactic Restriction on Locative Inversion	165
5.1.6. Implications	167
5.2. Locative Inversion in Japanese	171
5.2.1. Basic Facts	171
5.2.2. Deriving Japanese Locative Inversion	174
5.2.3. Supporting Evidence	177
5.3. Summary	179

6. Ergativity and Its Typological Variation — 180

6.1. Introduction: Ergativity	181
6.1.1. Morphological Ergativity	181
6.1.2. Syntactic Ergativity	183
6.1.3. Split-Ergativity	187
6.2. Problems of Ergativity	191
6.2.1. Problems of Morphological Ergativity	192
6.2.2. Problems of Syntactic/Shallow Ergativity	194
6.2.3. Problems of Split-Ergativity	195
6.2.4. Ergativity and GF-Splitting	196
6.2.5. Prospect under the Theory of Multiple Feature Checking	197
6.3. Approaches to Ergativity	198
6.3.1. Marantz (1981, 1984) and B. Levin (1983)	198
6.3.2. Other Pre-Minimalist Approaches	199
6.3.3. Two Minimalist Approaches	200
6.4. Theory of Ergativity and Multiple Feature Checking	205
6.4.1. Parameter for the Ergative/Accusative Distinction	206

6.4.2. Typological Varieties of Ergative Languages	207
6.4.3. Intransitives and Case-Marking of SUBJ(I)	220
6.4.4. Anti-Passive	224
6.4.5. Nonexistence of Anti-Passive in Accusative Languages	228
6.5. Summary	228

7. Double Object Constructions — 230

7.1. Larsonian VP-Shell in Agr-Based Case Theory	230
7.2. Underlying Structure for DOC	232
7.3. Deriving Typological/Dialectal Differences in DOC	234
7.3.1. Norwegian/Swedish vs. Danish	235
7.3.2. British vs. American English	244
7.3.3. Explanation of the Crosslinguistic Generalization	249
7.4. Summary	249
Appendix: Typological Variety of DOC	250

8. Object Shift in Japanese — 255

8.1. Word Order in Japanese Ditransitive Clauses	256
8.2. Object Shift in Ditransitive Clauses	258
8.2.1. Object Shift to an A-Position	258
8.2.2. Whither Is the Object Shifted?	259
8.2.3. Optionality of Object Shift and Violability of Procrastinate	268
8.2.4. Passivizability of DO and Violability of Procrastinate	271
8.3. Object Shift out of Desiderative Complements	272
8.3.1. Desiderative Complement in Japanese	272
8.3.2. Violability of Procrastinate	275
8.4. Object Shift in Transitive Clauses	276
8.4.1. Impossibility of Object Shift in Transitive Clauses	276
8.4.2. Lexical Difference in Violability of Procrastinate	280
8.5. Summary	280
Appendix: Optional vs. Obligatory Object Shift	281

9. Conclusion and Further Issues — 283

References — 287
Index — 311

Abbreviations

The following abbreviations are used in this book:

ABL	ablative	GEN	genitive
ABS	absolutive	GER	gerund
ACC	accusative	HAB	habitual marker
ACT	active (Apachean)	HON	honorification marker
ADJ	adjectivizer (Tamil)	IMP	impersonal
ANT	anti-passive	IMPF	imperfective
AOR	aorist	IND	indicative
ART	article	INF	infinitive
ASC	associative	INST	instrumental
ASP	aspect marker	INTR	intransitive
AUX	auxiliary	INV	inverse (Apachean)
CL	classifier	LOC	locative
COM	comitative	M	masculine
COMP	complementizer	N	neuter
COP	copula	NEG	negation
DAT	dative	NOM	nominative
DEC	declarative (Korean)	NOMINL	nominalizer
DEL	delimitative (Quechua)	NONFUT	non-future (Australian)
DES	desiderative	OBJ	objective (Dutch)
DET	determiner	PART	particle
DUB	dubitative	PARTIC	participle
EP	epicene	PASS	passive
ERG	ergative	PAST	past tense/past perfect
EXP	expletive	PERF	perfect
F	feminine	PL	plural
FOC	focus infix (Bantu)	POSS	possessor or possissive
FUT	future tense	POT	potential
FV	final vowel (Bantu)	PRES	present tense

PRET	preterite	GF	grammatical function
PROG	progressive	GR	grammatical relation
PROX	proximate		
Q	interrogative marker	EXP	experiencer
REC PST	recent past (Bantu)		
REL	relative marker	OBJ	logical, underlying object
REF	reflexive		(see §1.4.3)
PURP	purposive		
SG	singular	SUBJ	logical, underlying subject
TNS	tense		(see §1.4.3)
TOP	topic marker		
TRNS	transitivizer/transitive	SS	same-subject marker
VAL	validator (Quechua)		
vbl	variable		
VERBL	verbalizer		
Ø	phonologically null element		
1,2,3	first, second, third person		

Checking Theory and Grammatical Functions in Universal Grammar

1

Introduction

Generative grammar, initiated by Noam Chomsky more than forty years ago, has been developed as a program to characterize the knowledge of a native speaker about his/her natural language as a formal and explicit system to generate all and only the representations that underlie the grammatical sentences in a natural language. Thus, it is primarily concerned with states of the language faculty, which is supposed to be some array of cognitive traits and capacities, that is a particular component of the human mind/brain. Here, it is curious to note that the so-called Principles-and-Parameters approach (PP approach) (cf. Chomsky and Lasnik 1993) has been trying to reach its goal by abstracting patterns within a single language or by comparing a few languages, which are sometimes very similar (cf. Kayne 1996) and sometimes genetically different from each other (cf. Fukui 1995).

As Croft (1990) notes, however, the school of language (or linguistic) typology attempts to analyze linguistic patterns that are cross-linguistically found—in particular, patterns that can be discovered solely by cross-linguistic comparison. From this comparison they try to derive a set of generalizations like "if the demonstrative follows the head noun, then the relative clause also follows the head noun." Typology in this sense began with Greenberg's (1966) discovery of the universal correlation of morphology and word order. It is noteworthy here that both the Chomskyan approach and the Greenbergian approach consider the central question of linguistics to be "What is a possible human language?" and believe that there are universal constraints and principles that define the answer to this question (cf. Croft 1990). It should be noted, however, that the former uses a rationalist (i.e., deductive) and the latter an empiricist (i.e., inductive) method to discover those constraints and principles (see Chomsky 1966, 1975, 1986b, and, also, Katz and Bever 1976, Shibatani and Bynon 1995, Smith 1987).

What is important for the PP approach is that, in order to discover such universal principles and constraints, it is necessary that they should make cross-linguistic examinations that are broad enough to comprehend how they are varied. As mentioned, it is historically obvious that cross-linguistic studies within the framework of the PP approach have been far scarcer than those within the school of language typology, though there was indeed some important work that brought some consequential insights into the theory of Universal Grammar (UG) by conducting broadly cross-linguistic studies under the PP-approach (e.g., Marantz 1984 and Baker 1988, to mention a few). Since Chomsky (1992), however, a fair amount of work that conducts widely cross-linguistic studies under the PP approach has emerged. It is true that rich legacies from the GB era practically enable us to make cross-linguistic comparisons within the theory of formal syntax as Kayne (1984, 1996) and Fukui (1995) stress, but the architecture of the MINIMALIST PROGRAM characterized by Chomsky (1992, 1994a, 1995a) makes it possible for us to try much more; that is, it enables us to accomplish rationalist/deductive studies of typological variations among languages. Under the minimalist program, which stipulates that there is only one universal constraint (namely, the ECONOMY CONDITION) in UG and that a finite array of options exists as to how it applies (namely, PARAMETERS), what is required in order to find how natural languages differ in syntactic respects is to determine the possible parameters permissible in UG.[1] We need not care how rules or principles apply to each language or each construction. Put differently, if only we can figure out the variations of the possible parameters, we can also figure out how the human languages of the world differ syntactically and how UG matures in a given natural language.

This book, through a cross-linguistic investigation of natural language, studies two issues under the theory of syntax whose aim is to investigate and explore the architecture of UG under the framework of the minimalist program outlined in Chomsky (1992, 1994a) and, especially, Chomsky (1995a). One issue is a quite theory-internal one: The possibilities and limits of an extension of the feature-checking theory proposed by Chomsky (1995a) will be explored to the full. The other is a rather empirical issue: How grammatical functions/relations can be expressed under a syntactic theory within the minimalist program, a theory that can no longer rely on any conceptually unnecessary devices (Chomsky 1992, 1994a, 1995a), will be examined through studying GRAMMATICAL FUNCTION SPLITTING PHENOMENA, in which some of the grammatical functions alleged to be associated with a certain grammatical relation are split up. The examination of the latter issue will be conducted through analyses of a broad range of data from a variety of languages. The main purpose of this book, thus, is to demonstrate that the minimalist program, with an appropriate extension, gives a natural explanation to grammatical function splitting phenomena and to empirical facts concerning grammatical functions/relations found in a variety of languages, both in a very consistent way and with a limited set of parameters.

---

[1] According to Chomsky (1992), all parametric differences in natural languages lie in morphology (cf. Borer 1984 and Fukui 1995).

In this chapter, I will first sketch out the fundamental properties of grammatical function splitting phenomena, which will be extensively examined and investigated in this book. In §1.2 I will present my proposal about the theory of grammatical functions. In §1.3 I will outline the theory of multiple feature checking, which is proposed here as an extension of Chomsky's (1995a) theory of formal feature checking, and I will preview, in §1.4, the core rationales/technologies of some major theoretical proposals presented in this book, leaving full discussion of them to relevant chapters. This is intended to help the reader concentrate his/her attention on the description of the data to be examined in the subsequent chapters, especially when he/she confronts unaccustomed data in less-familiar languages.[2] The organization of this book will be presented in §1.5.

1.1. Grammatical Function Splitting

The notion GRAMMATICAL RELATION/FUNCTION has its own long history. Even within the frameworks of modern theoretical linguistics many studies have devoted their attention to the issues around it. In this section, however, I will sketch out the issues I am addressing in this book with regard to grammatical functions (GFs) and grammatical relations (GRs), referring the reader to Ura (1996b: chapter 1) for a general, theoretical discussion on GFs and GRs.

1.1.1. Grammatical Functions and Grammatical Relations

It is commonly held in the literature that every element (mostly, argument) in a clause has its own GFs. The ability to launch a quantifier floating, the ability to control a missing subject in a subordinate-adjunct clause, the ability to bind a (subject-oriented) reflexive, the ability to induce a subject-agreement on the finite verb of the clause, to stand in nominative, etc. are regarded as GFs.[3] GRs such as SUBJECT and OBJECT have been used as cover terms to refer to a set of some of those GFs that a single argument in a clause is supposed to have in general. A widely held view is that, if some argument *A* in a clause counts as having the GR subject (i.e., *A* assumes SUBJECTHOOD), then *A* is supposed to have the set of the GFs that are linked with the GR subject. And it is also widely assumed that, if *A* has one of the GFs linked to subjecthood, then *A* counts as the subject of the clause. In English, for example, if a DP counts as having the GR subject, the DP is expected to have the GFs linked to subject such as the ability to induce

---

[2] Each subsection in §1.4 thus can be skipped until it becomes relevant in the following chapters.

[3] Thus, grammatical functions should be distinguished clearly from grammatical roles, semantic functions, or semantic roles, all of which are called θ-roles in the PP-approach. There are vast numbers of studies concerning grammatical functions in general. See, among many others, Partee (1965), Johnson (1974b), Anderson (1976), Keenan (1974, 1976b), Perlmutter (1982), Harley (1995b), and references cited therein.

agreement on the finite verb in the clause and the ability to control the missing subject of a *without*-clause (cf. Postal 1990: 373–374):

(1.1)   a.   They$_k$ *has/have hired John$_i$ [without PRO.$_{*i/k}$ having to commit themselves$_k$/*himself$_i$ to that salary].

b.   John$_i$ has/*have been hired (by them$_k$) [without PRO$_{i/*k}$ having to commit *themselves$_k$/himself$_i$ to that salary].

Inversely, by differentiating which argument has one of the GFs linked to subject, we can tell which argument should be the subject of the clause.

An interesting question to ask here is: Is the set of the GFs that an argument with a certain GR is supposed to have universally or cross-linguistically invariant? Many researchers (e.g., Schachter 1976, 1977; Foley and Van Valin 1977, 1984; Andrews 1985; Keenan 1987; Comrie 1989; Bhat 1991; and Palmer 1994) have found that the answer should be negative on empirical grounds; that is, it has been discovered that, given any definition of GRs, there are plenty of cases where the GFs of *A* in a language L_1 differ from those of *B* in another language L_2 even though *A* and *B* should count as having the same GR. Moreover, it has also been revealed that even in a single language, there are cases where the GFs of *A* differ from those of *B* even though *A* and *B* should count as having the same GR. Let us take a closer look at the latter case, leaving open the more general questions concerned with the notion GRAMMATICAL RELATIONS/FUNCTIONS.[4]

1.1.2. Grammatical Function Splitting Phenomena

The so-called dative subject construction found in Tamil suitably exemplifies the case mentioned above:

(1.2)   *Tamil* (Lehmann 1993: 189)

    Kumaar-ukku irantu paiyan-kal-Ø iru-kkir-**aarkal**.
    Kumar-DAT two   boy-PL-NOM be-PRES-3PL.EP
    'Kumar has two boys.'

This is a typical example of the dative subject construction in Tamil. Compare (1.2) with (1.3), which illustrates a standard Tamil transitive clause with Nominative-Accusative pattern:

(1.3)   *Tamil* (Lehmann 1993: 181)

    Kumaar-Ø   raajaav-ai ati-tt-**aan**.
    Kumar-NOM Raja-ACC   beat-PAST-3SG.M
    'Kumar beat Raja.'

---

[4] For example, we should ask how to properly define grammatical relations/functions, how useful or necessary the notion grammatical relation is, etc. Cf. Ura (1996b: chapter 1) and references cited therein.

Tamil is a Dravidian language with SOV word order in the nominative-accusative system (see Lehmann 1993 and references cited therein).

In a Tamil ordinary transitive clause with Nominative-Accusative pattern like (1.3), the nominative-marked DP bears the ability to induce agreement on the finite verb in the clause as illustrated in (1.3), and it also bears the ability to control the missing subject in a subordinate-adjunct clause and the ability to bind a subject-oriented reflexive in the clause, as shown in (1.4):

(1.4) *Tamil* (Lehmann 1993: 185–186)

    a.   Kumaar-Ø$_i$ raajaav-ukkut$_k$ panam kotu-ttu, PRO$_{i/*k}$
           Kumar-NOM Raja-DAT money give-PARTIC
           cantoosappat-t-aan.
           feel-happy-PAST-3SG.M
           'Kumar$_i$ gave Raja$_k$ money [PRO$_{i/*k}$ to feel happy].'

    b.   Kumaar-Ø$_i$ raajaav-ukkut$_k$ [$_{DP}$ [$_{PP}$ tann-aip$_{i/*k}$ parri] oru
           Kumar-NOM Raja-DAT self-ACC about one
           katturai-aik] koti-tt-aar.
           article-ACC give-PAST-3SG
           'Kumar$_i$ gave Raja$_k$ [one article [about himself$_{i/*k}$]].'

As also shown in (1.4), the dative-marked DP in an ordinary transitive clause has none of these abilities. Let us suppose that the nominative-marked DP in (1.3) counts as subject in the clause because of the fact that it bears these abilities. This is intuitively very plausible because the nominative-marked DP that is alleged to count as subject in English and many other European languages also bears the same abilities. In other words, we are tentatively assuming that those GFs (i.e., to stand in nominative, to induce agreement on the finite verb, to control the missing subject in a subordinate-adjunct clause, and to bind a subject-oriented reflexive) are tightly linked to the GR subject in Tamil.

Interestingly enough, the dative-marked DP in the Tamil dative subject construction bears some of those GFs and the nominative-marked DP in the same construction bears the rest of the GFs. More specifically, in the Tamil dative subject construction, the dative-marked DP, but not the nominative-marked DP, has the ability to control the missing subject in a subordinate-adjunct clause (as shown in (1.5)), and the ability to bind a reflexive (as shown in (1.6)):

(1.5) *Tamil* (Lehmann 1993: 191–192)

    a.   Kumaar-ukkuk$_i$ koopam-Ø va-ntu, PRO$_i$ raajaav-api
           Kumar-DAT anger-NOM come-PARTIC Raja-ACC
           ati-tt-aan.
           beat-PAST-3SG.M
           'Kumar$_i$ got angry [PRO$_i$ to beat Raja].'

b. *Kempeni-kkup panam-Ø$_k$ kitai-ttu, PRO$_k$ vatti
company-DAT money-NOM get-PARTIC interest
perruk-kon-t-iru-kkir-atu.
get-hold-PARTIC-be-PRES-3SG.N
'The company got money$_k$ [PRO$_k$ to receive interest now].'

(1.6)   *Tamil* (Lehmann 1993: 190–191)

a. Kumaar-ukkut$_i$ [tann-aip$_i$ parrik kavalai]-Ø ill-ai.
Kumar-DAT self-ACC about concern -NOM be-not-3PL.N
'Kumar$_i$ has no concern about himself$_i$.'

b. Kumaar-ukkut$_i$ katattappatt-a uumaa-Ø$_k$ [tan$_{i/*k}$ viitt]-il
Kumar-DAT get-kidnappped-ADJ Uma-NOM self house -LOC
miintum kitai-tt-aal.
back get-PAST-3SG.F
'Kumar$_i$ got the kidnapped Uma$_k$ back in his$_i$/*her$_k$ house.'

On the other hand, only the nominative-marked DP induces the agreement on the finite verb in the Tamil dative subject construction, as shown in (1.7):

(1.7)   *Tamil* (Lehmann 1993: 189)

Kumaar-ukku irantu paiyan-kal-Ø iru-kkir-**aarkal**/*-**aan**.
Kumar-DAT two boy-PL-NOM be-PRES-**3PL.EP**/*-**3SG.M**
'Kumar has two boys.'

Therefore, the conclusion deducible from these observations is that in Tamil, the GFs that can be possessed by a single element in an ordinary transitive clause are split up into two elements in a clause with a dative subject. Due to this remarkable property, I call it GF-splitting.

Another example of GF-splitting phenomena comes from Navajo. According to Hale (1973), the word order in Navajo is strictly fixed as SOV. The active sentence in (1.8) can only be interpreted as represented in (1.9a), and it is never interpreted as in (1.9b):

(1.8)   *Navajo* (Palmer 1994: 210)

łíí' dzaanééz **yi**-ztal.   (active)
horse mule ACT-kick

(1.9)   a. 'The horse kicked the mule.'
        b. *'The mule kicked the horse.'

Thus, it is not unnatural to pretend that a DP counts as subject if it occupies the clause-initial position (cf. Hale 1973, Klaiman 1991, and Palmer 1994). Another possible GF that can be regarded as a GF linked to subject in Navajo is the ability to induce the plural agreement on the verbal element in the clause. In the Navajo active voice, the plural agreement is always induced by the DP occupying the clause-initial position, as shown in (1.10):[5]

---

[5] See Hale et al. (1977) for more about the plural agreement in Navajo.

(1.10) *Navajo* (Hale et al. 1977: 54)

a. Ashiiké at'ééd **da**-y-oo'í.   (active)
the boys the girl PL-ACT-see
'The boys see the girl.'

b. Ashkii at'ééké (***da**-)y-oo'í.   (active)
the boy the girls (*PL-)ACT-see
'The boy sees the girls.'

Navajo has a voice-changing (grammatical function changing) operation "active/inverse voice alternation" (cf. Hale 1973, Klaiman 1991, and Palmer 1994). Note that the inverse sentence in (1.11), which is derived from (1.8) by permuting the order of S and O, receives the same logical interpretation as (1.8):

(1.11) *Navajo* (Palmer 1994: 210)

dzaaééz łíí' **bi**-ztal.   (inverse)
mule   horse INV-kick
'The mule was kicked by the horse.' ($\Leftarrow$ logically equivalent to (1.9a))
*'The horse was kicked by the mule.' ($\Leftarrow$ logically equivalent to (1.9b))

Hence, the Navajo inverse voice is seemingly similar to passive voice in this respect (cf. Hale 1973). From this observation, one might be tempted to conjecture in the framework of Relational Grammar that object in active voice is promoted to subject in inverse voice (cf. Palmer 1994).

Then, it may come as a surprise to find that the clause-initial DP in inverse voice cannot induce the plural agreement on the verb; rather, the plural agreement is always induced by the second DP in inverse voice, as shown in (1.12):

(1.12) *Navajo* (Hale et al. 1977: 54)

a. At'ééd ashiiké **da**-b-oo'í.   (inverse)
the girl the boys PL-INVT-see
'The girl is seen by the boys.'

b. At'ééké ashkii (***da**-)b-oo'í.   (inverse)
the girls the boy (*PL-)INV-see
'The girls are seen by the boy.'

Therefore, the conclusion is that the GFs that are possessed by a single element in the Navajo active voice are split up into two elements in the Navajo inverse voice.

One of the most well-known GF-splitting phenomena is split-ergativity, though it has not been known by this hypocorism. Studies on ergativity (cf., among many others, Silverstein 1976; Comrie 1978, 1979; Dixon 1979, 1987, 1994; Marantz 1984; Bittner and Hale 1996a; and references cited therein) have revealed that ergative languages can be divided largely into two types: morphologically ergative languages and syntactically ergative ones. Languages of the former type have the so-called ergative Case system for morphological marking on nominals, but some of them have syntactic properties in common with those of the canonical accusative languages like English or Japanese.[6] According to Dixon (1994), no syntactically ergative language with the morphologically accusative Case system has ever been attested so far. Thus, all syntactically ergative languages are morphologically ergative, but some morphologically ergative languages are not syntactically ergative. To be brief, the ergative Case-marking pattern can be summarized in the following fashion: The logical subject in an active transitive clause (most typically, Agent) has a Case-marker morphologically different from the logical subject in an (active) intransitive clause, which has the same Case-marker as the logical object (typically, Patient or Theme) in an active transitive clause. The morphological Case-marking for Agent (or Actor) in an active transitive clause is called ERGATIVE, and the one for the subject in an intransitive clause and Patient in an active transitive clause is called ABSOLUTIVE.

In syntactically pure ergative languages like Dyirbal, DPs have in common a certain set of syntactic properties, most of which are believed to be possessed by a DP with the GR SUBJECT in ordinary accusative languages, if they are marked as absolutive. In languages with only morphological ergativity like Walmatjari (Dixon 1994), Chukchee (Comrie 1979), and Enga (Van Valin 1981), on the other hand, the ergative-marked DP in an active transitive clause and the absolutive-marked DP in an intransitive clause have some syntactic properties in common (such as the ability to control, to be a victim of omission, to be relativized, etc.), despite the evident fact that they are differently encoded from the morphological point of view. Interestingly to our concern, in some of these languages only the absolutive-marked DP, but not the ergative-marked DP, can induce subject agreement on the finite verb in the clause regardless of the transitivity of the clause (see Comrie 1978, 1979; DeLancey 1981; Dixon 1994; Palmer 1994; and references cited therein for more details). In other words, the GFs of the absolutive-marked DP in an intransitive clause are split up in an active transitive clause; some of them (the ability to induce subject agreement on the finite verb, the ability to stand in absolutive, etc.) are inherited by the absolutive-marked DP (i.e., Theme or Patient in an active transitive clause) and the rest (the ability to control, to be relativized, etc.) by the ergative-marked DP (i.e., Agent or Actor). This is clearly a kind of GF-splitting.

To recapitulate, it is possible to find that the GFs that are possessed by a single element in a construction in a language are split up into two (or more) elements in another construction in the same language. As Harley (1995b) correctly points out, GF-splitting phenomena pose empirically serious challenges against the theory with the assumption that GFs/GRs are defined in an absolutely deterministic fashion. Let us go farther into the details of this issue in the next section.

---

[6] As many authors point out, there are lots of morphologically ergative languages which have some syntactically accusative properties, yet have some syntactically ergative properties, too. See Dixon (1979, 1994), DeLancey (1981), and Manning (1996) for a survey.

1.2. A Minimalist Theory of Grammatical Functions

1.2.1. Grammatical Relations/Functions in the PP-approach

Putting aside the important question about the necessity/importance of the notion grammatical relation in the theory of grammar, there has been a big question about how to define it. Let us see how it has been defined in the PP approach.[7]

In the PP approach, grammatical relations have been continuously regarded as not absolute but derivative. This heritage stems from Chomsky (1965). Chomsky's basic idea was that grammatical relations (GRs) are very closely related to structural relations, and, hence, they should be structurally derived and defined. In Chomsky (1981), he substantiated this idea and proposed that the notion "subject of S (= the sentence)" is determined by the structural relation expressed by [NP, S]; that is, [NP, S] gives birth to the GFs associated with the GR subject. As Marantz (1984) and Williams (1984) indicated, structural relations in this era were unambiguously determined thanks to the Projection Principle (cf. Chomsky 1981) and the conventional X-bar theory (cf. Stowell 1981 and Chomsky 1981, 1986a).[8] Therefore, a GR, which is determined by a given syntactic position, as well as the GFs associated with the GR, is always invariant. Put differently, an argument *A* cannot bear the GFs associated with the GR SUBJECT unless it occupies the position immediately dominated by the node S. More generally, the theory of GFs and GRs under the PP-approach has held the hypothesis that an element with a particular GR has an invariant set of GFs that are peculiar to that GR.

Now it is important to note that it is very hard for this theory to give an account of the case where the GFs that are supposed to be linked with a certain GR are split up. A possible solution to this problem is to introduce other notions like "D-strucure positions" to the definition of GFs (cf. Belletti and Rizzi 1988). This enables us to say that some GFs are associated or determined by D-structure positions and others by S-structure positions. Put differently, in order for the theory with the structural definitions of GRs and GFs to grasp GF-splitting phenomena, it is imperative to refer to positions at "S-structure" and "D-structure."[9]

---

[7] See Ura (1996b: chapter 1) for discussion on approaches to GRs in other frameworks.

[8] Muysken (1982), who tried to derive the structural relation of a given element, not from its geometrical position in the structure, but from the relation it holds to other elements in the structure, is an exception in this regard. As will be evident, this is closely related to what I propose in this book. Thanks to Noam Chomsky (p.c.) for bringing this point to my attention.

[9] Cf. Williams (1984), where it is pointed out that θ-roles and nominal cases are also crucial in determining the GFs of a given element in the clause. Cf., also, Marantz (1984).

1.2.2. A Theory of GFs in the Minimalist Framework

1.2.2.1. Theoretical/Conceptual Problems

Under the minimalist framework that was initiated by Chomsky (1992), and which he has been developing and elaborating in subsequent works, the Projection Principle and the conventional X-bar theory have been discarded due to their lack of (virtual) conceptual necessity; as a consequence, the structural relations of a given element, under the minimalist syntax, are defined in terms of the relation the element has in connection with other elements in the structure (Chomsky 1994a and Ura 1994e). In other words, structural positions are defined not in an absolutely deterministic manner, but relationally. This gives rise to a situation in which we can no longer relate GRs and GFs to structural relations in a uniform and deterministic fashion. Now the question is: How can we define or determine GFs (and GRs) under Bare Phrase Structure Theory?

1.2.2.2. Possible Approaches to GF-Splitting Phenomena

The aforementioned theoretical question aside, GF-splitting phenomena pose an empirical problem to the theory of grammar as stated in §1.1.2. In the minimalist framework assumed in this book, we can no longer take advantage of the possible solution mentioned in §1.2.1. In this framework it is no use referring to structural positions like D-structure or S-structure for the reason described in §1.2.2.1. Moreover, the notions D-structure and S-structure cannot be referred to in this framework owing to the lack of their virtual conceptual necessity (Chomsky 1992).

Harley (1995b) and McClosky (1996) independently observe some kind of GF-splitting phenomena: They notice that the GFs of the element that is supposed to be regarded as subject in a construction may sometimes differ from those of the element that is supposed to be regarded as subject in another construction. The conclusion they have come to from their observations is that the DP with the GR subject in a construction may sometimes occupy a position different from the one where the DP with the GR subject is located in another construction. More specifically, they claim that some subject-DPs may occur at the Spec of IP; some may occur at the Spec of a certain functional category existing between IP and VP; and the others may linger at the Spec of VP, where they are base-generated. Note, however, that their claim still relies upon the structural relation in order to determine the GFs of a given DP. In this regard the critique mentioned when I criticized the GB approach to GFs applies again to the claim of Harley (1995b) and McClosky (1996): Structural determination for GFs cannot be available under the minimalist framework assumed in this book.

Now the problem is to formulate an appropriate definition of GFs under the minimalist framework without referring to structural relations, in order to give an explanation of GF-splitting phenomena under the minimalist framework presupposed in this book.

1.2.2.3. A Minimalist Theory of GFs

For the reason pointed out thus far, it is no longer possible to rely on structural relations under the minimalist framework assumed here. Nevertheless, there is a relationship that can be unambiguously determined in an absolutely deterministic way under this framework: namely, the relationship that is created by formal feature-checking. In the checking theory of Chomsky (1995a), it is assumed that formal features such as Case-features or categorial features are syntactic primitives and that they play the role of entering into checking relations (cf. §1.3.1.3). Therefore, it is quite natural to hypothesize a theory of GFs (and GRs) under this framework, a theory under which GFs (and GRs) are unambiguously defined or determined by checking relations. Here it is important to note that, as long as the feature-checking theory is free from conceptually unnecessary assumptions, the theory of GFs (and GRs) just sketched is also free from them.

Moreover, it should be emphasized that the theory of GFs proposed here has a good advantage on empirical grounds as well as on conceptual grounds, as will be demonstrated in subsequent chapters. In this book I will claim that, in addition to its superiority on conceptual grounds, this theory also has empirically wide advantages: As I will demonstrate in depth, it provides us with a good apparatus to handle GF-splitting phenomena appropriately, if the theory of multiple feature checking, which will be developed and elaborated in what follows, is supplied.

As argued earlier, I propose the hypothesis that GFs are determined by checking relations along the line suggested above. More specifically, I propose to hypothesize that a GF (such as the ability to control a missing subject in a subordinate clause) results from a certain feature-checking relation with a particular head.[10] It will be argued, for example, that the ability to control a missing subject results from a ϕ-feature checking relation with Infl (= T), and the ability to bind a (purely) subject-oriented reflexive, which has traditionally been linked to the GR subject, results from an EPP-feature checking relation with Infl. It is a matter of course that the ability to induce subject-agreement should be linked to the ϕ-feature checking relation with Infl (= T). Naturally, other types of feature-checking relations may result in other grammatical functions. Then, one should ask, what kinds of feature-checking relations yield the ability to control, to launch a floating quantifier, to be controlled, and so forth. There is no a priori answer to this question on conceptual grounds; rather, it should be answered in the light of empirical data.

However, once the theory of GFs along this line is established, one may as well ask the following question: Why is it that a given feature-checking relationship activates a particular grammatical function behavior. For example, why is a ϕ-feature checking relation with T crucial to being a controller, as opposed to checking some other feature with some other category? These are very difficult questions, but the minimalist program should provide principled answers to any

---

[10] See §1.3 for the theory of feature checking assumed in this book.

kind of question by reducing conceptually unnecessary stipulations. Even though I can discover some empirical correspondences between feature-checking relations and GFs, they are not more than stipulations on a case-by-case basis. If too many such stipulations are allowed, the framework will be too powerful to be explanatory. If there are several functional categories, each of which checks several features with each checking relationship then potentially licensing some arbitrary grammatical function behavior, there is a combinatorial explosion of possibilities. The danger then is that no interesting correlations or restrictions are predicted. In the final chapter I will touch on this question and try to give reasonable rationales to the theory of GFs developed in the chapters that follow.

Now let us examine how to explain GF-splitting phenomena by utilizing the theory of GFs proposed here. In order to give a minimalist explanation to GF-splitting, I rely crucially upon the system of multiple feature checking, an extension of Chomsky's (1995a) feature-checking theory. Let us first take a look at the theoretical basis of the theory of multiple feature checking.

1.3. Theory of Multiple Feature Checking

1.3.1. Minimalist Assumptions

Throughout this book I assume, as its main framework, the minimalist program for linguistic theory developed by Chomsky (1992, 1994a, 1995a, 1996), and I particularly adopt some of the leading ideas developed by Chomsky (1994a) and, especially, by Chomsky (1995a), in specific contexts. Putting aside the general issue of the entire validation of the minimalist theory as the theory of grammar of human language (cf. Chomsky 1992, 1994a,b 1995a,b, 1996), I will, in this section, briefly sketch out some of the major conceptions and assumptions of the minimalist theory, which will turn out to be prerequisite to the discussions in the chapters that follow.[11]

1.3.1.1. Conceptual Backgrounds

According to Chomsky (1992, 1994a, 1995a), the minimalist program for linguistic theory aims at establishing the theory of grammar of human language by postulating only minimal assumptions that are necessary and essential on conceptual grounds alone. As a consequence, there exist a few (hopefully, only one) sets of universal principles and a finite array of options as to how they apply (namely, parameters). This is the way to approach the so-called Plato's problem (Chomsky 1986a, 1991a,b), or the "perfectness" of language (or the language faculty of human beings) under the minimalist program (Chomsky 1992, 1994a, 1995a, 1996). Now the task of the minimalist program is to show, by utilizing these highly restricted options in UG, that the apparent richness and diversity of

---

[11] A more extensive introduction to the earlier minimalist program can be found in Lasnik (1993), Marantz (1995), Epstein, et al. (1996), and Wilder and Gärtner (1996).

linguistic phenomena is illusory and epiphenomenal and that it results from the interactions of the principle(s) and limited sets of fixed parameters.

In the minimalist theory advocated by Chomsky (1992, 1994a, 1995a), two linguistic levels are postulated and only those levels are assumed; they are necessary and essential for the linguistic theory as interface with the performance systems (namely, articulatory-perceptual (A-P) and conceptual-intentional (C-I) systems). It is also assumed that there is a single computational system C_{HL} for human language and only limited lexical variety; whereby, variations of language are essentially morphological (Chomsky 1994a: 3). C_{HL} should be interpreted as mapping some array A of lexical choices to a pair (π, λ), a linguistic expression of a particular language L, where π is a PF representation and λ is an LF representation, each consisting of legitimate objects that can receive an interpretation. Chomsky (1995a: 223) maintains that C_{HL} is strictly derivational, but not representational, in that it involves successive operations leading to (π, λ).[12] Thus, C_{HL} (namely, computation)

> typically involves simple steps expressible in terms of natural relations and properties, with the context that makes them natural "wiped out" by later operation, hence not visible in the representation to which the derivation converges. Thus in syntax, crucial relations are typically local, but a sequence of operations may yield a representation in which the locality is obscured. (Chomsky 1995a: 223)

A particular language L is an instantiation of the initial state of the cognitive system of the language faculty with options specified, and L determines a set of derivations (= computations). A derivation CONVERGES at one of the interface levels if it yields a representation satisfying Full Interpretation, a condition which requires that every entity at an interface level be interpreted. A derivation converges if it converges at both interface levels; otherwise, it CRASHES.

The array A of lexical choices, which is mapped to (π, λ) by C_{HL}, is the thing that indicates what the lexical choices are and how many times each is selected by C_{HL} in forming (π, λ). Let NUMERATION be a set of pairs (LI, i), where LI is an item of the lexicon and i is its index, which should be understood to be the number of times that LI is selected. Then, A is a numeration N; C_{HL} maps N to (π, λ). C_{HL} proceeds by selecting an item from N, reducing its index by 1. C_{HL} crashes if all indices are not reduced to zero (cf. Collins 1996).

At some point in the computation to LF (i.e., the computation from N to λ), there is an operation SPELL-OUT, which applies to the structure Σ already formed. Spell-out strips away from Σ those elements relevant only to π, leaving the residue Σ_L, which is mapped to λ by syntactic operations. The subsystem of C_{HL} that maps Σ to π is called the "phonological component," and the subsystem of C_{HL} that maps Σ to λ is called the "covert component." The pre-Spell-out component is called the "overt component." In this system, therefore, there is no direct relation between λ and π (see Brody (1995) for a different view in this regard).

---

[12] See Collins (1995b), Ura (1994b, 1995c), and, especially, Collins (1996) in addition to Chomsky (1995a, 1996) for more discussion on this successive nature of the derivation of structures and its relation to the Economy Condition. See §1.4.5.3.

1.3.1.2. Derivational Model for Structure Building

Given the numeration N, the operations of C_{HL} recursively construct SYNTACTIC OBJECTS from items in N and syntactic objects already formed (cf. Kitahara 1994). One of the operations of C_{HL}, what we will call SELECT, is a procedure that selects a lexical item LI from N, reducing its index by 1, and introduces it into the derivation. Another operation, what we will call MERGE, takes a pair of already formed syntactic objects and replaces them by a new combined syntactic object. The operation MOVE forms a new syntactic object Λ from two already formed syntactic objects κ and α, where κ is a target and α is the affected, by replacing κ with $\{\Gamma, \{\alpha, \kappa\}\}$ (= Λ).[13] Syntactic structures, being formed only by these three operations, are built derivationally in a bottom-to-top fashion.[14]

1.3.1.3. Theory of Formal Features and Their Checking

Following Chomsky (1992, 1994a, 1995a), this book premises the following assumptions concerning formal features:

1. Formal features (Fs) are the features that have the following properties:
   a. They are syntactic objects accessible in the course of C_{HL}.
   b. They are encoded in (or assigned to) a lexical item.

Among them, φ-features like gender, person, or number, Case-features like nominative or accusative, and categorial features like D-feature are important. In this book I use "nominal features" as a cover term for φ-features, Case-features, and D-feature; this cover term will be used when the distinction between these features is not important or when I would like to make the distinction obscure.

2. Fs undergo the operation FEATURE CHECKING, which motivates syntactic movements under the Last Resort Condition. By feature checking, a relation (called a CHECKING RELATION) is produced.

3. Feature checking always takes place between two features of the same sort.[15]

4. Feature checking is possible only when the element (= checkee) that possesses the feature to be checked is in the CHECKING DOMAIN

---

[13] Γ is the label of Λ. The label of K, which identifies the type to which K belongs, is determined derivationally (see Chomsky 1994a, 1995a for details).

[14] See Watanabe (1995a) for more discussion on structure building under the "bare" phrase structure theory of Chomsky (1994a, 1995a). Cf. Collins (1996) and Ura (1997a).

[15] Later it will be proposed that a checking relation should not necessarily be a one-to-one relation. One-to-many, many-to-one, or even many-to-many relations are possible for feature checking. For feature-mismatch, see Ura (1994e, 1995c) and Chomsky (1995a: §5.6).

of the element (= checker) that possesses the checking feature.[16] I assume, following Collins (1996), that checking is asymmetric.

5. Checked Fs are deleted when possible. Deleted Fs are erased when possible. Deleted Fs are invisible at LF, but accessible to syntactic operations. Erased Fs are not accessible at all in C_{HL}.

6. There are [+interpretable] and [−interpretable] Fs. The [−interpretable] Fs must be checked and deleted at LF, while [+interpretable] ones may not be checked or deleted because they are interpreted at LF; hence, the existence of them at LF does not yield a violation of Full Interpretation at LF. The [−interpretable] Fs that remain undeleted at LF cause the derivation to crash.

7. There are strong Fs and weak Fs. Strong Fs must be checked and deleted before Spell-out, while weak ones can be checked at LF. Strong Fs that remain unchecked at PF cause the derivation to crash.

8. Chomsky (1995a: §4.5.6) proposes the stipulation that an element introduced (base-generated) by Merge in its θ-position cannot undergo feature checking unless it moves somewhere other than its base-generated position. I will propose, however, that this should be parametrized. That is to say, in some languages, elements can undergo feature checking in their θ-positions, while they cannot in other languages. See §1.4.6.2 for more discussion.

In addition to these assumptions, I assume the following:

1'. There are [+multiple] Fs and [−multiple] Fs. The [+multiple] Fs can or must undergo more than one feature-checking operation, and, hence, they can or must enter into more than one checking relation (see §1.3.2 for the technical detail as to how [+multiple] Fs undergo multiple feature-checking operations).

---

[16] Relevant definitions are as follows: MAX(α) is the least full-category maximal projection dominating α. The category α dominates β if every segment of α dominates β. The category α contains β if some segment of α dominates β. The domain of α is the set of the nodes contained in Max(α) that are distinct from and do not contain α. The complement domain of α is the subset of the domain reflexively dominated by the complement of α. The residue of α is the domain of α minus the complement domain of α. X is in the minimal domain of α iff X is contained in MAX(α), and X is dominated by no elements in the domain of α other than itself and the elements not distinct from α. Thus, the minimal complement domain of α is the intersection of the minimal domain of α and the complement domain of α. Finally, the checking domain of α is the minimal residue of α. See Chomsky (1992: 15–16) for more discussion.

2'. Some Fs may tolerate one or more violations of Procrastinate, and others disallow any violation of Procrastinate (Chomsky 1995a: §10).

Assumptions 6, 7, and 1' are concerned with the properties that an F can have. Presumably the interpretability of Fs is universal and invariant among languages: It is universally true that nominative Case-feature is [–interpretable] and D-feature is [+interpretable], for example (Chomsky 1995a). On the other hand, I assume that the strong/weak distinction and the distinction between [±multiple] are subject to parametric variation: Nominative Case-feature in some languages can be strong and [+multiple], while it can be weak and [–multiple] in others. Parametric variation exists as to assumption 2': D-feature, for example, may tolerate multiple violations of Procrastinate in some languages, but only a single violation in others, and it may not tolerate any violation of Procrastinate in some others. More about 1' and 2' will be discussed in §1.3.2.

1.3.1.4. Agr-less Feature-Checking Theory

Following Chomsky's (1995a: §10) proposal that AGR-projections, which have played a very significant role in the earlier minimalist theory (Chomsky 1992, Lasnik 1993, and Watanabe 1993, inter alia), should be discarded on conceptual grounds, I assume the Agr-less feature-checking theory suggested by Chomsky (1995a: §10), according to which the nominal feature of SUBJ and that of OBJ in an active transitive clause are supposed to be checked off at a Spec of T and at a Spec of the higher head of the two-layered VP-shell, respectively, if these checkings are supposed to take place before Spell-out, as illustrated in (1.13).[17] (Throughout this book I use SUBJ and OBJ to refer to the logical, underlying subject and the logical, underlying object, respectively. See §1.4.3.)

(1.13)
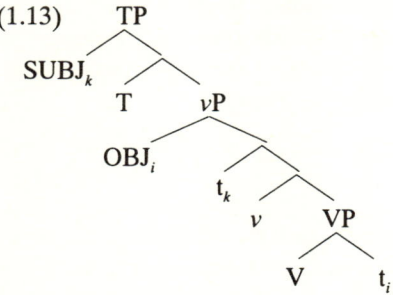

Following Chomsky (1995a), v is meant to stand for the higher head of the two-layered VP-shell for a simple transitive verb (cf. Hale and Keyser 1991, 1993).

---

[17] In (1.13) the position where OBJ is shifted is higher than the position where SUBJ is base-generated. It will be shown later in this book that there are cases in which the structural hierarchy of these positions is opposite. See appendix to chapter 8 for discussion on the placement of the shifted OBJ and the base-position of SUBJ. Cf. Jonas (1996).

1.3.1.5. Economy of Operations and the Theory of Attract

The leading idea of ECONOMY is as follows (cited from Chomsky 1995a: §2.1): At a particular stage Σ of a derivation, we consider only continuations of the derivation already constructed; in particular, only the remaining parts of the numeration N. Application of the operation OP to Σ is barred if this set contains a more optimal (convergent) derivation in which OP does not apply to Σ (cf. Ura 1994b, 1995c; and Collins 1995b, 1996). Chomsky (1995b) assumes that the operations SELECT and MERGE are "costless" in terms of economy considerations (cf. Bobaljik 1995a; Collins 1995b, 1996; and Ura 1997a,b).

In the system of Chomsky (1992, 1994a), several kinds of economy condition were independently stipulated. GREED and MINIMAL LINK CONDITION (MLC) were such conditions, and they individually played a role in constraining the operation MOVE (cf. Lasnik 1993 and Takahashi 1994). Incorporating Frampton's (1996) proposal to reinterpret the operation of movement as "attraction" (cf. Ura 1994b,e, 1995c), Chomsky (1995a) claims that the required effects of those conditions have been encompassed in the definition of ATTRACT, as in the following fashion:[18]

(1.14)   K ATTRACTS F if F is the CLOSEST feature that can enter into a checking relation with a sublabel of K. (Chomsky 1995a: §5.6)

Now it is evident that the notion "closeness" is essential for the economy condition (on operation). Chomsky (1995a: §10.2) defines it in the following fashion:

(1.15)   If β c-commands α and τ is the target of raising, then β is CLOSER to τ than α unless β is in the same minimal domain as (i) τ or (ii) α.

In the chapters that follow it will be shown that there are many cases where both (i) and (ii) should be true on empirical grounds (cf. Oka 1993a,b, 1995; and Ura 1994b, 1995c). The definition of Attract in (1.14) incorporates the effect of the MLC into "closeness" and the effect of the Last Resort Condition into its restriction on feature-matching, as stated in footnote 18.

Chomsky (1992) assumed the stipulation that, if a head H_1 head-moves onto the head H_2 that selects the maximal projection of H_1 as its complement, the minimal domain of H_1 extends to the minimal domain of H_2. Importantly, I do not assume this stipulation on a par with Chomsky (1995a); that is, I assume that there is no such extension of H's minimal domain even though H head-moves onto another head.

I assume another independently stipulated economy condition: PROCRASTINATE. This condition states that covert movement is more economical than overt

---

[18] Note that this definition also encompasses the LAST RESORT CONDITION, the core part of which can be epitomized as follows: Move raises α to target K only if a feature of α enters into a checking relation with a sublabel of K. Incidentally, a sublabel of K is a feature of the zero-level projection of the head H(K) of K (Chomsky 1995a: §4.4).

movement. Although Chomsky (1995a: §4.4) hints that, given the theory of movement of Fs, this condition can be deduced, I will leave to future research the issue of how Procrastinate is subsumed under the more general economy condition.[19]

1.3.2. Theory of Multiple Feature Checking

1.3.2.1. Multiple Specs and Violability of Procrastinate

As Chomsky (1994a, 1995a) repeatedly notes, the minimalist assumptions about phrase structure (i.e., the assumptions under the "bare" phrase structure), unlike the conventional X-bar theory, permit multiple specifiers (Specs) to be projected by a single head. Koizumi (1994a, 1995) and Ura (1993a, 1994e) provide some pieces of evidence in favor of the existence of multiple Specs projected by a single head.

Here it is important to define a specifier of a head X^0. Incorporating the intuition of Ura's (1993b) definition of Specs into the present assumptions, I propose the following definition:

(1.16) α is located in a Spec of X^0 iff (i) and (ii):

(i) α is excluded by X^0 (i.e., α is not dominated by X^{0max}).[20]

(ii) (a) α enters into a feature-checking relation with X^0, or
(b) α is assigned an external θ-role by X^0.

Exclusion is defined in the following manner:

(1.17) α is excluded by β iff no segment of β dominates α.

(Chomsky 1986a: 9)

Remember that feature checking takes place only within the minimal domain of H. Therefore, all elements that check one of their features against a feature of X^0 count as being in a Spec of X^0 if they are excluded by X^0, but contained by XP (= X^{max}).

In Ura (1994e) I claimed (1) that multiple Specs of a head H are possible only when H has multiple sets of Fs, and (2) that the ability of H to have multiple sets of Fs is determined by a (lexical) property: In a language L_1, for example, T may have multiple sets of Fs but v may not; on the other hand, neither T nor v may have multiple sets of Fs in another language L_2. This idea can be recaptured

---

[19] Chomsky (1995a: 264) attributes this idea to Hisa Kitahara and Howard Lasnik. Collins (1996), pointing out that Procrastinate has a very global nature, proposes that the effects of Procrastinate should be captured by conditions on chain-formation. See Ura (1997a,b) for an attempt to reduce Procrastinate to the local/strictly derivational economy condition.

[20] X^0 is a zero-level projection of X^{min} (= terminal element) and X^{0max} is the maximal zero-level projection of the head X^{min}. X^{min} projects to X^0 if another head Y or a formal feature of another element moves onto X^{min}.

by the introduction of the notion [±multiple] as was observed in §1.3.1.3. While a feature with the property of [+multiple] can enter into more than one checking relation, a feature with the property of [−multiple] can enter into only a single checking relation.

On the other hand, Chomsky (1995a), basically maintaining this idea about the parametric variation of the possibility of multiple Specs, refines the mechanism of multiple Specs to accommodate it to the theory of formal features he proposes: The guiding idea is that there is a parameter concerning the "violability of Procrastinate." Now let us suppose that H has a strong feature that must be checked off before Spell-out. If H does not have the parameter-setting that allows H to tolerate an unforced violation of Procrastinate, then H can project only one Spec, to which the checker for H's strong feature is attracted. If H may tolerate a single unforced violation of Procrastinate, another element ε may be attracted to an outer Spec of H after H's canonical (i.e., innermost) Spec is filled with the element that entered into the first checking relation with H, under the condition where ε enters into a checking relation with H.

As I stated in §1.3.1.3, I assume in this book that an F may have both the property of [+multiple] and the property that tolerates (more than) one unforced violation of Procrastinate. Now it is evident, however, that there emerges some redundancy concerning these properties of Fs. It is true that a [+multiple] F as well as an F that may tolerate (more than) one violation of Procrastinate can give birth to multiple Specs. But there are some differences between them; therefore, I assume both properties of Fs in this book: A [+multiple] F can enter into multiple feature-checking relations at LF, though an F with a tolerance for (more than) one violation of Procrastinate cannot establish multiple feature-checking relations at LF unless it also has the property of [+multiple]. Note that the property that tolerates (more than) one unforced violation of Procrastinate can be possessed only by an F of the head that attracts something. The property of [+multiple] can be possessed either by an F of the category that is attracted before Spell-out or by an F that is attracted at LF. Thus, it is possible that a Case-feature of DP, which is universally [−interpretable], has a [+multiple] property. If this hypothetical case happens, the DP can enter into multiple Case-feature checking relations. This means that the DP can move through multiple Case positions. I reported in Ura (1994a,e, 1996b) that this case can indeed be found in a construction I called HYPER-RAISING, in which a DP moves from a Case-checking position to another Case-checking position.[21] But it is senseless to say that a Case-feature of DP may tolerate an unforced violation of Procrastinate, because it cannot attract anything under the asymmetric checking theory (cf. Collins 1996).

The other important difference between [+multiple] and violability of Procrastinate is as follows: A feature with a [+multiple] property may force a violation of Procrastinate if it is also strong. In my analysis of Apachean inverse voice, I will argue that some feature must enter into multiple checking relations before Spell-out; that is, in order for it to be deleted (and erased) before Spell-

---

[21] See Schütze (1996) for a further application of this kind of idea to other phenomena.

out, it must enter into not a single, but multiple checking relations. It is true, as argued so far, that a feature with the property that tolerates unforced violations of Procrastinate may give birth to multiple checking relations before Spell-out, but it should be noted that the multiple checking relations that are created by this property are always optional before Spell-out. The property of [+multiple] can give rise to a situation where multiple checking relations before Spell-out are obligatory.

As repeatedly mentioned in this chapter, the notion "violability of Procrastinate" derives multiple Specs. The following question soon arises: What is the intuition behind the "violability of Procrastinate"? It seems that this kind of notion leads us to the question as to which principles of UG are violable and which are not. Given that some principles of UG are "violable," one might be tempted to conjecture that the notion of "violability" is parallel to the similar notion in Optimality Theory (cf. McCarthy and Prince 1993 and Prince and Smolensky 1993).[22]

The notion "violability of Procrastinate" should not be viewed as a conception like the ones in Optimality Theory. First, it is very clear that this conception is not applied to representation as a kind of "filter." Second, to admit this conception does not lead us to say "such and such principles of UG are violable and the others are not." As we stated, the notion "violability of Procrastinate" simply implies that, when a head H may tolerate an unforced violation of Procrastinate, H has a formal feature such that it is not required, but allowed to be checked off before Spell-out.

1.3.2.2. Multiple Feature Checking and Parameter-Setting

Collins (1995a) was the first article that explicitly elaborated the theory of multiple feature checking under the feature-checking theory of Chomsky (1994a, 1995a). After extending Ura's (1994e) idea about the feature-checking relation between multiple Specs and their head to the feature-checking relations between two heads, he has recast it under the feature-checking theory of Chomsky (1995a) and, finally, reached the conclusion that the one-to-many (i.e., multiple) checking relations should hold between individual formal features, but not between a head and positions (specifiers) or not between a head and another head. Therefore, the parameter concerning multiple checking should be set not upon each head, as Ura (1994e) assumed, but upon each formal feature of a head, as has been implicitly assumed in the discussion so far.

This gives rise to a situation in which a head H has formal features, each of which differs from the others in terms of its parameter concerning its ability to enter into multiple checking relations. For example, whereas the Case-feature of T in Imbabura Quechua may enter into multiple feature-checking relations, its ϕ-feature cannot, and this asymmetry results in some GF-splitting (see chapter 3). Moreover, it is natural to extend this idea to strong features: I propose that each

---

[22] Thanks to Naoki Fukui for bringing my attention to this point.

feature (of a single head) may differ from the others in terms of its strength. Therefore, it may be the case that, whereas (finite) T in a given language has a weak Case-feature, its EPP-feature is strong. I will claim that this case, indeed, happens in Bantu, which results in active/inverse alternation.

1.3.2.3. Variety of Multiple Feature Checking by [+Interpretable]-Features

In addition to a [+multiple] feature and a feature with the property that may tolerate an unforced violation of Procrastinate, there is another kind of property, [+interpretable], that enables the feature with that property to enter into multiple checking relations.

As mentioned in §1.3.1.3, if a feature is [+interpretable], its existence at LF does not cause a violation of Full Interpretation (FI), or more precisely, its existence at LF is required by FI because it must be interpreted at LF. In other words, it must not be deleted or erased at LF. Thus, a [+interpretable] feature, if being weak, need not enter into any checking relation. Recall that a checked feature is deleted if possible, and that a deleted feature is erased if possible (Chomsky 1995a: 280). Then, it follows from the nature of the property [+interpretable] that a [+interpretable] feature can enter into multiple checking relations. This is because a [+interpretable] feature cannot be deleted even if checked.

Chomsky (1995a) cites an example of multiple checking relations caused by a [+interpretable] feature. In several Romance and Slavic languages a DP induces agreement both on the finite verb and on the adjective in a raising construction like the one corresponding to the following English sentence: $John_i$ looks $[\ t_i\ tired\ ]$. The φ-feature of DP is [+interpretable]; thus DP can enter into multiple φ-feature checking relations, a situation which can be morphologically attested in those languages. This is a case where an element to be attracted has a [+interpretable] feature. Multiple feature checking is also possible if a head attracting something has a [+interpretable] feature. One example comes from multiple wh-phrases in a clause. Suppose that a wh-phrase is attracted to a Spec of C by the feature Q (or [+wh]).[23] It is natural that Q is [+interpretable] universally (see footnote 23; cf. Watanabe 1992). Then, Q can enter into multiple feature-checking relations. Thus, absorption in the sense of Higginbotham and May (1981) can be naturally reinterpreted as multiple checking by (the Q-feature of) C. In some Slavic languages, all the wh-phrases in an interrogative clause move to the clause-initial position (see Rudin 1988, Bošković 1994, Koizumi 1994a, and references cited therein). From the assumption that the Q-feature of C in those languages has the property of [+multiple] and [+strong] in addition to the universal property of [+interpretable], the fact of multiple wh-fronting in those languages follows. In English-type languages with single wh-fronting, only a

---

[23] Q is the source of interrogation (cf. Katz and Postal 1964 and Cheng 1991). Sometimes it is argued that Q should be regarded as a kind of the categorial feature D.

single *wh*-phrase is attracted to a Spec of C before Spell-out because the Q-feature of C in these languages has the property of [+strong] but [−multiple]. In French-type languages, a *wh*-phrase may raise to a Spec of C or may stay in situ because the Q-feature of C in these languages is weak in addition to the property that tolerates a single unforced violation of Procrastinate, but it is [−multiple]. In Japanese-type languages, no *wh*-phrase may raise because the Q-feature of C in these languages is weak, [−multiple], and does not tolerate a violation of Procrastinate.[24]

1.3.3. Multiple Feature Checking and GF-Splitting Phenomena

In §1.2.2.3 I introduced the theory of GFs, according to which a GF (such as the ability to control a missing subject in a subordinate clause) results from a certain feature-checking relation with a particular head. Given this theory of GFs in addition to the theory of multiple feature checking just sketched above, a natural explanation can be given to GF-splitting phenomena, which seem to be highly resistant to the theory of grammar in the minimalist program, as pointed out in §1.2.

Recall that, according to the theory of multiple feature checking, there may be a case where a head H enters into more than one feature-checking relation. Hence, the theory of multiple feature checking allows a situation where two DPs *A* and *B* independently check a different feature of Infl. Now suppose that *A* enters into a φ-feature checking relation with Infl and *B* enters into an EPP-feature checking relation with Infl. Then, we expect that some GF-splitting occurs in this case if we assume, according to our hypothesis about GFs, that the ability to control a missing subject in a subordinate-adjunct clause results from a φ-feature checking relation with Infl, and the ability to bind a (purely) subject-oriented reflexive results from an EPP-feature checking relation with Infl. That is to say, we expect that *A*, but not *B*, has the ability to control, and that *B*, but not *A*, has the ability to bind a subject-oriented reflexive. This is a merely putative case, but it is sufficient to show that this mechanism can provide a natural explanation of GF-splitting phenomena under the minimalist framework. In the chapters that follow, a good deal of empirical evidence in favor of this mechanism will be offered.

Moreover, the theory of multiple feature checking advocated in this book provides a natural account of another kind of GF-splitting. Marantz (1991: 234) holds that "recent investigations of languages with rich morphological case and agreement systems strongly indicate that the relationship between abstract Case and morphological case and agreement is indirect, at best." This kind of disparity

---

[24] Assuming that T's tense-feature, which is [+interpretable], can enter into multiple checking relations, Collins (1995a) explains the fact that verbs in a serial verb construction have the same full-fledged inflection of tense. This counts as another example of a [+interpretable] feature which attracts something that can enter into multiple checking relations.

between case morphology and agreement is naturally expected under the theory of multiple feature checking, according to which several formal features of a single head can be checked by an independent element. As we will see in chapter 4, the φ-feature and the nominative Case-feature of T in Japanese, for example, can be checked independently; therefrom, the so-called Dative Subject Construction, where the dative DP checks the φ-feature of T and the nominative DP checks the nominative Case-feature of T, results naturally.

This approach to grammatical functions (GFs) by means of the theory of (multiple) feature checking has a consequence with regard to the notion GRAMMATICAL RELATION (GR). Under the theory of (multiple) feature checking advocated in this book, the notion GR is, at best, of little use. To tell what kind of grammatical (syntactic) function a given argument bears under this theory, it is sufficient for us to discern what kind of checking relation it enters into with what kind of functional head. Recall that it has been traditionally held that an argument with a GR like subject or object has its own invariant GFs, and that GRs are regarded as intermediary abstract entities that relate these (syntactic) functions to the argument with a particular thematic role. Now that we can establish the relation between GFs and an argument without referring to GR, the notion GR is of no use in this regard.

1.4. Preview of Major Proposals

In this section I will preview some of the major theoretical proposals to be presented in this book, leaving the discussions on their empirical validity to the following sections.

1.4.1. Strong Features and Violability of Procrastinate

Chomsky (1995a: §2.1) proposes that, given that the derivation D has formed a category C that contains α with a strong feature F, D terminates if (1) F remains unchecked, and (2) C is not projected by α. I will propose another more restricted condition on the checking of strong features:

(1.18)   D terminates if F has not been checked at the stage of derivation where F can be checked off by some operation.

This proposal brings an interesting consequence to the issue concerning the base-position of SUBJ and the placement of overtly shifted OBJ, which has recently given rise to much controversy in the minimalist literature (e.g., Bobaljik 1995b; Koizumi 1993, 1995; and Jonas 1996). According to Chomsky's (1995a) Agr-less feature-checking theory, SUBJ is generated at a Spec of v and OBJ has its nominal feature checked off at a Spec of v if the checking takes place before Spell-out, as mentioned in §1.3.1.4. Then, a question arises: Which one comes in the canonical (i.e., innermost) Spec of v and which comes in its outer Spec?

Now suppose that *v* has a strong nominal feature, which attracts OBJ overtly to its Spec. The question is: What must happen after the stage in the derivation where this *v* has been introduced by Merge?

(1.19)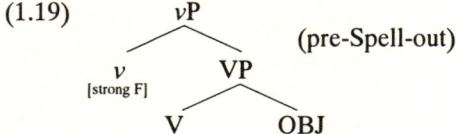

One might think that, because Merge is cost-free, the application of Merge to SUBJ targeting *v*P in (1.19) should happen, deriving (1.20) from (1.19):

(1.20)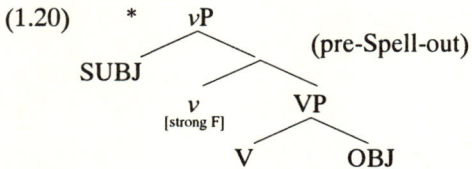

This derivation is precluded by (1.18), however; for, the strong nominal feature of *v* in (1.20) remains unchecked after this operation[25] in spite of the fact that it would be checked off by OBJ if OBJ moved to the Spec of *v*, as illustrated in (1.21):

(1.21)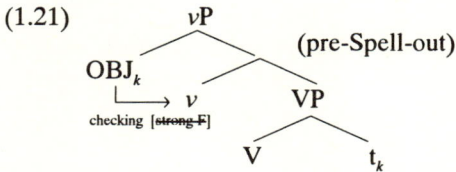

After (1.21), SUBJ is introduced by Merge into an outer Spec of *v*, as in (1.22). It is reasonable to assume that the (thematic) relation between SUBJ and *v* is properly established in (1.22) because SUBJ is in a Spec of *v*, given the definition of Spec, which was introduced in §1.3.2.1.[26]

(1.22)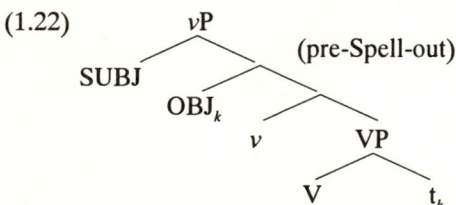

It is important to note that at the stage where OBJ is attracted to the canonical Spec of *v*, the general economy condition is violated because Move/Attract is selected over Merge, which is always more economical than Move/Attract. But one

[25] Recall the stipulation 8 in §1.3.1.3.

[26] This possibility was first suggested (to me) by Jonathan Bobaljik in personal communication.

should notice that this violation of economy is permissible because it is the only way to save the derivation from crash.

To summarize, our hypothesis predicts that, where v has a strong nominal feature, the position to which OBJ is overtly shifted is always lower than the base-position of SUBJ. Interestingly enough, this result corresponds exactly to what the so-called SPLIT VP HYPOTHESIS (Koizumi 1993, 1995 and Bobaljik 1995b) is trying to argue for.[27] According to Chris Collins (personal communication), the base position of SUBJ is always higher than the shifted OBJ in Ewe and some other African languages. Koizumi (1995) draws good evidence in favor of this from Zarma, a language spoken in Niger.

Instead, suppose that v in (1.19) has a weak nominal feature, but this nominal feature may tolerate an unforced violation of Procrastinate. The situation is illustrated in (1.23):

(1.23)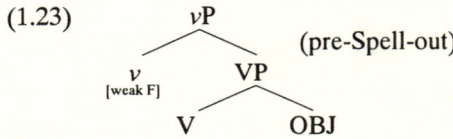

Then, the application of Merge to SUBJ targeting vP in (1.23) always beats the application of Move/Attract to OBJ to vP in the economy competition at the stage illustrated in (1.23). This is because Merge is more economical than Move/Attract. Notice that the application of Move/Attract to OBJ to vP in (1.23) is not required, though it is allowed due to the parameter of v, which allows v to tolerate an unforced violation of Procrastinate. Therefore, (1.24) is permitted, but (1.25) is not permitted in this situation:

(1.24)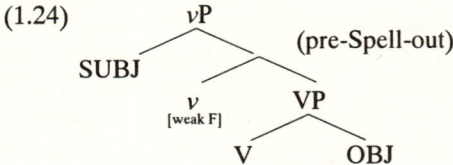

(1.25)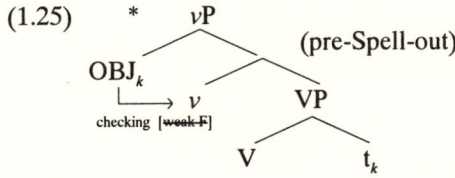

After (1.24), the application of Move/Attract to OBJ targeting vP in (1.24) is allowed thanks to the parameter of v, deriving (1.26):

---

[27] Jonas (1996) has discovered that in Icelandic, the base-position of SUBJ is always lower than the position of the shifted OBJ, contrary to the claim of the Split VP Hypothesis. I will demonstrate, however, that we can give a consistent account of the Icelandic case, too. See appendix to chapter 8.

(1.26)

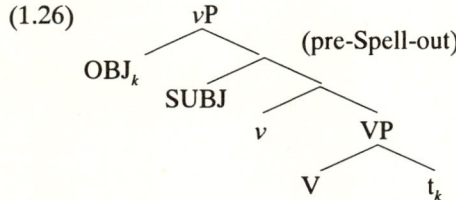

Hence, our hypothesis predicts that the base position of SUBJ is always lower than the shifted OBJ in a language L if v in L has a weak nominal feature, but it may tolerate, at least, one unforced violation of Procrastinate. In the appendix to chapter 8, I will demonstrate that this state of affairs is empirically attested.

1.4.2. Syntactic Mapping of Argument Structure

As mentioned in §1.3.1.4, this book adopts the two-layered VP-shell for the underlying structure of a simple transitive verb, which is delineated in (1.27):[28]

(1.27)

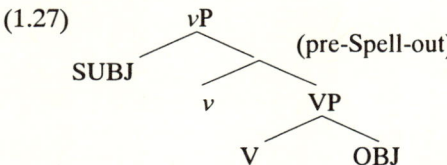

Here it is rather obscure, however, exactly what SUBJ and OBJ in (1.27) correspond to: with what kind of θ-roles are they generated at those positions?

I will assume, following Chomsky (1994a, 1995a), that v, the higher V in the two-layered VP-shell for a simple transitive verb, is a kind of light verb that has the ability to assign Agent, and that Theme is discharged within the minimal domain of the lowest V in a given VP-shell (cf. Hale and Keyser 1991, 1993). I am further assuming that Locative, too, is discharged within the minimal domain of the lowest V in a given VP-shell. Presumably, Locative is discharged to the Spec of the V and Theme is discharged to the complement of V, as illustrated in (1.28):

(1.28)

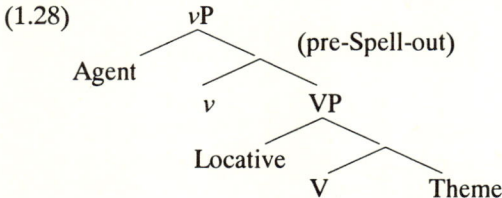

---

[28] As was argued in §1.4.1, the base position of SUBJ in (1.27) is not accurate if OBJ is required to be attracted to the canonical Spec of v. It is, however, true that SUBJ is generated at one of the possible Specs of v.

This is compatible with Jackendoff's (1972) and Grimshaw's (1990) Thematic Hierarchy in which Locative is ranked more highly than Theme, given that an argument A_1 is base-generated at a position higher than another argument A_2 if the θ-role of A_1 is ranked more highly than that of A_2 in the Thematic Hierarchy (cf. Speas 1990).[29]

Where is a θ-role such as Experiencer, Goal, or Benefactive discharged in the underlying structure? I propose that there is an individual (light) verb with the ability to assign those θ-roles to its Spec, and that this light verb (what will hereafter be called V_{mid}) selects the verb with the ability to discharge Theme as its complement (i.e., V in (1.28)) and is selected by the light verb assigning Agent to its Spec if Agent is to appear in the structure. Thus, for example, the full underlying structure in which Agent, Goal, and Theme are discharged looks like this:

(1.29)

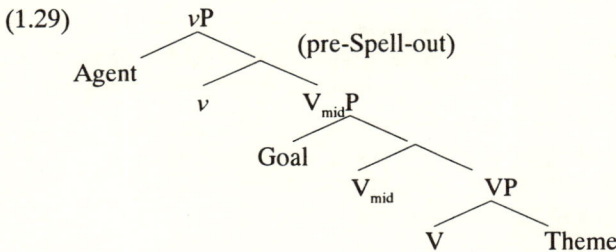

This represents the underlying structure for a ditransitive verb like *give* in English. In chapter 7 it will be demonstrated that this structure offers a natural explanation of several cross-linguistic and language-particular phenomena with respect to the double object construction.

One of the consequences of this proposal is as follows: In a simple transitive clause, Theme cannot be attracted to an A-position that is higher than Agent unless it beforehand moves to a position within the minimal domain in which Agent is located. This is because Agent is always the closest to the target unless Theme enters the minimal domain in which Agent is located. (Recall that we are assuming that there is no extension of a minimal domain (§1.3.1.5).) Another interesting prediction is that either Locative or Theme can be equally attracted to a certain target if there is nothing intervening between the target and these elements. This is because they are already in the same minimal domain (of V) in the

---

[29] It is not crucial for me to insist that Locative be generated at a higher position than Theme. In fact, many authors, including Speas (1990) and Mohanan (1994), assume that Locative is lower than Theme in the Thematic Hierarchy. The discussions that follows, however, will not be affected if Theme is generated at the Spec of V and Locative at the complement of V, as will become evident later, though I will keep assuming (1.28) for expository purposes. In passing, this kind of mapping of θ-roles with the aid of the Thematic Hierarchy should be reduced owing to the lack of its virtual conceptual necessity. I believe that it can be deduced from Hale and Keyser's (1991, 1993) approach, though I leave it to future research to pursue this possibility.

underlying structure. It will be shown in chapter 5 that this prediction is indeed borne out with other interesting results.

1.4.3. What Is SUBJ/OBJ?

In this book I use SUBJ and OBJ to refer to the logical, underlying subject and the logical, underlying object in a given clause, respectively. But it is necessary to clearly define what the logical, underlying subject and the logical, underlying object are.

In §1.4.2 I claimed that an argument A_1 is base-generated at a position higher than another argument A_2 if the θ-role of A_1 is ranked higher than that of A_2 in the Thematic Hierarchy. I will use the cover term SUBJ (which should be read as the logical, underlying subject) to refer to the argument that is introduced by Merge at the highest position in a given clause (or, more precisely, Complete Functional Complex in the sense of Chomsky 1986b), and OBJ (i.e., the logical, underlying object) for the argument that is introduced at the lowest position in the clause. If a clause contains arguments other than SUBJ and OBJ, I will use their own θ-role like Experiencer, Goal, or Benefactive to refer to them. Conventionally, I will use DO (direct object) and IO (indirect object) to refer to Theme and Goal, respectively, in a so-called double object construction.

According to this definition of SUBJ/OBJ, there occur cases where SUBJ and OBJ do not match with the conventional/intuitive use of subject and object, which is determined by the GR that each argument is supposed to bear. Consider (1.30):

(1.30) a. John fears horses. (*John* = Experiencer, *horses* = Theme/Patient)
b. Horses scare John. (*horses* = Theme/Patient, *John* = Experiencer)

Since I am assuming that Experiencer is higher than Theme in the Thematic Hierarchy, *John* in (1.30b) as well as *John* in (1.30a) is base-generated at a position higher than *horses*, regardless of its surface position. Thus, *John* and *horses* invariantly count as SUBJ and OBJ, respectively, in both sentences. Moreover, Theme counts as SUBJ in my terminology in an unaccusative sentence like *John arrived*, though it might be better to call it the logical, underlying object.[30]

In the literature on language typology, the following terminology is frequently used: S represents the intransitive subject, A the transitive subject, and O (or P) the transitive object (cf. Dixon 1979, 1989, 1994 and Comrie 1978, 1989). Informally, OBJ corresponds to O (or P) and SUBJ corresponds to A in a transitive clause and S in an intransitive clause (cf. Martin 1991). Furthermore, it should be noted that SUBJ and OBJ have nothing to do with GR subject and GR object in principle.

---

[30] In chapter 5 I will return to the issue as to why *horses* in (1.30b) appears at a higher position than *John* in the surface structure despite the fact that it is base-generated at a position lower than the base-position of *John*.

1.4.4. Equidistance, Multiple Specs, and DP-Movement over DP

As was mentioned in the preceding subsection, Theme (i.e., OBJ) in (1.31), which represents the underlying structure for a simple transitive verb, cannot be attracted by H beyond Agent (i.e., SUBJ) unless it beforehand enters the minimal domain in which SUBJ is located:

(1.31)

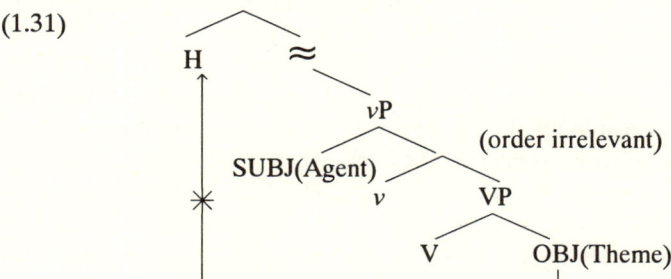

Instead, if OBJ is attracted by v in (1.31) for some reason and SUBJ is introduced by Merge, the structure where H has been introduced looks like (1.32):

(1.32)

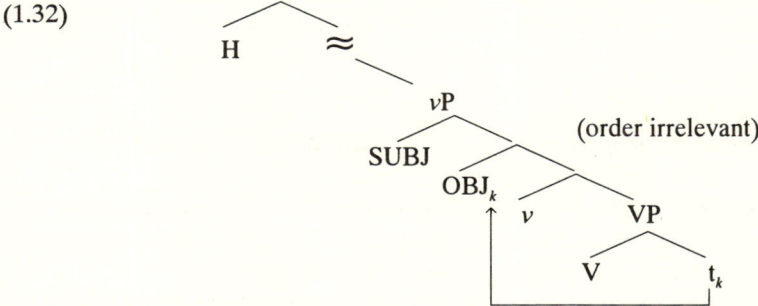

If H in (1.32) has a feature that can attract OBJ, and if OBJ retains the ability to check off the feature, then OBJ in (1.32) can be properly attracted by H without violating the "MLC" part let alone the "Last Resort" part in the definition of Attract/Move; for, SUBJ and OBJ in (1.32) are in the same minimal domain and, hence, they are equidistant from H.[31]

To generalize this story, the conclusion follows that an argument A_1 can jump over another argument A_2 that is located in the minimal domain D if A_1 beforehand moves into D. This is the theory of DP-movement over another DP to be advocated in this book. In what follows, it will be observed that many in-

---

[31] α and β are equidistant (from Γ) iff they are in the same minimal domain. If α and β are equidistant from Γ, movement of α to Γ and movement of β to Γ are equally economical with respect to the general economy condition. See Chomsky (1992). But note that, as stated in §1.3.1.5, I adopt throughout this book Chomsky's (1995a) proposal that Chomsky's (1992) idea that the extension of the minimal domain of α due to α's head-movement be discarded.

stances of argument-overpassing (e.g., active/inverse voice alternation (chapter 2), locative inversion (chapter 5), etc.) can be naturally accounted for by this theory.[32]

1.4.5. Optionality

Given the theory of formal features and Procrastinate (an economy condition that requires the application of Move/Attract to take place at covert syntax unless its application before Spell-out is the only way to save the derivation from crash), one might be tempted to draw the conclusion that overt movement applies only when a feature responsible for the movement is strong. One might gather from this conclusion that overt movement applies only when it is required (by feature checking); otherwise, overt movement never applies. This leads to the conclusion that optional movement (i.e., movement that can apply optionally before Spell-out) never exists. On the contrary, this kind of reasoning/conclusion is not the sole logical possibility under the theory of feature checking assumed in this book.

Needless to say, a lot of instances of optional movement can be found in natural language, some of which will be discussed in this book. Here I will sketch out the leading idea as to how to explain optional Move/Attract application.

1.4.5.1. Optionality of Raising and Violability of Procrastinate

As mentioned in §1.3.2.1, the notion "violability of Procrastinate" plays a very important role in this book. Now let us suppose that a head H has a weak nominal feature and that it may tolerate an unforced violation of Procrastinate. Then, an element ε with the nominal feature that matches with H's nominal feature *may* be attracted to a Spec of H before Spell-out. In other words, the overt movement of ε to a Spec of H is not required but allowed. This movement, not being required, violates Procrastinate if it takes place before Spell-out; however, one should note that it is permissible thanks to the property of H's nominal feature that may tolerate an unforced violation of Procrastinate. Upon the condition that H may tolerate an unforced violation of Procrastinate, the existence of optional movements is quite natural. In the chapters that follow many instances in which optional movement takes place under this mechanism will be observed.

---

[32] The analysis of argument-overpassing which was sketched here is an extension of Ura's (1993a,c, 1994e) under the more articulated theory of feature checking proposed by Chomsky (1995a). To the best of my knowledge, Tada (1993) is the first to provide an idea of multiple Specs for argument-overpassing phenomena (in a minimalist program), though he reached the idea through examples totally different from mine under the non-bare phrase structure theory.

1.4.5.2. *Optional Attraction before Spell-out and Equidistance*

Another instance of optionality comes from the following case: Given a target τ, either of the two elements ε_1 and ε_2 can move to τ. Oka (1993a,b) (and, also, Ura 1994e, 1995c) claims that the illusory cancellation of superiority (as in (1.33)) is an instance of this optionality:

(1.33)   a.   Where$_k$ did you buy what t_k.
         b.   What$_k$ did you buy t_k where.

Since the [+wh]-feature of C in English is strong (cf. Watanabe 1992 and Chomsky 1992), the *wh*-phrase that is closest to C is required to be attracted to the Spec of C before Spell-out. Suppose that the adjunct *wh*-phrase *where* is base-generated at a position adjoined to the maximal projection within which the argument *wh*-phrase *what* is also base-generated.[33] Then, the fact shown in (1.33) follows from the theory of Attraction, that either of the *wh*-phrases in (1.33) can be attracted by C; for, the *wh*-phrases in question are equidistant from C in (1.33).[34]

To summarize, two elements within the same minimal domain have the equal possibility to be attracted to τ. In other words, the choice as to whether ε_1 or ε_2 is to be attracted to τ is totally optional only if ε_1 and ε_2 are in the same minimal domain at the stage of derivation where the application of Attract to either of them is executed.

One of the most direct consequences of this proposal can be found in the following examples:

(1.34)   *English* (Guéron 1994: 173)
         a.   e is [$_{SC}$ John$_k$ my best friend$_l$]
         b.   John$_k$ is [t_k my best friend$_l$].
         c.   My best friend$_l$ is [John t_l].

Moro (1991) argues that (1.34b) and (1.34c) are derived from the common underlying structure (1.34a) (cf. Stowell 1981). Suppose, following Rothstein (1987), that the copula involved in (1.34) is equative and that the underlying structure of the small clause in (1.34) looks like:

(1.35)

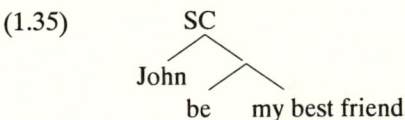

---

[33] See Oka (1993a,b) and Ura (1994e, 1995c) for details.

[34] I will not touch upon *wh*-movement again in this book, though. For a treatment of *wh*/operator-movement under the feature checking theory, see Branigan (1992), Oka (1993a,b, 1995), Takahashi (1994, 1995), Tsai (1994), Lee (1995), Maki (1995), Zwart (1996), Fukui (1997), and references cited therein.

That is to say, the small clause is headed by the equative *be*. Example (1.36) is derived from (1.35) if T is introduced by Merge:

(1.36)   [$_{TP}$ T [$_{SC}$ John be my best friend]]

In English the EPP-feature is strong; as a consequence, something is attracted to the Spec of T in overt syntax. In (1.36) *John* and *my best friend* are equidistant from T because they are in the same minimal domain of *be*. Then, we predict that either of them can be attracted to the Spec of T, resulting in either (1.34b) or (1.34c).[35]

1.4.5.3. Strictly Derivational/Local Economy

I will adopt throughout this book a strictly derivational/local economy condition on syntactic operations in C_{HL}. More specifically, I adopt Collins's (1996) local economy, the core of which can be summarized in the following fashion: At a particular stage Σ of a derivation, we consider only continuations of the derivation already constructed; in particular, only the remaining parts of the numeration *N*. Application of the operation OP to Σ is barred if this set contains a more optimal (convergent) derivation in which OP does not apply to Σ.[36]

With this in mind, consider the following situation in overt syntax:

(1.37)   [$_{XP}$ X(f_1, f_2) ... [$_{YP}$ WP(f_1) ZP(f_1, f_2) Y ...   (before Spell-out)

In (1.37), the head V has formal features f_1 and f_2, and WP has only f_1 but ZP has both f_1 and f_2. Since WP and ZP in (1.37) are in the same minimal domain of the head Y, they are equidistant from X. Now suppose (1) that the feature f_1 of X, like the EPP-feature of Infl in English, is a strong feature, (2) that the feature of f_2, like the φ-feature of Infl in English, is a weak [–interpretable]-feature, and (3) that the feature f_2 of ZP, like the φ-feature of DP, is [+interpretable]. Then, what should happen in (1.37) at the next step?

---

[35] As Pollock (1989) and Chomsky (1989) extensively argue, the English copular *be* moves overtly. Now note the following examples:

(i)   a.   Bill considers [$_{SC}$ Mary a doctor].
      b.   Mary$_k$ is [$_{SC}$ t$_k$ a doctor].
      c.   *A doctor$_k$ is [$_{SC}$ Mary t$_k$].

The prohibition of the alternation between (i)b and (i)c may be due to the fact that the NP *a doctor* in these examples acts as a predicate. See Rothstein (1987) and Stowell (1989) for the structure of the clause with a predicative NP. See Moro (1991), Heycock (1994), and Guéron (1994) for more discussions on the impossibility of the alternation shown in (i). For more discussion on relevant constructions, see Heycock (1995).

[36] See Collins (1996) for detailed discussion on derivational/local economy vs. global economy. He proposes a more rigorous definition of derivational/local economy, which brings broader consequences to the theory of feature checking as well as the theory of movement (see, also, Collins 1995b and Ura 1994b, 1995c). See Fukui (1996) and Ura (1997a) for conceptual/mathematical arguments for local economy.

As argued so far, either WP or ZP can be attracted by X's strong feature f_1 to the Spec of X without violating the "MLC" part let alone the "Last Resort" part of the definition of Attract/Move, because they are equidistant from X. Suppose that WP is attracted to that position in (1.37). Then, in order for the derivation to converge, the feature f_2 of ZP must move up onto X to check off the feature f_2 of X at LF. Instead, suppose that ZP is attracted to the Spec of X in (1.37). Then, there is no extra movement necessary for convergence; for, ZP at the Spec of X can check off the feature f_2 of X (at LF). Now compare those two derivations; whereas there is one extra step at LF necessary for convergence if WP is overtly attracted to the Spec of X in (1.37), such an extra step at LF is not necessary if ZP is overtly attracted.

Thence, advocates of global economy might conclude that the general economy condition demands that the former derivation (i.e., the derivation in which WP is overtly attracted in (1.37)) should be blocked by the latter one (i.e., the derivation in which ZP is overtly attracted in (1.37)), because the former needs more steps than the latter for convergence. On the contrary, in the chapters that follow, I will provide several pieces of empirical evidence that both derivations should be allowed. More specifically, I will demonstrate that both derivations depicted above should be possible in Bantu active/inverse alternation, Bantu locative inversion, Dutch experiencer inversion, and so forth.[37]

One should notice that both derivations are properly allowed if one adopts the local economy condition, which was stated above; this is because the movement of WP to the Spec of X and the movement of ZP to the Spec of X are equally economical at the stage in the derivation illustrated in (1.37) and there is no need to worry about any operation that could happen at a later stage in the derivation under the local economy condition.

1.4.6. Feature Checking as a Syntactic Operation

In this book, I will sometimes use the terminology CHECKING instead of "to enter a checking relation with" in Chomsky's (1995a) terminology. The reason for its use is that I would like to emphasize feature checking as a syntactic operation like Merge or Attract/Move. By explicitly counting Checking as an operation, I propose that Checking, like Attract/Move, be subject to the general economy condition. This means that Checking takes place only when it is required for convergence.

According to Chomsky (1995a), if F is in the checking domain of a head H, F can check off f, a sublabel of K, and if, furthermore, F and f match, then F is in a checking relation with f. Now that Checking is an operation subject to the general economy condition, it is not always the case that F automatically checks off (i.e., enters into a checking relation with) f when F is in a checking configuration with f. F checks off f only if it is required for convergence.

---

[37] Drawing data from the so-called English quotative inversion construction, Collins (1996) provides good evidence in favor of derivational/local economy.

Let us consider the following hypothetical case: T has a strong EPP-feature and a (weak) Case-feature. Due to the strong EPP-feature, a DP is attracted to the Spec of T, and checks off T's strong EPP-feature. Naturally, the DP has Case-feature, too. Does the Case-feature of the DP always checks off the (weak) Case-feature of T in this context? The answer is no under the hypothesis that Checking is an operation subject to the economy condition. This is because the Case-feature of T, not being strong, is not required to be checked off before Spell-out. The DP, therefore, may undergo further raising and enter into a Case-feature checking relation with something somehow. The Case-feature of T can be checked off by the Case-feature of another DP at LF. This derivation can be delineated as in the following:

(1.38)

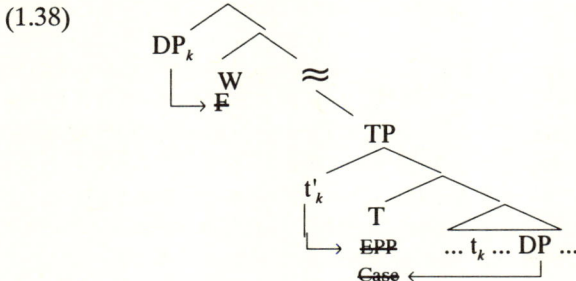

1.4.7. Some Parameters

1.4.7.1. The Impersonal Parameter

I will propose a new parameter, which is expected to cope with the problem involved in the following kind of examples:

(1.39)   a.   *German* (Safir 1984: 211)
           Er sagte, daß getanzt werden wird.
           he said COMP danced be will
           'He said that there will be dancing.'

       b.   *Arabic* (Postal 1986: 9)
           Julisa fi al-dari.
           sat(PASS) in the-house
           'There was sitting in the house.'

       c.   *Modern Hebrew* (Hermon 1984: 214)
           Kar/Harm/Tov/Mesha'amoen li.
           cold/hot/good/boring me(DAT)
           'I am cold/hot/well/bored.'

       d.   *Turkish* (Postal 1986: 144)
           Harp-te vur-ul-un-ur.
           war-LOC shoot-PASS-PASS-AOR
           Lit. 'In the war is been shot.'

e. *Sanskrit* (Ostler 1979: 367)
   Mayα (mαsam) αsyate.
   me(INST) month(ACC) sat(PASS)
   'There is sitting for a month by me.'

f. *Hindi* (Mohanan 1994: 183)
   Cor-ko pakdaa gayaa.
   thief-ACC catch(PERF) go(PERF)
   'The thief was caught.'

g. *Icelandic* (Andrews 1982: 462)
   Drengina vantar mat.
   the-boys(ACC) lacks food(ACC)
   'The boys lack food.'

As shown by the above examples, in a lot of so-called nominative-accusative languages, it may sometimes be the case that there is no element with nominative Case in a tensed clause, whose T is expected to assign/check nominative Case in an ordinary context. What checks off T's nominative Case-feature in these examples?

I would like to simply assume such a parameter as the following: There is a parameter concerning the checking of the nominative Case of T. If the setting of this parameter is positive in a language L, the nominative Case-feature of T need not be checked off in L.[38] In fact, this is merely a statement/description of what is going on in the examples concerned. It is conceivable that this parameter could be deduced by implementing an appropriate device, such as a use of (phonologically) null expletives, which plays the role in checking off T's nominative Case-feature, and so forth. But, in this book, I will not go into any detail in the implementation of the above parameter, leaving it to future research to explore it. For the purpose of this book, it suffices to note that there is a phenomenon that can be described with the above parameter.[39]

It is noteworthy that the situation at issue can be typically found in a certain type of construction, called the IMPERSONAL PASSIVE (Perlmutter and Postal 1984; Postal 1986), as observed in (1.39). If an intransitive (unergative/unaccusative) clause is passivized together with the demotion of SUBJ, it gives rise to a situation in which no nominative element appears in the clause. In this book, I will therefore call the aforementioned parameter the IMPERSONAL PARAMETER.

1.4.7.2. The Theta-Position Checking Parameter

Chomsky (1995a: §4.5.6) proposes the stipulation that an element introduced (base-generated) by Merge in its θ-position cannot undergo feature checking unless it moves somewhere other than its base-generated position. This stipulation indicates that the syntactic operation Checking does not coincide with θ-

---

[38] This is reminiscent of Safir's (1984, 1985) "NOM-drop parameter."

[39] See Ura (1995b) for discussion on this issue.

assignment/interpretation for some reason. As stated at 8 in §1.3.1.3, I will propose that this does not hold universally; that is, whereas Checking may coincide with θ-assignment in some languages, it may not in others. This parameter will be called THETA-POSITION CHECKING PARAMETER (henceforth, ΘPC-parameter). If a language L is [+ΘPC], then elements can undergo feature checking at their θ-positions in L, and if L is [–ΘPC], then elements cannot check anything at their θ-positions in L.

Consider the following vP-structure:

(1.40)

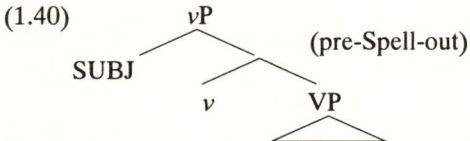

(pre-Spell-out)

SUBJ is introduced by Merge at a Spec of v. In this structure SUBJ is provided with its θ-role by v. Since v, selecting VP as its complement, is transitive, it has some nominal features such as accusative Case-feature. SUBJ at this position cannot check v's nominal features in languages like English or other European languages because these languages are [–ΘPC]. On the other hand, I will argue in chapter 6 that there are some languages in which SUBJ at this position can check v's nominal features just because these languages are [+ΘPC]. It will be demonstrated that these languages correspond to what are called ergative languages. Put differently, [±ΘPC] is the key to the distinction between nominative-accusative languages and ergative-absolutive languages, a big topic to which numerous studies have been devoted.

1.4.8. Definition of [±Construable]-Features

As stated in §1.2.2 this book is devoted to developing and elaborating the hypothesis that a GF (such as the ability to control a missing subject in a subordinate clause) results from a certain feature-checking relation with a particular head. In establishing the concrete theory of GFs in the light of empirical data, I will use the notion [±CONSTRUABLE]. A [+construable]-feature is the one that remains undeleted at LF in either or both elements involved in the checking relation. For instance, the EPP-feature (= D-feature) of T is deleted if it is checked off, but it remains undeleted in the DP that checks it off; hence, D-feature counts as a [+construable]-feature, even though it is deleted from T after its checking. It is useful to note that the EPP-feature (= D-feature) of T, though [+construable], is [–interpretable], because it must be deleted at LF due to Full Interpretation (Chomsky 1995a). In short, all the [+interpretable]-features are [+construable]. Therefore, EPP-features (= D-feature) and φ-features always count as [+construable] regardless of whether they are deleted or not from the element that possesses them, but Case-features are [–construable].[40]

---

[40] There is another type of [+construable]-feature: namely, [±wh]-feature. See Tsai

Interestingly, it will be shown that [±construable] is the key to distinguishing the so-called nominative-oriented phenomena from subject-oriented phenomena, distinction that has been often noticed in the literature (cf. Hale 1970, Dixon 1972, Marantz 1984, Bittner and Hale 1996a, and references cited therein).

1.5. Organization

From chapter 2 to chapter 6 I will concentrate on exploring the theory of GFs though studying several GF-splitting phenomena. Active/inverse voice alternation found in Bantu and Apachean will be dealt with in chapter 2, anti-impersonal passives in Lango and Imbabura Quechua in chapter 3, dative/quirky subject constructions in Japanese/Korean, Tamil, and Icelandic in chapter 4, locative inversion with GF-splitting in Bantu and Japanese in chapter 5, and ergativity and the typology of ergative languages in chapter 6. In chapter 7 and chapter 8 I will devote myself to discussions on some further applications of the theory of multiple feature checking, extending it to phenomena with no GF-splitting. Cross-linguistic studies on double object constructions will come in chapter 7, and optional object shift found in Japanese will be discussed in chapter 8. Concluding remarks together with remarks on some implications of the proposals presented in this book will appear in chapter 9.

(1994), Maki (1995), and Watanabe (1997) for relevant discussion on this feature and its checking.

2

Active/Inverse Voice Alternation

The construction that I will call here INVERSE almost corresponds to what has been called Subject-Object Inversion (e.g., Hale 1973) or Subject-Object Reversal (e.g., Kimenyi 1980) in the literature. According to Fox and Hopper (1994), an inverse clause is an active transitive clause in which the patient/theme/object has certain subject properties. In this chapter I am particularly concerned with an inverse construction that possesses the following remarkable properties: (1) The word order of the logical subject (SUBJ) and the logical object (OBJ) in the active transitive clause is changed so that the positions of OBJ and SUBJ are inverted (with V as the pivot in Bantu); (2) the inverted logical object (OBJ) acquires some of the properties of subject (i.e., subjecthood); and (3) the logical subject (SUBJ) partially loses its subjecthood but it is not demoted in the sense that it stands as nominative Case without any preposition (or postposition). The name inverse stems from the property (1). Because of the properties in (2) and (3), it has been held in the literature that inverse is a kind of voice alternation (cf. Klaiman 1991 and Palmer 1994). These properties (i.e., (2) and (3)) are of particular interest to us, because we can think of inverse as a GF-splitting phenomenon due to these properties.[1]

This chapter is organized as follows: In §2.1 I consider the syntactic basis of the active/inverse voice alternation, through analyzing the inverse voice construction found in some Bantu languages. In §2.2 I will turn to the inverse voice in Apachean languages. Concluding remarks, together with a brief comment on the inverse systems in other languages like Algonquan, Tanoan, and Tibeto-Burman, are in §2.3.

---

[1] For other types of inverse constructions found in a variety of languages, see the articles gathered in Givón (1994) and references cited therein.

2.1. Bantu Inverse Voice

In most Bantu languages, the basic word order is fixed as SVO, and this order is believed to be quite rigid. Several authors have pointed out, however, that in some Bantu languages, there is a case where this rigid order is collapsed without any morphological sign. This construction has been sometimes dubbed Subject-Object Reversal (Kimenyi 1980, 1988; Kinyalolo 1991) or (grammatical function changing) Topicalization (Givón 1975, 1979; Bokamba 1979; Palmer 1994). I will call it inverse since it has almost the same properties as the "inverse" system in North American Indian languages, as we will see later in this chapter. It has been reported in the literature that the construction in question can be found in Lingala, Likala (Givón 1975, 1979), Dzamba, Swahili (Bokamba 1979), Kinyarwanda (Kimenyi 1980, 1988), KiLega (Kinyalolo 1991), Kirundi (Ndayiragije 1996), and other languages.

2.1.1. Basic Properties of Bantu Inverse System

Now let us take a closer look at the basic properties of the inverse system in Bantu. As mentioned, the word order of an active clause in Bantu is SVO, as shown in (2.1):

(2.1)   Active

    a. *Dzamba* (Givón 1979: 189)
        oPoso a-tom-aki   mukanda.
        Poso HE-send-PAST letter
        'Poso sent a letter.'

    b. *Kinyarwanda* (Kimenyi 1980: 141)
        Umuhuûngu a-ra-som-a   igitabo.
        boy   HE-PRES-read-ASP book
        'The boy is reading the book.'

    c. *KiLega* (Kinyalolo 1991: 28)
        Mutu   t-á-ku-sol-ág-á   maku wéneéné.
        1person NEG-1-PROG-drink-HAV-FV 6beer alone
        'A person does not usually drink beer alone.'

    d. *Kirundi* (Ndayiragije 1996: 267)
        Yohani a-á-ra-somye   ivyo bitabo.
        John   3SG-PAST-FOC-read(PERF) those books
        'John read those books.'

In inverse, on the other hand, OBJ precedes V, which is followed by SUBJ; that is, the word order of an inverse clause is OVS, as in (2.2):

(2.2) Inverse
- a. *Dzamba* (Givón 1979: 189)
  I-mukanda mu-tom-aki oPoso. (cf. (2.1a))
  the-letter IT-send-PAST Poso
  'The letter was sent by Poso.'
- b. *Kinyarwanda* (Kimenyi 1980: 141)
  Igitabo cyi-ra-som-a umuhuûngu. (cf. (2.1b))
  book IT-PRES-read-ASP boy
  'The book is being read by the boy.'
- c. *KiLega* (Kinyalolo 1991: 28)
  Maku ta-ma-ku-sol-ág-á mutu wéneéné. (cf. (2.1c))
  6beer NEG-6-PROG-drink-HAV-FV 1person alone
  'Beer is not usually drunk by a person alone.'
- d. *Kirundi* (Ndayiragije 1996: 267)
  Ivyo bitabo bi-á-somye Yohani. (cf. (2.1d))
  those books 3PL-PAST-read(PERF) John
  'Those books were read by John.'

According to Kimenyi (1980, 1988), this operation gives a (kind of) passive reading to the sentence.[2] This construction in Bantu languages has the following common properties with the inverse voice in Amerindian languages (cf. Hale 1972 and Klaiman 1991): (1) the word order interchange of SUBJ and OBJ, and (2) the passive(-like) reading.

It is important to notice that the fronted OBJ in an inverse clause induces subject-agreement. Inverse therefore shares this property with passive. In a passive clause, the word order is also OVS. But SUBJ must be accompanied by some preposition in passive; that is, SUBJ in a passive clause must be syntactically demoted, as shown in (2.3):

(2.3) a. *Dzamba* (Bokamba 1979: 10)
- i. Passive
  I-mw-ete mu-kpet-*em*-eki {*Ø / **n'**}-o-mw-azi waabo.
  the-tree IT-cut-PASS-PAST **by**-the-woman here
  'The tree was chopped down by the woman here.'
- ii. Active
  o-mw-azi a-kpet-eki i-mw-ete waabo.
  the-woman SHE-cut-PAST the-tree here
  'The woman chopped down the tree here.'

---

[2] It is, however, very difficult to figure out what "passive reading" is. See Foley and Van Valin (1984), Siewierska (1984), Givón (1990), Palmer (1994), and articles collected in Keenan (1987), Shibatani (1988), and Givón (1994) for relevant discussion.

b. *Kinyarwanda* (Kimenyi 1988: 363)

   i. Passive

   Mweébwe mw-aa-boon-y-**w**-e {*Ø / **n'**}-âbagóre.
   you YOU-PAST-see-ASP-PASS-ASP **by**-women
   'You were seen by the women.'

   ii. Active

   Abagóre ba-a-boon-ye mweébwe.
   women THEY-PAST-see-ASP you
   'The women saw you.'

Moreover, it is noteworthy that inverse differs from passive in that no morphological sign shows up in an inverse clause, whereas a passive morpheme must be attached to V in a passive clause, as shown in (2.3).

In the literature it has been held that inverse, like passive, is a grammatical function changing operation: It has been claimed, rather reasonably, that the strongest evidence for the claim that the inverse system in Bantu is a grammatical function changing operation comes from the fact that the fronted OBJ in inverse, like in passive, obligatorily induces subject agreement, as we noted (Bokamba 1979; Givón 1979, 1986, 1990; Kimenyi 1980, 1988; Ndayiragije 1996).

Inverse also differs from topicalization/left-dislocation or relativization. In a clause with topicalization/left-dislocation as in (2.4), SUBJ precedes V with OBJ fronted into the clause-initial position, and it is SUBJ that induces subject-agreement. Compare (2.4) with the inverse clause in (2.2a), repeated here as (2.4b):

(2.4) *Dzamba* (Givón 1979: 189)

   a. TOPICALIZATION/LEFT-DISLOCATION

   I-mukanda$_i$ oPoso a-mu-tom-aki t$_i$.
   the-letter Poso HE-IT-send-PAST
   'The letter$_i$, Poso sent t$_i$.'

   b. INVERSE

   I-mukanda **mu**-tom-aki oPoso.
   the-letter IT-send-PAST Poso
   'The letter was sent by Poso.'

In Bantu, it is possible to say either that elements that undergo A-bar movement always leave their pronominal copy in their original position, the pronoun which cliticizes onto V, or that they always induce object-agreement (cf. Givón 1972, Bokamba 1976, and Kinyalolo 1991). In either way, it is noteworthy that SUBJ retains the ability to induce subject-agreement in a clause with topicalization/left-dislocation, as in (2.4); therefore, (2.5), where the topicalized OBJ induces agreement, is precluded:

(2.5)   *Dzamba* (Givón 1979: 189)

    *I-mukanda$_i$ oPoso **mu**-tom-aki t$_i$. (cf. (2.4))
    the-letter   Poso IT-send-PAST

This is natural because topicalization/left-dislocation is not a grammatical function changing operation. Inverse crucially differs from topicalization/left-dislocation in this respect: If SUBJ induces subject-agreement, instead of the fronted OBJ in an inverse clause, then the sentence is totally unacceptable:

(2.6)   *Dzamba* (Givón 1979: 189)

    *I-mukanda **a-mu**-tom-aki oPoso. (cf. (2.2a))
    the-letter   HE-IT-send-PAST Poso

Relativization in Bantu looks more like inverse than topicalization/left-dislocation does, because Bantu relativization causes both the word order change from SVO to OVS and the (subject-)agreement with the logical object that undergoes relativization (cf. Meeussen 1971, Givón 1972, and Bokamba 1976). In inverse, however, any kind of relative-marker does not appear, which may or must appear in Bantu relativization in general.

(2.7)   *Dzamba* (Givón 1972: 194)

    I-mukanda$_k$ **i-*mu*-**tom-aki   oPetelo t$_k$. (cf. (2.2a))
    the-letter   REL-*it*-send-PAST Peter
    'the letter that Peter sent' (relative reading)
    *'The letter was sent by Poso.' (*inverse reading)

This fact suggests that in a relativized clause, the verbal complex overtly moves to C due to the strong *wh*-feature of C (which is morphologically realized as the relative-marker), resulting in the word order OVS (cf. Kinyalolo 1991). Although it is still interesting to inquire why the OBJ fronted by relativization, instead of SUBJ, induces subject-agreement in Bantu, it is totally out of the scope of this book.[3] It is our purpose here to show that inverse differs from topicalization/left-dislocation or relativization. And this has been accomplished in the above discussion by the facts shown in (2.4)–(2.7).[4]

In the next section we will go on to the issue concerning the internal structure of an inverse clause in Bantu. In other words, we will explore how the inverse in Bantu is derived from the active.

---

[3] Cf. Givón (1972), Bokamba (1976, 1979), and, especially, Kinyalolo (1991) for relevant discussion. See Watanabe (1993, 1996) for extensive discussion about *wh*-agreement on a verbal complex under the minimalist framework.

[4] Ndayiragije (1996) provides further evidence that OBJ's movement to the clause-initial position in an inverse clause is not an A-bar movement but an A-movement: (1) The neg-element introduced in an inverse clause differs from the one introduced in a clause with an A-bar movement; (2) OBJ's fronting by inverse is clause-bound (within a tensed CP), but A-bar movement is not; and (3) OBJ's fronting by inverse never induces weak-crossover effect.

2.1.2. Mechanism of the Active/Inverse Alternation in Bantu

Thus far, we observed that inverse in Bantu has the following remarkable properties: (1) The logical object (OBJ) fronted to the clause-initial position in inverse, unlike the OBJ fronted by topicalization/left-dislocation, induces subject agreement; (2) unlike passive, however, the logical subject (SUBJ) is not syntactically demoted in the sense that there is no preposition attached to SUBJ in inverse; and (3) there is no morphological or phonological sign for inverse. In other words, active and inverse freely alternate. Passive does not freely alternate with active in the sense that adding a passive morphology to V is necessary in passive. Since no syntactic or morphological force is involved in inverse, inverse is regarded as a perfectly *optional* operation in syntactic respects. Moreover, (1) implies that OBJ in inverse acquires some of the subject properties. In this regard, inverse is regarded as a grammatical function changing operation like passive, though it is distinguished from passive as stated in (2).

In passing, some researchers point out that some pragmatically functional force must be involved in inverse, as can be conceived (see Bokamba 1979; Kimenyi 1980, 1988; and, especially, Ndayiragije 1996). This is by no means surprising since this state of affairs can also be seen in passive. Just as in the case of passive, I will proceed without taking any pragmatic/functional effect into consideration.

2.1.2.1. Optionality of the Bantu Inverse System

First, let us begin by taking a look at the initial structure of the VP-system, for which the two-layered VPs are assumed under Chomsky's (1995b: §10) theory of feature-checking, which dispenses with any Agr-system, as is illustrated in (2.8):

(2.8)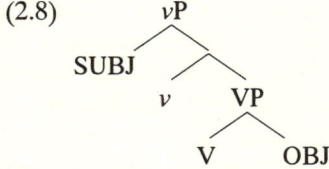

Under this framework, the accusative Case of OBJ in a transitive clause is checked off at a Spec of the higher head of the two-layered VP-shell (i.e., v), if the checking is required to happen before Spell-out (see §1.3.1.4).

Now suppose that the nominal feature of v in Bantu languages with active/inverse voice alternation is strong. Then, as we argued in §1.4.1, OBJ moves up to the innermost Spec of v before Spell-out. By the movement of OBJ to the innermost Spec of v, (2.9) is derived from (2.8):

(2.9)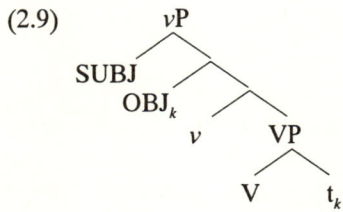

Here it is very important to notice that OBJ and SUBJ in (2.9) are now in the same minimal domain (of v).[5] According to Chomsky's (1995a: §10) definition of "closeness," both OBJ and SUBJ are EQUIDISTANT from somewhere else. Note that this means that either of them can move to a target if the movement satisfies the "Last Resort" part of the definition of Attract/Move (see §1.3.1.5).

Now Infl (or T) is introduced in (2.9) by Merge, deriving (2.10):

(2.10) $[_{IP}$ Infl $[_{vP}$ SUBJ $[_{v'}$ OBJ$_k$ $[_{v'}$ v $[_{VP}$ V t_k]]]]]

Here I propose that Infl in the Bantu languages with active/inverse alternation has a *strong* EPP-feature as well as a strong φ-feature, but its Case-feature is *weak*. It is important to notice that I am assuming, following Collins (1995a), that features of a single head (for example, Infl in this case) may have a value different from each other in their strength (see §1.3.2.2). The strong EPP-feature of Infl requires something with a D-feature to be moved overtly to the (canonical) Spec of Infl.

It should be noted, however, that the element to be moved is not necessarily a DP with a nominative Case-feature, because it is not the (weak) nominative Case-feature of Infl, but its strong EPP-feature that invokes this overt movement. Now notice that there are two elements available for checking off the strong EPP-feature of Infl in (2.10): namely, OBJ and SUBJ, both of which are equidistant from Infl due to the fact that they are in a Spec of v and they have a D-feature.

Here it is noteworthy that, although OBJ in (2.10) has entered into a feature-checking relation at an outer Spec of v, its D-feature is still available for checking the strong EPP-feature of Infl. This is precisely because a D-feature is [+interpretable] and [+interpretable] features may not be deleted even if they have been checked off (Chomsky 1995a). That is, OBJ as well as SUBJ in (2.10) has the same potential to check off the strong EPP-feature of Infl. It should be noted, again, that both are now in the same minimal domain; thus, either of them can be attracted to the (canonical) Spec of Infl to check Infl's EPP-feature without violating the requirement of Attract/Move. Put differently, OBJ at the inner-

---

[5] It should be noted that, as will be evident, it does not matter for the discussion that follows in this chapter whether OBJ is attracted to the innermost Spec of v, as I assume here, or to an outer Spec of v with SUBJ generated at its innermost Spec. In order for the discussion below to hold good, it is only imperative for OBJ to move to a position in the minimal domain where SUBJ is generated before Spell-out. See Ura (to appear b) for the discussion on the Bantu inverse construction without the former assumption, under which a forced Move beats an unforced Merge in the economy competition.

most Spec of v and SUBJ at an outer Spec of v in (2.10) can be attracted, with equal possibility, by the EPP-feature of Infl since both are equidistant from Infl.

Now suppose that SUBJ in (2.10) is attracted by Infl; that is, SUBJ, instead of OBJ, is moved overtly to the Spec of Infl to check off the strong EPP-feature of Infl. Then, (2.11) is derived:

(2.11) $[_{IP}$ SUBJ$_j$ Infl $[_{vP}$ t$_j$ $[_{v'}$ OBJ$_k$ $[_{v'}$ v $[_{VP}$ V t$_k$ $]]]]]$ (active)

This corresponds exactly to an active clause, if we assume, following Kinyalolo (1991), that V in Bantu languages moves overtly onto Infl. In (2.11), all the relevant features are satisfactorily checked off: Infl's EPP-feature, φ-feature, and Case-feature are checked off by SUBJ, SUBJ's nominal features (φ-feature and Case-feature) are checked against Infl, and OBJ's nominal features are checked off by v; whereby, (2.11) converges.

Suppose, instead, that OBJ in (2.10) is attracted by Infl; that is, OBJ, instead of SUBJ, is moved overtly to the Spec of Infl to check off the strong EPP-feature of Infl. Then, (2.12) is derived:

(2.12) $[_{IP}$ OBJ$_k$ Infl $[_{vP}$ SUBJ $[_{v'}$ t$'_k$ $[_{v'}$ v $[_{VP}$ V t$_k$ $]]]]]$ (inverse)

This corresponds exactly to an inverse clause. (Note that we are assuming that V in Bantu moves overtly onto Infl.) In (2.12) OBJ checks off Infl's strong EPP-feature (= D-feature) as well as Infl's φ-feature (OBJ's φ-feature as well as its D-feature is [+interpretable]; hence, it is able to enter into multiple checking relations (see §1.3.2.4)), but it cannot check Infl's nominative feature. OBJ's Case-feature has been checked off by v and has been deleted and erased at the same time because it is [–interpretable]; therefore, it is no longer available for checking Infl's Case-feature, though OBJ can check Infl's D-feature (i.e., EPP-feature) and φ-feature thanks to the [+interpretable] nature of those features. Note, also, that the Case-feature of SUBJ also remains unchecked in (2.12). Recall, however, that we are assuming that the Case-feature of Infl in those languages is not strong. Thus, it may be checked off at LF. Thus, if the Case-feature of Infl is checked against that of SUBJ in some way at LF, then the whole derivation of (2.12) converges. Now the question is: How can SUBJ in (2.12) enter into a Case-feature checking relation with Infl at LF?

Under the feature-checking theory of Chomsky (1995a), only features, but not categories, move at LF, and it is also assumed that an LF feature-movement is always a movement onto a head that attracts the feature. Thus, the (nominative) Case-feature of SUBJ in (2.12) head-moves onto Infl at LF to check off the weak (nominative) Case-feature of Infl; whence, all the relevant features involved in the derivation for (2.12) are satisfactorily checked off (Infl's EPP-feature and φ-feature are checked off by OBJ at the canonical Spec of Infl before Spell-out, the (nominative) Case-feature of Infl is checked against SUBJ's Case-feature at LF, and OBJ's accusative Case-feature (as well as φ-feature) is checked off by v before Spell-out).[6] Thereby, the whole derivation for an inverse

---

[6] Note that SUBJ's φ-feature need not be checked off because it is [+interpretable].

voice clause converges, as required. This is our analysis of the Bantu inverse voice system.

What is important here is that under our analysis of Bantu inverse voice, no morphological sign like the English passive morpheme -*en* (cf. Baker, Johnson, and Roberts 1989) plays any role for the active/inverse voice alternation: At the stage in the derivation illustrated in (2.10), which active and inverse have in common, Infl can attract either SUBJ at an outer Spec of *v* or OBJ at the innermost Spec of *v* with equal possibility owing to the definition of closeness with the notion "equidistance." In other words, the fact that SUBJ and OBJ are in the same minimal domain before Spell-out results in the total optionality of the active/inverse alternation in Bantu languages.

To sum up, there are three prerequisites for the derivation of Bantu inverse: (1) *v* has a strong nominal feature, which gives rise to a stage in the derivation where SUBJ and OBJ are equidistant from Infl; (2) Infl's EPP-feature is strong; and (3) Infl's nominative Case-feature is weak. Without the satisfaction of condition (1), OBJ's movement to a Spec of *v* violates Procrastinate.[7] Without the satisfaction of condition (2), OBJ's movement from the innermost Spec of *v* to the canonical Spec of Infl violates the "Last Resort" part of the definition of Attract/Move. Without the satisfaction of condition (3), SUBJ cannot linger at an outer Spec of *v* at Spell-out.

2.1.2.2. Grammatical Function Splitting in Inverse Voice

Our conclusion is that in an inverse clause, OBJ has the φ-feature checking relation with Infl. Thus, the fact naturally follows that the fronted OBJ in an inverse clause induces subject-agreement, instead of SUBJ, which lingers at an outer Spec of *v* before Spell-out.

Moreover, under our analysis, SUBJ in an inverse clause has its Case-feature checked off at LF by feature-movement onto Infl at LF. This is why SUBJ is not syntactically demoted in an inverse clause, unlike in a passive clause.[8] We can also explain why SUBJ in an inverse clause has no subject properties, by hypothesizing that only an element X that has a [+construable]-feature checking relation with Infl bears subject properties.[9] Although SUBJ in an inverse clause has a Case-feature checking relation with Infl, it has no [+construable]-feature checking relation with Infl.

On the other hand, the promoted OBJ in an inverse clause has some subject properties in addition to its ability to induce subject-agreement. According to

---

[7] As argued so far, (1) is stipulated in order to give birth to the pre-Spell-out stage illustrated in (2.10) for the derivation of inverse. But (1) is not the only possible way to guarantee (2.10) before Spell-out. If the nominal feature of *v* has the property that tolerates an unforced violation of Procrastinate, then (2.10) can be produced as well. I will return directly to this issue in §2.1.2.4.

[8] More on this difference between inverse and passive will be discussed in §2.1.2.3.

[9] For the definition of [±construable]-features, see §1.4.7.

Ndayiragije (1996), who also argues that the inverse OBJ occupies the Spec of Infl before Spell-out, the promoted OBJ in an inverse clause may be a victim of "pro-drop" and may undergo "raising." From our hypothesis that only an element X that has a [+construable]-feature checking relation with Infl bears subject properties, it naturally follows that the subjecthood of the inverse OBJ results from the fact that it has an EPP-feature and a φ-feature checking relation with Infl; for, an EPP-feature and a φ-feature are both [+construable].

2.1.2.3. Why Is SUBJ in a Passive Clause Obligatorily Demoted?

Interestingly enough, the fact concerning SUBJ in a Bantu inverse clause is not merely that SUBJ is not syntactically demoted, but also that it *must not* be demoted and it *must not* be omitted from the clause (see Kimenyi 1980 and Kinyalolo 1991).

(2.13) *Kinyarwanda inverse* (Kimenyi 1988: 358)
    a. Ibíshyíimbo by-aa-ri bî-teet-se abagóre.
         beans THEY-PAST-be THEY-cook-ASP women
        'The beans were being cooked by the women.'
    b. *Ibíshyíimbo by-aa-ri bî-teet-se **n'**abagóre.
         beans THEY-PAST-be THEY-cook-ASP **by**-women
       (cf. Ibíshyíimbo by-aa-ri bî-teet-s-*w*-e **n'**abagóre.
           beans THEY-PAST-be THEY-cook-*PASS*-ASP **by**-women)
    c. *Ibíshyíimbo by-aa-ri bî-teet-se Ø.
         beans THEY-PAST-be THEY-cook-ASP
       (cf. Ibíshyíimbo by-aa-ri bî-teet-s-*w*-e Ø.
           beans THEY-PAST-be THEY-cook-*PASS*-ASP)

This behavior of SUBJ in an inverse clause sharply contrasts with that of SUBJ in a passive clause, which must be demoted and may be omitted. The proposed mechanism for the Bantu inverse voice system plainly explains this fact.

In our theory of the Bantu inverse voice, it is not OBJ but the nominative Case-feature of SUBJ that checks off the (weak) nominative Case-feature of Infl (at LF). Since the finite tense always has a nominative Case-feature, this nominative Case-feature must be somehow checked off at LF, at the latest. But the Case-feature of OBJ (accusative Case-feature) in an inverse clause has already been checked off by v at a Spec of v when OBJ was attracted there, and, hence, it has been deleted (and erased) before it moves up to the canonical (i.e., innermost) Spec of Infl, as argued in §2.1.2.1; therefore, it is not available for checking off the nominative Case-feature of Infl. Thus, if SUBJ is syntactically demoted and lacks a structural Case, or if it does not exist in an inverse clause, the (weak) nominative Case-feature of Infl in an inverse clause remains unchecked at LF, resulting in crash at LF. This is why SUBJ in an inverse clause must not be demoted or omitted.

By the same reasoning, we can also account for the fact that SUBJ in an inverse clause cannot be incorporated into V in those Bantu languages (see Kimenyi 1980 and Kinyalolo 1991). Assuming that V-incorporation is a checking operation by which V's nominal feature is checked off by the incorporated element (cf. Baker 1988), we may say that if SUBJ at an outer Spec of v is incorporated into V, there remains nothing that can check off the (weak) nominative Case-feature of Infl at LF in an inverse clause.[10] This results in an LF crash.

Now let us consider why SUBJ in a passive clause in the Bantu languages that allow active/inverse alternation must be syntactically demoted or can be omitted. First, take the pre-Spell-out construction in which the two-layered VP-shell is introduced:

(2.14)   [$_{vP}$ v-PASS [$_{VP}$ V   OBJ]] (PASS: passive morpheme)

Recall that we are assuming that v in those languages has a strong nominal feature, which attracts OBJ to the innermost Spec of v before Spell-out. Let us assume, following the spirit of Baker (1988) and Baker, Johnson, and Roberts (1989), that the passive morpheme that is attached to a verb behaves like a DP, depriving the verb (= v) of its nominal feature (see Watanabe 1996 for more recent discussion on Case-absorption under the minimalist framework). Then, OBJ in passive is not attracted to a Spec of v, unlike in the case of inverse, where OBJ is attracted to that position before Spell-out. Now that OBJ is not attracted by v before Spell-out in a passive clause, SUBJ is generated at the canonical Spec of v, resulting in the stage in the derivation illustrated in (2.15):

(2.15)   [$_{vP}$ SUBJ [$_{v'}$ v-PASS [$_{VP}$ V   OBJ]]] (passive)

As the next step, Infl is introduced in (2.15) by Merge; thereby, (2.16) is derived:

(2.16)   [$_{IP}$ Infl [$_{vP}$ SUBJ [$_{v'}$ v-PASS [$_{VP}$ V   OBJ]]]] (passive)

It is important to note that in (2.16), SUBJ is obviously closer to Infl than OBJ is. Since we are assuming that Infl in those languages has a strong EPP-feature (see §1.2.2.1), the element with a D-feature that is closest to Infl is attracted by Infl to the canonical Spec of Infl before Spell-out. For this reason, SUBJ in (2.16) is inevitably attracted by Infl to the canonical Spec of Infl if SUBJ has a D-feature, as illustrated in (2.17):

(2.17)   *[$_{IP}$ SUBJ$_k$ Infl [$_{vP}$ t$_k$ [$_{v'}$ v-PASS [$_{VP}$ V   OBJ]]]] (passive)

The (strong) EPP-feature of Infl is properly checked off this way before Spell-out. But OBJ in (2.17) fails to have its Case-feature checked off. Notice that v in (2.17) is deprived of its nominal features including a Case-feature due to the attachment of the passive morpheme to it. Hence, there is nothing available for checking OBJ's Case-feature in (2.17); as a result, the derivation crashes. The

---

[10] See McGinnis (1995) for a proposal concerning the mechanism of word-internal feature checking.

conclusion is that the derivation inevitably crashes if SUBJ in a passive clause is generated at the (canonical) Spec of v with a D-feature.

In order to save the derivation for a passive clause in those Bantu languages, it is sufficient that SUBJ in a passive clause is not generated at the (canonical) Spec of v. This condition is achieved if SUBJ is not expressed in the sentence at all (i.e., totally omitted in the sentence), or if SUBJ is generated somewhere else as an adjunct with a preposition (i.e., retreat from 1 to 3 in the terminology of Relational Grammar (cf. Blake 1990)). In either case, OBJ in (2.16) can be properly attracted by Infl, as required, as illustrated in (2.18):

(2.18) $[_{IP}$ OBJ$_j$ Infl $[_{vP}$ Ø $[_{v'}$ v-PASS $[_{VP}$ V t_j]]] (*by*-SUBJ)]]

This is because in (2.18), there is nothing between Infl and OBJ at the V-complement that has the potential to check off the (strong) EPP-feature of Infl; accordingly, the closest element to Infl that has a D-feature is OBJ at the V-complement. As a result, OBJ with a D-feature can enter into a Case-checking relation with Infl, as required. In other words, the derivation for passive can escape from an LF crash only if (1) SUBJ is not expressed in the sentence at all (i.e., totally omitted from the sentence), or (2) SUBJ is generated somewhere else as an adjunct with a preposition.

2.1.2.4. Property of v's Nominal Feature

In §2.1.2.1 I claimed that v's strong nominal feature is prerequisite for inverse. The reason is that this guarantees that the stage in the derivation illustrated in (2.10) comes into existence before Spell-out:

(2.10) $[_{IP}$ Infl $[_{vP}$ SUBJ $[_{v'}$ OBJ$_k$ $[_{v'}$ v $[_{VP}$ V t_k]]]]]

Recall that (2.10) is crucial for the derivation for inverse, because it gives rise to the situation where SUBJ and OBJ are equidistant from Infl, the situation which, in turn, makes it possible for OBJ to be attracted to a Spec of Infl before SPELL-OUT. But, as I pointed out in footnote 7 above, to assume v's strong nominal feature is not the only possible way to guarantee (2.10) before Spell-out. If the nominal feature of v has the property that tolerates an unforced violation of Procrastinate, then (2.10) may come into existence before Spell-out as well. To recap, (2.10) may theoretically arise if v has a strong nominal feature or if v's nominal feature has the property that tolerates an unforced violation of Procrastinate. Now let us examine which of them is empirically correct.

According to Ndayiragije (1996), Kirundi allows the transitive expletive construction. Interestingly, OBJ always precedes SUBJ in this construction in Kirundi:[11]

---

[11] See Jonas and Bobaljik (1993), Chomsky (1995a), Bobaljik and Jonas (1996), and, especially, Jonas (1996) for transitive expletive constructions. Jonas (1996) presents extensive studies on this construction in Icelandic with special reference to the ordering between SUBJ and OBJ. I will touch on this issue in the appendix to chapter 8.

(2.19) *Kirundi* (Ndayiragije 1996: 272)
    a. *pro*(EXPLETIVE) ha-á-nyoye amatá abâna.
        EXP   LOC-PST-drink(PERF) milk children
       Lit. '(There) drank milk children.' ('Children drank milk.')
    b. **pro*(EXPLETIVE) ha-á-nyoye abâna amatá.
        EXP   LOC-PST-drink(PERF) children milk
       Lit. '(There) drank children milk.'

The fact shown in (2.19a) indicates that OBJ may move over the base-position of SUBJ. I assume that this is derived by object shift in a transitive expletive clause just like the case attested in Icelandic:

(2.20) *Icelandic* (Jonas 1996: chapter 2)
    Það borðuðu [$_{vP}$ ostinn$_k$ [$_{vP}$ margar m'ys [$_{VP}$ t$_k$]]].
    EXP ate   the cheese   many mice
    Lit. 'There ate [$_{vP}$ the cheese$_k$ [$_{vP}$ many mice [$_{VP}$ t$_k$]].'
    ('Many mice ate the cheese.')

Given the theory of strong features presented in §1.4.1 (see appendix to chapter 8 for more discussion), the precedence of the shifted OBJ over (the base-position of) SUBJ means that v's nominal feature, which motivates the object shift, is weak but has the property that tolerates an unforced violation of Procrastinate. The conclusion is that v's nominal feature has the property that tolerates an unforced violation of Procrastinate in Kirundi, which gives birth to (2.10).

Now that v's nominal feature, though tolerating an unforced violation of Procrastinate, is weak in Kirundi, we predict that object shift in Kirundi is optional. This prediction is borne out:

(2.21) *Kirundi* (Ndayiragije 1996: 274)
    a. Yohani a-á-oógeje imiduga néezá.
       John 3SG-PAST-wash(PERF) cars   well
       'John washed cars well.'
    b. Yohani a-á-oógeje néezá imiduga.
       John 3SG-PAST-wash(PERF) well   cars
       (logically same as (2.21a))[12]

As predicted, OBJ may precede or may follow a VP-adverb in Kirundi.[13]

---

[12] Ndayiragije (1996) claims that (2.21a) differs from (2.21b) in terms of focus, as is often the case when OBJ is shifted.

[13] The ill-formedness of (2.19b) might be a problem. I speculate that it might be attributed to Bobaljik and Jonas's (1996) theory of the licensing of [Spec, TP], according to which SUBJ in a transitive expletive construction must occupy the Spec of TP in overt syntax, though this approach inevitably fails to explain the Icelandic facts that Jonas (1996) has discovered. See Jonas (1996) for discussion.

In other Bantu languages with active/inverse alternation, examples can be found in which OBJ that is shifted precedes the base-position of SUBJ. The following comes from KiLega and Kinyarwanda:

(2.22) a. *KiLega* (Kinyalolo 1991: 81)

Mutu$_i$ t-á-ku-sol-ág-á [$_{vP}$ maku$_k$ [$_{vP}$ wéneéné$_i$ [$_{VP}$ t$_k$]]].
1person NEG-1-PROG-drink-HAB-FV 6beer 3SG:alone
'A person does not usually drink beer alone.'

b. *Kinyarwanda* (Kimenyi 1980: 58)

Umukoôbwa$_i$ a-ra-som-a [$_{vP}$ igitabo$_k$ [$_{vP}$ gusa$_i$ [$_{VP}$ t$_k$]]].
girl SHE-PRES-read-ASP book alone
'The girl is reading the book alone.'

In (2.22) the shifted OBJ moves over the base-position of SUBJ, which is represented by the adverb semantically associated with SUBJ. From these examples it is concluded that *v*'s nominal feature is weak and has the property that tolerates an unforced violation of Procrastinate in KiLega and Kinyarwanda.

Among the Bantu languages with active/inverse alternation, I have never found languages in which OBJ is obligatorily shifted. But, very importantly, as far as those languages are concerned, I have so far found no language in which object shift is obligatorily blocked (in overt syntax). That is, as far as I can see, all the Bantu languages with active/inverse alternation always allow OBJ to be shifted in overt syntax. Insofar as the observation is right, this confirms the theory of Bantu inverse voice proposed in this chapter. This is because OBJ is allowed to be shifted in overt syntax only if (1) *v* has a strong nominal feature, or (2) *v*'s nominal feature has the property that tolerates an unforced violation of Procrastinate.

2.1.3. Deriving the Parametric Differences

Thus far I argued that the following three factors are prerequisite for inverse: (1) OBJ is moved overtly to a Spec of *v*; (2) Infl's EPP-feature is strong; and (3) Infl's Case-feature is weak (see §2.1.2.1). The question I raise in this section is: Are these three sufficient for inverse? The answer is no. I am arguing that there is one more necessary condition that makes inverse possible.

Take Icelandic, for example. From the fact that Icelandic has an overt expletive equivalent to *there* in English, it is evident that the EPP-feature of T in Icelandic is strong. It is also evident from this that T's Case-feature is weak; for, according to Chomsky (1995a), the English-type expletive cannot check any Case-feature (before Spell-out). Thus, Icelandic satisfies (2) and (3). Now, does *v* in Icelandic have the property that allows OBJ to move overtly to its Spec? The answer is yes; all OBJs can undergo object shift in Icelandic (see, among many others, Holmberg 1986, Déprez 1994, Vikner 1994, and Jonas 1996), though a pronoun in Icelandic must be shifted (see Vikner 1994, Jonas 1996, and references cited therein).

In chapter 4 I will argue that the optionality of object shift stems from the fact that v may tolerate an unforced violation of Procrastinate, and that the fact that v tolerates an unforced violation of Procrastinate in Icelandic correlates with the fact that the shifted OBJ is always located at a position higher than the base position of SUBJ in Icelandic (see Jonas 1995).

Given this parameter-setting of v in Icelandic, OBJ may be attracted overtly to a Spec of v. Since all the prerequisites for inverse are met, it would be expected that inverse is also possible in Icelandic. But the fact is that inverse is not allowed in Icelandic. Why?

In his class lecture in the Fall of 1995, Noam Chomsky suggested that there are two types of language, in terms of the parameter concerning the Case- and φ-feature checking of T: In one type, T's Case-feature checking is always executed by the same element that executes T's φ-feature checking, whereas T's Case-feature checking and its φ-feature checking may be executed independently in the other type. Suppose that Icelandic, as well as English, French, and so forth are classified as the former type and the Bantu languages as the latter. Then, we can straightforwardly account for the difference between Icelandic and Bantu in terms of the existence of the inverse construction, as Chomsky himself pointed out.

Recall that in an inverse clause, T's Case-feature is checked off by (the Case-feature of) SUBJ (at LF) and its φ-feature is checked off by OBJ (before Spell-out). That is, T's Case-feature checking and its φ-feature checking are executed independently in the inverse construction. Given the above parameter, this independent checking of those two features of T is impossible in Icelandic. This is the reason why Icelandic disallows inverse, though it satisfies conditions (1), (2), and (3).[14]

2.1.4. Summary: Bantu Inverse Voice

Thus far I have shown how the inverse voice in Bantu is derived. I have argued that Bantu inverse voice results from the following four factors: (1) v has the nominal feature with the property that allows OBJ to move overtly to a Spec of v; (2) the EPP-feature of Infl is strong; (3) the nominative feature of Infl is weak; and (4) Infl's Case checking and its φ-feature checking may be executed inde-

---

[14] As a matter of fact, this account is not sufficient. It is true that the type of inverse construction found in Bantu, where the promoted OBJ induces subject-agreement, is not possible for the very reason described here. But the nonexistence of the following type of inverse construction in Icelandic cannot be explained:

(i) $[_{TP}$ OBJ(ACC)$_k$ T $[_{vP}$ t$'_k$ SUBJ(NOM) v $[_{VP}$ V t$_k$]]]

If SUBJ in (i) induces subject-agreement, then we incorrectly predict that the derivation for (i) converges in Icelandic: OBJ is attracted to the Spec of T in overt syntax to check T's strong EPP-feature, and the Case- and φ-feature of SUBJ enter into a proper checking relation with T at LF. This derivation cannot be blocked only by the parameter introduced here. In §5.4.2 I will discuss this issue in depth.

pendently. Were it not for any of these factors, the total optionality of the Bantu active/inverse alternation without any morphological sign could not be accounted for. It is noteworthy that all these factors are totally compatible with a stricter view of parameter-setting in UG (cf. Borer 1984 and Fukui 1995): All the aforementioned parameters except the last one are concerned exclusively within the parameter of strength of functional categories. And the last one, too, is concerned with the property of the functional category Infl (= T).

Owing to the above four factors, the following derivation can be materialized before Spell-out: OBJ first moves to a Spec of v, checking its Case-feature against v, and then, it moves up to the Spec of IP, entering into an EPP-feature checking relation as well as a φ-feature checking relation with Infl, and SUBJ stays in a Spec of v. In this derivation, the Case-feature of SUBJ can be checked off against the weak Case-feature of Infl at LF; thereby, the whole derivation converges both at LF and at PF. This derivation results in Bantu inverse. Hypothesizing that only an element X that has a [+construable]-feature checking relation with Infl can bear subject properties, I concluded (1) that the subject functions of OBJ in a Bantu inverse clause (to induce subject-agreement, to be a victim of "pro-drop," to control, etc. (cf. Ndayiragije 1996)) result from the fact that OBJ in inverse has an EPP-feature and a φ-feature checking relation with Infl; for, an EPP-feature and a φ-feature are both [+construable]; and (2) that the reason that SUBJ in inverse has no subject function follows from the fact that it has no [+construable]-feature checking relation with Infl.

In this section I explored the mechanism of the totally optional active/inverse voice alternation. In the next section I will investigate the active/inverse voice alternation that is mediated by some morphology.

2.2. Apachean Inverse Voice

2.2.1. Basic Properties of the Apachean Inverse System

In Apachean languages like Navajo and Apache, the active/inverse voice alternation is mediated by some morphological change on V. It has the following properties: (1) the interchange of the positions of SUBJ and OBJ, (2) the passive(-like) meaning (Hale 1973), and (3) SUBJ is not syntactically demoted despite the loss of some of its subjecthood.

Examples in (2.23) show the active/inverse voice alternation in Navajo:[15]

(2.23)   *Navajo* (Palmer 1994: 210)

    a. łíí́ dzaanééz **yi**-ztal. (active)
        horse mule   ACT-kick
        'The horse kicked the mule.'
        *'The mule kicked the horse.'

---

[15] In the literature on Amerindian languages, the voice that is contrasted with inverse voice is commonly called *direct voice*. But I will keep using *active voice* for the sake of consistency.

b. dzaaééz łíí́ **bi**-ztal. (inverse)
   mule horse INV-kick
   'The mule was kicked by the horse.'

The word order is crucial for interpretation in Apachean languages, because it is strictly fixed as SOV (cf. Perkins 1978). Thus (2.23a) never means 'The mule kicked the horse,' nor does it ever mean 'The horse was kicked by the mule,' as long as the active-morpheme (i.e., the prefix *yi-*) is attached to V.[16] If the active-morpheme in (2.23a) is replaced by the inverse-morpheme (i.e., the prefix *bi-*) without changing the word order as illustrated in (2.24), it is interpreted to mean 'The horse was kicked by the mule.'

(2.24) łíí' dzaanééz **bi**-ztal. (inverse) (cf. (2.23a))
       horse mule INV-kick
       'The horse was kicked by the mule.'

That is to say, it is the first DP that is identified as the Agent in an active clause, while it is the second in an inverse clause (Palmer 1994: 210).

Another remarkable property of the inverse system in Apachean is the strict constraint concerning the hierarchy of animacy.[17] Hale (1973) discusses the following conditions on the active/inverse alternation in Navajo: (1) If SUBJ and OBJ are equal in the animacy hierarchy, the alternation is totally optional; (2) if SUBJ outranks OBJ in the animacy hierarchy, then inverse voice is blocked; and (3) if OBJ outranks SUBJ in the animacy hierarchy, then inverse voice is obligatory. These conditions are illustrated by the following examples:[18]

(2.25) SUBJ = OBJ (Hale 1973: 301)

a. 'ashkii 'at'ééd yiyi-iłtsá. (active)
   boy   girl   ACT-see
   'The boy saw the girl.'

a'. 'at'ééd 'ashkii bi-iłtsá. (inverse)
    girl   boy   INV-see
    'The girl was seen by the boy.'

---

[16] See McDonough (1990) for a detailed analysis of Navajo verbal morphology from the phonological point of view.

[17] Due to the as yet unaccounted-for nature of the prefixes *yi-* and *bi-*, both of which were traditionally treated as the special third-person object markers that require SUBJ to be third person (Sapir and Hoijer 1967), the active/inverse voice alternation in Apachean languages occurs only when both SUBJ and OBJ are third person. Cf. Perkins (1978), Shayne (1982), Klaiman (1991), and references cited therein.

[18] Hale (1973) further argues that there is another constraint on the active/inverse alternation in Navajo concerning the humanity hierarchy. It works the same way as the animacy hierarchy, but its effects are much weaker than the animacy hierarchy as far as I can see from Hale's (1973) examples. Cf., also, Frishberg (1972), Creamer (1974), and Jelinek (1990) for discussion on the hierarchy in question.

b. łééchaa'í mósí yi-shxash. (active)
   dog   cat   ACT-bite
   'The dog bit the cat.'

b'. mósí łééchaa'í bi-shxash. (inverse)
    cat   dog   INV-bite
    'The cat was bittten by the dog.'

(2.26) SUBJ > OBJ (Hale 1973: 302)

a. diné dził y-oo'í. (active)
   man mountain ACT-see
   'The man sees the mountain.'

a'. *dził diné b-oo'í. (inverse)
    mountain man INV-see
    'The mountain was seen by the man.'

b. dzaanééz tsé yi-ztał. (active)
   mule   stone ACT-kick
   'The mule kicked the stone.'

b'. *tsé dzaanééz bi-ztał. (inverse)
    stone mule   INV-kick
    'The stone was kicked by the mule.'

(2.27) SUBJ < OBJ (Hale 1973: 302)

a. *tó 'ashkii yiyi-isxí. (active)
   water boy   ACT-kill
   'The water killed the boy.'

a'. 'ashkii tó bi-isxí. (inverse)
    boy   water INV-kill
    'The boy was killed by the water.'

b. *yas łééchaa'í yi-stin. (active)
   snow dog   ACT-freeze
   'The snow froze the dog.'

b'. łééchaa'í yas bi-stin. (inverse)
    dog   snow INV-freeze
    'The dog was frozen by the snow.'

In the next two subsections, I will show how an inverse clause is derived from its active counterpart in Apachean, and in §2.2.4, I will turn to the issue as to how to implement the device to cope with the constraint concerning the animacy hierarchy involved in the Apachean inverse system.

2.2.2. Mechanism of the Active/Inverse Alternation in Apachean

Now let us consider how an active clause alternates with its inverse counterpart in Apachean languages. Recall that the alternation in Apachean, unlike in Bantu, is mediated by a morphological sign. As mentioned in footnote 17, the prefixes *yi-* and *bi-* were traditionally treated as (special) third person affixes (Sapir and Hoijer 1967). Thus, it is safe for us to treat them as a kind of Infl with a certain φ-feature (it is safe to assume that the verbal affixes come from Infl).

Take the basic structure of the two-layered VP-shell before Spell-out:

(2.28) [$_{vP}$ [$_{VP}$ OBJ V] v]

I assume that, since their word order is strictly fixed as SOV in active clauses, Apachean languages, like Japanese, are {head-final, Spec-initial} in terms of the head-Spec parameter.

Now I propose (1) that (the nominal feature of) v in Apachean is weak and does not tolerate any unforced violation of Procrastinate, and (2) that the EPP-feature of Infl, regardless of whether it is *yi-* or *bi-*, is strong in Apachean. With this in mind, let us consider the derivations for an active clause and an inverse one step by step. Now that v is weak, OBJ must stay in situ (i.e., V-complement position) before Spell-out and SUBJ is generated at the innermost Spec of v, regardless of whether the clause is active or inverse:

(2.29) [$_{vP}$ SUBJ [$_{VP}$ OBJ V] v] (active/inverse)

After (2.29), Infl is introduced by Merge, deriving (2.30):

(2.30) [$_{IP}$ [$_{vP}$ SUBJ [$_{VP}$ OBJ V] v] Infl] (active/inverse)

Since Infl, whether it is *yi-* or *bi-*, is strong, something with D-feature must be moved to the canonical (i.e., innermost) Spec of Infl to check the strong EPP-feature of Infl before Spell-out. SUBJ, but not OBJ, is attracted to that position because SUBJ is the DP closest to Infl in (2.30):

(2.31) [$_{IP}$ SUBJ$_k$ [$_{vP}$ t$_k$ [$_{VP}$ OBJ V] v] Infl] (active/inverse)

Until this stage, the derivation for an active clause is the same as the derivation for an inverse clause.

Now suppose that (2.31) is an active clause (i.e., Infl is *yi-*). Then, nothing further is required to happen before Spell-out under our assumptions. This corresponds exactly to the surface structure of an active clause in Apachean. At LF, the nominal features (i.e., accusative Case-feature and φ-feature) of OBJ enter into a checking relation with v; thereby, the derivation converges. This is the derivation of an active clause in Apachean.

Suppose, instead, that (2.31) is an inverse clause (i.e., Infl is *bi-*). And suppose, furthermore, that OBJ at V-complement is moved overtly to an outer Spec of Infl, though this movement clearly violates the "Last Resort" part of the definition of Attract/Move insofar as the assumptions presented above are concerned. But note that it does not violate the "MLC" part of the definition of Attract/Move. For OBJ at V-complement is the argument closest to Infl once SUBJ has moved to the canonical Spec of Infl. This derivation is illustrated in (2.32):

(2.32) [$_{IP}$ OBJ$_l$ [$_{I'}$ SUBJ$_k$ [$_{vP}$ t$_k$ [$_{VP}$ t$_l$ V] v] Infl]] (inverse)

This corresponds exactly to the surface order of an inverse clause in Apachean. Thus, it is necessary to ensure that OBJ's movement from V-complement to an outer Spec of Infl does not violate the "Last Resort" part of the definition of Attract/Move. At present, however, I proceed further, just assuming that the movement in question fulfills the "Last Resort" part of the definition of Attract/Move.[19] The derivation illustrated in (2.32) converges if v head-moves onto Infl (at LF) and enters into a Case-feature checking relation with OBJ, which is now at an outer Spec of Infl; thereby, all the formal features required for convergence in (2.32) are checked off.

This is my analysis of active/inverse alternation in Navajo (Apachean). A question remains, however. What feature of Infl in an inverse clause attracts OBJ from V-complement to an outer Spec of Infl in (2.32)? If there were no feature that attracts OBJ to an outer Spec of Infl, the derivation illustrated in (2.32) would never exist; for, it violates the "Last Resort" part of the definition of Attract/Move.

Now I propose that the answer to the question should be the EPP-feature of the inverse Infl *bi*-. That is, the EPP-feature of the inverse Infl *bi*- is [+multiple] in the sense that it must enter into multiple checking relations. More specifically, I propose to assume that the EPP-feature of the inverse Infl *bi*-, which is strong, is deleted only if it is checked twice. Being strong, it must be checked and deleted (and erased) before Spell-out. Owing to the above assumption, (2.31), if that represents a stage in the derivation for an inverse clause, crashes at PF unless OBJ moves to an outer Spec of Infl to delete the EPP-feature of the inverse Infl *bi*- by executing the second checking of it (the first checking was executed by SUBJ at the canonical Spec of Infl). Thus, OBJ is always attracted overtly to an outer Spec of Infl in an inverse clause in Apachean, as illustrated in (2.32).

Here, it is very important to note that in an inverse clause in Navajo, SUBJ is always in the canonical (i.e., innermost) Spec of Infl and OBJ is always in an outer Spec of Infl. This is because (1) two DPs are necessary to delete the strong EPP-feature of the inverse Infl *bi*- before Spell-out, and (2) OBJ is never attracted to a Spec of Infl unless SUBJ is beforehand attracted to the innermost Spec of Infl, thanks to the "MLC" part of the definition of Attract/Move (SUBJ is always closer to Infl than OBJ is, unless SUBJ is moved to a Spec of Infl).

---

[19] Soon I will return to the question as to what feature of Infl (= *bi*-) attracts OBJ in (2.32).

2.2.3. Animacy Hierarchy and the Deletion of Infl's EPP-feature

In §2.2.1 I argued that there is a certain constraint on the animacy hierarchy in the active/inverse voice alternation in Apachean. To recapitulate, (1) If SUBJ and OBJ are equal in the animacy hierarchy, the alternation is totally optional; (2) if SUBJ outranks OBJ in the animacy hierarchy, then inverse voice is blocked; and (3) if OBJ outranks SUBJ in the animacy hierarchy, then inverse voice is obligatory. (Examples relevant to these effects are found in (2.25)–(2.27).) Now the question is how this constraint on the animacy hierarchy can be captured under our analysis of the Apachean active/inverse voice alternation.

My proposal is that the fact concerning the animacy hierarchy in Apachean can be captured by imposing a constraint on the deletion of the EPP-feature of Infl. In the preceding subsection I argued that the EPP-feature of Infl is strong in both active and inverse clauses. I also argued that the EPP-feature of the inverse Infl *bi-* in Apachean is deleted only if checked twice. Notice that the EPP-feature of the active Infl *yi-* is deleted if checked once. Thus, the element that executes the second checking, namely, OBJ accomplishes the deletion of the EPP-feature of Infl in an inverse clause. And SUBJ executes the deletion of the EPP-feature of Infl in an active clause.

Now I propose the following condition:

(2.33) CONDITION ON EPP-FEATURE DELETION IN APACHEAN

What deletes the EPP-feature of Infl in Apachean must not be lower than any other argument in the clause in the animacy hierarchy. (Animacy hierarchy: Animate > Non-animate)

Take the examples in (2.26), which are repeated here as (2.34):

(2.34) SUBJ > OBJ (Hale 1973: 302)

    a. diné   dził   y-oo´í. (active)
        man   mountain ACT-see
        'The man sees the mountain.'

    a'. *dził   diné b-oo´í. (inverse)
        mountain man INV-see
        'The mountain was seen by the man.'

    b. dzaanééz tsé   yi-ztał. (active)
        mule   stone ACT-kick
        'The mule kicked the stone.'

    b'. *tsé   dzaanééz bi-ztał. (inverse)
        stone mule   INV-kick
        'The stone was kicked by the mule.'

These examples show that inverse voice is blocked if in an inverse clause, SUBJ (i.e., the logical subject) outranks OBJ (the logical object) in the animacy hierarchy. Examples in (2.34a', b') are properly ruled out by the condition in (2.33) because OBJ, which deletes the EPP-feature in these sentences, is lower than SUBJ in the animacy hierarchy. On the other hand, (2.34a,b) are properly ruled in; for, SUBJ, which deletes the EPP-feature of Infl in these sentences, is higher than OBJ in the animacy hierarchy.

The examples where SUBJ is lower than OBJ in the animacy hierarchy in an active clause (as in (2.27a,b), repeated here as (2.35)) are ruled out by the condition in (2.33) because it is SUBJ that completes the deletion of the φ-feature of Infl in active voice.

(2.35) SUBJ < OBJ (Hale 1973: 302)

    a.   *tó   ´ashkii yiyi-isxí. (active)
           water boy   ACT-kill
           'The water killed the boy.'

    a'.   ´ashkii tó   bi-isxí. (inverse)
           boy   water INV-kill
           'The boy was killed by the water.'

    b.   *yas łééchaa´í yi-stin. (active)
           snow dog   ACT-freeze
           'The snow froze the dog.'

    b'.   łééchaa´í yas bi-stin. (inverse)
           dog   snow INV-freeze
           'The dog was frozen by the snow.'

On the other hand, when SUBJ is equal to OBJ in the animacy hierarchy, the condition is always satisfied trivially, and, hence, the active/inverse voice alternation is free, as in (2.25), repeated here as (2.36):

(2.36) SUBJ = OBJ (Hale 1973: 301)

    a.   ´ashkii ´at´ééd yiyi-iłtsá. (active)
           boy   girl   ACT-see
           'The boy saw the girl.'

    a'.   ´at´ééd ´ashkii bi-iłtsá. (inverse)
           girl   boy   INV-see
           'The girl was seen by the boy.'

    b.   łééchaa´í mósí yi-shxash. (active)
           dog   cat   ACT-bite
           'The dog bit the cat.'

    b'.   mósí łééchaa´í bi-shxash. (inverse)
           cat   dog   INV-bite
           'The cat was bittten by the dog.'

2.2.4. Subjecthood of SUBJ in Navajo Inverse Voice

In §2.2.2 I argued that SUBJ in a Navajo inverse clause is in the canonical (innermost) Spec of Infl with OBJ being in an outer Spec of Infl. I further argued that SUBJ in an inverse clause checks off the strong EPP-feature of Infl (before SPELL-OUT) in addition to the Case- and φ-features of Infl. Thus, in a Navajo inverse clause, SUBJ checks all of the nominal features of Infl, while OBJ checks only the EPP-feature of Infl (see §2.2.2). Given this, the hypothesis regarding GFs proposed in §2.1.2.2 leads us to predict that SUBJ in a Navajo inverse clause retains the subject properties. (For it has [+construable]-feature checking relations, i.e., EPP-feature and f-feature checking relations, with Infl.)

This prediction is, indeed, borne out. Hale et al. (1977: 52–55) show, with ample examples, that the plural agreement form in Navajo *da-* is always controlled by the logical subject (i.e., SUBJ), regardless of whether the clause involved is active or inverse. Consider the following examples:

(2.37) *Navajo* (Hale et al. 1977: 54)

a. Ashiiké at´ééd **da**-y-oo´í.
the boys the girl PL-ACT-see
'The boys see the girl.'

b. At´ééd ashiiké **da**-b-oo´í.
the girl the boys PL-INVT-see
'The girl is seen by the boys.'

c. Ashkii at´ééké y-oo´í.
the boy the girls ACT-see
'The boy sees the girls.'

d. *Ashkii at´ééké **da**-y-oo´í.
the boy the girls PL-ACT-see
'The boy sees the girls.'

e. At´ééké ashkii b-oo´í.
the girls the boy INV-see
'The girls are seen by the boy.'

f. *At´ééké ashkii **da**-b-oo´í.
the girls the boy PL-INV-see
'The girls are seen by the boy.'

These facts indicate that SUBJ in an inverse clause as well as in an active clause controls subject-agreement. This is what we expect, because under our analysis, only SUBJ has a φ-feature checking relation with Infl, irrespective of whether the clause is active or inverse. This, in turn, points to the validity of our analysis of the Navajo inverse system.

Furthermore, Ken Hale pointed out in personal communication that the implicit subject of the embedded predicate to which the participial form *-ii´* is attached is always controlled by the logical subject (SUBJ) in the matrix clause, regardless of whether the matrix clause is active or inverse (see Young and Morgan 1987). This fact indicates that SUBJ in an inverse clause retains the ability to control the missing subject of a subordinate-adjunct clause. Following Chomsky (1995a), I assume that a φ-feature checking relation with Infl is responsible for the ability to control the missing subject of a subordinate-adjunct clause.[20] Hence, this fact, too, is consistent with our analysis of Navajo inverse voice.

It is very interesting to note here that in Bantu inverse voice, OBJ gains some subject properties (like the ability to induce subject-agreement) and SUBJ loses its subject properties. I argued that this follows from the fact that OBJ, but not SUBJ, has a [+construable]-feature checking relation with Infl in Bantu inverse voice. In contrast, SUBJ retains the subjecthood in Apachean inverse voice, as observed above. This follows from the analysis presented here, according to which it is SUBJ that has a [+construable]-feature checking relation with Infl in Apachean inverse voice.

2.3. Summary

In this chapter I showed how the inverse voice in Bantu and the one in Apachean are derived under the theory of multiple feature checking. It was demonstrated that seemingly complicated phenomena involved in inverse in both types of languages can be consistently accounted for by postulating very simple parametric variations on the checking properties of some functional categories.

In the literature it has been reported that inverse constructions can be found in various languages: Tanoan languages like Arisona Tewa (Klaiman 1993), Northern Tiwa (Nichols 1995); and Algonquian languages like Plains Cree (Dahlstrom 1991), and Ojibwe (Rhodes 1994) (cf. Klaiman 1989); Athabascan languages like Koyukon (Thompson 1994); and other Amerindian languages like Nez Perce (Rude 1982), Tupí-Guaraní (Payne 1993), and Mapudungun (Arnold 1994); and Tibeto-Burman languages like Chepang (Thompson 1990).[21] From the syntactic point of view, it is safe to say that SUBJ is not syntactically demoted despite the fact that OBJ is syntactically promoted (i.e., OBJ becomes SUBJECT) in the inverse constructions found in those languages. Naturally, these inverse constructions have their own peculiarities, but they all involve GF-splitting phenomena that have, more or less, intermediate properties between the ones found in Bantu inverse and the ones in Apachean inverse. As noted above, Bantu inverse and Apachean inverse are opposite in terms of the subject properties that SUBJ loses: Whereas SUBJ loses all of its subject properties in Bantu inverse, it retains most of them in Apachean inverse. Since the mechanism presented in this chapter gives a rigorous account of these two inverse systems, it is

---

[20] In the chapters that follow I will demonstrate that this assumption holds true in a lot of cases.

[21] For inverse constructions in some other varieties of language, see Klaiman (1991) and articles gathered in Givón (1994).

expected that it will also provide an account of the inverse constructions in other languages. However, I leave it to future research to pursue this.

With regard to the theory of GFs, it is notable that I proposed to hypothesize that only an element that has a [+construable]-feature checking relation with Infl can bear subject properties. Moreover, I proposed the hypothesis that the ability to control the missing subject of a subordinate- adjunct clause results from a φ-feature checking relation with Infl. These two hypotheses will be scrutinized in subsequent chapters through the examination of other types of GF-splitting phenomena.

Appendix A
English Quotative Inversion

Collins (1996), extending and revising Collins and Branigan's (1995) analysis of quotative inversion in English, which is based on the interesting observations by Branigan and Collins (1993), provides a very interesting explanation of the phenomenon along the same line of analysis as I provided for the Bantu inverse construction. In this appendix I will summarize Collins's (1996) analysis of English quotative inversion with slight modifications. This is intended to elucidate the applicability of the mechanism of multiple feature checking that is utilized for my analysis of the Bantu inverse voice.

The examples in (2.38) are typical of English quotative inversion:

(2.38) *English* (Branigan and Collins 1993: 5–9)
    a. "I am so happy," thought Mary.
       (cf. "I am so happy," Mary thought.)
    b. "I am so happy," said Mary to John.
       (cf. "I am so happy," Mary said to John.)

According to Branigan and Collins (1993) and Collins and Branigan (1995), this construction has the following properties: (1) SUBJ in a clause with quotative inversion stays in situ (i.e., at the Spec of *v*); (2) V raises to T in overt syntax; and (3) it is SUBJ (or, more precisely, φ-feature of SUBJ) that enters into a φ-feature checking relation with T. Property (1) is confirmed by the following facts. Consider (2.39) and (2.40):

(2.39) *English* (Collins 1996: 32)
    a. "Where to?" asked the driver of the passenger.
    b. *"Where to?" asked of the passenger the driver.

(2.40) *English* (Collins 1996: 32)
    a. "John left," said the student to Mary.
    b. *"John left," said to Mary the student.

Take (2.38b), for example. The word order indicates either that the verb overtly moves to T with SUBJ lingering at the Spec of *v*, or that SUBJ undergoes rightward extraposition (regardless of the position of the verb). The facts shown in (2.39) and (2.40) indicate that the former is true. In fact, if SUBJ becomes "heavy" by the attachment of modifiers, SUBJ can be extraposed, as shown in (2.41):

(2.41) *English* (Collins 1996: 32)
    a. "Where to?" asked of us the driver with the blond hair.
    b. "John left," whispered to Joan the woman sitting at the end of the counter.

This observation leads to the conclusion that SUBJ remains at the Spec of *v* before Spell-out (i.e., property (1)). This, in turn, indicates that the verb in a clause with quotative inversion overtly moves to T beyond SUBJ at the Spec of *v* (i.e., property (2)).[22]

The examples in (2.42) show that SUBJ (or, more precisely, φ-feature of SUBJ) enters into a φ-feature checking relation with T:

(2.42) *English*
    a. "Mary has already left," says/*say John.
    b. "Mary has already left," *says/say the two men.

From property (1) and property (2), it follows that it is at LF that SUBJ (or, more precisely, φ-feature of SUBJ) enters into a φ-feature checking relation with T (i.e., property (3)). Besides, SUBJ enters into a nominative Case-feature checking relation with T (at LF). This is shown by the following example:

(2.43) *English* (Collins 1996: p.33)
    "Mary has already eaten", said ?he/*him.

Furthermore, Collins (1996) hypothesizes, departing from the assumption made by Branigan and Collins (1993) and Collins and Branigan (1995), that the Spec of T is filled with the operator associated with the quote preposed to the clause-initial position.[23] Now the structure of a clause with quotative inversion looks like:

(2.44)   TP   (overt syntax)

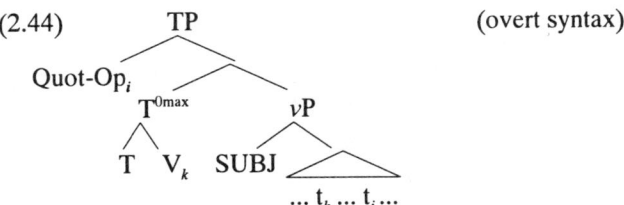

---

[22] The fact concerning the placement of adverbs confirms this conclusion. See Collins (1996) for more details about this. Cf., also, Branigan and Collins (1993) and Collins and Branigan (1995).

[23] See Collins (1996) for more on this hypothesis and related issues.

As Collins (1996) notes, this structure of English quotative inversion has several properties very similar to that of the Bantu inverse construction: (1) The logical (underlying) subject (i.e., SUBJ) remains in situ (i.e., the Spec of v); (2) V overtly moves to T; (3) OBJ (or its equivalent) moves to the Spec of T before SPELL-OUT; (4) SUBJ enters into a nominative Case-feature checking relation with T (at LF); and (5) without any morphological sign, a clause with quotative inversion freely alternates with the equivalent clause without quotative inversion (if some lexical/syntactic conditions are fulfilled; see the discussion below). The only difference between English quotative inversion and Bantu inverse is that, whereas it is SUBJ that checks the φ-feature of T in English quotative inversion, it is OBJ that checks it in Bantu inverse. These similarities and difference between English quotative inversion and Bantu inverse, according to Collins (1996), can be straightforwardly explained by a simple parametric difference.

Recall the derivation of the Bantu inverse construction: First, OBJ moves to a Spec of v due to the property of the nominal feature of v. This gives rise to a situation where SUBJ, which is generated at a Spec of v, and OBJ are equidistant from T. Given that the EPP-feature of T in Bantu is strong, either SUBJ or OBJ must be attracted to the (innermost) Spec of T before Spell-out to check off T's EPP-feature. If OBJ is attracted to the Spec of T and checks off T's EPP-feature, it also checks off the φ-feature of T thanks to the stipulation that the φ-feature of T in those languages is also strong. Then, at LF, (the nominative Case-feature of) SUBJ enters into a checking relation with T, and since all the features that must be checked off are properly checked off, this derivation converges as required.

Now suppose that verbs which can induce quotative inversion such as *say*, *tell*, *ask*, and so forth, can optionally have a strong nominal feature, which can attract OBJ (i.e., QUOTATIVE-OPERATOR (QUOT-OP) in this case) to a Spec of v before Spell-out. If it is attracted to that position, the Case-feature and φ-feature of Quot-Op are checked off there by v. The former is deleted (and erased) but the latter may remain due to its [+interpretable] nature. Now that SUBJ and Quot-Op are equidistant from T, either of them can be attracted to the Spec of T before Spell-out for checking the strong EPP-feature of T. If Quot-Op is attracted, a clause with quotative inversion emerges. At this position, Quot-Op checks off T's EPP-feature. Now one might conjecture that Quot-Op may induce subject-agreement just as OBJ induces subject-agreement in Bantu inverse. Now I propose to assume that the φ-feature of T in English, as well as the nominative-feature of T, is weak. Actually, this assumption has already been proposed (though implicitly) by Chomsky (1995a) in the context where he concludes that the expletive *there* in English checks only the EPP-feature of T before Spell-out and the Case-feature and φ-feature of T can be checked off by the associate at LF.

In §1.4.5 I proposed that Checking is a kind of operation that is subject to the general economy condition. If this proposal is correct, then Quot-Op at the Spec of T is not required to check off the φ-feature of T before Spell-out; as a result, Procrastinate requires that Quot-Op must not check off the φ-feature of T before Spell-out. This is the parametric difference between Bantu and English:

In Bantu, OBJ attracted to the Spec of T in overt syntax must check the φ-feature of T before Spell-out due to the strongness of T's φ-feature. In English, on the other hand, the nominative-feature and φ-feature of T remain unchecked before Spell-out. Then, the nominative Case-feature of SUBJ must be attracted at LF to check off T's (weak) nominative Case-feature. Assuming that English is a language in which nominative Case-checking and φ-feature checking must coincide (see §2.1.3), I would argue that it is the φ-feature of SUBJ, but not OBJ, that checks off T's φ-feature at LF. This is the derivation of English quotative inversion.[24]

One might think, incidentally, that this analysis of English quotative inversion would erroneously allow inverse voice even in English if the predicate of the clause is the type of verb that allows quotative inversion; for, we are assuming that these verbs allow their Theme-argument to be moved overtly to a position in the minimal domain where the Agent-argument is generated.

(2.45) *English*
    *It$_k$ said John t$_k$ (to Mary).
    (cf. "Bill left," said John (to Mary).)

To preclude this, I propose to stipulate that the nominal feature of *v* of a quotative verb, if it is strong, has such a special property that it can attract only an operator before Spell-out. It is noteworthy that a quotative verb, unlike V in the usual case in English, overtly moves to T in this construction, with SUBJ seemingly postposed to the right of the verb. As Collins and Branigan (1995) note, this is reminiscent of French stylistic inversion (cf. Kayne and Pollock 1978, Déprez 1990, Watanabe 1994a). Both constructions require an operator to be involved.

As for (2.45), it is ruled out in the following manner: Because *it* in (2.45) is not an operator, it cannot be attracted to a Spec of *v* before Spell-out; as a result, it cannot be attracted by T before Spell-out. Therefore, (2.45) is never derived.

In fact, if *it* in (2.45) is replaced with *so*, the sentences become acceptable (cf. Collins and Branigan 1995):

(2.46) *English*
    So said John (to Mary).

So, like the quotative operator, refers to an idea expressed elsewhere in the context; hence, it is reasonable to assume that *so* acts like an operator in this regard.[25]

Following, essentially, Collins (1996), I propose to stipulate that the overt movement of the quotative verb to T before Spell-out is necessary for the check-

---

[24] This analysis of English quotative inversion is slightly different from the one provided by Collins (1996). The original and leading idea of my analysis, however, is exclusively due to Collins (1996).

[25] See Stowell (1988) for relevant discussions on the operator-like behavior of *so*.

ing of T's EPP-feature by Quot-Op. Under Watanabe's (1993) three-layered Case theory, we could say that this checking yields another feature that must be checked by the follow-up operation within the domain of C. It is possible to identify this newly created feature as what Collins and Branigan (1995) call [+quot], which is to be checked by Quot-Op at the Spec of C.

Now it is interesting to note a consequence of my analysis of English quotative inversion with respect to the hypothesis of GFs presented in this chapter. From the hypothesis that the ability to control the missing subject of a subordinate-adjunct clause results from a ɸ-feature checking relation with T (= Infl), the prediction follows that it is SUBJ that has this property even in a clause with quotative inversion in English. This prediction is, indeed, borne out:

(2.47) *English*
      a. "I've made it," said John$_k$ [without PRO$_k$ smiling].
      b. *"I've made it," was repeated over and over by John$_k$ [without PRO$_k$ smiling].

Appendix B
Inversion and Local Economy

As explicitly stated in §1.4.4.3, the economy condition that I adopt throughout this thesis is a strictly derivational/local one in the sense that it applies only to a particular stage Σ of a derivation (see Collins 1995b; Ura 1994b, 1995e; and, especially, Collins 1996). The derivations of the Bantu inverse construction and of English quotative inversion lend strong support for this view, as Collins (1996) independently emphasizes.

I argued that active/inverse voice in Bantu and a clause with or without quotative inversion in English freely alternate under some conditions. Collins (1996) correctly points out that the free alternation observed in these constructions provides strong support for the strictly derivational view of the economy condition.

To see this, let us reconsider the derivation of each of the constructions. In Bantu, *v* has the nominal feature that allows OBJ to move to its Spec before Spell-out. And then T is inserted by Merge to this derivation. Example (2.48) illustrates the stage in the derivation where T has been inserted by Merge after OBJ's shift to a Spec of *v*:

(2.48)   [$_{TP}$ T [$_{vP}$ SUBJ [$_{vP}$ OBJ$_k$ *v* [$_{VP}$ V t$_k$]]]]

Since T has a strong EPP-feature in Bantu, something with D-feature must be attracted to the Spec of T before Spell-out. In (2.48) SUBJ and OBJ are equidistant from T; consequently, either of them can be attracted to that position. If SUBJ is attracted, the active clause is derived. If OBJ is attracted, then the inverse clause is derived. Now let us turn our attention to the whole derivation for each clause. In the derivation for the active clause, there is only one more step from (2.48) necessary for LF convergence; namely, SUBJ's movement to the Spec of T.[26] On the other hand, in the derivation for the inverse clause, there are two steps from (2.48) necessary for LF convergence: OBJ's movement to the Spec of T in overt syntax, plus the feature-movement of SUBJ's nominative feature to T at LF. The same holds true for English quotative inversion, as is evident from the discussion presented in appendix A.

If, as has sometimes been claimed in the literature, any derivation with more steps is blocked by a derivation with fewer steps, our analyses of the inverse construction in Bantu and the English quotative inversion fail. Therefore, as long as our analyses of those constructions are right, the economy condition should be defined as a strictly derivational/local condition that applies only to a particular stage Σ of a given derivation, as Collins (1996) proposes. One might conjecture, incidentally, that the Numeration for an inverse clause differs from the one for an active clause because of the difference in terms of the specification of T's ϕ-features involved. If the Numeration for inverse were different from the one for active, the comparison between inverse and active in terms of the economy condition would not materialize because of the difference of the Numeration (Chomsky 1992, 1996). It is true that SUBJ checks off the ϕ-feature in active and OBJ checks off the ϕ-feature in inverse, as I claimed. Provided that SUBJ's ϕ-feature specification differs from OBJ's, the Numeration for active is different from the one for inverse. But both Numerations should be the same in the case where SUBJ has the same ϕ-feature specification as OBJ has (e.g., a case where both SUBJ and OBJ are third-person, singular, and masculine). Even in such a case, active/inverse alternation is freely applicable.

---

[26] Here I ignore V-movement, which is irrelevant for the discussion.

3

Anti-Impersonal Passives

It is a widely held view that in a "passive" clause, the logical (underlying) object (i.e., OBJ) assumes the subject properties that the logical (underlying) subject (i.e., SUBJ) would assume in an "active" clause, and that passivization accompanies some syntactic and morphological changes (see Siewierska 1984, Keenan 1985, P. K. Andersen 1991, and Palmer 1994). Within the theory of Relational Grammar the derivation of a passive sentence involves two changes of syntactic relation to the underlying structure: On the one hand, the logical, underlying object (OBJ) is so changed by the passivization as to assume GR SUBJECT (i.e., OBJ PROMOTION); on the other, the logical, underlying subject (SUBJ) is so changed by the operation as to assume no GR (i.e., SUBJ DEMOTION) (cf. Perlmutter and Postal 1983, Postal 1986, and Blake 1990).

As Comrie (1977) points out, it is a logical possibility that there are languages in which these two processes exist independently. In the languages that possess a passive construction with only OBJ promotion, two subjects result from such a passivization, and in the languages that possess a passive construction with only SUBJ demotion, the so-called impersonal passive construction, in which there is seemingly no surface subject, results from such a passivization (cf. Perlmutter 1983, Perlmutter and Postal 1984, Postal 1986). Comrie (1977) enumerates several languages of the latter type of passive construction, though he acknowledges that he knows of no languages with the former type of passive construction.

In some (less-familiar) languages, however, it is possible to find a passive(-like) construction in which OBJ gains subject properties and, more interestingly to our concern, SUBJ is not syntactically demoted: That is to say, only OBJ promotion, but not SUBJ demotion, is involved in this passive(-like) construction. Owing to this peculiarity, which is opposite to the property of impersonal passives, in which only SUBJ demotion but not OBJ promotion is involved, this construction should be called ANTI-IMPERSONAL PASSIVE (AIP).

In this chapter, I will study a variety of this construction in some languages. It will be demonstrated that the theory of multiple feature checking advocated in this book offers a natural account of this construction.[1] This chapter is organized as follows: In §3.1, Lango, a Western Nilotic language, will be selected as a language with a prototype of anti-impersonal passive, and I will explore an account of the mechanism involved in the anti-impersonal passive in this language under the theory of multiple feature checking. In §3.2, I will take a closer look at the passive construction in Imbabura Quechua, another illustrative example of anti-impersonal passive. Concluding remarks will appear in §3.3. In the appendix, I will make a brief comment on impersonal passive constructions and briefly consider their implications under the theory of multiple feature checking.

3.1. Anti-Impersonal Passive in Lango

A prototype of anti-impersonal passive (hereafter, AIP) can be found in some Western Nilotic languages like Lango or (Bor) Dinka.[2] Despite the fact that OBJ in this construction gains some subject properties, SUBJ retains some of its subject properties without being syntactically demoted. In this section I will investigate the syntactic nature of the AIP in Lango and its implications in the theory of GF-splitting that has been advocated in this book under the theory of multiple feature checking.[3]

3.1.1. Basic Properties of "Long Object Shift" in Lango

Based on the ample data Noonan and Bavin Woock (1978) (henceforth, N&BW) provide, Woolford (1991) claims that OBJ in a Lango transitive clause can be permuted to an A-position beyond SUBJ. Given the fact that the basic word order is SVO in Lango (cf. Noonan 1981, 1992), such a permutation of OBJ in

---

[1] In this respect the inverse construction, which was studied in chapter 2, can be regarded as a special case of anti-impersonal passive, in which the word order of SUBJ and OBJ in active is reversed. In all the anti-impersonal passive constructions to be examined in this chapter, the word order of SUBJ and OBJ is not reversed in the same way as in the inverse constructions. In passing, ANTI-IMPERSONAL PASSIVE should be distinguished from IMPERSONAL ANTI-PASSIVE, which can be found such languages as Yaqui (cf. Escalante 1990).

[2] In this section I will draw data only from Lango. Judging from Gjerlow-Johnson and Ayom's (1986) study of the Bor dialect of Dinka, a Nilotic language spoken in Sudan, I believe that there are very few differences between Lango and Bor Dinka in terms of the syntactic mechanism of anti-impersonal passive.

[3] For detailed grammatical descriptions of Lango, a Nilotic language spoken in Uganda, see Michael Noonan's excellent grammar (Noonan 1992). For more discussion on Lango syntax, see Noonan (1981). Unless otherwise noted, all the examples of this section are extracted from these books in addition to Noonan and Bavin Woock (1978) and Woolford (1991).

Lango may be called LONG OBJECT SHIFT (hereafter, LOS) if Woolford's claim is correct: It is commonly held that OBJECT SHIFT is OBJ's movement to an A-position in overt syntax (cf. Wyngaerd 1989, Mahajan 1990, Déprez 1994, Vikner 1994, Bobaljik 1995b, Jonas 1996, and references cited therein), and "long" is added to the name of the permutation operation in Lango because it differs from the ordinary object shift, which is widely alleged to be permuted to an A-position in between the surface subject position and the base-position of SUBJ. According to N&BW (1978) and Noonan (1992), this operation can be regarded, from a functional point of view, as passive in Lango, which lacks the ordinary passive construction that is made by the attachment of a passive morpheme to a predicate. If it is a passive, it differs from the ordinary passive in that, as mentioned above, SUBJ is not syntactically demoted in this construction. Hence, LOS in Lango (and Dinka) counts as a kind of AIP.

Now let us briefly review Woolford's (1991) arguments for the claim that OBJ is permuted to an A-position beyond SUBJ by LOS in Lango. As the following examples show, OBJ can be permuted by LOS to the clause-initial position beyond the subject, regardless of whether the clause is the matrix one or an embedded one:[4]

(3.1) *Lango* (N&BW 1978: 128)

    a.   Dako   o-jwat-o   loca. (Active)
           woman 3SG-hit-PERF man
           'The woman hit the man.'

    b.   Loca$_i$ dako   o-jwat-o   t$_i$. (AIP)
           man   woman 3SG-hit-PERF

(3.2) *Lango* (N&BW 1978: 129)

    a.   Dako   o-tam-o [$_{CP}$ ni [$_{IP}$ atin o-jwat-o loca]]. (Active)
           woman 3SG-thought COMP child 3SG-hit   man
           'The woman thought that the child hit the man.'

    b.   Dako   o-tam-o [$_{CP}$ ni [$_{IP}$ loca$_i$ atin o-jwat-o t$_i$]]. (AIP)
           woman 3SG-thought COMP man child   3SG-hit

(3.3) *Lango* (N&BW 1978: 129)

    a.   Loca o-mi: atin   m:t. (Active)
           man 3SG-gave child gift
           'The man gave the child a gift.'

    b.   Atin$_i$ Loca o-mi: t$_i$ m:t. (AIP)
           child   man 3SG-gave   gift

---

[4] For the sake of simplicity alone, I omit assigning the diacritics for tone distinction in all of the Lango examples here. For the precise dictation of the examples, see the reference from which the relevant example is extracted.

Seemingly, AIP looks like topicalization/left dislocation. It will, however, turn out, according to Woolford (1991), that it does not involve such an A-bar-type movement if we look more closely at the construction.

As Woolford (1991) notes, the strongest evidence that LOS in Lango is an A-movement comes from the fact that it does not block any other A-bar movement. Consider the examples in (3.4):

(3.4)   *Lango* (N&BW 1978: 136)

    a.   Buk$_i$ [$_{CP}$ a'mɛ [$_{IP}$ dako   o-mi: loca t$_i$]] dwoŋ. (Active)
        book   REL   woman 3SG-gave man   big
        'The book$_i$ [that the woman gave the man t$_i$]] is big.'

    b.   Buk$_i$ [$_{CP}$ a'mɛ [$_{IP}$ loca$_k$ dako   o-mi: t$_k$ t$_i$]] dwoŋ. (AIP)
        book   REL   man   woman 3SG-gave   big
        'same as (3.4a)'

    c.   *Buk$_i$ [$_{CP}$ a'mɛ [$_{IP}$ loca$_k$ ɛn [$_{CP}$ a'mɛ [$_{IP}$ dako   o-mi: t$_k$ t$_i$]]]]
        book   REL   man   it   REL   woman 3SG-gave
        dwoŋ. (Cleft)
        big
        'The book [that it is the man [that the woman gave t$_k$ t$_i$]] is big.'

In (3.4a) the direct object of the subordinate active clause undergoes an A-bar movement by relativization. The example in (3.4b) is derived if the indirect object in (3.4a) undergoes LOS within the subordinate clause. As the well-formedness of (3.4b) indicates, LOS does not block relativization. But clefting indeed blocks relativization, as the ill-formedness of (3.4c) shows. This contrast can be easily explained, as Woolford (1991) points out, by assuming that LOS, unlike clefting, is a kind of A-movement. In fact, clefting as well as topicalization/left dislocation blocks another A-bar movement, as shown by the following English examples:

(3.5)   *English* (Woolford 1991: 234)

    a.   *[The book$_i$ [that it is the man$_k$ [that the woman gave t$_k$ t$_i$]]]
        is big.

    b.   *[The book$_i$ [that the man$_k$, the woman gave t$_k$ t$_i$]] is big.

    c.   *[The book$_i$ [that (as for) the man$_k$, the woman gave him$_k$ t$_i$]]
        is big.

Another difference between LOS and clefting/relativization comes from the fact that LOS out of the second clause of a paratactic construction is possible, while clefting/relativization out of the same context is not, as shown in (3.6):

(3.6)   *Lango*

    a.   Kal$_i$ dako o-dlo   ico   o-pyɛto   t$_i$.
        millet woman 3SG-pressed man 3SG-winnowed
        'The woman pressed the man to winnow millet.' (AIP)

b. *Ogwang$_i$ ɛn [$_{CP}$ a'mɛ [$_{IP}$ a-dlo   Okelo o-jwat-ɛ t$_i$]].
   Ogwang it   REL   1SG-pressed Okelo 3SG-hit-3SG
   'It is Ogwang$_i$ [that I pressed Okelo to hit t$_i$].' (Cleft)

c. *Loca$_i$ [$_{CP}$ a'mɛ [$_{IP}$ Okelo o-dlo   Ogwang o-jwat-[t$_i$]]
   man   REL   Okelo 3SG-pressed Ogwang 3SG-hit-3SG
   'The man$_i$ [that Okelo pressed Ogwang to hit t$_i$]' (Relative)

(I omit going into any detail of the paratactic serial verb construction in Lango; see Noonan and Bavin 1981, and Noonan 1992: 194–210.) It is true that, until clarifying the syntactic property of the paratactic serial verb construction in Lango, it is impossible to conclude only from the examples in (3.6) that LOS is an A-movement. But it suffices for our purpose here to notice that LOS differs in extractability from a paratactic serial verb construction, from clefting and relativization, both of which we can say involve A-bar movement (cf. Noonan 1992). It is easier and even more natural to assume that the contrast shown in (3.6) indicates that LOS is not an A-bar movement (and, hence, it is an A-movement) than to devise a complicated theory of A-bar dependencies in Lango, assuming that LOS is a kind of A-bar movement, but that it differs from clefting/relativization in extractability from a paratactic serial verb construction.[5]

Again, these facts are not sufficient to confirm the claim that OBJ permuted by LOS surely occupies an A-position.[6] Nevertheless, I proceed to the next step, assuming this claim to be valid: I will show that the claim gains further support because there are several facts that resist a natural and consistent account without the claim.

3.1.2. Whither Does Object Go by LOS?

Now that OBJ permuted by LOS occupies an A-position in an anti-impersonal passive clause, the next question to be answered is: What is that position? In this subsection I will try to solve this question by considering the syntactic property of the permuted OBJ in an anti-impersonal passive clause in Lango.

N&BW (1978) report a very interesting property of OBJ permuted by LOS: It gains some of the subject properties. To account for this peculiarity of the shifted OBJ, Woolford (1991) claims that OBJ occupies the Spec of Infl with SUBJ remaining at the Spec of VP in an anti-impersonal passive clause in Lango. I will, however, argue in this subsection that the first half of her claim is correct, but the latter is wrong; that is, I will show that SUBJ as well as the shifted

---

[5] According to Law and Veenstra (1992), a null operator must be involved in serial verb constructions in general. If this is the case, then the contrast shown in (3.6) more strongly suggests that LOS is an A-movement. Chris Collins (personal comminucation), however, pointed out to me that there is a difference between parataxis in Lango and the ordinary serial verb construction, in that it is always possible to extract the object of the second verb in the latter construction. See Bamgbose (1974) and Collins (1993, 1994, 1995a) for relevant discussion.

[6] See Woolford (1991) for some other evidence in favor of this claim.

OBJ occupies a Spec of IP under the theory of multiple feature checking. It will be demonstrated that this can provide a satisfactory account of the fact that OBJ permuted by LOS in an anti-impersonal passive clause gains some subject properties in Lango.

3.1.2.1. Switch Reference in Lango: Evidence for OBJ in Spec-IP

N&BW (1978) report that the shifted OBJ gains five subject-like properties in an anti-impersonal passive clause in Lango. The most convincing one is the fact that the shifted OBJ becomes able to control *pro* in an embedded clause with the non-switch reference marker.[7]

According to Noonan (1992: 225–226), the ordinary third person subject affixes in hypotactic complement clauses assume a new function. Thus, they are used to indicate that the subject of the complement is not the same as the subject of the matrix clause. In this sense the ordinary third person forms are regarded as having a switch reference function in hypotactic complements. If, however, it is intended that the subject of the matrix clause is coreferential with the subject of the complement clause, then the special non-switch reference affixes (i.e., same-subject affixes) must be attached to the inflected predicate in the complement. Consider (3.7):

(3.7)   *Lango* (Noonan 1992: 226)

    a. Rwot$_i$ o-kobo [ni   pro$_{*i/g}$ o-neko   abwor].
        king   3SG-said COMP   3SG-killed lion
        'The king$_i$ said that he$_{*i/g}$ killed the lion.'

    b. Rwot$_i$ o-kobo [ni   pro$_{i/*g}$ ɛ-neko   abwor].
        king   3SG-said COMP   SS-killed   lion
        'The king$_i$ said that he$_{i/*g}$ killed the lion.'

In (3.7a) the ordinary third person singular affix is attached to the embedded predicate. This means that the phonologically null subject in the embedded complement clause with the third person singular affix is different from the matrix subject. In (3.7b), on the other hand, the same-subject affix is used; whereby, the subject in the embedded clause must be coreferential with the matrix subject.

Now consider the following examples, the second of which includes the same-subject affix attached to the embedded predicates with the matrix anti-impersonal passive clause involving LOS:

---

[7] In addition to this property, according to N&BW (1978), the shifted OBJ becomes able to be coreferential with the null subject of another sentence in discourse, to be coreferential with the null subject in a conjunct clause, to be the clause-initial element in word order, and to launch a floating quantifier, all of which have been considered to be GFs linked to GR SUBJECT.

(3.8) *Lango* (N&BW 1978: 131)

a. Dako$_i$ o-kobbi loca$_k$ [ni pro$_{i/*k/*g}$ ɛ-bino dːk]. (Active)
woman 3SG-told man COMP SS-go back
'The woman$_i$ told the man$_k$ that pro$_{i/*k/*g}$ will go back.'

b. Loca$_k$ dako$_i$ o-kobbi t$_k$ [ni pro$_{i/k/*g}$ ɛ-bino dːk]. (AIP)
man woman 3SG-told COMP SS-go back
'The woman$_i$ told the man$_k$ that pro$_{i/k/*g}$ will go back.'

As shown in (3.8a), the null subject in the complement clause must be coreferential with SUBJ in the matrix clause when the same-subject affix appears in the complement clause; hence, OBJ in the matrix clause cannot control *pro* in (3.8a). Interestingly enough, OBJ in the matrix clause, however, can control the null subject of the embedded clause whose predicate has the same-subject affix if the clause is an anti-impersonal passive one with its OBJ permuted by LOS, as shown in (3.8b). It should be noted here that the null subject of the complement clause whose predicate has the same-subject affix cannot be controlled by OBJ in the matrix clause that undergoes A-bar movement such as clefting or relativization:

(3.9) *Lango*

a. Loca$_k$ ɛn [am'ɛ dako$_i$ o-kobbi t$_k$ [ni pro$_{i/*k/*g}$ ɛ-bino dːk]].
man it REL woman 3SG-told COMP SS-go back
'It is the man$_k$ that the woman$_i$ told t$_k$ that pro$_{i/*k/*g}$ will go back.'

b. Loca$_k$ [am'ɛ dako$_i$ o-kobbi t$_k$ [ni pro$_{i/*k/*g}$ ɛ-bino dːk]]
man REL woman 3SG-told COMP SS-go back
'the man$_k$ that the woman$_i$ told t$_k$ that pro$_{i/*k/*g}$ will go back'

Therefore, the fact that the permuted OBJ in Lango anti-impersonal passive can control *pro* in the subordinate clause with the same-subject affix indicates that OBJ in the anti-impersonal passive gains one of the subject properties. Notice, also, that SUBJ in the matrix clause in (3.8b), too, can control *pro* in the embedded clause. This clearly shows that LOS invokes a GF-splitting.

Now recall our hypothesis that only the element that has a [+construable]-feature checking relation with Infl bears the GFs that have been traditionally regarded as the subject-oriented properties, which are contrasted with the nominative-oriented properties (see chapter 6; cf. Bittner and Hale 1996a). One of the most remarkable subject-oriented properties is the ability to control the missing subject in a subordinate-adjunct clause (cf. Perlmutter 1984). In fact, Chomsky (1995) argues that a φ-feature checking relation with Infl is the source of the ability to control. Given this hypothesis, the fact shown in (3.8b) indicates that OBJ as well as SUBJ in the Lango anti-impersonal passive has a [+construable]-feature checking relation with Infl.

Here it should be emphasized that OBJ in addition to SUBJ in an anti-impersonal passive clause in Lango has the subject property that enables it to control. In this regard SUBJ in this construction is not syntactically demoted.

Furthermore, the fact that it is SUBJ that induces subject-agreement in an anti-impersonal passive clause in Lango, as shown in (3.10), lends further support to this conclusion.

(3.10) *Lango* (N&BW 1978: p.132)

    a. Gwɛn o-cel-a   pro. (Active)
        stone 3SG-hit-1SG
        'The stone hit me.'

    b. An$_i$ gwɛn o-cel-a   t$_i$. (AIP)
        I   stone 3SG-hit-1SG

    c. *An$_i$ gwɛn a-celo   t$_i$. (AIP)
        I   stone 1SG-hit

This clearly shows that SUBJ is not syntactically demoted in an anti-impersonal passive clause in Lango in the sense that it retains subject properties. In addition, this shows that SUBJ enters into a ϕ-feature checking relation with Infl even in an anti-impersonal passive clause.

3.1.2.2. Surface Position of SUBJ

Now that OBJ as well as SUBJ has a [+construable]-feature checking relation with Infl in an anti-impersonal passive clause in Lango, it is necessary to ask where OBJ and SUBJ in this construction are located in overt syntax. Woolford (1991), as mentioned above, claims that OBJ occupies the Spec of Infl with SUBJ remaining at the Spec of VP in an anti-impersonal passive clause in Lango.

Contrary to Woolford's (1991) claim, I will show that there is some evidence which shows that SUBJ moves overtly to a Spec of Infl even in an anti-impersonal passive clause with LOS. First, let us consider the surface position of SUBJ and the predicate in an ordinary active indicative clause. Then we will turn to the question about the surface position of SUBJ in a clause with its object permuted by LOS in a Lango anti-impersonal passive clause.

According to Noonan (1992), SUBJ in an ordinary active clause *always* precedes auxiliaries/neg-elements/adverbs like 'yet' or 'just':

(3.11) *Lango* (N&BW 1978: 132 and Noonan 1992: 122)

    a. Dako 'bino nenno loca.
        woman will   see   man
        'The woman will see the man.'

    b. Lɔca (pe) o-bino   paco.
        man   NEG   3SG-came home
        'The man (did not come) came home.'

It is a widely held view that it is universally true that auxiliaries and the neg-head are structurally higher than the VP in a clause (cf. Pollock 1989 and Ouhalla

1991). Given the fact that Lango is a fairly strict SVO language, as Noonan (1992) claims, the fact shown in (3.11) suggests that SUBJ moves overtly out of the VP. Moreover, if it is true that auxiliaries are base-generated at Infl, as is also widely assumed, then the word order shown in (3.11a) suggests that SUBJ moves overtly from the Spec of VP to the Spec of Infl (cf. Koopman and Sportiche 1991).

Furthermore, the fact shown in (3.12) below indicates that V moves overtly out of the VP in Lango, as in French.

(3.12)   *Lango* (Woolford 1991: 241)
   a. [Awobe duci] ocɛmɔ.
       boys   all   ate
       'All the boys ate.'
   b. Awobe ocɛmɔ duci.

According to Noonan (1992: 169–170), the floated quantifier associated with SUBJ is stranded at the immediate post-verbal position, as in (3.12b). Sportiche (1988) argues that a floated quantifier marks original/landing sites of the A-movement of SUBJ. Assuming the VP-internal subject hypothesis, we may interpret the fact in (3.12b) as showing that both SUBJ and V move overtly out of VP in Lango. In addition, Noonan (1992: 181) reports the fact that manner/degree adverbials *always* follow a finite verb in Lango. This fact lends further support to the claim that V moves overtly out of VP in Lango.

I conclude from these facts that SUBJ and V both move overtly out of VP in an ordinary active indicative clause in Lango. Under the minimalist theory of feature checking assumed in this book, this means that the nominal feature (presumably, an EPP-feature) of T (= Infl) and the verbal feature of T are both strong, requiring overt subject movement and overt V-raising, respectively.

Next, let us consider where SUBJ appears in an anti-impersonal passive clause in which OBJ is permuted by LOS. As the following example shows, SUBJ precedes auxiliaries even in an anti-impersonal passive clause:

(3.13)   *Lango* (N&BW 1978: 133)
   Loca$_i$ dako 'bino nenno t$_i$.
   man   woman will see
   'The woman will see the man.'

By the same reasoning as in the case of (3.11), I conclude from this fact that not only does SUBJ move overtly out of VP, even in an anti-impersonal passive clause, but also that it moves overtly to a Spec of Infl.

Furthermore, one should recall our conclusion (1) that OBJ in an anti-impersonal passive clause occupies an A-position, and (2) that OBJ has a [+construable]-feature checking relation with Infl. Given these conclusions, in addition to the one that SUBJ in an anti-impersonal passive clause occupies a Spec of Infl before Spell-out, then the fact concerning the word order shown in (3.13) and (3.14) suggests that OBJ in an anti-impersonal passive clause, too, occupies an outer Spec of Infl with SUBJ located at the inner Spec of Infl before Spell-out.

(3.14) *Dako loca$_i$ 'bino nenno t$_i$.
woman man will see
'under the same interpretation as (3.13)'

Thus far I have demonstrated that in an anti-impersonal passive clause in which OBJ is permuted by LOS, SUBJ, as well as the shifted OBJ, occupies a Spec of Infl.

Therefore, although Woolford (1991) is right in claiming that OBJ permuted by LOS in Lango anti-impersonal passive occupies a Spec of Infl in overt syntax, her claim that SUBJ in that construction remains in VP in overt syntax is inaccurate. For her, OBJ's overt movement to a Spec of Infl inevitably implies that the subject in an anti-impersonal passive clause is not in a Spec of Infl, because she assumes the "conventional" X-bar theory, which disallows multiple Specs per head (cf. Chomsky 1986a). It leads her to the conclusion that SUBJ lingers at the Spec of VP where it is base-generated. But under the theory of multiple feature checking, this situation is totally possible (Chomsky 1994a; Koizumi 1994a, 1995; and Ura 1994e). In the next section I will show how to cope with LOS in Lango under the theory of multiple feature checking.

3.1.3. Derivation of Anti-Impersonal Passive in Lango

Now that OBJ as well as SUBJ in an anti-impersonal passive clause occupies a Spec of Infl in overt syntax, let us consider how they move to their positions.

Thus far, it was concluded that SUBJ in an anti-impersonal passive clause has a [+construable]-feature (more precisely, ϕ-feature) checking relation with Infl; for, it also has the ability to control. Moreover, it was observed that OBJ permuted by LOS can control *pro* in a subordinate clause with the same-subject affix. Thus, it follows from our hypothesis concerning GFs, that OBJ permuted by LOS in an anti-impersonal passive clause, too, has a [+construable]-feature checking relation with Infl. In agreement with Chomsky (1995a), I further argue that OBJ as well as SUBJ in a Lango anti-impersonal passive clause has a ϕ-feature checking relation with Infl. How is it possible for both SUBJ and OBJ to enter into a ϕ-feature checking relation with Infl at the same time?

3.1.3.1. Infl's [+Multiple] ϕ-feature

Now let us consider how an anti-impersonal passive clause is derived in Lango. In §3.1.2.2, I showed that in an anti-impersonal passive clause in Lango, SUBJ is at the canonical Spec of Infl and OBJ at an outer Spec of Infl before Spell-out. The question is: How are they forced to move to their respective positions before Spell-out?

Given the fact that SUBJ is moved overtly to the (innermost) Spec of Infl in Lango irrespective of whether the clause is active or anti-impersonal passive (see §3.1.2.2), it is natural to assume that the EPP-feature of Infl (= T) in Lango is always strong. With this in mind, consider the stage in the derivation illustrated in (3.15):

(3.15)   [$_{IP}$ Infl [$_{vP}$ SUBJ v [$_{VP}$ V OBJ]]]

Since the EPP-feature of Infl is strong regardless of whether the clause is active or anti-impersonal passive, SUBJ, which is the DP closest to T, is always attracted to the innermost Spec of Infl to check off the strong EPP-feature of Infl before Spell-out, deriving (3.16) from (3.15):

(3.16)   [$_{IP}$ SUBJ$_k$ Infl [$_{vP}$ t$_k$ v [$_{VP}$ V OBJ]]]

If nothing happens further to (3.16), it expresses the surface structure of an active clause in Lango.

Now I propose (1) that Infl's φ-feature, as well as its EPP-feature, is strong in a Lango anti-impersonal passive clause, and (2) that the strong φ-feature of Infl in an anti-impersonal passive clause is a [+multiple]-property that requires two checking operations for its deletion. This is reminiscent of our proposal that the strong EPP-feature of the inverse Infl *bi-* in Apachean is deleted only if it is checked twice (see §2.2). Let us return to (3.16) and suppose that the clause is an anti-impersonal passive one. Then, Infl's φ-feature attracts OBJ to an outer Spec of Infl for the purpose of the second execution of its checking. This derives (3.17) from (3.16):

(3.17)   [$_{IP}$ OBJ$_i$ [$_{IP}$ SUBJ$_k$ Infl*(AIP)* [$_{vP}$ t$_k$ v [$_{VP}$ V t$_i$]]]]   (AIP)

This expresses the surface structure of an anti-impersonal passive clause in Lango. In other words, LOS in Lango is induced by the strong φ-feature of the anti-impersonal passive Infl that requires two checking operations for its deletion before Spell-out.

This derivation of an anti-impersonal passive clause in Lango converges, as required, if V overtly head-moves up onto Infl and enters into a Case-checking relation with OBJ, which is at an outer Spec of Infl; whereby, all the [–interpretable] features involved in (3.17) are properly checked off. Indeed, this conforms to the fact that V overtly raises to Infl in Lango (see §3.1.2.2).

3.1.3.2. Morphophonological Agreement in Anti-Impersonal Passive

It is important to recall the fact that SUBJ, but not OBJ, induces subject-agreement in an anti-impersonal passive in Lango, as was noted in (3.10). Thus, one might be tempted to claim (cf. Ura 1996b) that this clearly indicates that SUBJ, but not OBJ, has a φ-feature checking relation with Infl. Contrary to this claim, I argued above that OBJ in a Lango anti-impersonal passive clause has a φ-feature checking relation with Infl.

Given that OBJ has a φ-feature checking relation with Infl, why is it that only SUBJ induces morphological agreement upon the finite verb in the anti-impersonal passive? Here I simply speculate, without any evidence, that this is due merely to a morphophonological reason: It is the element linearly/morphophonologically closest to the finite verb that induces the agreement that is morphophonologically visible. It is safe to say that this is a general tendency, judging from the fact that the innermost subject always induces morphophonologically visible agreement in almost all languages with so-called multiple subjects, like Japanese, Korean, and Uzbek (see Ura 1994e).[8]

A comment on control and switch-reference is in order. I argued that a φ-feature checking relation with Infl, irrespective of its morphophonological visibility, is the source of the ability to control the missing subject in a clause with the same-subject affix. This may count as a restatement of Hale's (1992) proposal about the determination of the controller involved in switch-reference. He proposes that φ-feature and c-command are its only crucial factors (cf., also, Borer 1989 and Lasnik 1992). So it is natural to extend the hypothesis that a φ-feature checking relation with Infl is the source of the ability to control the missing subject in a subordinate-adjunct clause, and to say that the ability to control in switch-reference is possessed by the element that has a φ-feature checking relation with Infl (see Watanabe 1995b for more discussion).

Thus far I claimed that Infl in a Lango anti-impersonal passive clause is different from Infl in an active clause. Unfortunately, there is no morphophonologically visible/audible sign available which shows that they are really distinct from each other. For the case of Apachean, it was observed that there is a clear morphological distinction between the inverse Infl and the active Infl: The former morphophonologically appears as *bi-* and the latter as *yi-* (cf. chapter 2). In Bor Dinka, another Western Nilotic language which has an active/anti-impersonal voice alternation very similar to the one in Lango as mentioned in footnote 2, there is a morphophonologically clear distinction between the anti-impersonal passive Infl and the active Infl: According to the description given in Gjerlow-Johnson and Ayom (1986), a verb's vowel and tone are altered in a systematic way in Bor Dinka if the clause is changed from active into anti-impersonal passive.[9] Hence I presume that the lack of the morphophonologically visible/audible distinction between the anti-impersonal passive Infl and the active Infl in Lango is accidental.

---

[8] According to Grønbech (1936), a few Turkic languages may allow multiple agreements on the finite verb induced by multiple subjects, though it is impossible to find the same type of anti-impersonal passive as Lango in those languages.

[9] See, also, Nebel (1947) for details. For further discussion on what we call anti-impersonal passives in Dinka, see T. Andersen (1991).

3.1.4. Grammatical Function Splitting by LOS

In this subsection let us consider a problem that one might raise with respect to our claim that OBJ in an anti-impersonal passive clause in Lango is in a Spec of Infl. N&BW (1978) and Woolford (1991) report that OBJ permuted by LOS cannot bind any subject-oriented reflexive within its clause as shown in (3.18), in spite of the fact that it acquires the ability to control *pro* in the complement clause with the same-subject affix as observed in §3.1.2.1.

(3.18) *Lango*

    a. Loca$_i$ o-kwao   dako$_k$ pir-ɛ   kɛnɛ$_{i/*k}$. (Active)
        man   3SG-asked woman about-3SG self
        'The man asked the woman about himself/*herself.'

    b. [$_{IP}$ Dako$_k$ [$_{IP}$ loca$_i$ o-kwao   t$_k$ pir-ɛ   kɛnɛ$_{i/*k}$]]. (AIP)
        woman   man   3SG-asked   about-3SG self
        'The man asked the woman about himself/*herself.'

Hitherto I claimed that a [+construable]-feature checking relation with Infl is crucial for subject-oriented phenomena (such as control). I also claimed that OBJ as well as SUBJ in (3.18) has a [+construable]-feature (more precisely, φ-feature) checking relation with Infl. Then, it might be predicted that OBJ as well as SUBJ in an anti-impersonal passive clause in Lango can bind a subject-oriented reflexive. The fact shown in (3.18) is therefore contrary to this prediction.

Ura (1996b) discovered that the element in an outer Spec of Infl cannot bind *zibun-zishin*, a (purely) subject-oriented reflexive, in Japanese, though the element in the canonical Spec of Infl can properly bind it.[10] This is illustrated in (3.19):

(3.19) *Japanese*

    John$_k$-ga [$_{DP}$ t$_k$ imooto$_j$]-ga [$_{DP}$ **zibun-zishin**-no*k/j heya]-de
    -NOM   sister   -NOM self-self-GEN   room -at
    koros-are-ta.
    kill-PASS-PAST
    Lit. 'John's$_k$ sister$_j$ was killed in self's*$_{k/j}$ room.'

Through studying the possessor-raising construction in Japanese, I argued in Ura (1996b) that the outer SUBJ as well the inner one in (3.19) has a φ-feature checking relation with Infl in addition to a nominative Case-feature checking relation with Infl. But only the inner one has an EPP-feature checking relation with Infl. The conclusion I drew in Ura (1996b) from this observation was that an EPP-feature checking relation with Infl is exclusively necessary for the ability to bind a (purely) subject-oriented reflexive.[11]

---

[10] For discussion on *zibun-zishin* in Japanese, see Katada (1991), among others.

[11] See Ura (1996b) for more discussion on the binding ability of *zibun-zishin* vs. that of *zibun*, another (not so purely) subject-oriented reflexive in Japanese.

Here recall our analysis of the Lango anti-impersonal passive: In an anti-impersonal passive clause in Lango, although both the element at the outer Spec of Infl (i.e., OBJ) and the one at its inner Spec (i.e., SUBJ) have a φ-feature checking relation with Infl, only the latter has an EPP-feature checking relation with Infl. Therefore, given Ura's (1996b) conclusion that an EPP-feature checking relation with Infl is the source of the ability to bind a (purely) subject-oriented reflexive, the Lango fact shown in (3.18) naturally follows and gives strong support to our analysis of the Lango anti-impersonal passive.

3.1.5. Summary for Lango Anti-Impersonal Passive

In this section I argued that LOS in Lango involved in an anti-impersonal passive clause is induced by T's strong φ-feature that requires two executions of its checking, and that this explains the facts concerning the GF-splitting phenomena involved in a Lango anti-impersonal passive clause. In the next section I will examine the syntactic nature of a somewhat different type of anti-impersonal passive, which is found in Imbabura Quechua.

3.2. Anti-Impersonal Passive in Imbabura Quechua

3.2.1. Basic Properties of Imbabura Quechua Passive

Another type of anti-impersonal passive is found in Imbabura Quechua.[12] Morphologically, passive in Imbabura Quechua is made from the corresponding active by the attachment of the past participle suffix to the main verb together with the introduction of *-ca* 'be', which, in place of the main verb, represents tense and subject agreement (Cole 1982: 133–134).[13] By passivization OBJ is moved overtly to the clause-initial position, which is the surface subject position in Imbabura Quechua, an SOV language (cf. Cole 1982 and Lefebvre and Muysken 1988), and it accordingly becomes marked as nominative. Very remarkable as to passive in Imbabura Quechua is the fact that SUBJ retains its nominative Case-marking in a passive clause, which indicates that SUBJ in a passive clause in Im-

---

[12] According to Jake (1985), the passive construction, which is of sole interest to our concern in this chapter (i.e., anti-impersonal passive), is not found in other Quechua dialects. In Huallaga Quechua, for example, SUBJ in passive must be marked as ablative (or genitive or commitative, in some cases), according to Weber (1989: 245), though the morphological changes involved in active/passive alternation are the same as in Imbabura Quechua (see below). This is clearly a sign of SUBJ demotion. Cf., also, Lefebvre and Muysken (1982) for passive in Cuzco Quechua.

[13] According to Cole (1982), there is another way to derive passive from active: By the attachment of an infinitive suffix to the main verb together with the introduction of *-tuki* 'become'. See Cole (1982) for the differences between those two passives in Imbabura Quechua, differences that seem irrelevant to our concern in this chapter (cf. Siewierska 1984 and Watanabe 1996 for relevant discussion). We will concentrate our attention on the *ka*-passive.

babura Quechua is not syntactically demoted, as Cole (1982) and Jake (1985) explicitly state. In this regard the Imbabura Quechua passive counts as an anti-impersonal passive.

The following examples are illustrative for Imbabura Quechua (anti-impersonal) passive:

(3.20)   *Imbabura Quechua* (Jake 1985: 54)

    a. Active
        [Chai jari]-Ø-ca   [hura aswa]-ta ufya-rca-Ø-mi.
        that man -NOM-TOP hura beer -ACC drink-PAST-3-VAL
        'That man drank hura beer.'

    b. AIP
        [hura aswa]-Ø-ca   ([chai jari]-Ø) ufya-shca-mi ca-rca-Ø.
        hura beer -NOM-TOP   that man -NOM drink-PASS-VAL be-PAST-3
        'The hura beer was drunk (by that man).'

(3.21)   *Imbabura Quechua* (Jake 1985: 57)

    a. Active
        Alcu-cuna-Ø-ca ñuca-nchi-ta cani-rca-Ø-mi.
        dog-PL-NOM-TOP   1-PL-ACC   bite-PAST-3-VAL
        'The dog bit us.'

    b. AIP
        Ñuca-nchi-Ø-ca   alcu-cuna-Ø cani-scha-mi ca-rca-**nchi**.
        1-PL-NOM-TOP   dog-PL-NOM   bite-PASS-VAL be-PAST-**1PL**
        'We were bitten by the dog.'

In Quechua all grammatical cases are expressed by the attachment of a Case-particle; for example, *-ta* is attached to an accusative DP, *-paj* to a genitive DP, and so forth (see Cole 1982 for details). It is notable that, as shown in the above examples, the nominative Case-particle is morphologically null (cf. Cole 1982, Hermon 1984, and Jake 1985).

Also remarkable is the fact that the subjects in all the above examples are topicalized, which is evident from the attachment of the topic-marker *-ca* to them. In Quechua, as in Japanese or Korean, there is a (strong) tendency, under natural contexts, to mark an argument (most often, the subject) in the matrix clause as a topic. It is, however, possible to leave out a topic argument in the sentence (Cole 1982: §1.12); the examples in (3.22) are thus perfectly acceptable (grammatical):[14]

---

[14] See Cole (1982: chapter 1 §1.11.2), Jake (1985: chapter 2 §5), and Hermon (1984: chapter 2) for the validator suffixes and their functions. Roughly speaking, they are used for emphasis.

(3.22) *Imbabura Quechua* (Cole 1982: 98 and Hermon 1984: 21)

    a.   José-Ø   María-ta   juya-n-mi.
           -NOM   -ACC   love-3-VAL
       'Jose loves Maria.'

    b.   Juan-Ø   aycha-ta   miku-rka-Ø.
           -NOM   meat-ACC eat-PAST-3
       'Juan ate meat.'

When a DP is topicalized with the topic-marker *-ca*, the topicalized DP must retain its original Case suffix, as shown in (3.23) (cf. Cole 1982 and Lefebvre and Muysken 1988):

(3.23) *Imbabura Quechua* (Jake 1985: 24)

    a.   María*(-ta)-ca$_k$ José-Ø t$_k$ juya-n-mi.
           -ACC-TOP   -NOM   love-3-VAL
       'Maria$_k$, Jose loves t$_k$.'

    b.   Urcu*(-mande)-ca supai-cuna-Ø   t$_k$ shamu-nga-Ø-chari.
           mountain-ABL-TOP devil-PL-NOM   come-FUT-3-DUB
       'Maybe the devil will come from the mountain.'

From this it is concluded that in a(n anti-impersonal) passive clause like (3.20b) or (3.21b), the underlying (logical) object (i.e., OBJ) is marked as nominative. In fact, it is not impossible for OBJ in a(n anti-impersonal) passive clause to appear without the topic-marker:[15]

(3.24) *Imbabura Quechua* (Jake 1985: 58)

    Ñuca-nchi-Ø   alcu-cuna-Ø   cani-scha-mi   ca-rca-nchi.
    1-PL-NOM   dog-PL-NOM   bite-PASS-VAL   be-PAST-1PL
   'We were bitten by the dogs.'

This counts as strong evidence that OBJ in passive is indeed marked as nominative in an Imbabura Quechua (anti-impersonal) passive clause, as Cole (1982) and Jake (1985) indicate.

Furthermore, the fact that subject-agreement is induced only by OBJ in a(n anti-impersonal) passive clause (as shown ealier by (3.21)) confirms that OBJ is syntactically promoted and gains some subjecthood in an Imbabura Quechua (anti-impersonal) passive clause. To recap, in an Imbabura Quechua (anti-impersonal) passive clause, (1) both SUBJ and OBJ stand in nominative, and (2) passive morphology is involved, and (3) OBJ, but not SUBJ, induces agreement. From these facts, it is safe to conclude that SUBJ is not completely demoted despite the promotion of OBJ in Imbabura Quechua (anti-impersonal) passive. This

---

[15] Though, according to Cole (1982: §1.12), the topic-marking of the promoted OBJ in a(n anti-impersonal) passive clause seems nearly obligatory in natural contexts, because the two sequential nominative-marked DPs are liable to be interpreted as being conjoined.

is the reason that we identify the passive construction in Imbabura Quechua as an anti-impersonal passive.

3.2.2. Grammatical Function Splitting

Now let us consider what grammatical functions OBJ and SUBJ have in an anti-impersonal passive clause in Imbabura Quechua.

3.2.2.1. Subjecthood of the Promoted OBJ in Anti-Impersonal Passive

Most remarkable is the fact that the promoted OBJ induces subject-agreement in an Imbabura Quechua anti-impersonal passive clause. This sharply contrasts with a Lango anti-impersonal passive clause, in which the nondemoted SUBJ induces subject-agreement as observed in §3.1.

Furthermore, according to Jake (1985), the promoted OBJ in the Imbabura Quechua anti-impersonal passive gains the ability to be coreferential with SUBJ in an adverbial clause with the same-subject affix attached to its predicate.

(3.25) *Imbabura Quechua* (Jake 1985: 59)
[Wawa-Ø$_k$ shamu-**shpa**-ca], pai-lla-Ø$_k$ alcu-Ø cani-shca-mi
child-NOM come-SS-TOP he-DEL-NOM dog-NOM bite-PASS-VAL
ca-rca-Ø. (AIP)
be-PAST-3
'[When the child$_k$ came], he$_k$ was bitten by the dog.'

Following, essentially, Hale (1992) and Watanabe (1995b), I am assuming that proximation (same-subject value or coreference) and obviation (different subject value or disjoint reference) in the so-called switch-reference system are closely linked to control (see §3.1.3). Then, the above fact suggests that the promoted OBJ in an anti-impersonal passive clause gains the ability to control. It is noteworthy that OBJ in an active clause does not have the ability to control; consequently, (3.26) is not acceptable:

(3.26) *[Wawa-Ø$_k$ shamu-**shpa**-ca], alcu-Ø pai-lla-ta$_k$
child-NOM come-SS-TOP dog-NOM he-DEL-ACC
cani-rca-Ø-mi. (Active)
bite-PAST-3-VAL
'[When the child$_k$ came], he$_k$ was bitten by the dog.'

In the previous section, I claimed that the fact that the promoted OBJ in the Lango anti-impersonal passive gains the same ability implies that the OBJ enters into a [+construable]-feature (more precisely, φ-feature) checking relation with Infl. The same reasoning, thus, leads to the conclusion that the promoted OBJ in the Imbabura Quechua anti-impersonal passive, too, has a φ-feature checking relation with Infl. In contrast, the fact that SUBJ in an anti-impersonal passive clause cannot control indicates that SUBJ has no φ-feature checking relation with Infl in this construction in Imbabura Quechua.

3.2.2.2. Grammatical Functions of SUBJ in Anti-Impersonal Passive

First of all, the nondemoted SUBJ in the Imbabura Quechua anti-impersonal passive never induces subject-agreement, as noted in §3.2.2.1. Second but of more interest, the nondemoted SUBJ in the anti-impersonal passive cannot control, in remarkable contrast with the Lango anti-impersonal passive. Consider the following examples:

(3.27) *Imbabura Quechua* (Jake 1985: 60)
   a. [PRO$_k$ milma-ta randi-shpa-mi], taita-Ø$_k$ ruwana-ta
              wool-ACC buy-SS-VAL   father-NOM   poncho-ACC
       awa-rca-Ø. (Active)
       weave-PAST-3
       Lit. 'After PRO$_k$ bought wool, father$_k$ wove a poncho.'
   b. *[PRO$_k$ milma-ta randi-shpa-mi], ruwana-Ø   taita-Ø$_k$
              wool-ACC buy-SS-VAL   poncho-NOM father-NOM
       awa-shca   ca-rca-Ø. (AIP)
       weave-PASS be-PAST-3

In light of the hypothesis proposed thus far, this means that SUBJ in the Imbabura Quechua anti-impersonal passive has no [+construable]-feature checking relation with Infl, though it is evident from its nominative-marking that it has a feature-checking relation with Infl which is mediated by nominative Case-feature, a [–construable]-feature.

To sum up, it was observed (1) that the promoted OBJ in an anti-impersonal passive clause in Imbabura Quechua gains the ability to control, and (2) that the nondemoted SUBJ in an anti-impersonal passive clause in Imbabura Quechua loses the ability to control. From (1) and (2) it was concluded that in the Imbabura Quechua anti-impersonal passive, the promoted OBJ has a φ-feature checking relation with Infl, but the nondemoted SUBJ does not.

Note that this conclusion is, indeed, confirmed by the fact that OBJ, but not SUBJ, induces subject-agreement in an Imbabura Quechua anti-impersonal passive clause. Now that we know what kinds of feature checking are involved in an Imbabura Quechua anti-impersonal passive clause, the next question is: How is an anti-impersonal passive clause derived in Imbabura Quechua?

3.2.3. Explanation

Now I propose the following: (1) The nominative Case-feature of Infl in Imbabura Quechua can enter into multiple checking relations; (2) the nominative Case-feature of Infl in Imbabura Quechua is strong; (3) the EPP-feature and φ-feature of Infl in Imbabura Quechua are both weak;[16] and (4) the nominative Case-feature of Infl in an Imbabura Quechua anti-impersonal passive clause needs double checking, just like the EPP-feature of the inverse Infl in Apachean or the φ-feature of the Infl in an anti-impersonal passive clause in Lango. Besides, I propose that (1), (2), and (3) (but not (4), of course) hold irrespective of the voice of the clause. With these assumptions in mind, let us now consider the derivation for the anti-impersonal passive in Imbabura Quechua.

Suppose that (3.28) below is an anti-impersonal passive clause:

(3.28) $[_{IP}$ Infl(PASS) $[_{vP}$ SUBJ(NOM) v-pass $[_{VP}$ V OBJ(NOM)]]] (AIP)

I assume that the passive-morpheme attached to V absorbs the nominal features of v including the accusative Case-feature (see Baker, Johnson, and Roberts 1988, and, especially, Watanabe 1996 for Case-feature absorption). Thanks to (2), SUBJ is attracted to T to execute the first checking of the nominative Case-feature of the anti-impersonal passive Infl.[17] This derives (3.29) from (3.28):

(3.29) $[_{IP}$ SUBJ(NOM)$_k$ Infl(PASS) $[_{vP}$ t_k v-pass $[_{VP}$ V OBJ(NOM)]]] (AIP)

It should be noted that at this stage in the derivation, SUBJ checks the nominative Case-feature of Infl, but it need not check the EPP-feature and φ-feature of Infl. This is because they are weak in Imbabura Quechua (due to (3)). Under the hypothesis that Checking is a kind of syntactic operation that is subject to the general economy condition, a weak feature is allowed not to be checked off before Spell-out if it is not required for convergence (see §1.4.6).

Owing to (4), the nominative-marked OBJ in (3.29) is attracted overtly to an outer Spec of Infl to execute the second checking of the strong nominative Case-feature of the anti-impersonal passive Infl in Imbabura Quechua. This derives (3.30) from (3.29):

(3.30) $[_{IP}$ OBJ(NOM)$_l$ $[_{IP}$ SUBJ(NOM)$_k$ Infl(PASS) $[_{vP}$ t_k v-pass $[_{VP}$ V t_l]]]]
(AIP)

This represents the surface structure of an anti-impersonal passive clause in Imbabura Quechua. This derivation results in convergence in the following fashion: Before Spell-out, the strong nominative Case-feature of Infl is properly deleted by the checking executed by SUBJ plus the subsequent checking executed by OBJ; v's nominal features are absorbed by the passive morpheme; and OBJ at the outer Spec of Infl checks off Infl's weak EPP-feature and φ-feature at LF.[18]

---

[16] Since the weakness of T's EPP-feature (i.e, D-feature) virtually means that the so-called Extended Projection Principle does not hold in this language, it may be possible to say that T has no EPP-feature in Imbabura Quechua. This is supported by the nonexistence of expletives in Imbabura Quechua (cf. Cole 1982).

[17] OBJ is never attracted to v, because v's nominal features are absorbed by the passive morpheme.

[18] I will return directly to the question why SUBJ has neither EPP-checking relation nor

Anti-Impersonal Passives 89

In the previous subsection I concluded, from the observation concerning GF-splitting in the Imbabura Quechua anti-impersonal passive, that the promoted OBJ has a φ-feature checking relation with Infl, but the nondemoted SUBJ does not. Then, a question arises: Why is it that OBJ in (3.30) always checks off the weak φ-feature of Infl at LF despite the fact that SUBJ in (3.30), too, has the potential to check it off (that is, SUBJ is in the checking configuration for Infl's φ-feature checking)? SUBJ and OBJ in (3.30) seem to have the same potential to check off the weak φ-feature of Infl at LF because both are in a Spec of Infl. There is, however, a reason to presume that the φ-feature of OBJ, but not that of SUBJ, must check off Infl's weak φ-feature (and, also, EPP-feature) in (3.30).

Elsewhere in this book I repeatedly emphasized that the economy condition should be applied strictly derivationally (or strictly stepwise) (Collins 1995b, 1996; Ura 1994b, 1995c). Under the hypothesis that Checking is a syntactic operation subject to the general economy condition, more economical Checking should be selected over less economical one. Returning to (3.30), I now aim to show that the checking of Infl's weak φ-feature and EPP-feature by OBJ is more economical than the one by SUBJ. How can we measure the economy of Checking at LF?

Watanabe (1995a), utilizing Chomsky's (1994a) set-theoretic notation of terms, claims that all the (syntactic) operations at LF always result in redefinition of a term that has already been created in overt syntax.[19] With this notion of redefinition, we can measure the economy of Checking at LF in the following manner: At LF, a more economical Checking results in fewer redefinitions of terms than a less economical one. If this is correct, then less economical Checkings are blocked by a more economical one with Watanabe's (1995a) Avoid Redefinition Condition:

(3.31) **Avoid Redefinition Condition** (Watanabe 1995a: 275)
Avoid redefinition of terms as much as possible.

Now I propose that Checking at LF redefines already existing terms in the following fashion: Take, for example, (3.32), where XP has a feature F1, which is to check a weak feature f_w of a head H:

(3.32)
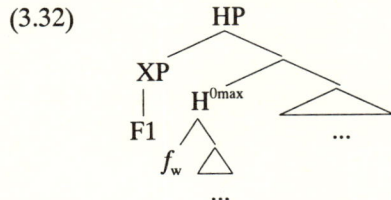

φ-feature checking relation with Infl in (3.30).

[19] Watanabe's (1995a) original idea excludes the possibility of Checking as a syntactic operation. However, if all checking operations involve movement of features, as Chomsky (1995 fall lectures) proposes, Checking (at LF) always results in redefinition of already existing terms, as claimed here.

According to Chomsky (1995a), only formal features are moved at LF. Hence, it is not so unnatural to extend this by assuming that only formal features can enter into a checking relation at LF.[20] If so, then F1 cannot check f_w unless f_w enters into a checking relation with F1 by moving to a position adjoined to XP. This situation can be delineated as in (3.33):

(3.33)
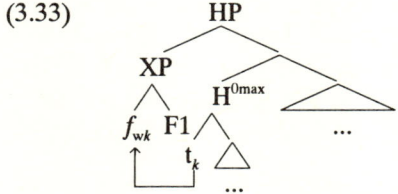

This Checking at LF causes the redefinition of the terms {XP, HP} in (3.33).

With this in mind, let us return to (3.30), which represents the pre-Spell-out stage in the derivation of the Imbabura Quechua anti-impersonal passive. It can be delineated as follows:

(3.34)   IP   (= (3.30))
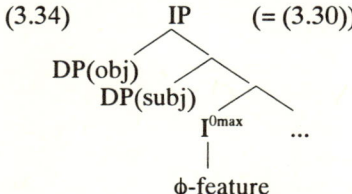

Let us assume, for the sake of brevity of discussion, that the nominative Case-feature of OBJ and that of SUBJ enter into a checking relation with Infl before Spell-out. Then, the only [−interpretable] formal feature that remains unchecked in (3.34) is the (weak) φ-feature of Infl (if we ignore the (weak) EPP-feature of T). How is this feature checked off? Under the mechanism of LF Checking sketched above, there are two possibilities: The φ-feature of Infl in (3.34) enters into a checking relation with the DP (i.e., SUBJ) at the innermost Spec of Infl by moving to a position adjoined to it, or it enters into a checking relation with the DP (i.e., OBJ) at an outer Spec of Infl by moving to a position adjoined to it. Both Checkings are illustrated in (3.35):

(3.35)   a.
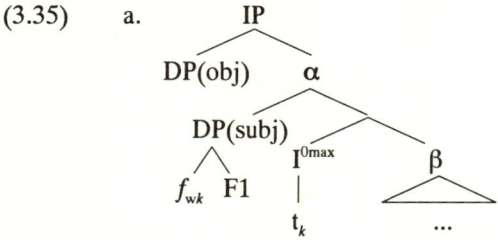

---

[20] In fact, Chomsky suggested an even stronger assumption in his 1995 fall class lectures, proposing that a checking relation should hold within X^{0max} even before LF as well as at LF. The reader is referred to his ongoing work, according to which the fundamentals of XP-movement in overt syntax can be maintained. See, also, Ura (1997a).

b.
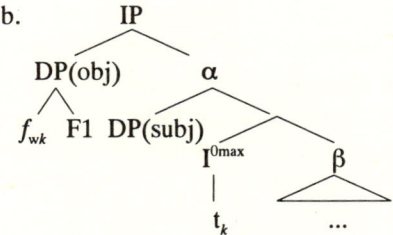

In (3.35) f_w stands for the (weak) φ-feature of Infl and F1 stands for the φ-feature of DP. It is important to notice that the movement of f_w in (3.35a) is as long as that of f_w in (3.35b) because SUBJ and OBJ are equidistant from I^{0max}; hence, both movements are equally economical in terms of the length of movement.

In (3.35a), which represents the checking of Infl's φ-feature by SUBJ at LF, the term α, in addition to the terms DP(subj) and IP are redefined by this operation.[21] However, only the terms DP(subj) and IP are redefined in (3.35b), which represents the checking of Infl's φ-feature by OBJ at LF. Hence, (3.35a) involves more redefinition of terms than (3.35b). Consequently, the former is blocked by the latter, given the condition in (3.31).

As shown in (3.30), we therefore have a good reason to conclude that OBJ, but not SUBJ, checks off Infl's weak φ-feature (and its (weak) EPP-feature, too) at LF in an Imbabura Quechua anti-impersonal passive clause. This, in turn, explains the fact that OBJ always induces subject-agreement in the Imbabura Quechua anti-impersonal passive.

3.2.4. Parametric Variations

Thus far, I have argued that the strong nominative Case-feature of the Infl in an anti-impersonal passive clause that needs to be checked twice for its deletion is the cause of the anti-impersonal passive in Imbabura Quechua. As observed, this derives the following situation:

(3.36) *Imbabura Quechua Anti-Impersonal Passive*

[$_{IP}$ OBJ$_l$ [$_{IP}$ SUBJ$_k$ Infl(*PASS*) [$_{vP}$ t$_k$ *v*-pass [$_{VP}$ V t$_l$]]]]

Furthermore, I demonstrated that the weak φ-feature and EPP-feature of the anti-impersonal passive Infl in Imbabura Quechua are always checked off by OBJ at an outer Spec of Infl at LF; as a result, OBJ always induces subject-agreement in the Imbabura Quechua anti-impersonal passive.

It is noteworthy that the nondemoted SUBJ as well as the promoted OBJ in the Lango anti-impersonal passive can control, as observed in the previous section. Here, on the other hand, it was observed that only the promoted OBJ, but

---

[21] The term α at the stage in the derivation before the redefinition should be {I, {DP(subj), {I, {I, β}}}}.

not the nondemoted SUBJ, can control in the Imbabura Quechua anti-impersonal passive. How can this parametric variation be accounted for?

Elsewhere in this book, I have exploited the hypothesis that the ability to control results from a ϕ-feature checking relation with Infl. With this hypothesis in mind, let us recall that the nondemoted SUBJ at the canonical Spec of Infl in the Imbabura Quechua anti-impersonal passive has no ϕ-feature checking relation with Infl, though it has a nominative Case-feature checking relation with Infl. Instead, the promoted OBJ in the Imbabura Quechua anti-impersonal passive has a ϕ-feature checking relation and an EPP-feature checking relation with Infl. It follows from the above hypothesis that the promoted OBJ, but not the nondemoted SUBJ, can control in the Imbabura Quechua anti-impersonal passive. On the other hand, I concluded that the permuted OBJ as well as the nondemoted SUBJ in the Lango anti-impersonal passive has a ϕ-feature checking relation with Infl; whereby, both can control in a Lango anti-impersonal passive clause.

In chapter 2, I illustrated that the strong EPP-feature of the inverse Infl that need to be checked twice for its deletion is the cause of inverse in Apachean, and showed that this derives the following situation:

(3.37) *Apachean Inverse*

$[_{IP} \ OBJ_l \ [_{IP} \ SUBJ_k \ Infl(INV) \ [_{vP} \ t_k \ v \ [_{VP} \ V \ t_l \ ]]]]$

Recall that it was observed that SUBJ in the innermost Spec of Infl always induces subject-agreement in the Apachean inverse. This sharply contrasts with the Imbabura Quechua anti-impersonal passive. As I argued in the previous section, the reason that OBJ always induces subject-agreement in Imbabura Quechua comes from the fact that the ϕ-feature of Infl in Imbabura Quechua is weak. Now suppose that the ϕ-feature of Infl in Apachean is strong. Then, the theory requires that SUBJ at the innermost Spec of Infl should always check it off in overt syntax before OBJ moves to an outer Spec of Infl. This is because a strong feature must be checked off immediately after its introduction in the derivation under our hypothesis of strong features (see §1.4.1). To conclude, the parametric variation concerning the strength of the ϕ-feature of Infl differentiates the Imbabura Quechua anti-impersonal passive and the Apachean inverse in terms of subject-agreement.

3.2.5. Summary for Imbabura Quechua Anti-Impersonal Passive

In this section, I illustrated how the anti-impersonal passive in Imbabura Quechua is derived. I argued that there are four parameters crucially responsible for its derivation: (1) The nominative Case-feature of Infl in Imbabura Quechua can enter into multiple checking relations,[22] (2) the nominative Case-feature of Infl in

---

[22] See Ura (1994e) for independent evidence in favor of the claim that Infl in Imbabura

Imbabura Quechua is strong, (3) the EPP-feature and φ-feature of Infl in Imbabura Quechua are both weak, and (4) the nominative Case-feature of Infl in an Imbabura Quechua anti-impersonal passive clause needs double checking.

3.3. Summary

In this chapter I demonstrated how the theory of multiple feature checking can account for the derivation of the anti-impersonal passive constructions in Lango and Imbabura Quechua. It was also demonstrated that, with the aid of the hypothesis concerning GFs, the GF-splitting phenomena involved in those constructions can be fully accounted for. Furthermore, I made the following proposal regarding the ability to bind a (purely) subject-oriented reflexive: An element has the ability to bind a (purely) subject-oriented reflexive if the element has an EPP-feature checking relation with Infl. In addition, I claimed, extending Watanabe's (1995a) idea of redefinition of terms, that the general economy condition requires that, in a situation where two elements, both of which have a feature f, occur at Specs of a head H, a weak feature of a head H should be checked off by the corresponding feature of the element that occupies the outer Spec of H.

As I reported in Ura (1995b), anti-impersonal passive constructions can be found in Malay (Indonesia) (Chung 1976, 1983), Javanese (Davies 1993, 1995), Chamorro (Cooreman 1984), Western Muskogean languages such as Chickasaw and Choctaw (Munro and Gordon 1982), and so forth, and Ura (1995b) argued that these anti- impersonal passive constructions, despite their differences, can be consistently accounted for with the theory of multiple feature checking with a small set of parameter-settings.

Appendix:
A Very Short Note on Impersonal Passives

This chapter studied a passive(-like) construction, which I call anti-impersonal passive, in which only OBJ promotion, but not SUBJ demotion, is involved. As Comrie (1977) points out, it is easy to find, in many languages, a passive(-like) construction in which only SUBJ demotion, but not OBJ promotion, is involved. Traditionally, this passive construction is called IMPERSONAL PASSIVE (Perlmutter 1983, Perlmutter and Postal 1984, and Postal 1986). This appendix is devoted to make a brief mention on this construction under the theory of multiple feature-checking advocated in this book.

Roughly speaking, there are two types of impersonal passives in the world's languages. As for one type, overt movement of OBJ to the surface subject position is not involved, but the nonpromoted OBJ shows some subject properties. In

---

Quechua can check multiple nominative features.

contrast, OBJ gains no properties of subject in the other type of impersonal passive. There have been many studies on the former type (Perlmutter 1978, Perlmutter and Postal 1984, Levin 1985a, Burzio 1986, Hestvik 1986, Postal 1986, Åfarli 1992, and Watanabe 1996, to list a few). On the other hand, only a few theoretical investigations have been done on the latter type (Sobin 1985, Postal 1986, Baker, Johnson, and Roberts 1989, and Goodall 1993, among others), though the existence of such an impersonal passive construction has long been documented in the literature (e.g., Langacker 1976 for Uto-Aztecan, Awbery 1976 for Welsh, Ostler 1979 for Sanskrit, Klaiman 1981 for Bengali, Knecht 1986 for Turkish, Marantz 1988 for Nepali, O'Connor 1992 for Nothern Pomo, inter alia; cf. Keenan 1976b, 1985; Comrie 1977; Nerbonne 1982; Siewierska 1984; and Postal 1986 for lists of languages with this type of impersonal passive).

Although I will not go into any detail of these constructions in this book, it is expected that the theory of multiple feature checking advocated here offers a natural account of the impersonal passive construction in which OBJ gains no subject properties with SUBJ syntactically demoted, as well as a consistent account of the impersonal passive construction in which OBJ gains some of the subject properties.[23]

---

[23] See Ura (1995b) for a treatment of varieties of impersonal passive under the theory of multiple feature checking.

4

Dative Subject Constructions

In this chapter I will investigate the syntactic properties of the so-called "Dative/Quirky Subject Construction," which has recently been attracting much attention in the literature, because it poses some very interesting problems to the theory of Case and agreement. In addition, still more interesting to our concern is the fact that some GF-splitting phenomena are involved in this construction.

It has been often claimed in the literature that the Dative Subject Construction (DSC) typically occurs in a clause whose predicate expresses an emotion, attitude, or situation of one's mind. Predicates that occur in this construction, thus, almost correspond to what are called "Experiencer (Psych) Verbs." Following most of the analyses for this construction proposed in the PP-approach (Belletti and Rizzi 1988, among others), I will demonstrate that the peculiarity of the "experiencer" predicates in terms of argument structure is responsible for the promotion of the Experiencer argument to the Spec of T in overt syntax, but the analysis to be presented in this chapter differs from those analyses in that it provides a uniform account of the cross-linguistic variation of this construction with small sets of parametric differences. Furthermore, it also naturally accounts for the GF-splitting involved in the DSC under the theory of multiple feature checking.

In section 1, I will take a closer look at the DSC in Japanese and Korean and give an explanation of it under the theory of multiple feature checking. It will be observed that the analysis of the DSC provided for Japanese and Korean encounters some problems if DSCs in other languages are examined. In section 2 and the subsequent sections, through studying varieties of DSCs, I will show how the crosslinguistic variety of DSC is accounted for under the theory of multiple feature checking.

4.1. Japanese (and Korean)

4.1.1. Basic Properties

4.1.1.1. Case Arrays

It has been established in the literature on Japanese that the DSC in Japanese may occur when the predicate in the clause is a kind of so-called psych-predicate, or when some kind of stative suffix such as the potential suffix *-(rar)e* is attached to it (cf. Kuroda 1965, Inoue 1976, Tonoike 1979, and Sugioka 1985, among many others):

(4.1)   *Japanese* (Sugioka 1985: 156)

      a. Taroo-ni   hebi-ga   kowa-i. (adjective)
          Taroo-DAT snake-NOM fearful-PRES
          'Taroo is fearful of snakes.'

      b. Taroo-ni   eigo-ga   dekir-u. (verb)
          Taroo-DAT English-NOM understand-PRES
          'Taroo understands English.'

(4.2)   *Japanese* (Sugioka 1985: 156)

      Taroo-ni   eigo-ga   hanas-e-ru. (potential)
      Taroo-DAT English-NOM speak-POT-PRES
      'Taroo can speak English.'

It is interesting to note that the Theme argument in the DSC in Japanese (and Korean) is always marked as nominative; thus, the following examples in which the Theme object is marked as accusative with the dative subject are ungrammatical:

(4.3)   *Japanese*

      a. *Taroo-ni   hebi-o   kowa-i. (cf. (4.1a))
          Taroo-DAT snake-ACC fearful-PRES
          'Taroo is fearful of snakes.'

      b. *Taroo-ni   eigo-o   dekir-u. (cf. (4.1b))
          Taroo-DAT English-ACC understand-PRES
          'Taroo understands English.'

(4.4)   *Korean* (E.-J. Lee 1992: 240)

      a. Chelswu-eykey   ton-i/*-ul   philyoha-ta.
          Chelswu-DAT   money-NOM/-ACC need-DEC
          'Chelswu needs money.'

      b. Chelswu-eykey   umak-i/*-ul   coh-ta.
          Chelswu-DAT   music-NOM/-ACC fond-DEC
          'Chelswu is fond of music.'

Recently, the syntactic behavior of "nominative object" in Japanese has attracted much attention in the literature under the PP-approach because it raises very interesting problems in terms of Case theory (e.g., Saito 1982; Takezawa 1987; Kubo 1992; Tada 1992, 1993; Morikawa 1993; Koizumi 1994b; Harley 1995b; and Zushi 1995, among many others). Under the Agr-based Case theory, Tada (1992, 1993) claims that the nominative object has its nominative Case-feature checked off at the Spec of AgrO in the clause, and Koizumi (1994b) and Zushi (1995) independently provide several pieces of supporting evidence in favor of Tada's claim. Later in this section I will argue that this analysis of the DSC in Japanese (and Korean) by means of AgrO can be reanalyzed under the Agr-less Case theory without any loss if the theory of multiple feature checking is provided.

It is interesting, in passing, to note that it is not the case that all of the predicates that allow the nominative object allow the dative subject, as Kuno (1973), Shibatani and Cotton (1976), Sugioka (1985), and Morikawa (1993) point out:

(4.5)   *Japanese* (Morikawa 1993: 133)

    a. Joe-ga/*-ni   unagi-ga   suki-da.
        -NOM/-DAT   eels-NOM   fond-COP
        'Joe is fond of eels.'

    b. Watashi-ga/*-ni susi-ga   tabe-ta-i.
        I-NOM/-DAT   sushi-NOM eat-DES-PRES
        'I want to eat sushi.'

This means that the DSC is lexically idiosyncratic in nature.

As noted before, the potential suffix *-(rar)e* in Japanese makes it possible for a predicate to allow its SUBJ and OBJ to be marked as dative and as nominative, respectively:

(4.6)   *Japanese*

    a. Taroo-ni   eigo-ga   hanas-e-ru.
        Taroo-DAT English-NOM speak-POT-PRES
        'Taroo can speak English.'

    b. *Taroo-ni eigo-ga   hanas-u.
        Taroo-DAT English-NOM speak-PRES

Even when the potential suffix is attached to the predicate of the clause with a dative subject, there must be a nominative object in the clause in Japanese (Kuroda 1965, Kuno 1973). Owing to this requirement, the following examples are excluded:

(4.7)   *Japanese*

    a. *Taroo-ni eigo-o   hanas-e-ru. (cf. (4.6a))
        Taroo-DAT English-ACC speak-POT-PRES
        'Taroo can speak English.'

b. *Taroo-ni hasir-e-ru.
   Taroo-DAT run-POT-PRES
   'Taroo can run.'

   (cf. Taroo-ga hasir-e-ru.
         Taroo-NOM run-POT-PRES
         'Taroo can run.'   )

This leads Shibatani (1978) to stipulate that there must be a nominative element in a tensed clause in Japanese. This stipulation can be easily recast under the feature-checking theory by saying that the nominative feature of T must be checked in Japanese (and Korean). If this is correct, then it further leads us to the conclusion that the nominative object in the DSC checks its nominative Case-feature against T. In §4.1.2, I will indeed pursue this line of analysis.

4.1.1.2. Subjecthood of Dative Subject

In this section I will examine how much the "dative subject" in a DSC in Japanese and Korean is really subject-like. It has been established that it must count as a SUBJECT in syntactic respects (Shibatani 1977, 1978; Kageyama 1978; Perlmutter 1984; among many others, for Japanese, and Gerdts and Youn 1988, Kim 1990, and O'Grady 1991 for Korean). First, it can bind a subject-oriented anaphor:

(4.8)   *Japanese*

   a. John-ni$_k$ zibun-ga$_k$/zibun-zishin-ga$_k$ simpai-da.
         -DAT   self-NOM/self-self-NOM   worry-COP
      'John$_k$ worries about himself$_k$.'

   b. John-ni$_k$ Mary-ga$_i$ [zibun$_{k/*i}$/zibun-zishin-no$_{k/*i}$ sensei]-ni
         -DAT   -NOM   self/self-self-GEN   teacher -to
      hikiawase-(ra)re-ru.
      introduce-POT-PRES
      Lit. 'John$_k$ can introduce Mary$_i$ to self's$_{k/*i}$ teacher.'

The subject-oriented anaphora *zibun* and *zibun-zishin* cannot be coreferential with any nonsubject even if it is c-commanded, as the ill-formedness of (4.9) shows:

(4.9)   *Japanese*

   John-ga$_k$ Mary-o$_i$ [zibun$_{k/*i}$/zibun-zishin-no$_{k/*i}$ sensei]-ni
      -NOM   -ACC   self/self-self-GEN   teacher -to
   hikiawase-(ra)re-ru.
   introduce-POT-PRES
   Lit. 'John$_k$ can introduce Mary$_i$ to self's$_{k/*i}$ teacher.'

As the well-formedness of (4.10), where the nonsubject oriented reflexive *kanojo-zishin* is properly bound by *Mary*, shows, *Mary* in (4.9) indeed c-commands, but does not bind, *zibun/zibun-zishin*:

(4.10) *Japanese*

John-ga Mary-o$_i$ [kanojo-zishin-no$_i$ sensei]-ni hikiawase-(ra)re-ru.
-NOM -ACC herself-GEN teacher -to introduce-POT-PRES
Lit. 'John can introduce Mary$_i$ to herself's$_i$ teacher.'

The conclusion is that the dative subject can bind a subject-oriented anaphor in Japanese. This also holds true in Korean, as shown in (4.11):

(4.11) *Korean* (O'Grady 1991: 102)

John-eykey$_i$ Harry-ka$_k$ [[casin-uy$_{i/*k}$ sengkong]-ul]-wihayse
-DAT -NOM self-GEN success -ACC -for
philyoha-ta.
need-DEC
Lit. 'John$_i$ needs Harry$_k$ for self's$_{i/*k}$ success.'

Second, the dative subject in DSC can control.

(4.12) *Japanese* (Perlmutter 1984: 321)

a. [PRO$_k$ sutoraiki-o yat-tei-nagara], roodoosya-ni(-wa)$_k$ sono
strike-ACC do-PROG-while workers-DAT(-TOP) its
mokuteki-ga wakara-nakat-ta.
purpose-NOM understand-NEG-PAST
Lit. 'Although PRO$_k$ being on strike, the workers$_k$ did not understand its purpose.'

b. [PRO$_k$ ongaku-o kiki-nagara], John-ni$_k$ hon-ga yom-e-ru.
music-ACC listen to-while -DAT book-NOM read-POT-PRES
'While PRO$_k$ listening to music, John$_k$ can read books.'

(4.13) *Korean* (O'Grady 1991: 103)

[PRO$_k$ haksayng-i-myense], John-eykey$_k$ [manhun ton]-i
student-be-though -DAT much money -NOM
philyoha-ta.
need-DEC
'Although PRO$_k$ being a student, John$_k$ needs much money.'

As the ill-formedness of (4.14) shows, PRO in the Japanese *-nagara* construction and in the Korean *-myense* construction cannot be controlled by any nonsubject (see Perlmutter 1984 for Japanese and O'Grady 1991 for Korean):

(4.14) *Japanese*

[PRO$_{k/*i}$ ongaku-o kiki-nagara], John-ga$_k$ Mary-o$_i$ damasi-ta.
music-ACC listen to-while -NOM -ACC cheat-PAST
'While PRO$_{k/*i}$ listening to music, John$_k$ cheated Mary$_i$.'

(4.15) *Korean* (O'Grady 1991: 103)

[PRO$_{k/*i}$ haksayng-i-myense], John-i$_k$ Harry-lul$_i$ salhayhay-ss-ta.
student-be-though   -NOM   -ACC   kill-PAST-DEC
'Although PRO$_{k/*i}$ being a student, John$_k$ killed Harry$_i$.'

As has been claimed elsewhere in this book, an element's ability to control indicates that the element has a φ-feature checking relation with T; accordingly, the fact shown by (4.12) and (4.13) leads to the conclusion that the dative subject in the Japanese and Korean DSC enters into a φ-feature checking relation with T.

Indeed, there is strong evidence which shows that it enters into a φ-feature checking relation with T. Consider (4.16), in which subject-honorification is involved:

(4.16) *Japanese*

a. Yamada-sensei-ga   seito-o   o-tasuke-ni   nar-ta.
   Prof. Yamada-NOM   student-ACC   HON-help-to   become-PAST
   'Prof. Yamada helped a student.'

b. *Seito-ga   Yamada-sensei-o   o-tasuke-ni   nar-ta.
   student-NOM   Prof. Yamada-ACC   HON-help-to   become-PAST
   'A student helped Prof. Yamada.'

(4.17) *Korean* (O'Grady 1991: 156–157)

a. Kyoswu-nim-i   haksayng-tul-ul   ttayli-si-ess-ta.
   professor-HT-NOM   student-PL-ACC   beat up-HON-PAST-DEC
   'The professor beat up the students.'

b. *Haksayng-tul-i   kyoswu-nim-ul   ttayli-si-ess-ta.
   student-PL-NOM   professor-HT-ACC beat up-HON-PAST-DEC
   'The students beat up the professor.'

Harada (1976) and Shibatani (1977) claim that the so-called subject-honorification in Japanese (and Korean)[1] is induced solely by the element with the SUBJECT function.[2] Toribio (1990), recasting their claim under the PP-approach, argues that subject-honorification is induced by Spec-head agreement mediated by φ-feature. If this is correct (and I assume so), then the well-formedness of the following examples shows that the dative subject in the Japanese and Korean DSC enters into a φ-feature checking relation with T, as expected:

---

[1] For detailed discussion on subject-honorification in Korean, see Sohn (1994: §2.1.3.6.4) and references cited therein.

[2] For an approach to the technical implementation of the syntactic property of subject-honorification, see Toribio (1990).

(4.18) a. *Japanese* (Perlmutter 1984: 323)

Yamada-sensei-ni [sono mondai]-ga o-wakari-ni
Prof. Yamada-DAT that problem -NOM HON-understand-to
nar-u.
become-PRES
'Prof. Yamada understands that problem.'

b. *Korean* (O'Grady 1991: 102)

Sensayng-nim-ekey ton-i philyoha-si-ta.
professor-HT-DAT money-NOM need-HON-DEC
'The professor needs money.'

To sum up, it was observed that the dative subject in the Japanese and Korean DSC shows some properties of SUBJECT; that is, it has the ability to bind a subject-oriented reflexive, the ability to control, and the ability to induce subject-honorification. Under the theory of GFs advocated in this book, these facts strongly suggest that the dative subject in Japanese and Korean enters into a [+construable]-feature checking relation with T.

4.1.1.3. Nonsubject Properties of Nominative Object

Now let us see how much the nominative object in the Japanese and Korean DSC is object-like. First, it cannot bind a subject-oriented anaphor:

(4.19) *Japanese*

*Zinzibu-ni Mary-ga$_i$ [zibun$_*/$zibun-zishin-no$_i$ jooshi]-ni
 personnel section-DAT -NOM self/self-self-GEN boss -to
ima-sugu hikiawase-(ra)re-ru.
right now introduce-POT-PRES
Lit. 'The personnel section can introduce Mary$_i$ to self's$_{*i}$ boss right now.'

(4.20) *Korean* (O'Grady 1991: 102)

John-eykey$_i$ Harry-ka$_k$ [[casin-uy$_{i/*k}$ sengkong]-ul]-wihayse
 -DAT -NOM self-GEN success -ACC -for
philyoha-ta.
need-DEC
Lit. 'John$_i$ needs Harry$_k$ for self's$_{i/*k}$ success.'

The following fact shows that the nominative object can bind a non-subject-oriented reflexive. Compare (4.19) with (4.21) :

(4.21) *Japanese*

Zinzibu-ni Mary-ga$_i$ [kanojo-zishin-no$_i$ jooshi]-ni
personnel section-DAT -NOM her-self-GEN boss -to
ima-sugu hikiawase-(ra)re-ru.
right now introduce-POT-PRES
Lit. 'The personnel section can introduce Mary$_i$ to herself's*$_i$ boss right now.'

Second, the nominative object cannot control PRO in the Japanese *-nagara* construction or the Korean *-myense* construction:

(4.22) a. *Japanese*

[PRO$_{k/*i}$ sake-o nomi-nagara], John-ni$_k$ Mary-ga$_i$ damas-e-ru.
 sake-ACC drink-while -DAT -NOM cheat-POT-PRES
'While PRO$_{k/*i}$ drinking sake, John$_k$ can cheat Mary$_i$.'

b. *Korean* (Gerdts and Youn 1988: 157)

[PRO$_{k/*i}$ Mikuksimin-i-myense], apeci-eykey$_k$ thongyekkwan-i$_i$
 US citizen-be-though father-DAT interpreter-NOM
philyoha-si-ta.
need-HON-DEC
'Although PRO$_{k/*i}$ being a US citizen, father$_k$ needs an interpreter$_i$.'

Third, the nominative object cannot induce subject-honorification, which is an overt manifestation of subject-agreement in Japanese and Korean under our assumption. This fact is shown by (4.23) below. Compare (4.23) with (4.16a) and (4.17a), in which the nominative subject properly induces subject-honorification:

(4.23) a. *Japanese*

*Gakusei-ni Yamada-sensei-ga o-kiniiri-da.
students-DAT Prof. Yamada-NOM HON-fond-COP
'Students are fond of Prof. Yamada.'

b. *Korean* (O'Grady 1991: 102)

*Ku haksayng-eykey kyoswunim-i philyoha-si-ta.
the student-DAT professor-NOM need-HON-DEC
'The student needs the teacher.'

It is noteworthy that this fact indicates that T's nominative Case-feature and its φ-feature can be checked independently in Japanese and Korean; for, it is natural to assume that T's nominative Case-feature is checked off by the nominative object and T's φ-feature is checked off by the dative subject, as observed in the previous subsection.

To conclude, it follows from the hypothesis of GFs elaborated in this book that all those facts indicate that the nominative object in the Japanese and Korean DSC has no [+construable]-feature checking relation with T.

Nevertheless, there is a fact which suggests that the nominative object in the Japanese DSC behaves like an ordinary subject: Tada (1993) and Uchibori (1994) report that possessor-raising from the nominative object (in a DSC) is possible in Japanese, despite the fact that possessor-raising from OBJ is precluded in Japanese in general (see Ura 1996b: chapter 4):

(4.24) *Japanese* <Subj(NOM)-Obj(NOM) pattern> (Tada 1993: 132)

    a. Boku-ga [John-no atama]-ga tatak-e-na-i.
        I-NOM   -GEN head -NOM hit-POT-NEG-PRES
        'I cannot hit John's head.'

    b. Boku-ga John-ga$_k$ [t_k atama]-ga tatak-e-na-i.
        I-NOM   -NOM   head -NOM hit-POT-NEG-PRES

(4.25) *Japanese* <Subj(DAT)-Obj(NOM) pattern> (Uchibori 1994)

    a. Boku-ni [John-no atama]-ga tatak-e-na-i.
        I-DAT   -GEN head -NOM hit-POT-NEG-PRES
        'I cannot hit John's head.'

    b. Boku-ni John-ga$_k$ [t_k atama]-ga tatak-e-na-i.
        I-DAT   -NOM   head -NOM hit-POT-NEG-PRES

This fact seems prima facie to be inconsistent with the above conclusion that the nominative object (in a DSC) has no [+construable]-feature checking relation with T; on the contrary, I will show that this fact is, indeed, predicted by the analysis of DSC in Japanese that will be presented in the next section.

4.1.2. Proposals

Now I propose the following: (1) the EPP-feature of T in Japanese and Korean is strong;[3] (2) the Experiencer argument (hereafter, EXP) of a psych-verb that can occur in a DSC is generated at the Spec of a kind of light verb, which takes a VP with Theme in its complement position (see (4.26));

(4.26)   The light verb in this structure has a stative meaning.

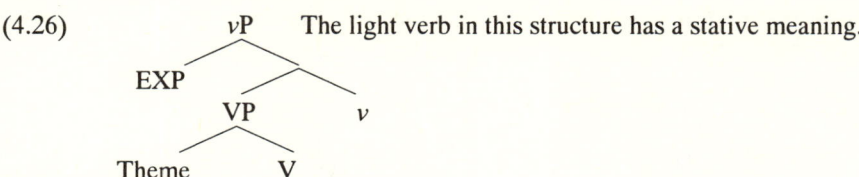

(3) the light verb in the two-layered VP-shell of the psych-verb that can occur in the Japanese and Korean DSC may assign a dative Case to EXP as an inherent Case, and it is allowed not to have accusative Case-feature as a lexical idiosyncrasy; (4) in Japanese and Korean, T's φ-feature checking may be executed independently of T's nominative Case checking, as in Bantu (see chapter 2); (5) T's

---

[3] This is independently proposed or assumed by Ueda (1990), Nemoto (1993), Watanabe (1993), and Koizumi (1995).

φ-feature is strong, but its nominative-feature is weak in Japanese and Korean; and (6) T's nominative feature may enter into multiple feature-checking relations (see Ura 1994e).

Assumption (2) is essentially an extension of Belletti and Rizzi's (1988) idea about the argument structure of psych-verbs. Assuming that it is well-established that EXP is higher than Theme in the Thematic Hierarchy (cf. Carrier-Duncan 1985, Grimshaw 1990, and Speas 1990), I assume, according to the mapping theory proposed in §1.4.2, that EXP is generated at a position higher than the Theme argument. As for (3), it was intuitively noted by Shibatani and Cotton (1976); they held that the dative subject in a DSC is subcategorized by the predicate in the DSC clause. Following their intuition, Saito (1982), Takezawa (1987), and Morikawa (1993) maintain that the subcategorized dative subject is generated not as an NP (or DP), but as a PP. This is almost equivalent to the claim that the dative subject is assigned an inherent Case, because they treat the dative subject as the element that needs no structural Case assignment/checking. Nonetheless, I will insist that the dative subject should be a DP (or, more precisely, that it has a D-feature). As we will see later, this assumption plays a crucial role in our explanation of the DSC in Japanese and Korean. It has already been observed that (4) is evident from the fact that the dative subject, but not the nominative object, induces subject-honorification, a kind of subject-agreement in Japanese and Korean. Assumption (6) is motivated independently by the fact that Japanese and Korean allow multiple subjects in a single clause (cf. Ura 1994e, 1996b, and references cited therein).

4.1.3. Analysis

Now let us take a look at the derivation of the DSC in Japanese and Korean, keeping the above assumptions in mind. First, consider the derivation of a DSC with a psych-verb as its predicate. The initial structure looks like this:

(4.27) $[_{vP}$ EXP(DAT) $[_{VP}$ Theme V $]$ v $]$

Note that EXP is assigned dative as its inherent Case (according to assumption (3)). Then, T is introduced by Merge, deriving (4.28) from (4.27):

(4.28) $[_{TP}$ $[_{vP}$ EXP(DAT) $[_{VP}$ Theme V $]$ v $]$ T $]$

According to assumption (1), something with D-feature is attracted to the (innermost) Spec of T to check T's strong EPP-feature (i.e., D-feature). EXP (i.e., the dative subject) is the closest to T; consequently, it is attracted to the Spec of T before Spell-out, deriving (4.29) from (4.28):

(4.29) $[_{TP}$ EXP(DAT)$_k$ $[_{vP}$ t_k $[_{VP}$ Theme V $]$ v $]$ T $]$

Note that EXP has a D-feature and, hence, can be attracted by the EPP-feature of T, though its Case-feature can never be available for Case-checking because of its inherent nature. At the stage in the derivation illustrated in (4.29), EXP checks off T's strong EPP-feature and strong φ-feature.

If Theme has a nominative Case, as illustrated in (4.30), it corresponds to the surface structure of the DSC in Japanese and Korean.

(4.30) $[_{TP}$ EXP(DAT)$_k$ $[_{vP}$ t$_k$ $[_{VP}$ Theme(NOM) V] v] T]
(DSC before Spell-out)

The step shown in (4.30) results in a convergent derivation if Theme, which has a nominative Case-feature, properly checks off T's weak nominative Case-feature at LF.[4] This can be achieved if the nominative Case-feature of Theme (i.e., the nominative object) moves onto T at LF to enter into a checking relation with T. Note that there is no need to worry about the accusative Case-feature of the psych-verb, because it is allowed not to have accusative Case-feature (due to assumption (3)).

This is our analysis of the derivation of the Japanese and Korean DSC whose predicate is a psych-verb.[5] In the next section it will be demonstrated how this analysis enables us to account for the facts concerning the DSC in Japanese and Korean observed in §4.1.1.

4.1.4. Explanation

4.1.4.1. Grammatical Functions

In §4.1.1 it was observed that the dative subject (i.e., EXP) can control, can bind a subject-oriented anaphor, and can induce subject-honorification, while the nominative object (i.e., Theme) can do none of these things. I have argued for the hypothesis that these abilities are yielded by a [+construable]-feature checking relation with T (= Infl).[6] If this hypothesis is correct, the above properties of the dative subject and the nominative object in the Japanese and Korean DSC are straightforwardly accounted for; as I argued in §4.1.3, it is EXP (i.e., the dative subject) that checks off T's EPP-feature and φ-feature (before Spell-out), and Theme (i.e., the nominative object) has no [+construable]-feature checking relation with T, though it enters into a nominative Case-feature checking relation with T at LF. This therefore leads to the conclusion that the dative subject, but not the nominative object, can have the aforementioned GFs in Japanese and Korean.

---

[4] I ignore V-movement in overt syntax. See Koizumi (1995) for V-movement in Japanese and Park (1991) for Korean.

[5] See §4.1.4.4 for the Japanese DSC whose predicate has had the potential suffix *-(rar)e* attached.

[6] The conclusion we reached so far was (1) that the ability to control the missing subject in a subordinate-adjunct clause results from a φ-feature checking relation with T (cf. chapters 2 and 3), and (2) that the ability to bind a (purely) subject-oriented reflexive results from an EPP-feature checking relation with T (chapter 3).

Moreover, it was noted in §4.1.1 that Theme must be marked as nominative when EXP is marked as dative. Reconsider (4.29), which is the pre-Spell-out stage in the derivation for DSC:

(4.29) $[_{TP}$ EXP(DAT)$_k$ $[_{vP}$ t_k $[_{VP}$ Theme V] v] T] (before Spell-out)

Now suppose that Theme is marked as accusative. Then, the structure looks like (4.31):

(4.31) $[_{TP}$ EXP(DAT)$_k$ $[_{vP}$ t_k $[_{VP}$ Theme(ACC) V] v] T] (cf. (4.30))

The structure in (4.31), unlike (4.30), can never result in a convergent derivation anyway. The fact that Japanese and Korean have no construction corresponding to the impersonal construction suggests that the IMPERSONAL PARAMETER (see §1.4.7.1) is negative in those languages; if the impersonal parameter is set as negative in a language L, then the finite T in L always has a nominative Case-feature to be checked off. Now that the parameter is negative in Japanese and Korean, T's nominative Case-feature, though weak, must be checked off in those languages. In (4.31), however, there is no element with nominative Case-feature; consequently, T's (weak) nominative Case remains unchecked at LF, resulting in crash at LF. This is the reason that Theme must be marked as nominative when EXP is marked as dative. In this fashion Shibatani's (1978) observation that there must be, at least, one nominative element in a finite clause in Japanese can be accommodated.

4.1.4.2. Case Arrays

It is parenthetically interesting to note that there is a group of psych-predicates that allow the following Case arrays:[7]

(4.32)   *Japanese*

    a. Subj(NOM)-Obj(NOM) pattern

        John-ga Mary-ga shimpai-da.
          -NOM   -NOM anxious-COP
        'John is anxious about Mary.'

    b. Subj(NOM)-Obj(ACC) pattern

        John-ga Mary-o shimpai-da.
          -NOM   -ACC anxious-COP

    c. Subj(DAT)-Obj(NOM) pattern

        John-ni Mary-ga shimpai-da.
          -DAT   -NOM anxious-COP

---

[7] Some speakers, especially the elder generation, do not allow the Nom-Acc pattern for *shimpai* 'anxious', though. To my ear (4.32b) sounds perfectly acceptable.

d. *Subj(DAT)-Obj(ACC) pattern
      *John-ni   Mary-o   shimpai-da.
       -DAT   -ACC   anxious-COP

Thus far the patterns illustrated in (4.32c) and (4.32d) were examined. How about the derivations for (4.32a) and (4.32b)?

Let us look back on assumption (3) in §4.1.3: The light verb in the two-layered VP-shell of some of the psych-verbs that can occur in the Japanese and Korean DSC may assign a dative Case to EXP as an inherent Case, and they are allowed not to have accusative Case-feature as a lexical idiosyncrasy. Given this assumption, (4.32a) can be derived when the psych-predicate fails to assign an inherent dative Case to EXP and fails to have accusative Case-feature. If this situation arises, then EXP is attracted to the Spec of T to check off T's strong EPP-feature and φ-feature. Now that EXP has a nominative Case-feature, it also checks off T's weak Case-feature (at LF). The nominative Case-feature of Theme can be checked against the nominative Case-feature of T at LF because the nominative Case-feature of T in Japanese and Korean may enter into multiple feature-checking relations (due to assumption (6)). In this situation, EXP can never be marked as accusative, though it can be marked as dative, as argued before; for, there is no accusative feature available for its checking in this situation.

If the psych-predicate fails to assign an inherent dative Case to EXP, but it has an accusative Case-feature, (4.32b) is derived. The convergent derivation for this construction is the same as the derivation for an ordinary simple active transitive clause. If EXP is marked as accusative and Theme is marked as nominative in this situation, the derivation crashes in just the same way as Agent is marked as accusative and Theme is marked as nominative in an ordinary simple active transitive clause.

Notice that assumption (3) states that it is lexically determined whether a given psych-predicate is allowed to assign an inherent dative Case to its EXP and whether it is allowed not to have an accusative Case-feature. Thus it is predicted that there are some lexical variations in terms of the Case arrays that are permitted by a particular psych-predicate. As noted in §4.1.1, some psych-predicates like *suki* 'like' or *kirai* 'dislike' allow the Nom-Nom and the Nom-Acc patterns, but disallow the Dat-Nom pattern:[8]

(4.33) *Japanese*

   a. Joe-ga/*-ni   unagi-ga   suki/kirai-da.
       -NOM/-DAT   eels-NOM   like/dislike-COP
      'Joe likes/dislikes eels.'

   b. Joe-ga   unagi-o   suki/kirai-da.
       -NOM   eels-ACC   like/dislike-COP

---

[8] As is frequently pointed out in the literature on Japanese traditional grammar, the elder generation tends to hate the Nom-Acc pattern, though the younger generation freely allows it.

Thus, this type of psych-predicate is allowed not to have an accusative Case-feature, but it is not allowed to assign an inherent dative Case to its EXP.[9] Another type of psych-predicate like *odoroki* 'surprise' allows the Nom-Nom pattern as well as the Dat-Nom, but disallows the Nom-Acc pattern:

(4.34) *Japanese*

    a. Joe-ga/-ni   [sono nyuusu]-ga   odoroki-da.
         -NOM/-DAT that news -NOM surprise-COP
        'Joe is surprised at that news.'

    b. *Joe-ga   [sono nyuusu]-o   odoroki-da.
         -NOM   that news -ACC surprise-COP

Thus, this type is allowed to assign an inherent dative Case to its EXP, but it is not allowed to have an accusative Case-feature. Yet another type of psych-predicate is expected, as a logical possibility, to allow only the Dat-Nom, disallowing the Nom-Nom and the Nom-Acc patterns. According to Shibatani and Cotton (1976) and Uchibori (1994), however, there is no such type of psych-predicate. But this is fully predictable; for, the parameter-setting assumed in (3) implies that, if a given psych-predicate is allowed to assign an inherent dative Case, it is also allowed not to assign an inherent dative Case. Therefore, it must be the case that the Nom-Nom pattern is allowed whenever the Dat-Nom pattern is allowed.

4.1.4.3. Possessor-Raising from Nominative Object

As was noted in §4.1.1, possessor-raising is possible from the nominative object in Japanese in spite of the fact that possessor-raising is impossible from any accusative-marked object in Japanese (see Ura 1996b: chapter 3). Relevant examples are:

(4.35) *Japanese* (Uchibori 1994)

    a. Boku-ni/-ga [John-no   imooto]-ga   shimpai-da.
        I-DAT/-NOM   -GEN sister   -NOM anxious-COP
        'I am anxious about John's sister.'

    b. Boku-ni/-ga John-ga$_k$ [t$_k$ imooto]-ga   shimpai-da.
        I-DAT/-NOM   -NOM   sister   -NOM anxious-COP

(4.36) *Japanese*

    a. Boku-ga [John-no   imooto]-o   shimpai-da.
        I-NOM   -GEN sister   -ACC anxious-COP
        'same meaning as (4.35a)'

---

[9] The lexical items *suki* and *kirai* in the grammar of the Japanese elder generation do not assign an inherent dative Case to their EXP, nor do they have an accusative Case-feature.

b. *Boku-ga John-o$_k$ [t$_k$ imooto]-o shimpai-da.
   I-NOM   -ACC   sister -ACC anxious-COP

These examples show that possessor-raising from OBJ is possible if OBJ is marked as nominative in Japanese.

This can easily be accounted for under the analysis of the Japanese DSC presented thus far. I claimed that the nominative feature of the nominative object in the Japanese DSC enters into a nominative Case-feature checking relation with T at LF by moving onto T at LF. Given assumption (6) in §4.1.3, which states that T's nominative feature may enter into multiple feature-checking relations in Japanese, the nominative Case-feature of the raised possessor as well as the nominative Case-feature of the possessed DP can properly enter into a Case-feature checking relation with T at LF, as required; whence, the well-formedness of (4.35b) follows. On the other hand, if the accusative feature in Japanese never enters into multiple checking relations, as I extensively argued in Ura (1996b: chapter 3), one of the accusative DPs in (4.36b) can never enter into a checking relation, resulting in an LF crash.

4.1.4.4. Potential Suffix in Japanese

As observed in §4.1.1, the potential suffix *-(rar)e* in Japanese makes it possible for a transitive or ditransitive verb to allow its SUBJ and OBJ to be marked as dative and as nominative, respectively:

(4.37) *Japanese*

a. Transitive

   i. Taroo-ni   eigo-ga   hanas-e-ru.
       Taroo-DAT English-NOM speak-POT-PRES
       'Taroo can speak English.'

   ii. *Taroo-ni   eigo-ga   hanas-u.
        Taroo-DAT English-NOM speak-PRES
        'Taroo speaks English.'

       (cf. Taroo-ga   eigo-o   hanas-u.
            Taroo-NOM English-ACC speak-PRES
            'Taroo speaks English.'   )

b. Ditransitive

   i. Taroo-ni   ningyoo-ga Hanako-ni ager-e-ru.
       Taroo-DAT doll-NOM   Hanako-DAT give-POT-PRES
       'Taroo can give Hanako a doll.'

   ii. *Taroo-ni   ningyoo-ga Hanako-ni ager-u.
        Taroo-DAT doll-NOM   Hanako-DAT give-PRES
        'Taroo gives Hanako a doll.'

(cf. Taroo-ga ningyoo-o Hanako-ni ager-u.
Taroo-NOM doll-ACC Hanako-DAT give-PRES
'Taroo gives Hanako a doll.'   )

Now let us consider how a DSC is made from a (di)transitive clause by the attachment of the potential suffix.

My proposal concerning the potential suffix is as follows: (1) It takes the two-layered VP-shell for a transitive verb as its complement; (2) it has a null Case[10] and it assigns a θ-role to be discharged to its Spec; (3) it optionally absorbs the accusative Case-feature of a transitive verb; and (4) it optionally has an inherent dative Case to be assigned to its Spec when it absorbs the accusative Case. Thus, two structures are imaginable for the underlying structure. The diagram in (4.38) illustrates the underlying structure in which the potential suffix does not absorb the accusative Case-feature:[11]

(4.38)

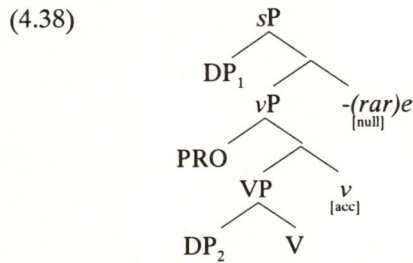

In (4.38) PRO and DP_2 are assigned Agent by v and Theme by V, respectively. Since v in (4.38) retains its accusative Case-feature, DP_2 is required to check it off for convergence. Owing to (2), PRO is required to check off the null Case of the potential suffix. Thus, there is no way for DP_1 to be marked as anything other than nominative. For if it has any Case other than nominative, there is no element that can check off the (weak) nominative Case-feature of T in Japanese, resulting in crash.[12] Thereby (4.39) is derived:[13]

(4.39) [$_{TP}$ Taroo-ga$_k$ [$_{sP}$ PRO$_k$ eigo-o hanas-er-u]].

It is predicted that this is acceptable because it converges. Indeed, the Case array shown in (4.39) is factually allowed.[14] Besides, in this situation, there is no way

---

[10] See Chomsky and Lasnik (1993) and, especially, Martin (1992) and Watanabe (1993) for discussions on null Case. The idea that PRO (or control) is involved in the potential construction was originally suggested by Saito (1982).

[11] sP stands for the maximal projection of the potential suffix -(rar)e.

[12] Recall that Japanese is [–impersonal] in that T's nominative feature must be checked somehow in the derivation.

[13] In (4.39) I omit depicting the trace of *Taroo*. It is moved from a Spec of s. Besides, I ignore V-movement here.

[14] Some method must be devised to ensure that DP_1 in (4.38) and (4.40) are coreferential with PRO. Although it is easy to say that the potential suffix is a kind of obligatory control predicate, its theoretical implementation is not so easy (cf. Watanabe 1995b). I will

for DP₂ to be marked as anything but accusative; otherwise, there would be no element that can check off the accusative Case-feature of *v*.

The diagram in (4.40) illustrates the underlying structure in which the potential suffix absorbs the accusative Case-feature:

(4.40)
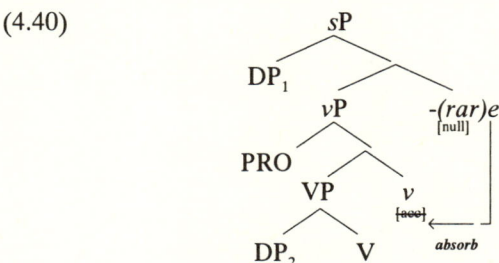

Although it may be assigned an inherent dative Case by the potential suffix, DP₁ in (4.40) must be attracted to the Spec of T before Spell-out due to T's strong EPP-feature in Japanese. There is no way for DP₂ to be marked as any structural Case other than nominative; otherwise, in the clause, there would be no element that could enter into a Case-checking relation with DP₂. The structure in (4.40) thus results in (4.41):

(4.41)   Taroo-ni/-ga eigo-ga/*-o hanas-er-u.

It is noteworthy that PRO does not prohibit the nominative Case-feature of DP₂ from entering into a checking relation with T at LF, despite its intervention between them. This is because PRO is invisible for the LF attraction/checking by T's weak nominative-feature; for, PRO's Case-feature (i.e., null Case) does not match with T's Case-feature (i.e., nominative). (That is to say, PRO has no nominative-feature that prevents the nominative-feature of DP₂ from being attracted by T at LF. Cf. Ferguson 1996 and Ura 1996a)

It should be emphasized that the nominative DP₂ (i.e., Theme) has no [+construable]-feature checking relation with T when the clause is a DSC made by the attachment of the potential suffix. On the other hand, the dative DP₁ has a [+construable]-feature checking relation with T; as a result, it follows from the hypothesis concerning GFs that, whereas the dative DP₁ can control, can bind a subject-oriented anaphor, and can induce subject-honorification, the nominative DP₂ can do none of these things. This is what was observed in §4.1.1.

Moreover, according to the above analysis of the DSC made by the attachment of the potential suffix, there is no room for the lexical variation of the Case arrays that are permitted in the DSC made by the attachment of the potential suffix. This contrasts with the DSC made by a psych-predicate. Indeed, as is expected, the Nom-Nom pattern, the Nom-Acc pattern, and the Dat-Nom pattern are all permitted, irrespective of the type of (di)transitive predicate involved in the DSC made from the attachment of the potential suffix.

---

leave pursuing the implementation to future research.

4.1.5. Supporting Evidence

To summarize the discussion so far, I have claimed that the DSC in Japanese and Korean is derived as in the following way: (1) EXP (or DP_1) with an inherent dative Case is attracted to the Spec of T before Spell-out for the purpose of checking off T's strong EPP-feature and ϕ-feature; and (2) the nominative Case of Theme (or DP_2) enters into a checking relation with T at LF. In this section I will provide further evidence in favor of this claim.

4.1.5.1. Scope of Nominative Object

Tada (1992, 1993) has discovered that the nominative object can take its scope over the potential suffix *-(rar)e*:

(4.42)   *Japanese* (Koizumi 1994b: 214)

       John-ga   migime-**dake-ga**   tumur-e-ru.
       -NOM   right eye-**only**-NOM   close-POT-PRES
       'John can close only his right eye.'

According to Tada (1992, 1993) and Koizumi (1994b), this sentence has the following interpretation:

(4.43)   It is only his right eye that John can close. (interpretation of (4.42))

That is to say, *dake* 'only' takes its scope over the potential suffix *-(rar)e* 'can' in (4.42). This sharply contrasts with (4.44), a counterpart of (4.42) whose object is marked with accusative, instead of nominative:

(4.44)   *Japanese* (Koizumi 1994b: 214)

       John-ga   migime-**dake-o**   tumur-e-ru.
       -NOM   right eye-**only**-ACC   close-POT-PRES
       'John can close only his right eye.'

According to Tada (1992, 1993) and Koizumi (1994b) again, (4.44) has only the reading on which *dake* 'only' is within the scope of the potential suffix *-(rar)e* 'can'. That is, (4.44) has the following interpretation:

(4.45)   It is possible for John to close his right eye only.
                                                                                                                (interpretation of (4.44))

To put it differently, the object cannot take its scope over the potential suffix if it is marked as accusative, but it can if marked as nominative.

Even when the subject in (4.42) becomes marked as dative, the nominative object is still able to get the wide-scope reading. Thus, (4.46) has the reading expressed in (4.43):

(4.46) *Japanese*

John-*ni* migime-**dake**-ga tumur-**e**-ru.
-DAT right eye-**only**-NOM close-POT-PRES
'John can close only his right eye.'

From these observations, the conclusion can be drawn that the nominative object, but not the accusative object, is located at a position higher than the position of the potential suffix at LF. Now suppose, following, essentially, Kitahara (1996), that the feature-checking position of α counts as α's LF position relevant to its scopal interpretation.[15] Then, the above data indicate that the feature-checking position of the nominative object is higher than the potential suffix at LF, as Tada (1992, 1993) and Koizumi (1994b) point out.

This contrast between the nominative object and the accusative object in terms of their scopal domain at LF is thoroughly explainable under the analysis of DSC and the potential construction proposed so far: According to it, (the nominative Case-feature of) the nominative object (in a DSC) moves up onto T at LF in order to enter into a checking relation with T; as a result, the (nominative Case) feature checking position of the nominative object is as high as the position of T at LF. Therefore, the scopal domain of the nominative object is equivalent to the c-commanding domain of T at LF. Since T c-commands (at least, the trace of) the potential suffix at LF, the theory correctly predicts that the nominative object has its scope over the potential suffix, as required. (Cf. Aoun and Li 1994 for the determination of scopal domains.)

On the other hand, under the analysis of the potential construction presented in §4.1.4.4, the accusative object has its accusative Case-feature checked against *v* in the tree illustrated in (4.47):

(4.47) 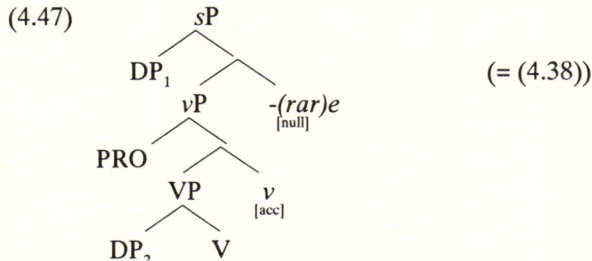 (= (4.38))

Although it may be the case that *v* is merged with the potential suffix by head-movement, resulting in the structure shown in (4.48a), the accusative Case-feature of the accusative object cannot c-command the potential suffix at LF, as is evident from the structure shown in (4.48b):[16]

---

[15] See Fox (1995), Reinhart (1995), and Watanabe (1997) for a detailed study on scope interpretation in the minimalist program.

[16] *s* stands for the potential suffix and "acc-f" in (4.48) stands for the accusative Case-feature of the accusative object.

(4.48) a.  b. (at LF)

Therefore, the accusative object cannot take its scope over the potential suffix. In passing, note that (4.49) below illustrates the head-internal structure of T at LF where the nominative object enters into a checking relation with T:[17]

(4.49) (at LF)

This lucidly illustrates that the nominative Case-feature of the nominative object c-commands the potential suffix at LF, resulting in its wide scope over the potential suffix.

The following facts cited from Koizumi (1994b) more strikingly point to the adequacy of the present analysis:

(4.50) *Japanese* (Koizumi 1994b: 221–222)

    a. John-ga migime-**dake-o** tumur-**e-na**-i.
       -NOM right eye-**only**-ACC close-POT-NEG-PRES
       'John cannot close only his right eye.'

    b. John-ga migime-**dake-ga** tumur-**e-na**-i.
       -NOM right eye-**only**-NOM close-POT-NEG-PRES
       'John cannot close only his right eye.'

According to Koizumi (1994b), the scopal relation of the three elements *dake* 'only', the potential suffix *-(ar)er* 'can', and the negative suffix *-nai* 'not'[18] in (4.50a) and the one in (4.50b) are as follows:

(4.51)   a. neg > can > only (= (4.50a))

      b. only > neg > can (= (4.50b))

Even though the nominative subject in (4.50b) is replaced with a dative subject, its reading shown in (4.51b) remains the same.

This fact clearly shows that the nominative object (in a DSC) has its Case-feature checked against T at LF, as I claimed. It, in turn, lends support to the analysis of the DSC in Japanese presented in this section.

---

[17] "nom-f" stands for the nominative Case-feature of the nominative object.

[18] For discussion on the Japanese neg-head *-nai* and its interaction with head-movement, see Ura (1995a, to appear c). See Kato (1985) for negation in Japanese in general.

4.1.5.2. Long-Distance Feature-Movement

Further supporting evidence comes from the fact that the nominative object can occur at a position distant from a potential suffix. Consider the following examples:

(4.52) *Japanese*

a. John-ni(-wa) [Mary-o musuko-ga shimpai-ni] omo-e-ru.
   -DAT(-TOP)   -ACC   son-NOM anxious-COP(INF) think-POT-PRES
   'It seems to John that Mary is anxious about her son.'
   (Lit. 'John can think Mary (to be) anxious about her son.')

b. *John-ga [Mary-o musuko-ga shimpai-ni] omo-u.
   -NOM   -ACC   son-NOM anxious-COP(INF) think-PRES
   'John thinks Mary (to be) anxious about her son.'

c. John-ga [Mary-ga musuko-ga shimpai-da to] omo-u.
   -NOM   -NOM   son-NOM   anxious-COP COMP think-PRES
   'John thinks that Mary is anxious about her son.'

Following Takezawa (1987), I assume that *-ni*, the particle attached to *shimpai* 'anxious' in the above examples, is a nonfinite form of the copular *-da*.[19] According to Takezawa (1987) and Kikuchi and Takahashi (1991), the embedded clauses in (4.52a,b) count as a Japanese counterpart of the English small clause [$_{SC}$ *Mary (to be) anxious about her son*]. Thus, there is no [+tense] in the embedded clauses in (4.52a,b). As Takezawa (1987) extensively argues, nominative Case in Japanese is not available in tenseless clauses in general:

(4.53) *Japanese*

a. John-ga [Mary-o/*-ga manuke-ni] omo-u.
   -NOM   -ACC/-NOM   stupid-COP(INF) think-PRES
   'John thinks Mary (to be) stupid.'

b. John-ga [Mary-ga manuke-da to] omo-u.
   -NOM   -NOM   stupid-COP COMP think-PRES
   'John thinks that Mary is stupid.'

As Takezawa (1987: 152–156) points out, however, it is possible to mark the subject of a tenseless clause as nominative if the potential suffix is attached to the matrix epistemic verb:

(4.54) *Japanese*

John-ni(-wa) [Mary-ga manuke-ni] omo-e-ru. (cf. (4.53a))
-DAT(-TOP)   -NOM   stupid-COP(INF) think-POT-PRES
Lit. 'John can think Mary (to be) stupid.'

This can be explained as follows under the assumptions in this section: The matrix dative subject checks off the EPP-feature and φ-feature of the matrix T, but

---

[19] See Okutsu (1978) and Kikuchi and Takahashi (1991) for more discussion on *-ni/-da*.

the weak nominative Case-feature of the matrix T wants for checking. The nominative Case-feature of the subject in the embedded tenseless clause enters into a checking relation with the matrix T by moving beyond the clause boundary at LF to check off the weak nominative Case-feature of the matrix T. Since the accusative Case-feature of the matrix epistemic verb can be absorbed by the potential suffix, the derivation converges.

Now let us return to (4.52a). Just as in the case of (4.54), the strong EPP-feature and φ-feature of the matrix T are checked off by the matrix dative subject in overt syntax, but the weak nominative Case-feature of the matrix T wants for checking. Recall the assumption that the potential suffix is allowed not to absorb an accusative Case-feature. Now suppose that the potential suffix in (4.52a) does not absorb the accusative Case-feature of the matrix epistemic verb. Then, the accusative subject of the embedded tenseless clause in (4.52a) checks it off. Furthermore, the weak nominative Case-feature of the matrix T can properly attract the nominative Case-feature of the nominative object in the embedded tenseless clause at LF; for, the accusative subject in the embedded tenseless clause does not block this attraction at LF because the Case-feature of this intervening accusative DP has been checked, deleted, and erased (Chomsky 1995a) when the attraction is applied.[20] Therefore, the derivation for (4.52a) converges, resulting in its well-formedness.

Notice that this explanation crucially utilizes the assumption that the feature checking of the nominative object is executed by the (finite) T. Thus, it lends further support to the analysis of the DSC in Japanese presented in this section.

4.1.6. Summary and Problems

In this section, in order to cope with the DSC in Japanese and Korean, I proposed the following: (1) The EPP-feature of T in Japanese and Korean is strong; (2) the EXP of a psych-verb that can occur in a DSC is generated at the Spec of a kind of light verb, which takes a VP with Theme in its complement position; (3) the light verb in the two-layered VP-shell of the psych-verb that can occur in Japanese and Korean DSC may assign a dative Case to EXP as an inherent Case, and it is allowed not to have accusative Case-feature as its lexical idiosyncrasy; (4) in Japanese and Korean, agreement may be independent of nominative Case just as in Bantu; (5) T's φ-feature is strong, but its nominative Case-feature is weak in Japanese and Korean; and (6) T's nominative Case-feature may enter into multiple feature-checking relations. I argued that, given these assumptions, the GF-splitting involved in the Japanese and Korean DSC can be explained together with other welcome consequences. Moreover, I showed that there are some pieces of supporting evidence in favor of the analysis proposed.

As will be observed in the sections that follow, however, the explanation I proposed in this section for the Japanese and Korean DSC does not always hold good for DSCs found in other languages. Recall that the dative subject in Japa-

---

[20] Provided that LF cyclicity is assumed (cf. Watanabe 1995a).

nese and Korean induces subject-honorification, a kind of manifestation of subject-agreement. And this is crucial for the explanation: Elsewhere in this book I claimed, following Chomsky's (1995a) suggestion, that the ability to control results from a φ-feature checking relation with T. The Japanese and Korean fact is compatible with this. But in many languages with the DSC, the ability to control is possessed by the dative subject that does not induce subject-agreement.[21] More specifically, in Tamil, Icelandic, Hindi, and so forth, the dative subject gains subjecthood despite the fact that it does not induce subject-agreement. (Subject-agreement is induced by the nominative object, or the third person singular neuter (masculine) agreement (impersonal agreement) appears as the default.) This problem will be explained in the sections that follow.

Another problem is that, in languages like Tamil and Hindi, the Dat-Acc pattern is allowed as well as the Nom-Acc and the Dat-Nom patterns. In this section I argued that the Dat-Acc pattern is systematically precluded in Japanese and Korean. Then, why is it allowed in those languages? Or, what kind of parameter allows it? This is the other problem discussed in what follows.[22]

4.2. Tamil

As mentioned above, there are two types of DSC in Tamil and other Dravidian languages (cf. Lehmann 1993 for Tamil, Sridhar 1976, 1979 for Kannada; Mohanan 1982 and Jayaseelan 1983 for Malayalam); namely, the Dat-Acc pattern and the Dat-Nom pattern. They may differ from each other in the subject properties that the dative subject gains. In this section, drawing data exclusively from Tamil, I will study these types of DSC in Dravidian languages and their syntactic behaviors concerning GF-splitting.

4.2.1. DAT-ACC Pattern

In Tamil, the dative subject in the Dat-Acc pattern does not induce subject agreement. Instead, the default third person singular neuter agreement (or impersonal agreement) always appears in this pattern, according to Lehmann (1993). Some examples are:

(4.53) *Tamil* (Lehmann 1993: 184)

    a. Kumaar-ukku raajaav-aip pitikk-**um**.
          Kumar-DAT   Raja-ACC   like-IMP
          'Kumar likes Raja.'

---

[21] A survey of the variety of DSCs in the world's languages can be found in Masica (1976).

[22] As far as I can see, it seems that the Nom-Nom pattern is allowed only in the languages that allow multiple subjects in a single clause. This suggests that the [+multiple] nominative Case-feature of T is responsible for this pattern, as can readily be conceived.

b. Kumaar-ukku   inta   uur-ait   teriy-**um**.
    Kumar-DAT   this   place-ACC   know-IMP
    'Kumar knows this place.'

(Cf. Kumaar-Ø   raajaav-ai   ati-tt-**aan**.
    Kumar-NOM   Raja-ACC   beat-PAST-3SG.M
    'Kumar beat Raja.'   (Lehmann 1993: 181))

The suffix *-um* is equivalent to the third person singular neuter agreement morpheme, which I express here as impersonal. Take (4.53a) for example. From the fact that both *kumaar* 'Kumar' and *raajaav* 'Raja' are third person singular masculine, it is evident that the verb agrees with neither of them.

Here it is important to note that Tamil has a genuine impersonal construction, as in (4.54):

(4.54) *Tamil* (Lehmann 1993: 175)

a. [kumaar-Ø   raajaav-aip   kaarkk-a]   neer-nt-atu.
    Kumar-NOM   Raja-ACC   see-INF   happen-PAST-IMP
    'It happens that Kumar saw Raja.'

b. [kumaar-Ø   varu-v-aan]   pool-um.
    Kumar-NOM   come-FUT-3SG.M   seem-IMP
    'It seems that Kumar will come.'

According to Lehmann (1993: 175f.), there is ample evidence which shows that there is no (morphophonologically overt) subject in those sentences. Put differently, those are impersonal sentences with a null expletive, or with no subject at all. This implies that Tamil is a [+impersonal] language,[23] which means that there is no need to worry about the checking of the nominative Case-feature of T in Tamil (see §1.4.7.1).

Keeping this in mind, let us consider what GFs the dative subject in the Dat-Acc pattern shows. First, it can bind a subject-oriented reflexive, as shown in (4.55):

(4.55) *Tamil* (Lehmann 1993: 186)

Kumaar-ukkut$_i$ tann-ai$_i$ mattum   pitikk-um.
Kumar-DAT   self-ACC   only   like-3IMP
'Kumar$_i$ likes himself$_i$.'

Notice that the subject-oriented reflexive *tann* in Tamil cannot be bound by the dative-marked indirect object, as (4.56) shows:[24]

---

[23] See, also, Perlmutter (1983) for a comment on Tamil impersonal constructions.

[24] For *tann* and other facts with regard to its subject-orientation in Tamil, see Lehmann (1993) and Sarma (1994).

(4.56) *Tamil* (Lehmann 1993: 185–186)

Kumaar-Ø$_k$ raajaav-ukkut$_i$ [$_{DP}$ [$_{PP}$ tann-aip$_{k/*i}$ parri] oru katturai-aik]
Kumar-NOM Raja-DAT   self-ACC   about one article-ACC
koti-tt-aar.
give-PAST-3SG.HON
'Kumar$_k$ gave Raja$_i$ [one article [about himself$_{k/*i}$]].'

The conclusion is that, among the dative-marked arguments, only the one appearing as SUBJ in a DSC can have the ability to bind a subject-oriented reflexive.

Second, the dative subject in the Dat-Acc pattern can control. In (4.57) it controls the missing subject in a tensed coordinate clause:

(4.57) *Tamil* (Lehmann 1993: 187)

Kumaar-ukku$_i$ antap penn-aip piti-ttu, PRO$_i$ aval-aik kaliyaanam
Kumar-DAT that girl-ACC like-PARTIC   she-ACC marriage
cey-t-aan.
do-PAST-3SG.M
'Kumar$_i$ liked that girl and PRO$_i$ married her.'

It should be noted that the dative-marked indirect object cannot control the missing subject in a tensed coordinate clause, as shown in (4.58):

(4.58) *Tamil* (Lehmann 1993: 186)

Kumaar-Ø$_i$ raajaav-ukkut$_k$ panam kotu-ttu, PRO$_{i/*k}$
Kumar-NOM Raja-DAT   money give-PARTIC
cantoosappat-t-aan.
feel-happy-PAST-3SG.M
'Kumar$_i$ gave Raja$_j$ money and PRO$_{i/*k}$ felt happy.'

Moreover, the dative subject can control PRO in a tensed subordinate clause:

(4.59) *Tamil* (Lehmann 1993: 187)

[PRO$_i$ niraiyac caappit-tu] kumaar-ukku$_i$ vayirr-ai vali-tt-atu.
      a lot   eat-INF   Kumar-DAT   stomach-ACC pain-PAST-IMP
'[PRO$_i$ eating a lot], Kumar$_i$ got stomach pain.'

This shows that the dative-marked arguments do not have the ability to control unless they appear as SUBJ in a DSC in Tamil.

To sum up, the dative subject in the Dat-Acc pattern has the ability to bind a subject-oriented reflexive and the ability to control, despite the fact that it does not induce subject-agreement. In the Dat-Acc pattern, subject-agreement is impersonal in Tamil, as noted at the beginning of this section.

4.2.2. DAT-NOM Pattern

In this section, let us see what properties the Dat-Nom pattern of the Tamil DSCs has. First, the dative subject in the Dat-Nom pattern does not induce subject-agreement, just as the dative subject in the Dat-Acc pattern does not. Interestingly, subject-agreement in the Dat-Nom pattern is induced by the nominative object, which remarkably contrasts with the case where subject-agreement appears as default (i.e., impersonal) in the Dat-Acc pattern. This fact is exemplified by (4.60):

(4.60)   *Tamil* (Lehmann 1993: 189f.)

    a. Kumaar-ukku irantu paiyan-kal-Ø   iru-kkir-**aarkal**.
        Kumar-DAT   two   boy-PL-NOM   be-PRES-**3PL.EP**
        'Kumar has two boys.'

    b. Kumaar-ukku cila   ninaivu-kal-Ø   va-nt-**ana**.
        Kumar-DAT   a few memory-PL-NOM come-PAST-**3PL.N**
        'Kumar got some memories..'

Although the Dat-Nom pattern differs from the Dat-Acc pattern in this regard, the dative subject in the Dat-Nom pattern behaves the same as the dative subject in the Dat-Acc pattern in other respects: It can control the missing subject in a tensed coordinate clause, as shown in (4.61):

(4.61)   *Tamil* (Lehmann 1993: 191)

    Kumaar-ukkuk$_i$ koopam-Ø va-ntu,   PRO$_i$ raajaav-api ati-tt-aan.
    Kumar-DAT   anger-NOM come-PARTIC   Raja-ACC beat-PAST-3SG.M
    'Kumar$_i$ got angry and PRO$_i$ beat Raja.'

In contrast, the nominative object cannot control, as the ill-formedness of (4.62) shows:

(4.62)   *Tamil* (Lehmann 1993: 192)

    *Kempeni-kkup panam-Ø$_k$ kitai-ttu, PRO$_k$ vatti
    company-DAT   money-NOM   get-PARTIC   interest
    perruk-kon-t-iru-kkir-atu.
    get-hold-PARTIC-be-PRES-3SG.N
    'The company got money$_k$ and PRO$_k$ receives interest now.'

The dative subject in the Dat-Nom pattern, just like the one in the Dat-Acc pattern, can bind a subject-oriented reflexive:

(4.63)   *Tamil* (Lehmann 1993: 190)

    Kumaar-ukkut$_i$ [tann-aip$_i$ parrik kavalai]-Ø   ill-ai.
    Kumar-DAT   self-ACC   about   concern -NOM be-not-3PL.N
    'Kumar$_i$ has no concern about himself$_i$.'

The nominative object, in contrast, cannot bind a subject-oriented reflexive, as shown in (4.64):

(4.64) *Tamil* (Lehmann 1993: 191)

Kumaar-ukkut$_i$ katattappatt-a uumaa-Ø$_k$ [tan$_{i*k}$ viitt]-il
Kumar-DAT get-kidnappped-ADJ Uma-NOM self house -LOC
miintum kitai-tt-aal.
back get-PAST-3SG.F
'Kumar$_i$ got the kidnapped Uma$_k$ back in his$_i$/her$_k$ house.'

To recap, the dative subject in the Dat-Nom pattern, just like the dative subject in the Dat-Acc pattern, has the ability to control and the ability to bind a subject-oriented reflexive, though subject-agreement in the Dat-Nom pattern is induced by the nominative object. In the next section, I will propose the parameter-settings involved in the Tamil DSCs and demonstrate that the facts observed here can be satisfactorily accounted for.

4.2.3. Analysis

4.2.3.1. Parameter-Settings

Now I propose the following: (1) T's EPP-feature is strong in Tamil; (2) T's nominative Case-feature and φ-features are both weak in Tamil; (3) EXP is generated at the Spec of a kind of light verb, which selects VP with Theme in its complement position (see (4.65));

(4.65)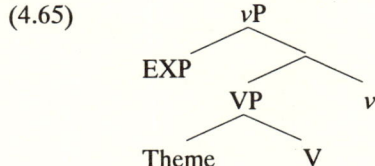

(4) (i) the light verb (i.e., *v*) in the two-layered VP-shell for a psych-verb that occurs in the Dat-Acc pattern assigns a dative Case to EXP as an inherent Case, and it also has an accusative Case-feature, and (ii) *v* in the two-layered VP-shell for a psych-verb that occurs in the Dat-Nom pattern assigns a dative Case to EXP as an inherent Case, but it has no accusative Case (n.b.: these properties of the verbs are lexically determined); (5) T's nominative Case-feature checking must be executed together with the φ-feature checking in Tamil (i.e., it cannot be checked off independently); (6) T's nominal features in Tamil may escape checking, because Tamil is a [+impersonal] language, as noted in §4.2.1.

4.2.3.2. Explanation

Now let us begin with the initial structure illustrated in (4.66) to see how the Tamil DSCs are derived:

(4.66)   [$_{vP}$ EXP(DAT) [$_{VP}$ Theme V] *v*]

Note that EXP is assigned a dative Case as its inherent Case (due to proposal (4)) irrespective of the type of psych-verb involved in the clause. Then, T is introduced by Merge, deriving (4.67) from (4.66):

(4.67)   [$_{TP}$ [$_{vP}$ EXP(DAT) [$_{VP}$ Theme V] v] T]

Due to assumption (1), something with a D-feature is attracted to the (innermost) Spec of T to check T's strong EPP-feature (i.e., D-feature). EXP (i.e., the dative subject) is the closest to T; consequently, it is attracted to the Spec of T before Spell-ooout, deriving (4.68) from (4.67):

(4.68)   [$_{TP}$ EXP(DAT)$_k$ [$_{vP}$ t$_k$ [$_{VP}$ Theme V] v] T]

Note that EXP has a D-feature and, hence, can be attracted by the EPP-feature of T, though its Case-feature can never be available for Case-checking because of its inherent nature. At the stage in the derivation illustrated in (4.68), EXP checks off T's strong EPP-feature. It should be noted that the ϕ-feature of T, as well as its nominative Case-feature, being weak, remains unchecked before Spell-out under the hypothesis that Checking is a syntactic operation subject to the general economy condition.[25] Note, also, that the derivation up to this stage is the same regardless of whether Theme is marked as accusative or nominative.

If Theme is marked as nominative, as illustrated in (4.69), it corresponds to the surface structure of the Dat-Nom pattern:

(4.69)   [$_{TP}$ EXP(DAT)$_k$ [$_{vP}$ t$_k$ [$_{VP}$ Theme(NOM) V] v] T]
                                                                    (Dat-Nom pattern)

Example (4.69) results in a convergent derivation if Theme, which has a nominative Case-feature, properly checks off the weak ϕ-feature and nominative Case-feature of T at the same time (due to (5)). This can be achieved if the corresponding formal features of Theme move onto T at LF to enter into a checking relation with T. Note that there is no need to worry about the accusative Case-feature of v in this case; for, the psych-verbs that occur in the Dat-Nom pattern inherently lacks an accusative Case-feature (due to assumption (4(ii))).

A comment on the checking of T's weak ϕ-feature at LF is in order. Before Spell-out, EXP at the Spec of T does not check it off because it is weak, as claimed above. At LF, the nominative Case-feature of Theme is attracted by the weak nominative Case-feature of T. According to Chomsky (1995 fall class lectures), the ϕ-feature of Theme together with the nominative Case-feature of Theme can be moved onto T for free by the free-ride strategy with pied-piping. Then, one might think that either the ϕ-feature of EXP, which is located at the Spec of T, or the ϕ-feature of Theme, which is pied-piped onto T along with the nominative Case-feature of Theme, can enter into a ϕ-feature checking relation with T at LF. But the fact is that the latter always enters into a ϕ-feature checking relation with T, as observed above. Why should this be so?

---

[25] As argued in depth in §3.2.3, Procrastinate requires Checking to take place as late as possible.

As I hinted in §3.2.3, the LF feature checking between a head H and an element located at the Spec of H is mediated by feature-movement (Chomsky 1995 fall class lectures). Given this, the checking of T's weak ϕ-feature by EXP is less economical than its checking by the ϕ-feature of Theme. This is because, whereas no operation is needed for the latter (the ϕ-feature of Theme is pied-piped onto T^0 as a free-rider together with the movement of the nominative Case-feature of Theme onto T^0), an operation (i.e., the movement of a ϕ-feature from within T^0 to EXP) must be invoked for the former. (Note that the economy condition applied here is strictly derivational/local in the sense of Collins 1996). Hence, the conclusion is that it is (the ϕ-feature of) Theme that always enters into a ϕ-feature checking relation with T in the Tamil DSC with the Dat-Nom pattern.

Let us return to (4.68) and suppose that Theme in (4.68) is marked as accusative as illustrated in (4.70):

(4.70) $\quad$ [$_{TP}$ EXP(DAT)$_k$ [$_{\nu P}$ t$_k$ [$_{VP}$ Theme(ACC) V] ν] T]
$\hfill$ (Dat-Acc pattern)

This corresponds to the surface structure of the Dat-Acc pattern. At this stage, T's ϕ-feature and nominative Case-feature, ν's Accusative Case-feature, and Theme's accusative Case-feature remain unchecked. The structure in (4.70) results in a convergent derivation if the accusative Case-feature of Theme moves onto ν at LF and checks against ν's accusative Case-feature. Notice, again, that we do not worry about T's ϕ-feature and nominative Case-feature in Tamil, due to proposal (6). It seems technically possible that the ϕ-feature of the accusative-marked Theme checks off the ϕ-feature of T at LF in this case, but it is indeed prohibited owing to proposal (5).

4.2.3.3. Grammatical Functions

Thus far it has been observed that the dative subject (i.e., EXP) in the Tamil DSCs has the ability to control and the ability to bind a subject-oriented reflexive, irrespective of whether Theme is marked as accusative or nominative. Moreover, whereas the nominative object induces subject-agreement in the Dat-Nom pattern, the default impersonal agreement appears in the Dat-Acc pattern.

Recall the hypothesis that these abilities result from a [+construable]-feature checking relation with T (= Infl). More precisely, I claimed that the ability to control results from a ϕ-feature checking relation with T, and the ability to bind a subject-oriented reflexive results from an EPP-feature checking relation with T. Given this hypothesis, the above properties of the dative subject in the Tamil DSCs are straightforwardly accounted for. As argued above, it is EXP (i.e., the dative subject) that checks off T's EPP-feature before Spell-out regardless of the case-marking of Theme. For the Dat-Acc pattern, Theme (i.e., the accusative object) has no [+construable]-feature checking relation with T. Accordingly, it leads to the correct prediction that the accusative object has neither the ability to control nor the ability to bind a subject-oriented reflexive in the Tamil DSC with the Dat-Acc pattern.

A problem arises for the Dat-Nom pattern, however. In §4.2.3.2 I argued that the nominative object in the Tamil DSC with the Dat-Nom pattern enters into a φ-feature checking relation with T at LF. Hence, it is predicted that the nominative object bears the ability to control. This prediction, however, is contrary to the fact: The nominative object in the Tamil DSC cannot control; rather, it is the dative subject that has the ability to control, as observed above.

Here I propose to make a slight modification of the hypothesis concerning the ability to control. Relaxing the former hypothesis that the ability to control results from a φ-feature checking relation with T, I propose (1) that the ability results from a [+construable]-feature checking relation with T, and (2) that, if there is more than one argument with a [+construable]-feature checking relation with T in a single clause, the ability to control is possessed by the argument that is ranked as the highest according to the following hierarchy: argument with a φ-feature checking relation with T before Spell-out ≫ argument with an EPP-feature checking relation with T before Spell-out ≫ argument with a φ-feature checking relation with T at LF ≫ argument with an EPP-feature checking relation with T at LF.

Returning to the Tamil DSC with the Dat-Nom pattern, we know that the dative subject (i.e., EXP) enters into an EPP-feature checking relation with T before Spell-out and the nominative object (i.e., Theme) enters into a φ-feature checking relation with T at LF. Thus, the newly introduced hypothesis concerning the ability to control leads to the conclusion that it is the dative subject with an EPP-feature checking relation with T before Spell-out that holds the ability to control in the Tamil DSC with the Dat-Nom pattern.

As for the ability to bind a subject-oriented reflexive, the fact observed so far conforms to the hypothesis that it stems from an EPP-feature checking relation with T: It was revealed that the dative subject in the Tamil DSC with the Dat-Nom pattern enters into an EPP-feature checking relation with T before Spell-out; whereby, the dative subject can bind a subject-oriented reflexive. On the other hand, the nominative object in the construction at issue has no EPP-feature checking relation with T; hence, it cannot bind a subject-oriented reflexive.

4.2.4. Evidence for the Difference between Dat-Acc and Dat-Nom

Thus far I have claimed that (the Case-feature of) Theme in the Dat-Acc pattern does not move up to T, but that it does move up to T in the Dat-Nom pattern at LF. Indeed, there is supporting evidence in favor of this claim.

Vaijayanthi Sarma (personal communication) pointed out to me that, whereas Theme in the Dat-Acc pattern cannot take scope over the sentential negation, Theme in the Dat-Nom pattern can. Consider the following examples:

(4.72) *Tamil*

a. Kumaar-ukku irantu paiyan-kal-aip puriy-av-**ill**-ai.
   Kumar-DAT two boy-PL-ACC understand-INF-NOT-IMP
   'Kumar didn't understand two boys.'

b. Kumaar-ukku irantu paiyan-kal-Ø tirumpak kitai-av-**ill**-ai.
   Kumar-DAT two boy-PL-NOM back get-INF-NOT-3PL
   'Kumar didn't get two boys back.'

We cannot get the reading under which (4.72a) is interpreted as meaning "There were two boys who Kumar did not understand." In contrast, (4.72b) can be interpreted as meaning "There were two boys who Kumar did not get back." These facts indicate that the nominative object, but not the accusative object, can take its scope over the neg-element *ill* in the Tamil DSCs.[26] It follows from the analysis of the Tamil DSCs presented here that the (accusative Case-feature of the) accusative object cannot be higher than the neg-element at LF, while the (nominative feature of the) nominative object in the Tamil DSC with the Dat-Nom pattern can c-command the neg-element at LF, because it is attached onto T at LF, as I argued. Therefore, the fact shown in (4.72) lends good support to my analysis of the two types of Tamil DSCs.

4.2.5. Summary and Dative Subjects in Kannada

In this section I illustrated how the two types of Tamil DSC are derived. Specifically, I proposed the following: (1) T's EPP-feature is strong in Tamil; (2) T's nominative Case-feature and φ-features are both weak in Tamil; (3) EXP is generated at the Spec of a kind of light verb, which selects VP with Theme in its complement position; (4) (i) the light verb (i.e., *v*) in the two-layered VP-shell for a psych-verb that occurs in the Dat-Acc pattern assigns a dative Case to EXP as an inherent Case, and it also has an accusative Case-feature, and (ii) *v* in the two-layered VP-shell for a psych-verb that occurs in the Dat-Nom pattern assigns a dative Case to EXP as an inherent Case, but it has no accusative Case (n.b.: these properties of the verbs are lexically determined); (5) T's nominative Case-feature checking must be executed together with the φ-feature checking in Tamil (i.e., it cannot be checked off independently); (6) T's nominal features in Tamil may escape checking, because Tamil is a [+impersonal] language.

Since Sridhar's (1976, 1979) extensive study, Kannada, another Dravidian language, has been often discussed as a typical example of a language with a DSC (e.g., Dryer 1982, Hermon 1984, Bhat 1991, and Harley 1995b, inter alia). According to Sridhar (1979), Kannada differs from Tamil in that the Dat-Acc pattern is not found in the former. But the Dat-Nom pattern is allowed if the

---

[26] For discussion on *ill*, see Lehmann (1993: 228ff.).

predicate in the clause is a stative predicate and/or psych-predicate. Sridhar (1976, 1979) shows that the dative subject in the Kannada DSC has the following properties: (1) It has the ability to bind a subject-oriented reflexive, and (2) it can control; whereas, the nominative object has no such properties except that it always induces subject-agreement.[27] These properties of the Kannada DSC are the same as those of the Tamil DSC with the Dat-Nom pattern. Hence I conclude that the parameters concerning the Kannada DSC are as follows: (1) T's EPP-feature is strong in Kannada; (2) T's nominative Case-feature and φ-features are both weak in Kannada; (3) EXP is generated at the Spec of a kind of light verb, which selects VP with Theme in its complement position; (4) the light verb of the verbs that occur in this construction assigns a dative Case to EXP as an inherent Case, but it has no accusative Case; and (5) T's nominative Case-feature checking must be executed together with the φ-feature checking in Kannada. The Kannada DSC, thus, is derived in the same manner as the Tamil DSC with the Dat-Nom pattern.

4.3. Icelandic

In this section I will address my full attention to the DSC in Icelandic, the most studied example of DSC in the literature.

4.3.1. Data

As is well known, Icelandic abounds with the so-called Quirky Subject Construction (hereafter, QSC), in which the "subject" stands in a non-nominative Case (Thráinsson 1979, Andrews 1982, Zaenen and Maling 1984, Yip, Maling, and Jackendoff 1987, Cowper 1988, Sigurðsson 1989, and Van Valin 1991, to name a few). Thus, the DSC is a subtype of the QSC. Some examples are:

(4.73) *Icelandic* (Andrews 1982: 461–463)
    a. Accusative Subject
        i. Mig   kelur. (intransitive)
           me(ACC) is-freezing
           'I am freezing.'
        ii. Drengina   vantar   mat. (transitive)
           the-boys(ACC) lacks   food(ACC)
           'The boys lack food.'
    b. Dative Subejct
        i. Mér   kólnar. (intransitive)
           me(DAT) is-getting-cold.
           'I am getting cold.'

---

[27] For a summary and discussion of the Kannada DSC, see Bhat (1991) and Harley (1995b).

ii. Barninu batnaði veikin. (transitive)
the-child(DAT) recovered-from the-disease(NOM)
'The child recovered from the disease.'

c. Genitive Subject

i. Verkjanna gætir ekki. (intransitive)
the-pains(GEN) is-noticeable NEG
'The pains are not noticeable.'

ii. Konungs var þangað von. (transitive)
the-king(GEN) was thither expectation(NOM)
'The king was expected there.'

In this section I will concentrate my attention to the DSC in Icelandic,[28] though the QSC in Icelandic can be treated in the same way as the DSC, as will become evident later in this section.[29]

As many authors have pointed out, the dative (or quirky) subject in the Icelandic DSC (or QSC), just like the dative subject in the Japanese DSC and the Tamil DSC, can bind a subject-oriented reflexive[30] and can control. Let us look at the first property. As shown in (4.74), the quirky subjects can bind a subject-oriented reflexive:[31]

(4.74) *Icelandic*

a. Honum leiðist [konan sín/[?]*hans].
him(DAT) bores wife self's / his (Sigurðsson 1989: 207)

b. Hverjum þykir [$_{SC}$[sinn fugel] gagur].
everyone(DAT) thinks self's bird beautiful
Lit. 'Everyone thinks self's bird beautiful.'

(Zaenen, Maling, and Thráinsson 1985: 450)

---

[28] Among the Germanic languages, DSCs similar to the one found in Icelandic can be found also in Faroese (Lockwood 1977), Dutch (den Besten 1984 and Levin 1985a,b), German (Haider 1984 and Hawkins 1986), Old English (Elmer 1981 and Allen 1995), and Old Norse (Faarlund 1990).

[29] See Thráinsson (1979), Zaenen, Maling, and Thráinsson (1985), Cowper (1988), Sigurðsson (1989), and Andrews (1990) for some discussions on the subjecthood of the accusative subject and the genitive subject. They all agree that all the quirky subjects behave like "subject" in Icelandic. See §4.3.3 for the dative (quirky) subject in a passive clause.

[30] It is somewhat controversial, though, to conclude that the Icelandic reflexive pronouns *sig* 'self(ACC)', *sér* 'self(DAT)', and *sín* 'self(GEN)' are really subject-oriented. In fact, Thráinsson (1979) cites examples in which they are bound by an object within the same clause (cf., also, Anderson 1986, Maling 1986, and Rögnvaldsson 1986). But, as Maling (1986: footnote 2) and Rögnvaldsson (1986) point out, many speakers do not accept object-bound reflexives. Besides, according to Maling (1986), the reflexive possessive, too, allows subject antecedents only (cf. Einarsson 1945).

[31] For the reflexives in Icelandic and their binding properties, see Thráinsson (1976/1990) and Sigurðsson (1989) in addition to the references cited in footnote 30.

Second, the dative subject in the Icelandic DSC can control, as shown in (4.75):

(4.75) *Icelandic*

a. Honum$_k$ leiddist [að PRO$_k$ na ekki profinu].
    him(DAT) bored   to   pass not the-exam
    'He was sorry not to pass the exam.'   (Sigurðsson 1989: 207)

b. Mer$_k$ likuðu bækurnar [an þess PRO$_k$ að buast við þvi].
    me(DAT) liked(PL) the-books without   to expect it
    'I$_k$ liked the books wihtout PRO$_k$ expecting to.' (Toribio 1993: 155)

These examples therefore indicate that the dative subject has a [+construable]-feature checking relation with T under the theory of GFs advocated in this book.[32]

Strikingly interesting is the fact that the dative (or quirky) subject cannot induce subject-agreement in Icelandic. The generalization is as follows: If there is no nominative-marked DP (i.e., nominative object) in the clause, the default impersonal agreement appears; if the nominative object appears in the clause, then it never fails to induce subject-agreement (Zaenen and Maling 1982, 1984 and Falk 1991).[33] These facts are shown in the following examples:

(4.76) *Icelandic* (Sigurðsson 1989: 240)

a. Okkur   *likuðu/likaði   við Olaf.
    us(DAT.PL) liked(3PL)/(IMP) with Olaf(ACC)
    'We are pleased with Olaf.'

b. Mir   likuðu/*likaði   hestarnir.
    me(DAT.SG) liked(3PL)/(3SG) the-horses(NOM.PL)
    'I liked the horses.'

A comment on the types of predicates that allow the DSC (QSC) in Icelandic is in order. Just like the Japanese and Korean DSC or the Tamil DSCs, almost all of the predicates that allow the DSC (QSC) in Icelandic are stative and take a nonagentive argument (cf. Andrews 1982 and Smith 1994). I assume, following many authors (e.g., Levin and Simpson 1981, Cowper 1988, and Harley 1995a,b), that these predicates can be classified as psych-predicates, whose external θ-role is discharged as EXP.

---

[32] For other pieces of evidence in favor of the claim that the dative (quirky) subject syntactically behaves like a "subject" in Icelandic, see Thráinsson (1979), Andrews (1982), Zaenen, Maling, and Thráinsson (1985), and Sigurðsson (1989), among others.

[33] Thráinsson (1979: 466) cites an example in which the nominative object optionally induces subject-agreement. Schütze (1993) points out, however, that most speakers prefer obligatory agreement with the nominative object and that the above optionality is allowed only for a very small set of verbs (cf. Jonas 1992 and Taraldsen 1995). I agree with Schütze (1993) that this is a highly idiosyncratic phenomenon that is outside the core grammar. The other exception can be found in the case where the nominative object is a first or second person pronoun. In this case the default impersonal agreement appears (cf. Jónsson 1994 and Taraldsen 1995).

To recap, the Icelandic DSC quite resembles the Tamil DSC with the Dat-Nom pattern in that the dative subject can bind a subject-oriented reflexive and can control, but the nominative object, instead of the dative subject, induces subject-agreement. Thus it is natural to expect that parameters quite similar to the ones involved in the Tamil DSC with the Dat-Nom pattern are also involved in the Icelandic DSC. I will explore this possibility in the next subsection.

4.3.2. Analysis

4.3.2.1. Parameter-Settings

Now I propose the following: (1) T's EPP-feature is strong in Icelandic; (2) T's nominative Case-feature and φ-feature are both weak in Icelandic; (3) EXP is generated at the Spec of a kind of light verb, which takes a VP with Theme in its complement position (see (4.77));

(4.77)   The light verb in this structure has a stative meaning

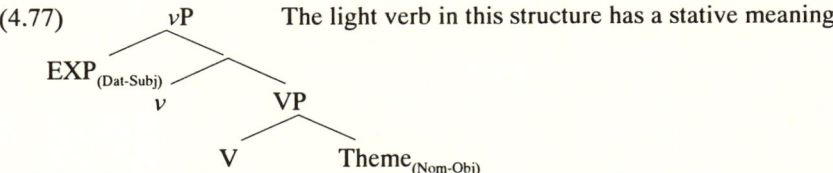

(4) the light verb in the two-layered VP-shell of a psych-verb that occurs in DSC assigns a dative Case to EXP as an inherent Case, and it has no accusative Case-feature (n.b.: these properties of the verbs are lexically determined);[34] (5) T's nominative Case-feature checking must be executed together with the φ-feature checking in Icelandic (i.e., it cannot be checked off independently);[35] and (6) T's nominal features in Icelandic may escape checking because Icelandic is a [+impersonal] language.

Notice that these parameters for the Icelandic DSC are quite similar to the ones for the Tamil DSCs. The only difference is (4), where lexical variations are allowed. In fact, QSCs other than the DSC found in Icelandic are derived in the same way as the DSC if parameter (4) is changed appropriately. For example, if the light verb assigns an accusative Case to EXP as an inherent Case and it retains a structural accusative Case-feature to be checked off by Theme, the accusative subject construction shown in (4.78) is derived:[36]

---

[34] As a matter of fact, (4) is not a parameter, but it states a lexical property of the psych-predicates at issue.

[35] Chomsky (fall 1995 class lectures) suggested the same parameter-setting for Icelandic.

[36] For the types of predicates that allow the QSC and their case arrays, see Andrews (1982), Sigurðsson (1989), Van Valin (1991), Smith (1994), and references cited there.

(4.78)   *Icelandic*
Drengina   vantar   mat.
the-boys(ACC) lacks   food(ACC)
'The boys lack food.'

In fact, it has been claimed by many authors (e.g., Levin and Simpson 1981, Cowper 1988, Sigurðsson 1989, Freidin and Sprouse 1991, Jónsson 1994, and Harley 1995a,b, inter alia) that quirky cases are tightly linked to particular lexical items or particular θ-roles.

According to Chomsky's (1995a) theory of expletives, (1) and (2) are both confirmed by the fact that Icelandic has an overt expletive. As for (3), it is a universal characteristic of psych-predicates. And (6) has been well documented in the literature and confirmed by the following examples, which are clearly regarded as an impersonal construction (cf. Thráinsson 1979, Zaenen, Maling, and Thráinsson 1985, Van Valin 1991, Holmberg 1994, and references cited there):

(4.79)   *Icelandic*
a. Honum   var   hjálpað (af mér).
    he(DAT)   was(IMP) helped by me(DAT)
    'He was helped (by me).'   (Van Valin 1991: 152)

b. Barninu$_k$ virðist [t$_k$ hafa   verið hjálpað].
    the-child(DAT) seems   have(INF) been helped
    'The child seems to have been helped.'
                                    (Freidin and Sprouse 1991: 404)

c. Í gær   var   (*það) dansað á skipinu.
    yesterday was(IMP) EXP   danced on the-ship
    Lit. 'Yesterday was danced on the ship.'
                                    (Holmberg and Platzak 1995: 100)

4.3.2.2. Explanation

Now that, as noted above, the parameters concerned in the DSC in Icelandic are virtually the same as the ones concerned in the Tamil DSC with the Dat-Nom pattern, the Icelandic DSC is derived in the same way as the Tamil DSC. First, consider (4.80), which represents the stage in the derivation where T is merged with the two-layered VP-shell of a psych-verb:

(4.80)   [$_{TP}$ T [$_{vP}$ EXP(DAT) v [$_{VP}$ V Theme(NOM)]]]

Due to assumption (1), something with a D-feature is attracted to the (innermost) Spec of T to check T's strong EPP-feature (i.e., D-feature). EXP (i.e., the dative subject) is the closest to T; consequently, it is attracted to the Spec of T before Spell-out, deriving (4.81) from (4.80):

(4.81)   [$_{TP}$ EXP(DAT)$_k$ T [$_{vP}$ t$_k$ v [$_{VP}$ V Theme(NOM)]]]

Note that EXP has a D-feature and, hence, can be attracted by the EPP-feature of T, though its Case-feature can never be available for Case-checking because of its inherent nature. At the stage in the derivation illustrated in (4.81), EXP checks off T's strong EPP-feature. It should be noted that the ϕ-feature of T, as well as its nominative Case-feature, being weak, remains unchecked before Spell-out under the hypothesis that Checking is a syntactic operation subject to the general economy condition.[37] The structure in (4.81) corresponds to the surface structure of the DSC in Icelandic.[38]

The stucture shown in (4.81) results in a convergent derivation if Theme, which has a nominative Case-feature, properly checks off both the weak ϕ-feature and the nominative Case-feature of T at the same time (due to (V)). This can be achieved if the corresponding formal features of Theme move onto T at LF to enter into a checking relation with T. Note that there is no need to worry about the accusative Case-feature of v in this case; for, the verbs that occur in the Dat-Nom pattern lack an accusative Case-feature, just like the Tamil DSC with the Dat-Nom pattern. Also as in the case of the Tamil DSC with the Dat-Nom pattern, the (strictly derivational/local) economy condition demands that the ϕ-feature of Theme, but not that of EXP, should enter into a ϕ-feature checking relation with T; as a result, the nominative Theme always induces subject-agreement (see §4.2.3.2 for detail).

4.3.2.3. Subjecthood of Dative (Quirky) Subjects

In §4.3.1 it was observed that the dative subject in the Icelandic DSC can bind a subject-oriented reflexive and can control. Under the theory of GFs advocated in this book, this can be easily accounted for: As argued in §4.3.2.2, the dative subject has an EPP-feature checking relation with T before Spell-out, and the nominative object enters into a ϕ-feature checking relation with T at LF by the movement of its corresponding feature onto T at LF.

Recall that an element has the ability to control only if it enters into a [+construable]-feature checking relation with T (see §4.2.3.3). Both the dative subject and the nominative object satisfy this; hence, they are endowed with the potential to control. But the nominative object is ranked lower than the dative subject in the hierarchy for the determination of the actual controller (see §4.2.3.3). Accordingly, the dative subject holds the ability to control.

As for the ability to bind a subject-oriented reflexive, the prediction is that it is possessed by the dative subject in the Icelandic DSC. Elsewhere in this book I hypothesized that the ability to bind a subject-oriented reflexive stems from an EPP-feature checking relation with T. Given this hypothesis, it follows that only

---

[37] As was noted before, the subject with a quirky case results from the idiosyncrasy of a particular verb; hence, the QSC with an accusative subject or a genitive subject is derived in the same way described here.

[38] Thus, the nominative object in the Icelandic DSC remains at the complement of the psych-verb in overt syntax. In fact, Harbert and Toribio (1991) provide evidence for this.

the dative subject, but not the nominative object or any other argument in the clause, can bind a subject-oriented reflexive in the Icelandic DSC.

As mentioned, the nominative object morphologically behaves like the ordinary "subject" in two respects: It is marked as nominative and it induces subject-agreement. These two behaviors of the nominative object are straightforwardly explained: The nominative object's Case-feature and ϕ-feature enter into a checking relation with T at LF. This results in the morphologically subject-like properties of the nominative object.

4.3.2.4. Licensing of Nominative Objects

An idea frequently proposed in the literature is that the Case of the nominative object is licensed somehow by Infl (e.g., Hermon 1984, Cowper 1988, Sigurðsson 1989, Harbert and Toribio 1991, Schütze 1993, Jónsson 1994, and Holmberg and Platzak 1995, inter alia), though the proposed implementations of the licensing mechanism differ. The analysis presented in the preceding subsection may be regarded as a variant of this idea.

Harley (1995a,b) argues against this idea, claiming that it leads to an incorrect prediction that the nominative object cannot be licensed in a nonfinite clause, because there is no doubt that T in a nonfinite clause (in Icelandic) has no nominative Case.[39] As the well-formedness of (4.82) shows, the nominative object can appear in a nonfinite clause:

(4.82) *Icelandic* (Andrews 1982: 464)
Barninu$_k$ virðist [t$_k$ hafa   batnað   veikin].
the-child(DAT) seems   have(INF) recovered-from the-disease(NOM)
'The child seems to have recovered from the disease.'

To maintain the idea that finite Infl licenses the nominative object, the dependency from the object position in an embedded clause to the matrix Infl must be established somehow. The apparent problem is, thus, how we can establish such a long-distance dependency. In fact, this may pose a real problem for some approaches, but it is not at all a problem for the analysis I presented here. There is no intervening formal feature between the matrix T (= Infl) and the nominative-marked object in the embedded clause in (4.82). Thus, the Case-feature and the ϕ-feature of the nominative object each can enter into a proper checking relation with T by moving onto T at LF, as required.[40]

---

[39] A similar claim is made by Sprouse (1989). Contrary to these claims, Schütze (1996) remarks that there is no reason to deny on theoretical grounds that a nonfinite T (in Icelandic) may have a nominative Case.

[40] Schütze (1996) points out that there is a problem yet to be solved: There is a case where long-distance agreement between the nominative object in a nonfinite clause and the matrix Infl is possible in spite of the existence of a possible intervenor. One of the solutions he suggested is to assume that a nonfinite T (in Icelandic) may have a nominative Case. If this is the case, the problem is resolved without adding any other proviso to

4.3.3. Passive and Dative Subjects in Germanic

In some Germanic languages (e.g., Icelandic and German), the dative subject appears when a verb that takes a dative-marked object is passivized:

(4.83) *Icelandic*

    a. Transitive (Sigurðsson 1989: 308)

        i. Pall bauð ykkur.
           Paul invited you(DAT.PL)
           'Paul invited you.'

        ii. Ykkur var boðið.
            you(DAT.PL) was(IMP) invited(IMP)
            'You were invited.'

    b. Ditransitive (Sigurðsson 1989: 347)

        i. Olafur sagði mer þessa sögu.
           Olaf(NOM) told me(DAT) this(ACC) story(ACC)
           'Olaf told me this story.'

        ii. Mér var sögð þessi saga.
           me(DAT) was(3SG) told this(NOM) story(NOM)
           Lit. 'Me was told this story.'

(4.84) *German*

    a. Transitive (Haider 1984: 88, 67)

        i. ... daß er ihm half
           COMP he(NOM) him(DAT) helped
           '...that he helped him'

        ii. ... daß ihm geholfen wurde
           COMP him(DAT) helped was(IMP)
           '... that him was helped'

    b. Ditransitive

        i. ... daß er ihm einen Kuchen schenkte
           COMP he(NOM) him(DAT) a cake(ACC) presented
           '...that he presented him a cake'

        ii. ... daß ihm ein Kuchen schenkte wurde.
           COMP him(DAT) a cake(NOM) presented was(3SG)
           '... that him was presented a cake'

In the passive of the ditransitive clause whose subject position is occupied by the dative-marked indirect object (IO), the subject-agreement is induced by the nominative-marked direct object (DO), just as in the case of the DSC:[41]

---

the analysis of the Icelandic DSC presented in this section.

[41] See den Besten (1981) and Müller (1995) for more data concerning passive ditransitive clauses in German.

(4.85) *Icelandic* (Sigurðsson 1989: 348)

    a. Okkur var sögð þessi saga.
       us(DAT) was(3SG) told(F.SG) this story(F.SG.NOM)
       'We were told this story.'

    b. Mér voru sagðar þessar sögur.
       me(DAT) were(3PL) told(F.PL) these stories(F.PL.NOM)
       'I was told these stories.'

(4.86) *German*

    ... daß ihm die Bücher zugeschickt wurden/*wurde
    COMP him(DAT) the books(PL.NOM) sent were(3PL)/was(3SG)
    '... that the books were sent to him'

Note, also, that DO in a passive ditransitive clause cannot stand in accusative, but it must be marked as nominative:

(4.87) a. *Icelandic* (Sigurðsson 1989: 348)

       *Okkur var sögð þessa sögu. (cf. (4.85a))
       us(DAT) was(3SG) told(F.SG) this story(F.SG.ACC)
       'We were told this story.'

    b. *German*

       *... daß ihm einen Kuchen schenkte wurde (cf. (4.84b(ii)))
       COMP him(DAT) a cake(ACC) presented was(3SG)
       '... that a cake was given to him'

These properties of the passive clause with a dative subject[42] can be accounted for with the same mechanism that was employed for the explanation of the Icelandic DSC.[43]

First, suppose that in these languages, IO is assigned dative as an inherent Case with its GOAL-role. This conforms to the fact that IO cannot be accompanied with any preposition such as the equivalent to *to* in English.[44]

(4.88) a. *Icelandic* (Holmberg and Platzak 1995: 188)

       *Ég gaf bók **til** Jóns.
       I gave a book **to** John

       (cf. Ég gaf Jóni bók.
           I gave John a book)

---

[42] The same construction can be found in Dutch (den Besten 1984) and in Faroese (Lockwood 1977).

[43] For the DSC detected in Old/Middle English and its demise in Present-day English, see the appendix to this chapter.

[44] According to Müller (1995), some verbs can take IO with the preposition *an* 'to', though the interpretation of the IO with it somewhat differs from that of the IO without it. Cf. Lederer (1969).

b. *German*

  *... daß Ich einen Kuchen **an** den Vermieter gegeben habe
  COMP I(NOM) a cake(ACC) **to** the landlord(ACC) given have
'... that I have given a cake to the landlord'

(cf. Lederer 1969: chapter D)

 (cf. ... daß Ich dem Vermieter einen Kuchen gegeben habe
   COMP I(NOM) the landlord(DAT) a cake(ACC) given have)

In chapter 7 I will argue that it holds universally good that IO is generated at a higher position than DO, as illustrated in (4.89):[45]

(4.89) [$_{TP}$ T ... [$_{vP}$ SUBJ v [$_{VmidP}$ IO(DAT) V$_{mid}$ [$_{VP}$ V DO]]]]
               (linear order irrelevant)

Given this (see, also, §1.4.2), IO is always closer to T than DO is unless DO is moved into the minimal domain where IO is located.[46] Now suppose that the passive morpheme is attached to v, absorbing its accusative Case-feature, and that SUBJ is syntactically demoted.[47]

(4.90) [$_{TP}$ T ... [$_{vP}$ v-PASS [$_{VmidP}$ IO(DAT) V$_{mid}$ [$_{VP}$ V DO]]]]
               (linear order irrelevant)

Since it is plausible that the EPP-feature of those languages is strong, something must be attracted to the Spec of T before Spell-out. IO, though marked as dative, can check off the EPP-feature (i.e., D-feature) of T, as maintained elsewhere in this chapter; as a consequence, it is attracted to the Spec of T before Spell-out, deriving (4.91):

(4.91) [$_{TP}$ IO(DAT)$_k$ T ... [$_{vP}$ v-PASS [$_{VmidP}$ t$_k$ V$_{mid}$ [$_{VP}$ V DO]]]]
               (linear order irrelevant)

This represents the surface structure of the passive clause with a dative subject in these languages.

 If DO is marked as nominative, (4.91) results in a convergent derivation in the same way as in the case of the Icelandic DSC. If DO is marked as accusative, then in the clause, there is no element that can check off the accusative Case-feature of DO; as a result, it crashes at LF. This is the reason that the nominative-

---

[45] Takano (1996) provides ample evidence in favor of the base-structure for the double object construction illustrated in (4.89). For more discussion, see Takano (1996) and chapter 7 and references cited therein.

[46] This further indicates that DO cannot be moved to the Spec of T by passivization unless DO is precedently moved into the minimal domain where IO is located. Indeed, I will demonstrate in chapter 7 that this is empirically attested.

[47] I am assuming that V$_{mid}$ in those languages has no structural Case (though it assigns an inherent dative Case to its Spec). In addition, following Baker, Johnson, and Roberts (1989), I am tentatively assuming that the external θ-role of v (i.e., Agent) is assigned to the passive morpheme. See Watanabe (1993, 1996) for an extensive study of the mechanism of passive in the minimalist feature-checking theory.

marked DO that is not located at the Spec of T in overt syntax can induce subject-agreement (cf. (4.85) and (4.86)), and that the examples in (4.87) are ill-formed.

It is noteworthy that other Germanic languages such as English and Swedish do not allow the non-nominative IO to occur at the Spec of T in overt syntax.

(4.92)   a.   *English*

*Him was/were given the dolls.   (cf. He was given the dolls.)

       b.   *Swedish* (Holmberg and Platzak 1995: 126)

*Honom blev givet/givna   hästarna.
him   was   give(SG)/give(PL)   the-horses
'He was given the horses.'

(cf. Han blev givet   hästarna.
      he   was   give(SG)   the-horses)

I would like to suggest that this is due to the fact that the Case of IO is structural in languages like English or Swedish. This sharply contrasts with Icelandic and German, in which IO is assigned an inherent dative Case. Thus, IO in Icelandic and German cannot be accompanied by the preposition 'to' if it appears as the Goal argument of the ditransitive predicate, as observed in (4.88). This is because the dative Case-assignment depends on the Goal-role assignment in Icelandic and German. It is also plausible that IO can appear together with the preposition 'to' in English and Swedish because the Case of IO is independent of the Goal-role assignment in these languages:

(4.93)   a.   *English*

Mary gave the dolls **to** Mary.   (cf. Mary gave Mary the dolls.)

       b.   *Swedish* (Holmberg and Platzak 1995: 188)

Jag gav en bok **till** Johan.
I   gave a   book **to** John

(cf. Jag gav Johan en bok.
      I   gave John   a   book)

Given that IO is marked structurally in English and Swedish, the ill-formedness of the examples in (4.92) naturally follows: Because the passive morpheme absorbs one of the structural Cases of the ditransitive verb, there is no way to assign/check more than one non-nominative structural Case in a passivized ditransitive clause in those languages.[48]

Before we go on to the next subsection, it is important to note that the nominative-marked DO also can occur at the Spec of T in Icelandic and Germanic (cf. Andrews 1982 and Zaenen, Maling, and Thráinsson 1985 for Icelandic,

---

[48] See chapter 7 for extensive discussion on passives of ditransitives in English and Swedish.

and den Besten 1984 and Grewendorf 1989 for German). Consider (4.94) and (4.95):

(4.94) *Icelandic* (Andrews 1982: 481)

    a. Bíllinn var syndur henni.
       the-car(NOM) was shown her(DAT)
       'The car was shown to her.'

    b. Henni var syndur bíllinn.
       her(DAT) was shown the-car(NOM)
       Lit. 'Her was shown the car.'

(4.95) *German*

    a. ... daß das Buch ihm gegeben wurde
       COMP the book(NOM) him(DAT) given was(3SG)
       '... that the book was given to him'

    b. ... daß ihm das Buch gegeben wurde
       COMP him(DAT) the book(NOM) given was(3SG)
       '... that him was given the book'

Why is it that either the nominative-marked DO or the dative-marked IO can be promoted to the Spec of T by passivization in those languages?

In chapter 7 I will argue that the promotion of DO to the Spec of T by passivization is possible only when DO can be moved to the minimal domain where IO is located. Take Norwegian and Danish, for example. In Norwegian, DO as well as IO can be promoted by passivization, as will be observed in chapter 7. In fact, there is evidence which shows that DO can be moved to the minimal domain where IO is located; that is, DO can undergo overt object shift in Norwegian. In contrast, DO cannot undergo overt object shift in Danish; therefore, DO cannot be promoted by passivization in Danish, as I will argue in chapter 7.

Returning to Icelandic and German, it is possible to find evidence which shows that DO can undergo overt object shift in those languages (see Collins and Thráinsson 1993, 1996 and Bobaljik 1995b for Icelandic, and Dikken 1995 and Müller 1995 for German):

(4.96) *Icelandic* (Collins and Thráinsson 1993: 34)

    a. Hann gaf konunginum ambáttina.
       he(NOM) gave the-king(DAT) the-maidservant(ACC)
       'He gave the king the maidservant.'

    b. Hann gaf ambáttina$_k$ konunginum t$_k$.
       he(NOM) gave the-maidservant(ACC) the-king(DAT)

(4.97) *German* (Dikken 1995: 220)

    a. Der Hans gav der Maria das Buch.
       ART Hans(NOM) gave ART Mary(DAT) the book(ACC)
       'Hans gave Mary the book.'

b. Der Hans   gav   das Buch$_k$ der Maria   t$_k$.
   ART Hans(NOM) gave the book(ACC) ART Mary(DAT)

As argued in chapter 7, I interpret this fact as showing that V_{mid} within the three-layered VP-shell for a ditransitive verb may tolerate an unforced violation of Procrastinate (see chapter 7 for detail). Given this, at some stage in the derivation of the passive clause of a ditransitive verb in those languages, the following structure may appear:

(4.98)   [$_{TP}$ T ... [$_{vP}$ v-PASS [$_{VmidP}$ DO(NOM)$_k$ IO(DAT) V_{mid} [$_{VP}$ V t$_k$]]]]
(linear order irrelevant)

In (4.98), DO and IO are equidistant from T; therefore, either of them can be attracted by T to T's Spec. This optionality results in the word-order alternation shown in (4.94) and (4.95).

Note, in passing, that not all of the ditransitive predicates in Icelandic and German take the Dat-Acc pattern as their complements. Interestingly, ditransitive verbs that do not take this pattern may not allow DO's overt object shift:

(4.99) *Icelandic*

   a. Ég   lofaði   Ólafi   bilnum.
      I(NOM) promised Olaf(DAT) the-car(DAT)
      'I promised Olaf the car.'

   b. *Ég   lofaði   bilnum$_k$ Ólafi   t$_k$.
      I(NOM) promised the-car(DAT) Olaf(DAT)

(4.100) *German*

   a. Sie   haben den Jungen   das Lied   gelehrt.
      they(NOM) have the boy(ACC) the song(ACC) taught
      'They have taught the boy the song.'

   b. *Sie   haben das Lied$_k$ den Jungen t$_k$ gelehrt.
      they(NOM) have the song(ACC) the boy(ACC)   taught
      'They have taught the boy the song.'

Our theory, thus, leads to the prediction that, while IO in those examples can be promoted by passivization, DO cannot. This prediction is, indeed, borne out:

(4.101) *Icelandic* (Andrews 1982: 480)

   a. Henni   var lofað   bilnum.
      her(DAT) was promised the-car(DAT)
      'She was promised the car.'

   b. *Bilnum   var lofað   henni.
      the-car(DAT) was promised her(DAT)
      Lit. 'The car was promised her.'

(4.102) *German*

    a. ... dann ist der Jungen   das Lied   gelehrt worden
         then is the boy(NOM) the song(ACC) taught been
         '... then the boy was taught the song'

    b. *... dann ist den Jungen   das Lied   gelehrt worden
         then is the boy(ACC) the song(NOM) taught been
         Lit. '... then the song was taught the boy'

This fact, too, lends support to the analysis presented here.

4.3.4. Experiencer Inversion in Dutch

Koster (1978) points out that a limited class of verbs allow their object to precede their subject in an active clause.[49] The class may correspond almost to psych-verbs, according to Levin (1985b).[50] Whereas ordinary transitive (unergative) predicates disallow this inversion (as in (4.103)), one type of psych-verbs (or ergative verbs) allow it, as shown in (4.104):[51]

(4.103) *Dutch* (Hoekstra 1984: 188)

    a. ... dat de jongen   een auto   zag
         COMP the boy(NOM) a   car(OBJ) saw
         '... that the boy saw a car'

    b. *... dat   een auto   de jongen   zag
         COMP a   car(OBJ) the boy(NOM) saw

(4.104) *Dutch* (Hoekstra 1984: 187)

    a. ... dat die fout   de schoolmeester   opviel
         COMP that mistake(NOM) the school-teacher(OBJ) struck
         '... that that mistake struck the school teacher'

    b. ... dat de schoolmeester   die fout   opviel.
         COMP the school-teacher(OBJ) that mistake(NOM) struck

From the fact that the clause at issue is embedded, it is evident that (4.104b) is not derived from (4.104a) by the topicalization of the objective-marked EXP and that (4.104a) is not derived from (4.104b) by the topicalization of the

---

[49] In a passivized ditransitive clause IO can precede SUBJ (i.e., Agent) in Dutch, as it can in Icelandic and German (cf. Koster 1978 and den Besten 1984). Cf. §4.3.3.

[50] According to den Besten (1984), Hoekstra (1984) and, especially, Broekhuis (1992), it is more precise to regard those verbs that allow this kind of OBJ's permutation not as psych-verbs, but as ergative verbs.

[51] There is no morphophonological distinction between accusative and dative in Dutch, which is the reason that I use OBJ 'objective' to refer to the case of objects in Dutch. Incidentally, a similar type of inversion can be found in German, too, under the same conditions (cf. den Besten 1984 and Safir 1985).

nominative-marked Theme. The following fact also confirms that Theme occupies the Spec of T in (4.104a) and that EXP occupies the Spec of T in (4.104b):

(4.105) *Dutch* (Levin 1985b: 38)

    a. Zullen deze boeken u bevallen?
        will these books(NOM) you(OBJ) please
        'Will these books please you?'

    b. Zullen u deze boeken bevallen?
        will you(OBJ) these books(NOM) please

If either EXP or Theme were topicalized, either of the examples in (4.105) would be ungrammatical; for, a yes-no question cannot coincide with topicalization (Levin 1985b).

It can therefore be concluded that either the objective-marked EXP or the nominative-marked Theme in a clause with a psych-verb in Dutch can appear at the Spec of T in overt syntax. Here it is important to note that, in spite of the fact just observed, it is the nominative-marked Theme that always induces subject-agreement irrespective of whether EXP or Theme occupies the Spec of T in overt syntax, as Levin (1985b) points out:

(4.106) *Dutch* (Levin 1985b: 37)

    a. Deze boeken bevallen hem.
        these books(NOM.PL) please(PL) him(OBJ.SG)
        'These books please him.'

    b. Hem bevallen deze boeken.
        him(OBJ.SG) please(PL) these books(NOM.PL)

Now I propose that v and V in the two-layered VP-shell for Dutch psych-verbs undergo restructuring in the manner delineated in (4.107):

(4.107) a. ... [$_{vP}$ EXP(OBJ) v [$_{VP}$ V Theme(NOM)]] (linear order irrelevant)

      b. ... [$_{v-VP}$ EXP(OBJ) v–V Theme(NOM)] (linear order irrelevant)

It is important to note that this process of restructuring should be distinguished from head-movement. Unlike the assumption made by Chomsky (1992), I am assuming, following Chomsky (1995a), that head-movement cannot extend a minimal domain. The important point here is that, as the result of restructuring, EXP and Theme fall into the same minimal domain.

Now suppose that, as in the Icelandic DSC, EXP is assigned an inherent dative Case by v and a psych-verb has no accusative Case in Dutch. Then, either of them can move overtly to the Spec of T in overt syntax to check off the strong EPP-feature; for, they are equidistant from T. If EXP is moved there in overt syntax, the Case-feature and φ-feature of Theme are moved onto T at LF to enter into a proper checking relation with T. If Theme is moved to the Spec of T in overt syntax, then nothing is moved at LF. In either case, T's φ-feature is checked off by the nominative-marked Theme; therefrom, it follows that the nominative-marked Theme always induces subject-agreement irrespective of its surface position.⁵²

4.4. Theoretical Implications of DSC

4.4.1. Inversion in Germanic and Local Economy

In §4.3.4 it was observed that the EXP(OBJ)-Theme(NOM) order and the Theme(NOM)-EXP(OBJ) order freely alternate in a clause with a psych-verb in Dutch; it was also observed, in §4.3.3, that the IO(DAT)-DO(NOM) order and the DO(NOM)-IO(DAT) order freely alternate in a passive ditransitive clause in Icelandic and German. I argued that in both cases, there is a stage in the derivation where the two arguments in question are in the same minimal domain. They are delineated as in (4.108):

(4.108) a. Experiencer Inversion in Dutch

$[_{TP}$ T ..... $[_{v\text{-}VP}$ EXP(OBJ) v–V Theme(NOM)]]
(linear order irrelevant)

b. Indirect Object Inversion in Icelandic and German

$[_{TP}$ T ..... $[_{vP}$ v-PASS $[_{VmidP}$ DO(NOM)$_k$ IO(DAT) V_{mid} $[_{VP}$ V t_k]]]]
(linear order irrelevant)

Note that the Theme-EXP order is derived from (4.108a) by the movement of Theme to the Spec of T before Spell-out; that is, only one step from the stage illustrated in (4.108a) is necessary for convergence at LF. In order to derive the EXP-Theme order, on the other hand, two steps from the stage in (4.108a) are necessary for convergence: One is the movement of EXP to the Spec of T before Spell-out and the other is the feature-movement of the Case and φ-features of Theme onto T at LF. The same holds true in the derivations of Icelandic and German indirect-object inversion: Only one step from the stage illustrated in (4.108b) is necessary to derive the convergent DO-IO order, but two steps are necessary to derive the convergent IO-DO order.

It is commonly alleged that the general economy condition prefers fewer steps. According to this view, the aforementioned account of the inversion phenomena cannot be tenable; the derivation with fewest steps blocks the derivations with more steps. However, one should notice that counting steps involved

---

⁵² Thus far I have neglected the reason for the impossibility of the alternation shown in (4.103); namely, the impossibility of the permutation of the SUBJ-OBJ order in a clause whose predicate is an ordinary transitive unergative verb (cf. Hoekstra 1984 and Broekhuis 1992). At first glance this is due to the property of unergative verbs which precludes the restructuring process. But the problem arises, because Dutch allows (optional) overt object shift (Bobaljik 1995b), which gives rise to a situation in which SUBJ and OBJ are in the same minimal domain even in a transitive unergative clause. This, in turn, leads to the incorrect prediction that the permutation of SUBJ-OBJ order is possible even in a transitive unergative clause. I will return directly to this issue in §4.4.2.

in a derivation obviously makes the economy condition global, which should be avoided in the minimalist program I am assuming in this book (see Collins 1995b, 1996 and Ura 1994b, 1995c, 1997a). It is important to note that if we take the general economy condition as strictly derivational/local, the above problem does not arise at all: At the next step from the stage illustrated in (4.108), the two possible operations are equally economical because they are Attract/Move from the same minimal domain to the same target (i.e., the Spec of T), which is motivated by the checking of the same feature (i.e., the strong EPP-feature). Although only one of the two derivations at issue necessarily involves another step at LF, this surplus step in the derivation is not considered by the general economy condition defined as strictly derivational/local. Therefore, the inversion phenomena observed in §4.3.3 and §4.3.4 lend strong support to the claim that the general economy condition should be defined as strictly derivational/local.

4.4.2. Icelandic DSC and Bantu Inverse

In §2.1.3 I discussed the reason that Icelandic disallows the type of inverse construction found in Bantu. Recall that the Bantu inverse results from the fact that OBJ overtly moves to a Spec of v owing to the strong nominal feature of v with SUBJ being generated at another Spec of v (see §2.1 for details). As I will extensively argue in chapters 7 and 8, my hypothesis concerning optional object shift is that it results from the fact that OBJ may be moved to a Spec of v owing to v's property that allows v to tolerate an unforced violation of Procrastinate. Now that Icelandic allows optional object shift (Holmberg 1986 and Vikner 1994), the following situation may emerge in Icelandic:[53]

(4.109) $[_{TP}$ T ... $[_{vP}$ OBJ$_k$ SUBJ v $[_{VP}$ V t_k]]]

Notice that this situation also emerges during the derivation for Bantu inverse, as argued in chapter 2.

The Bantu inverse is derived from (4.109) by the movement of OBJ to the Spec of T before Spell-out. Thanks to the stipulation that T's ϕ-feature as well as its EPP-feature in Bantu is strong, OBJ at the Spec of T induces subject-agreement. At LF, the nominative Case-feature of SUBJ moves onto T; thereby, the derivation converges.

As I argued in §4.3, T's EPP-feature is strong but its ϕ-feature, as well as its nominative Case-feature, is weak in Icelandic. Now let us return to (4.109) and suppose that it happens in Icelandic. Then, either OBJ or SUBJ in (4.109) can be attracted to the Spec of T by T's strong EPP-feature before Spell-out, because they are equidistant from T. If OBJ is attracted, the derivation converges if SUBJ's ϕ-feature and nominative Case-feature move onto T at LF to enter into a proper checking relation with T. This derivation results in a type of inverse construction, in which the accusative-marked OBJ occupies the Spec of T in surface

---

[53] Here I ignore the hierarchical/linear order of SUBJ and the shifted OBJ, which is irrelevant to the discussion that follows.

structure and the nominative-marked SUBJ induces subject-agreement. This construction does not exist in Icelandic, however. Therefore, this putative derivation should be precluded in Icelandic.

Chomsky (fall 1995 class lecture) suggested that the derivation for this putative Icelandic inverse construction is precluded by the economy condition. For it involves more steps than the derivation in which SUBJ in (4.109) moves overtly to the Spec of T. This latter derivation needs no LF movement. This account encounters two big problems, however: First, it employs global economy. Second, but more important, the same reasoning leads to the incorrect prediction that the economy condition applies also to the Bantu inverse, and it always selects active over inverse because active involves fewer steps than inverse. Then, how can we preclude the derivation of the putative Icelandic inverse sketched above without recourse to global economy?

Here I propose a parameter to cope with this problem.[54] There are two types of languages in terms of the parameter concerning DP's formal features and their morphological property. The parameter is set in the following manner: If a language L has a positive value in terms of this parameter, L must observe the condition on DP's formal feature checking, which is stated in (4.110); if L is negative in terms of this parameter, L may violate the condition.

(4.110) **Condition on DP's Formal Feature**

> If DP has a structural Case-feature, its D-feature cannot enter into a checking relation with any other element than the one that has a Case-feature checking relation with it.

The rationale of this condition is that it requires DP to have its D-feature checked off together with its structural Case-feature. This condition is not so unnatural because Case-features are assigned to or possessed by DP (but not N, D, or NP) and DP is a locus of D-feature. Hence the parameter proposed above states that there are two types of languages: DP's D-feature checking must go with its structural Case-feature checking in some languages, while it is allowed not to go with its structural Case-feature checking in the others.[55]

With this parameter in mind, let us return to the putative inverse construction in Icelandic. The parameter enables us to preclude its derivation, as required, if Icelandic has a positive value in terms of this parameter. Recall that in the derivation for the putative inverse in Icelandic, OBJ is first moved overtly to a Spec of v. OBJ may undergo this movement due to the fact that the nominal feature of v is weak but it tolerates an unforced violation of Procrastinate. But note that in order for OBJ to be attracted overtly to a Spec of v, OBJ must enter into an accusative Case-feature checking relation with v when it lands at that position; otherwise, the "Last Resort" part of the definition of Attract/Move is violated. Hence OBJ inevitably has its accusative Case-feature checked off at

---

[54] This solution, too, was originally suggested in Chomsky's fall 1995 class lecture.

[55] Crucially, the condition (4.110) allows DP's structural Case-feature checking to go independently of its D-feature checking.

this position. Given this, OBJ cannot move up from there to the Spec of T before Spell-out to check off the strong EPP-feature of T owing to the Icelandic parameter setting. Since the overt movement of OBJ from a Spec of v to the Spec of T in (4.109), repeated here as (4.111), is precluded this way, the reason follows that the putative inverse in Icelandic does not exist.

(4.111) [$_{TP}$ T ... [$_{vP}$ OBJ$_k$ SUBJ v [$_{VP}$ V t_k]]]

Case-feature checking

This account of the nonexistence of inverse in Icelandic does not preclude the Bantu inverse if the parameter setting in terms of the condition in (4.110) is negative in Bantu. In Bantu OBJ in (4.111) can move up to the Spec of T before Spell-out to check off the strong EPP-feature (and φ-feature) of T because DP's D-feature can safely enter into a checking relation with an element that is different from the element with which it enters into a Case-feature checking relation.

Moreover, the above account does not spoil the analysis of the DSC in Icelandic presented in this chapter. In §4.3 I demonstrated that the derivation for the Icelandic DSC involves the stage illustrated in (4.112):

(4.112) [$_{TP}$ T ... [$_{vP}$ EXP(DAT) v [$_{VP}$ V Theme(NOM)]]]

The dative-marked EXP is moved to the Spec of T before Spell-out to check off the strong EPP-feature of T. At LF the φ-feature and nominative Case-feature of the nominative-marked Theme move up onto T to enter into a checking relation with T. These operations trivially satisfy the condition in (4.110); for, the dative assigned to EXP is an inherent Case, so that EXP safely checks off the EPP-feature of T without violating (4.110). The nominative feature of Theme also safely enters into a checking relation with T. Even though Icelandic has a positive value for the parameter at issue, the structural Case-checking may be independent of the EPP-feature checking (but not vice versa (cf. footnote 55)).

Last, it is interesting to consider the problem mentioned in footnote 53: Why is it that the SUBJ-OBJ permutation is not allowed in a transitive unergative clause in Dutch? This was somewhat mysterious at that time, but by assuming that the aforementioned parameter is positive in Dutch, it can be easily explained.

As shown in (4.113), OBJ in a transitive unergative clause may optionally undergo overt object shift in Dutch (cf. Wyngaerd 1989, Neeleman 1994, Bobaljik 1995b, and references cited therein).[56]

---

[56] There is a controversy, though, as to whether object shift in Dutch is a real A-movement or not. It has an equivocal status between object shift in Scandinavian languages, which counts as a pure A-movement, and short object-scrambling in German, which counts as an A-bar movement (cf. Wyngaerd 1989, Vikner 1994, and Müller 1995 for relevant discussion).

(4.113) *Dutch* (Bobaljik 1995b: 75)
    a. ... dat veel mensen [$_{VP}$ gisteren [$_{VP}$ dat boek gekocht]] hennen
        COMP many people   yesterday that book bought   have
       '... that many people bought that book yesterday'
    b. ... dat veel mensen dat boek$_k$ [$_{VP}$ gisteren [$_{VP}$ t$_k$ gekocht]] hennen
        COMP many people that book   yesterday   bought   have

My hypothesis about optional object shift leads to the conclusion that SUBJ and OBJ are in the same minimal domain at some stage in the derivation before Spell-out, as illustrated in (4.114):

(4.114) [$_{TP}$ T ... [$_{vP}$ OBJ$_k$ SUBJ v [$_{VP}$ V t$_k$]]]

As I argued earlier, OBJ at a Spec of v in (4.114) has to have its structural (i.e., accusative) Case-feature checked off when it is moved there. As a consequence, it can never be attracted by the strong EPP-feature of T owing to the Dutch parameter that does not allow DP's D-feature to enter into a checking relation independently of its structural Case-feature checking relation. Then, the accusative-marked OBJ can never occupy the Spec of T with the nominative-marked SUBJ being within VP in a transitive unergative clause in Dutch.[57]

4.5. Summary

In this chapter I investigated the syntactic derivations of the DSCs found in various languages, and demonstrated that the GF-splitting phenomenon involved in the DSC in each type of language can be consistently accounted for by the hypothesis concerning GFs plus the theory of multiple feature checking. Moreover, I showed that the differences among the syntactic behaviors of the DSCs can be deduced from a very small set of simple parametric variations.

---

[57] In fact, there are cases in which the accusative OBJ and the nominative SUBJ freely alternate in terms of their surface position in Dutch (and German). However, even in those cases, it holds true that the verbs involved are transitive ergatives, according to den Besten (1984) and Broekhuis (1992). I leave it open here to investigate the issue further. See den Besten (1984), Hoekstra (1984), Grewendorf (1989), and Broekhuis (1992) for discussions.

Appendix A
Old English and Historical Change

As I mentioned in §4.3.1, there is a kind of DSC in Old/Middle English, which has been sometimes regarded as "impersonal" (cf. Elmer 1981, Fischer and van der Leek 1983, Lightfoot 1991, Denison 1993, Allen 1995, and Kim 1996, inter alia).[58] Some examples[59] are:[60]

(4.115) *Old English* (Denison 1993: 72)

    hu him se sige gelicade
    how him(DAT) the victory(NOM) pleased
    'how the victory had pleased him'

(4.116) *Middle English* (Allen 1995: 242)

    and þat hem likede here lodliche sinnes
    and COMP him liked their loathsome sins
    'and that their loathsome sins pleased them'

It is very interesting to note that, despite the fact that the dative EXP occurs at the clause-initial position (i.e., the Spec of T) in Old and Middle English (cf. Fischer and van der Leek 1983 and Lightfoot 1991),[61] the DSC in Old English differs strikingly from the one in Middle English in the following respect: Whereas it is the nominative Theme that induces subject-agreement in Old English, it is the dative EXP that induces it in Middle English. This contrast is shown by the examples in (4.117):

(4.117) a. *Old English* (Denison 1993: 74)

    þam cynge licondon peran
    the king(DAT.SG) pleased(PL) pears(NOM.PL)
    'the king liked pears'

---

[58] See, especially, Denison (1993) for ample examples and a detailed summary and discussion on the previous analyses of the construction at issue.

[59] Here I will merely cite the secondary source of each Old/Middle English example presented. For its primary source, see the reference cited.

[60] Note that Middle English lacks the dative Case morphology. The dative became marked morphologically as oblique and later as objective. Cf. Kemenade (1987) and Allen (1995).

[61] Allen (1995) extensively argues, with ample data, that the dative EXP in the clause-initial position in Old/Middle English bears subjecthood. In this book I assume that her claim is right, without any argument. Cf., also, Fischer and van der Leek (1983) and Lightfoot (1991).

b. *Middle English* (Allen 1995: 263)

   how that   hem   oughten   have greet repentaunce
   how COMP them(DAT) ought(PL) have great repentance
   'How they should have great repentance'

Here I am showing that this historical change in English can be accounted for by a simple parametric change in terms of DSC.[62]

It is noteworthy that the DSC in Old English resembles the DSC in Icelandic in that the dative EXP behaves syntactically as "subject" despite the fact that the nominative Theme induces subject-agreement. In contrast, the DSC in Middle English resembles the DSC in Japanese and Korean in that the dative EXP behaves syntactically and morphologically as "subject" in that it induces subject-agreement. Thus, it is natural to assume that the parameters involved in the Old English DSC are the same as in the Icelandic DSC; that is, (1) T's EPP-feature is strong; (2) T's nominative-feature and φ-feature are both weak; and (3) v in the two-layered VP-shell for a verb that occurs in the DSC assigns a dative Case to EXP as an inherent Case, and it has no accusative Case-feature. Given these parameters, the DSC in Old English is properly derived: The dative EXP is moved to the Spec of T in overt syntax to check off T's strong EPP-feature. Due to (2), the dative EXP does not check off the φ-feature and Case-feature of T. At LF, the φ-feature and Case-feature of the nominative Theme move onto T, resulting in its agreement with T.

And the parameters for the DSC in Middle English are: (1') T's EPP-feature is strong; (2') T's φ-feature is strong, but its nominative-feature is weak; (3') v in the two-layered VP-shell for a verb that occurs in the DSC assigns a dative Case to EXP as an inherent Case, and it has no accusative Case-feature; and (4') T's nominative Case-feature checking may be independent of its φ-feature checking. Given these parameters, the derivation for the DSC in Middle English are as follows: The dative EXP is attracted to the Spec of T in overt syntax due to T's strong EPP-feature. Due to (2') the dative EXP at the Spec of T checks off T's strong φ-feature, too; as a result, the subject-agreement is induced by the dative EXP. At LF the Case-feature of the nominative Theme moves onto T to enter into a proper checking relation with T.

Given the above parameters for the DSC in Old English and those for the one in Middle English, it is easy to find the parametric difference between them: (2) and (2') differ, and all others are the same. To put it differently, the diachronic change from Old English to Middle English proceeded in the following fashion:[63]

---

[62] As a matter of fact, the things concerned in this historical change of the English DSC (or impersonal in general) are more complicated, as is usually the case with diachronic syntax (cf. Lightfoot 1979). See Elmer (1981), Lightfoot (1991), and, especially, Allen (1995) for detailed discussion on the issue.

[63] Because the expletive *there* does not check off T's φ-feature in Present-day English (Chomsky 1995a), it is very important to assume that T's φ-feature becomes weak, once again, in Present-day English. I leave it to future research to investigate the highly in-

(4.118)

	Old English	Middle English
T's EPP-feature	strong	strong
T's f-feature	**weak**	***strong***
T's Case-feature	weak	weak

Now the next (big) question is: Why is it that the DSC has totally demised in Present-day English (PdE)? Here I would like to stipulate that it is due to the fact that the dative in PdE loses its former ability to check off an EPP-feature. Let us consider the derivation for a clause with a psych-verb in PdE:

(4.119) [$_{TP}$ T ... [$_{vP}$ EXP(DAT) v [$_{VP}$ V Theme(NOM)]]]

If the dative EXP in (4.119) has no ability to check off an EPP-feature, the element with a D-feature that is closest to T in (4.119) is the nominative Theme. Note that T's φ-feature is weak in PdE (Chomsky 1995a), the dative EXP is not attracted by that feature to the Spec of T before Spell-out even if it has the ability to check off a φ-feature. Thus, the nominative Theme is attracted to the Spec of T before Spell-out in PdE to check off T's strong EPP-feature; thereby, (4.120) is derived:

(4.120) [$_{TP}$ Theme(NOM)$_k$ T ... [$_{vP}$ EXP(DAT) v [$_{VP}$ V t_k]]]

The derivation in (4.120) converges because all the residual formal features that need checking can be properly checked off at LF (that is, the φ-feature and Case-feature of T are checked off by the nominative Theme). As exemplified by (4.121), (4.120) corresponds to a clause with a psych-verb in PdE, as expected:[64]

(4.121) *Present-day English*
    a. It(NOM.SG) pleases(SG) them(DAT.PL).
    b. These toys(Theme) please the baby(EXP).

This may count as a minimalist reformulation of Belletti and Rizzi's (1988) theory of psych-verb constructions.

One should notice that I am assuming that psych-verbs like *please, surprise*, and so forth, assign EXP dative as an inherent Case and that it has no accusative Case-feature (see Grimshaw 1990 for the list of this type of verb). Some psych-verbs, which diachronically assigned an inherent dative Case to EXP in the Old/Middle English period, no longer retain that property and have gained a new property as ordinary transitive unergative verbs. Verbs like *like, fear*, and so forth are examples of such verbs (see Grimshaw 1990 and, especially, Martin 1991 for the list of such verbs):

---

triguing question as to why it goes back to weak.

[64] Note that the dative in PdE is morphologically not differentiated from the accusative.

(4.122) *Present-day English*
    a. The baby(EXP) likes these toys(Theme).
    b. *These toys like(s) the baby.
    c. Mary(EXP) feared the situation(Theme).
    d. *The situation feared Mary.
       (cf. The situation scared Mary.)

Since I stipulate that the dative EXP in a clause with a psych-verb of the *please*-type in PdE cannot check off an EPP-feature, it leads to the prediction that the dative EXP in such a clause cannot be promoted to the Spec of T anyhow. This is borne out by the fact that it cannot be promoted by syntactic passivization.[65]

(4.123) *Present-day English*
    a. *John was surprised by that news.
    b. *John was pleased by that toy.
    c. *Mary was scared by the situation.
       (cf. The situation was feared by Mary.)

This fact thus conforms to the analysis of the *please*-type psych-verbs in PdE presented here.

Appendix B
DSCs (QSCs) in Other Languages

In this appendix I will just round up DSCs (and QSCs) from other languages. No attempt will be made to provide any detailed analysis of them, though brief comments will be made as to how they are accounted for under the theory of multiple feature checking. This appendix is intended to give a quick overview of the relevant facts cross-linguistically.

1. Russian and Polish

According to Bailyn (1991) and Kondrashova (1993), the dative EXP in the DSCs in Russian occupies the Spec of Infl (= T) in overt syntax. They indepen-

---

[65] These verbs can be used in an adjectival passive clause, as in (i) (cf. Wasow 1977, Belletti and Rizzi 1988, and Grimshaw 1990):
  (i) a. John was very (*much) surprised at that news.
      b. John was very (*much) pleased with that toy.

Though, see Pesetsky (1995) and Bouchard (1995) for arguments against this claim (cf., also, Postal 1971). For the distinction between syntactic passive and adjectival passive, see Wasow (1977) and Levin and Rappaport (1986).

dently provide the following arguments in favor of this claim: (1) The dative subject can control, and (2) it can bind a subject-oriented reflexive.[66] The relevant data are cited below:

(4.124) *Russian*

    a. Borisu$_k$ nravitsja igrat' muzyku [PRO$_k$ golym].
          Boris(DAT) like(IMP) play(INF) music(ACC) nude(INST)
          'Boris likes to play music nude.' (Bailyn 1991: 86)

    b. [PRO$_k$ pridja domaoji], Vove stalo
          coming(ASP) home Vova(DAT) get(PAST.ASP.IMP)
          skuchno.
          boring(IMP)
          'On coming home, Vova got bored.' (Kondrashova 1993: 210)

(4.125) *Russian* (Bailyn 1991: 88)

    Saše$_k$ ponravilsja vrač$_i$ u sebja$_{k/*i}$.
    Sasha(DAT) liked doctor(NOM) at self(OBL)
    Lit. 'Sahsa$_k$ liked the doctr$_i$ at self's place$_{k/*i}$.'

Furthermore, when Theme in a DSC, if any, is marked as nominative, it always induces subject-agreement; otherwise, the default impersonal agreement appears (Franks and Greenberg 1988):

(4.126) *Russian*

    a. i. Saše nravjatsja knigi.
             Sasha(DAT) like(3PL) book(PL)
             'Sasha likes books.' (Bailyn 1991: 81)

        ii. Borisu$_k$ nravitsja igrat' muzyku [PRO$_k$ golym].
             Boris(DAT) like(IMP) play(INF) music(ACC) nude(INST)
             'Boris likes to play music nude.' (Bailyn 1991: 86)

    b. i. Saše nužen vrač.
             Sasha(DAT.F) need(M.SG) doctor(NOM.M.SG)
             'Sasha needs a doctor.'

        ii. Saše nužno vrača.
             Sasha(DAT.F) need(IMP) doctor(ACC.M.SG) (Bailyn 1991: 82)

These properties indicate that the DSCs in Russian resembles the Tamil DSCs, which were observed in §4.2.[67]

---

[66] The Russian reflexive anaphora are strictly subject-oriented, according to Rappaport (1986).

[67] Like Icelandic, Russian allows QSCs (such as the one with an accusative- or genitive-marked EXP) in addition to pure DSCs. Interestingly, Preslar (1994) indicates that only the dative-marked EXP shows subjecthood in Russian QSCs/DSCs. Although this issue is worth pursuing, I will leave it to future research.

According to Dziwirek (1994), the DSCs in Polish, another familiar Slavic language, behave the same as the ones in Russian:[68] The dative subject in the Polish DSCs can control and can bind a subject-oriented reflexive.[69]

2. Hindi (and Other Indo-Aryan Languages)

Hindi(-Urdu) and other Indo-Aryan languages like Bengali (Klaiman 1981), Kashimir (Bhatt 1993), Marathi (Pandharipande 1990), and others. (cf. Masica 1976) abound with several types of DSCs and more radical QSCs (cf. articles gathered in Verma and Mohanan 1990). In Hindi, the subject-agreement in the DSC is induced by the nominative Theme if it appears in the clause; otherwise, the default (impersonal) agreement appears (Gair and Wali 1989 and Mohanan 1994). According to Davison (1985), Kachru (1990), and Mohanan (1994), however, the dative subject in Hindi (and other Indo-Aryan languages) possesses the ability to bind a subject-oriented reflexive and the ability to control.

These facts suggest that the DSCs in Hindi and other Indo-Aryan languages resemble the Tamil (and other Dravidian) ones, which were observed in §4.2. In fact, many authors (e.g., Masica 1976 and Abbi 1990, among others) have pointed out that both language groups are classified together in terms of the DSC. If so, it leads to the conclusion that the dative subject in Indo-Aryan occupies the Spec of T in overt syntax, just as in the case in Tamil. And some authors, such as Davison (1985) and Bhatt (1993), reached the same conclusion.[70]

3. Italian (and Spanish)

In the literature it has been reported that, although the dative subject (i.e., EXP) in the Italian DSC[71] possesses rich abilities to control (cf. Perlmutter 1984), it fails to bind a reflexive and fails to induce subject-agreement (cf. Perlmutter

---

[68] For the sake of space, I omit citing relevant data in Polish. See Dziwirek (1994) for ample data and discussion.

[69] Interestingly enough, according to Fried (1994), Czech, another Slavic language, allows a DSC, but the dative subject fails to show the properties such as the ability to control and the ability to bind a subject-oriented reflexive. A possible speculation is that the dative-marked EXP in Czech, like the one in PdE, cannot check an EPP-feature. More investigations are obviously needed. Cf. Franks (1995) for some relevant discussions on DSCs in Slavic languages.

[70] In Hindi a construction syntactically similar to the DSC can be found, which Mahajan (1995) calls "ACTIVE passive." See Mahajan (1995, to appear) for details. The transitive clause with an ergative-marked subject in Hindi has several syntactic properties in common with the DSC, too. Cf. Mohanan (1994) and Mahajan (1989, 1996) for discussion. See Chapter 6 where I will devote myself to investigating ergative languages under the theory of multiple feature checking.

[71] Some particular class of psych-verbs can allow a DSC in Italian (see Perlmutter 1984 and Belletti and Rizzi 1988).

1984 and Belletti and Rizzi 1988).[72] Under the hypothesis concerning GFs, if an element has an ability to control, then it has a [+construable]-feature checking relation with T. From the fact that Theme induces subject-agreement in the Italian DSC, it can be deduced that the dative subject has no ϕ-feature checking relation with T. This, in turn, implies that the dative subject has an EPP-feature checking relation with T in Italian. Indeed, this is compatible with the conclusion of Calabrese (1986) and Belletti and Rizzi (1988) that the dative subject occurs at the Spec of T (= Infl) in overt syntax. It is plausible that the dative subject's disability to bind comes from the fact that it counts as a kind of PP in those languages;[73] it is not unnatural to speculate that a binder and its bindee should be in the same category.

Another interesting thing to note about the Italian DSC is the fact that the word order of the dative EXP and the Theme freely alternate just as in Dutch experiencer inversion (cf. §4.3.4):

(4.127) *Italian* (Belletti and Rizzi 1988: 340)

    a. A Gianni piacciono   le tue idee.
       to Gianni please(PL)   your ideas
       'Your ideas please (to) Gianni.'

    b. Le tue idee   piacciono   a Gianni.
       your ideas please(PL)   to Gianni

Belletti and Rizzi (1988) propose that EXP and Theme are generated within the same maximal projection of V. Under the theory about the universal mapping of argument structure (§1.3.2), their claim cannot be maintained, but it can be captured by assuming that v and V in the two-layered VP-shell for the Italian psych-verbs that allow the DSC are restructured, resulting in (4.128):[74]

(4.128)   ... [$_{v-VP}$ EXP v–V Theme]

Given this, the word order alternation in the Italian DSC can be explained in the same manner as the Dutch DSC (see §4.3.4 for details).

4. Accusative Subjects in Quechua

According to Cole and Jake (1978), a peculiar type of QSC is found in Imbabura Quechua (and Huanca Quechua (Hermon 1984)), a nominative-accusative SOV

---

[72] According to Masullo (1992, 1993), the same holds true in the Spanish DSC. The subject-agreement in the Italian (and Spanish) DSC is induced by the (nominative) Theme, which is usually the case in DSCs cross-linguistically, as we observed in this chapter (the only exceptional cases to this come from Japanese, Korean, and Middle English).

[73] It is not an ordinary PP, however, because only the PP as a dative EXP can occur at the Spec of T (that is, can check off an EPP-feature) (cf. Belletti and Rizzi 1988).

[74] In §4.3.4, I argued that this process of the restructuring of psych-verbs also happens in Dutch.

language. When the desiderative suffix *-naya* (*-naa* in Huanca Quechua) is attached to a transitive verb, the subject of the clause is marked as accusative with the object still remaining marked as accusative:

(4.129) *Imbabura Quechua* (Cole and Jake 1978: 74)

    a. Ñuca-Ø can-da ricu-ni/*-ngui.
       I-NOM you-ACC see-1SG/-2SG
       'I see you.'

    b. Ñuca-ta can-da ricu-**naya-n**/*-ni/*-ngui.
       I-ACC you-ACC see-DES-IMP/-1SG/-2SG
       'I would like to see you.'

If the accusative subject occurs, then the subject-agreement must be impersonal, as shown in (4.129b). The case-marking pattern in the Quechua QSC suggests that the desiderative suffix *-naya* takes a control structure and assigns an inherent accusative Case to its Spec together with Experiencer role:

(4.130)

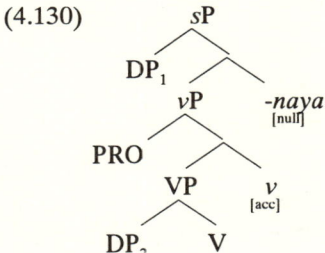

This structure is very similar to the structure of the Japanese potential construction, which I proposed in §4.1.4.4. The only difference is that, while the Japanese potential suffix may absorb the accusative Case-feature of *v*, the Quechua desiderative suffix has no effect on the Case-feature of *v*.

Cole and Jake (1978) and Hermon (1984) demonstrate in full that the accusative subject in the Quechua QSC syntactically behaves as "subject," despite its morphologically coding properties of its accusative-marking and its failure to induce subject-agreement. The fact that the accusative subject does not induce subject-agreement means that it has no φ-feature checking relation with T, and the fact that it has the ability to control the missing subject in a subordinate clause whose predicate contains the same-subject marker (Cole and Jake 1978)[75] indicates that it has a [+construable]-feature checking relation with T. Therefore, it follows that the accusative subject in the Quechua QSC has an EPP-feature checking relation with T.

In §3.2, where the Quechua anti-impersonal passive construction was examined, I argued that the EPP-feature (as well as φ-feature) of T in Quechua is weak, but its nominative Case-feature is strong. Notice that in the Quechua QSC,

---

[75] For switch-reference in (Imbabura) Quechua, see §3.2.

there is no nominative element. What checks it off before Spell-out in a Quechua desiderative clause?

Here I propose to assume that the desiderative suffix, instead of absorbing the accusative Case-feature of v, absorbs the (strong) nominative Case-feature of T. Given this assumption, the derivation for the QSC in Quechua converges in the following manner: The strong nominative Case-feature of T is properly checked off thanks to the assumption; the accusative Case of EXP need not be checked off because of its inherent nature; the EPP-feature is checked off by the (D-feature of the) accusative EXP at LF, resulting in its ability to control; and the Theme properly checks off the accusative Case-feature of v.

5. Georgian

Georgian also provides an instance of DSC. According to Harris (1981, 1984), a group of so-called affective predicates take their subject as dative with the object as nominative:

(4.131) *Georgian* (Harris 1984: 284)

Me   mašinve   momeconet   tkven.
me(DAT)   immediately   1SG-liked-2PL-IND   you(PL.NOM)
'I liked you immediately.'

The Georgian DSC is extremely interesting because the nominative Theme induces subject person-agreement and the dative EXP induces the indirect-object person-agreement.[76] Furthermore, the dative EXP induces number-agreement, which is supposed to be triggered by "subject" (Harris 1981, 1984). On the other hand, given the hypothesis concerning subject-oriented reflexives, it is possible to interpret the fact that the dative EXP, but not the nominative Theme, can bind a subject-oriented reflexive as indicating that the dative EXP in the Georgian DSC occupies the Spec of T before Spell-out, entering into an EPP-feature checking relation with T. The facts concerning the word order indicate that the nominative Theme remains within VP in overt syntax (see McGinnis, to appear, for discussion).

Given these facts, I tentatively propose the following for the Georgian DSC: T's subject person-agreement feature as well as its nominative Case-feature is weak, but its EPP-feature and number-agreement feature are strong. The affective verbs in Georgian have a three-layered VP-shell, just like the ordinary ditransitive predicates. EXP is generated at the Spec of V_{mid}. The topmost light verb v in the three-layered VP-shell in Georgian has a strong φ-feature. This φ-feature is realized as indirect-object person agreement. The EXP, which is assigned an inherent dative by the affective predicate, is attracted to the Spec of v

---

[76] As is well known, the Georgian verbal-agreement system is extremely complicated; it is not easily described here. See Marantz (1989) and Hewitt (1995) for discussion.

to check off the strong ϕ-feature of *v*. And then, it is also attracted farther to the Spec of T before Spell-out to check off the strong EPP-feature and number-agreement feature of T. At LF, T's weak nominative Case-feature and subject person-agreement feature can be checked off by the corresponding features of the nominative Theme.[77]

---

[77] There are still many unsolved questions/problems here. See McGinnis (to appear) for a detailed study on Georgian QSCs under the minimalist program.

5

Locative Inversion

In the previous chapters I have crucially utilized the notion EQUIDISTANCE under the theory of Attract proposed by Chomsky (1995a). Under this theory, the local and strictly stepwise economy condition (Collins 1996 and Ura 1995c) guarantees that the application of Attract to α is as economical as the application of Attract to β only if α and β are equidistant from the target. It follows that either a or b can be attracted by some feature to a position if they are in the same minimal domain at the stage in the derivation before that operation (see §1.4.4). In this chapter I will add a piece of evidence in favor of this, drawing examples from the locative inversion construction in Bantu and in Japanese.

5.1. Bantu Locative Inversion

5.1.1. Basic Facts

Recently, locative inversion in Bantu has attracted much interest in the theory of syntax. This construction is very similar to Bantu active/inverse voice alternation (see §2.1), in that there is no morphology involved in either construction, as shown by the Chichewa examples in (5.1):

(5.1) *Chichewa* (Bresnan and Kanerva 1989: 2)

    a. Ku-mu-dzi   ku-li   chi-tsime.
        17-3-village 17-be   7-well
        'In the village is a well.'

    a'. Chi-tsime chi-li   ku-mu-dzi.
        7-well   7-be   17-3-village
        'A well is in the village.'

b. Ku-mu-dzi ku-na-bwer-a a-lendo-wo.
   17-3-village 17-past-come-ind 2-vistor-those
   'To the village came those visitors.'

b'. a-lendo-wo a-na-bwer-a ku-mu-dzi.
    2-vistor-those 2-past-come-ind 17-3-village
    'Those vistors came to the village.'

With the (unaccusative) predicate as the pivot, the Theme-DP and the locative phrase are inverted by the operation called locative inversion. As will be observed later in this chapter, it is true that there is a lexical/syntactic condition on locative inversion. But, it is noteworthy that, if a given clause satisfies it, locative inversion freely applies to that clause without any morphological change showing the alternation. Furthermore, just like the fronted OBJ in an inverse clause, the locative phrase preposed by locative inversion acquires some of the subject properties.

Before considering what mechanism is involved in locative inversion, let us make a brief examination of the syntactic properties of the preposed locative phrase and the postposed Theme-DP in a clause with locative inversion. The clearest evidence that the locative phrase preposed by locative inversion gains subjecthood comes from the fact that it induces subject agreement:

(5.2) *Chichewa* (Bresnan and Kanerva 1989: 9)

a. *Ku*-mu-dzi *ku*-na-bwer-a a-lendo-wo.
   17-3-village *17*-PAST-come-IND 2-vistor-those
   'To the village came those visitors.'

b. *M*-nkhalango *mw*-a-khal-a mi-kango.
   18-9-forest *18*-PERF-remain-IND 4-lion
   'In the forest have remained lions.'

In the checking theory assumed in this thesis, this clearly shows that the locative phrase preposed by locative inversion has a φ-feature checking relation with Infl.

Another argument for the subjecthood of the locative phrase preposed by locative inversion comes from the fact concerning the attributive VP construction. According to Bresnan and Kanerva (1989), the attributive verb form in Chichewa is morphologically derived from the infinitive by the addition of the associative prefix *á-*. It is noteworthy that in the attributive verbal phrase, every argument of the basic verb may be expressed except for the syntactic subject. In (5.3), for instance, the active subject (in (5.3a)) and the passive one (in (5.3b)) of the bracketed verbal phrases are missing:

(5.3) *Chichewa*(Bresnan and Kanerva 1989: 13)

a. M-sodzi [$_{VP}$ w-o-ik-a nsomba pa-m-pando]
   1-fishman 1-ASC INF-put-IND 10 fish 16-3-chair
   'a fishman putting fish on a chair'

b. nsomba [$_{VP}$ z-o-ik-idw-a   pa-m-oando]
   10 fish   10-ASC INF-put-PASS-IND 16-3-chair
   'fish being put on a chair'

According to Bresnan and Kanerva (1989), the descriptive generalization is that this attributive VP expresses a semantic property that can be defined by abstracting over an open argument of the derived verb, which must correspond to the subject argument of the base verb.

Now consider the following example:

(5.4) *Chichewa* (Bresnan and Kanerva 1989: 14)

M-nkhalango [$_{VP}$ m-o-khal-a   mi-kango]
18-9 forest   18-ASC INF-live-IND 4-lion
Lit. 'in the forest where there live lion'

In this example it is the locative phrase that is the open argument and it is the Theme-argument that remains inside the VP. This indicates that the locative phrase can behave like a syntactic subject in Chichewa.[1]

On the other hand, as Polinsky (1993) points out, the Theme-DP postposed by locative inversion loses all of its subject properties that it assumes in an active unaccusative clause without locative inversion. First, it loses the ability to induce subject-agreement, as is evident from the contrast shown in (5.1) above. Second, it loses the ability to control (see Polinsky 1993 for detail):

(5.5) *Kinyarwanda* (Polinsky 1993: 346)

a. Aba-shiytsi$_k$ ba-ra-siinziir-a   muri iyi inzu [PRO$_k$ ku-guna
   2-guest   2-PROG-sleep-IMPF in this house   INF-rest
   mbere y'umurimo].
   before PRP   work
   'The guests$_k$ are sleeping in this house [PRO$_k$ to get some rest before work].'

b. *Muri iyi inzu   ha-ra-siinziir-a   aba-shiytsi$_k$ [PRO$_k$ku-guna].
   in   this house 16-PROG-sleep-IMPF 2-guest   INF-rest
   'In this house are sleeping guests$_k$ [PRO$_k$ to get some rest].'

From these facts it can be concluded that the Theme-DP postposed by locative inversion loses its subjecthood.[2]

Here it is important to note that the Theme-DP postposed by locative inversion, just like the inverted SUBJ in an inverse clause, does not have any object properties, either. In general, objects in Bantu can undergo relativization or clefting and can induce (optional) object agreement. As shown by Bresnan and Kanerva (1989) (for Chichewa) and Polinsky (1993) (for Kinyarwanda), however,

---

[1] See Bresnan and Kanerva (1989) for other arguments in favor of the subjecthood of the locative phrase inverted by locative inversion.

[2] See Polinsky (1993) for other pieces of evidence that the Theme-DP postposed by locative inversion has lost its subjecthood.

the Theme-DP postposed by locative inversion cannot undergo relativization or clefting (as shown in (5.6b)),[3] and it cannot induce object agreement (as shown in (5.7)):

(5.6) *Chichewa* (Bresnan and Kanerva 1989: 15)

    a. Pa-m-chenga p-a-im-a nkhandwe.
       16-3-sand 16-PERF-stand-IND 9 fox
       'On the sand is standing the fox.'

    b. *N'chi-yani chi-mene$_k$ pa-m-chenga p-a-im-a   t$_k$.
       COP 7-Q   7-REL   16-3-sand   16-PERF-stand-IND
       'Lit. What is it that$_k$ on the sand is standing t$_k$.'

(5.7) *Chichewa* (Bresnan and Kanerva 1989: 15)

    Ku-mu-dzi ku-na-(*wa-)bwer-a a-lendo-wo.
    17-3-village 17-REC PST-(2-)come-IND 2-visitor-2 those
    'To the village came those visitors.'

More interestingly, the Theme-DP postposed by locative inversion, just like the inverted SUBJ in an inverse clause, is not syntactically demoted. As observed in chapter 2, SUBJ in a Bantu passive clause must be syntactically demoted by attaching a preposition to it, or by not being expressed in the clause at all.

(5.8) *Chichewa* (Trithart 1977: 15)

    a. N-thochi zi-na-nyamul-idw-a *(*ndi*) Joni.
       10-banana 10-past-carry-pass-ind by John
       'The bananas were carried (by) John.'

    b. N-thochi zi-na-nyamul-idw-a (*Joni).
       10-banana 10-past-carry-pass-ind John
       'The bananas were carried (John).'

As shown in (5.9), however, the Theme-DP postposed by locative inversion must not be syntactically demoted:

(5.9) *Chichewa*

    a. *Ku-mu-dzi ku-na-bwer-a ndi a-lendo-wo.
       17-3-village 17-REC PST-come-IND by 2-visitor-2 those
       Lit. 'To the village came by those visitors.'

    b. *Ku-mu-dzi ku-na-bwer-a   Ø.
       17-3-village 17-REC PST-come-IND
       Lit. 'To the village came Ø.'

To summarize, the locative phrase preposed by locative inversion gains subjecthood by entering into a φ-feature checking relation with Infl, while the Theme-DP postposed by locative inversion does not have the properties of sub-

---

[3] See Bresnan and Mchombo (1985) for discussion on relativization and clefting in Chichewa and in Bantu in general.

ject, let alone the properties of object. Moreover, the Theme-DP in a clause with locative inversion is not syntactically demoted. These properties of locative inversion strikingly resemble those of inverse voice in Bantu, which were studied at length in chapter 2. Here it should be noted that all Bantu languages that allow the active/inverse voice alternation also allow locative inversion, but not vice versa. For example, Kinyarwanda allows both, but Chichewa allows only locative inversion.

In the next section I will demonstrate that the properties of locative inversion can be given a consistent account by the theory of multiple feature checking.

5.1.2. Explanation

5.1.2.1. Syntactic Mapping of Locative

In order to explain the aforementioned properties of locative inversion in Bantu, I propose to assume that in the underlying structure for an unaccusative verb, the θ-role Locative (or Location) is always assigned to the Spec of the V (see §1.4.2). Elsewhere in this book I assume the hypothesis which requires that every argument in a clause be hierarchically ordered according to its rank in the Θ-Hierarchy. According to the hypothesis, thus, an argument with a θ-role ranked higher in the hierarchy is generated at a higher structural position. In fact, several authors, such as Ostler (1979), Carrier-Duncan (1985), Belletti and Rizzi (1988), and Speas (1990), have proposed the same.[4]

In the two-layered VP-shell proposed by Chomsky (1995a), Agent is always generated at a Spec of the higher V in the shell (namely, *v*), which counts as a source of transitivity due to its function as a causative (Hale and Keyser 1991, 1993), and Theme is generated at the complement of the lower V. If Locative is higher than Theme, but lower than Agent in the Thematic Hierarchy, as Jackendoff (1972), Foley and Van Valin (1984), and Grimshaw (1990) argue, it should be generated at a Spec of the lower V in the shell, according to the above hypothesis.[5] This mapping of the argument structure within the lower VP in the two-layered VP-shell can be illustrated as in the following:

---

[4] Note, however, that this hypothesis is expected to be restated under Hale and Keyser's (1991, 1993) theory of the thematic relation.

[5] If it turns out that Locative is lower than Theme in the hierarchy, as several authors (such as Carrier-Duncan 1985, Speas 1990, and Bresnan and Kanerva 1992) contend, it should be the case that Theme is generated at a Spec of the lower V with Locative generated at the complement of that V. As will become evident, the discussion below in the text will not be affected even if this is the case. However, my analysis of locative inversion, which assumes Locative to be higher than Theme, differs crucially from the analysis of locative inversion proposed by Bresnan and Kanerva (1989). As Schachter (1992) points out, the hierarchy in which Locative is lower than Theme is imperative for Bresnan and Kanerva's (1989) analysis of Bantu inversion. Again, my analysis is independent of whether Locative is higher than Theme or vice versa.

(5.10)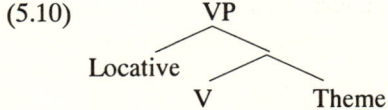

Here it is very important to notice that the position where Locative is generated is in the same minimal domain where Theme is generated.

5.1.2.2. Analysis of Bantu Locative Inversion

Now suppose that T (=Infl) is introduced in (5.10) by Merge without the projection of v. Then, (5.11) is derived:

(5.11)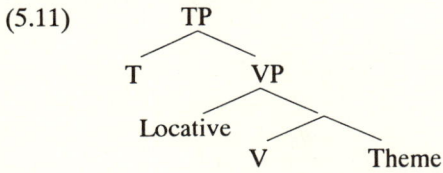

In chapter 2 I claimed that the EPP-feature (i.e., D-feature) of T in Bantu languages is strong. Thus, something with a D-feature must be attracted to the Spec of T to check off T's strong EPP-feature before Spell-out. Now that Locative and Theme in (5.11) are in the same minimal domain (of V), either of them can be attracted to the Spec of T without deviating from the MLC part of the definition of Attract, if they have a D-feature, satisfying the Last Resort part of the definition of Attract. If the latter condition is met (i.e., both Theme and Locative have a D-feature), (5.12) is derived if Locative in (5.11) is attracted to the Spec of T:

(5.12)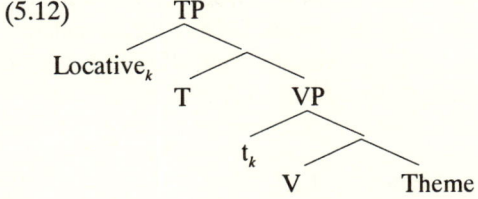

In (5.12) the EPP-feature is checked off by the D-feature of Locative before Spell-out, provided that locative phrases in Bantu can have a D-feature. Recall that I argued in chapter 2 that the ϕ-feature of T in Bantu, too, is strong; therefore, Locative can check off the ϕ-feature of T as well, provided that locative phrases in Bantu can have a ϕ-feature. The D-feature (and ϕ-feature) of Theme need not be checked because they are [+interpretable]. In order for this derivation to converge, the Case-feature of Theme and the weak Case-feature of T must be checked off at LF.[6] Those features can be properly checked off by rais-

---

[6] Recall that I am assuming that there is no v projection involved in this derivation. The single VP projection counts as an unaccusative verb. To put it differently, there is no (accusative) Case involved in this derivation because an unaccusative verb has no Case (cf. Burzio 1986). Thus, there is no need to check accusative Case in this derivation. I

ing the Case-feature of Theme onto T at LF; whence, the derivation converges. Note that this exactly represents the surface structure of a clause with locative inversion.[7]

(5.13) [$_{TP}$ ku-mu-dzi$_k$ ku-li$_g$ [$_{VP}$ t$_k$ [$_{V'}$ t$_g$ chi-tsime]]] (= (5.1a))
         17-3-village   17-be   7-well
    'In the village is a well.'

It is interesting to note, in passing, that this analysis of Bantu locative inversion is very pertinent to Bresnan and Kanerva's (1989) discovery that the Theme-DP in a clause with locative inversion lingers in the smallest projection of VP in overt syntax; they provide a few pieces of evidence which show that the Theme-DP in a clause with locative inversion remains in overt syntax at the position that corresponds to the ordinary object position in a transitive clause. See Bresnan and Kanerva (1989: 3–9) for details.

Now suppose that Theme is attracted to the Spec of T in (5.11). As already noted, this does not deviate from both the Last Resort part and the MLC part of the definition of Attract, because it has a D-feature and it (as well as Locative) is the element closest to T that can check the EPP-feature of T. Then, (5.14) is derived from (5.11):

(5.14)
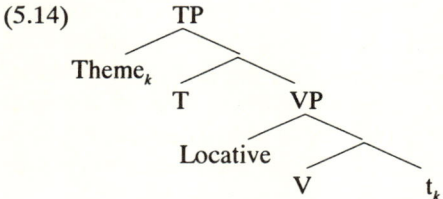

In (5.14) the Case and φ-features of T as well as its strong EPP-feature are checked off by Theme; as a result, the Case-feature of Theme, too, is deleted. Even if Locative may have a D-feature and φ-feature, they are allowed not to be checked because they are [+interpretable].[8] Thereby, (5.14) converges. This exactly corresponds to an unaccusative clause without locative inversion.

(5.15) [$_{TP}$ Chi-tsime$_k$ chi-li$_g$ [$_{VP}$ ku-mu-dzi [$_{V'}$ t$_g$ t$_k$]]]
         7-well   7-be   17-3-village
    'A well is in the village.'

5.1.2.3. D-feature and Φ-feature of Locative Phrases in Bantu

Returning to the analysis of locative Bantu inversion illustrated in (5.12) above, one should note that I crucially rely on the presupposition that Locative has a D-

---

will examine this issue more closely later in this chapter.

[7] Recall that I am assuming that V overtly moves up onto T in Bantu (see chapter 2 and references cited therein).

[8] I will return to this issue in §5.1.2.3.

feature and a φ-feature. Thus, the analysis hinges on whether this presupposition is true or not.

As for the φ-feature, it is quite clear from their morphology that locative phrases in Bantu have φ-features. In almost all Bantu languages locative phrases are morphologically marked in the same fashion as DPs. Take the Chichewa examples in (5.1a,a'), repeated here as (5.16), for instance:

(5.16) *Chichewa* (Bresnan and Kanerva 1989: 2)

    a. Ku-mu-dzi ku-li chi-tsime.
       17-3-village 17-be 7-well
       'In the village is a well.'

    a'. Chi-tsime chi-li ku-mu-dzi.
       7-well 7-be 17-3-village
       'A well is in the village.'

The locative phrase in these examples has the prefix *ku-*, which is classified as 17, just as the Theme-DP has the prefix *chi-*, which is classified as 7. These prefixes behave the same in both syntactic and morphological respects (cf. Carstens 1991, 1993), and it is commonly assumed in the literature on Bantu that they are regarded as number, a kind of φ-feature. It is, thus, natural to assume that locative phrases in Bantu have a φ-feature.

What about the question as to whether locative phrases in Bantu have a D-feature? According to Bresnan (1994), there is a good deal of evidence that locative phrases in Bantu have a D-feature. The clearest evidence comes from the fact that locative phrases in Bantu, unlike in English, can freely occur in the subject position of semantically compatible verbs:

(5.17) *Chichewa* (Bresnan 1994: 111)

    Ku San Jose ku-ma-ndi-sangalats-a.
    17-San Jose 17-PRES.HAB-1SG-please-FV
    '(Being in) San Jose pleases me.' (Lit. 'In San Jose pleases me.')

In (5.17), the locative phrase, just like locative phrases preposed by locative inversion, induces subject-agreement, showing that it enters a φ-feature checking relation with T (= Infl). Note that the object in (5.17) is incorporated into V as a clitic. Hence, in (5.17) there is no element but the locative phrase that can check off the EPP-feature (i.e., D-feature) of T; otherwise, (5.17) would crash, resulting in ungrammaticality.[9] It follows that locative phrases in Bantu may have a D-feature.

Moreover, according to Bresnan (1994), when a locative phrase appears at the object position of a transitive verb, it can induce (optional) object-agreement

---

[9] The same reasoning leads to the conclusion that the locative phrase checks off the Case-feature of T in (5.17). In other words, it behaves like a true DP in this case. In fact, Myers (1987) provides an analysis similar to this, proposing that locative phrases in Chishona need a Case. Carstens (1991, 1993) and Kinyalolo (1991), too, propose that the structure of Bantu locative phrases looks much like the structure of DP in a sense.

and it can be passivized. In addition, a locative phrase can have its possessor in its Spec, as shown by (5.18) (cf., also, Bresnan and Mchombo 1995):

(5.18) *Chichewa* (Bresnan 1994: 112)
      A-lendo   a-ma-pa-kond-a   pa mu-dzi   p-athu p-o-chititsa
      2-visitor 2-PRES.HAB-16-love-fv 16 3-village 16-our 16-ASC.INF-attract
      chi-dwi.
      7-interest
      'Visitors love it, our interesting village.'

Since, in general, a PP cannot take its possessor, this property of locative phrases in Bantu should be attributed to their structural nature as DPs.

From these observations it is safe to conclude that locative phrases in Bantu may have a D-feature.[10] This indicates that they can check off the strong EPP-feature of T. In other words, they can be attracted by the strong EPP-feature of T without violating the Last Resort part of the definition of Attract. Now that locative phrases may have a D-feature in Bantu, the movement of Locative presupposed in our analysis of locative inversion illustrated in (5.12) is validated. As noted before, this derivation of locative inversion converges as required: The EPP-feature of T, as well as its φ-feature, is checked off by the locative phrase at the Spec of T before Spell-out, the Case-feature of T can be checked off at LF by Theme's Case-feature which is moved onto T at LF, and the D-feature and φ-feature of Theme, being [+interpretable], need not be checked off. This is the mechanism of locative inversion in Bantu.

5.1.3. GF-Splitting by Bantu Locative Inversion

The analysis of Bantu locative inversion sketched above provides a natural account of the subjecthood of Locative and the loss of subjecthood of Theme in a clause with locative inversion.

It was observed in §5.1 that the locative phrase preposed by locative inversion gains the ability to control. Remember the hypothesis that the ability to control results from a [+construable]-feature checking relation with Infl (= T). Since, under the analysis of Bantu locative inversion presented here, the locative phrase in a clause with locative inversion checks T's EPP-feature and φ-feature, both of which are [+construable], it naturally follows from the above hypothesis, that the locative phrase preposed by locative inversion can control.

As was also observed in §5.1, Theme in an unaccusative clause without locative inversion has the ability to induce subject-agreement and the ability to control, while it loses these abilities when it appears in a clause with locative inversion. In the analysis of locative inversion, Theme does not have any [+construable]-feature checking relation with T throughout the derivation. It fol-

---

[10] See Bresnan (1994) for several other (minor) arguments for the claim that locative phrases may behave like DPs in Bantu. Cf., also, Myers (1987), Bresnan and Kanerva (1989), Carstens (1991), Kinyalolo (1991), and Bresnan and Mchombo (1995).

lows that Theme has no subject properties in a clause with locative inversion in Bantu, as expected.

5.1.4. Deriving the Parametric Variation

Now recall that there is an interesting generalization about the parametric variation concerning the relation of locative inversion and active/inverse alternation in Bantu languages.

(5.19) A Generalization in Bantu Languages:

If a language L in Bantu allows active/inverse voice alternation, then L also allows locative inversion, but not vice versa.

For example, Kinyarwanda allows both constructions, but Chichewa allows only locative inversion. To the best of my knowledge there is no Bantu language that allows only active/inverse voice alternation, though there are a lot of Bantu languages that allow only locative inversion.

My analysis of locative inversion and active/inverse voice alternation naturally accounts for the reason that languages like Chichewa allow locative inversion, but disallow active/inverse alternation. Recall that I argued in chapter 2 that in order for a language L to allow active/inverse voice alternation, L must have v whose property allows OBJ to move overtly to its Spec before Spell-out. Now, suppose that v in those Chichewa-type languages does not have such a property, so that OBJ can never move overtly to a Spec of v in those languages. Then, OBJ and SUBJ in a transitive clause are never in the same minimal domain throughout the derivation in those languages. This means that OBJ can never pass over SUBJ in those languages; whence, the inverse construction, in which OBJ moves over SUBJ to the Spec of T, never occurs in those languages. On the other hand, given the assumption concerning the base-position of locative phrases, either a locative phrase or Theme-DP can be attracted to the Spec of IP before Spell-out, regardless of the parametric difference of v in terms of its property that (dis)allows OBJ's overt movement to a Spec of v. Insofar as locative phrases have a D-feature in L, locative inversion is possible in L regardless of any parametric differences.

5.1.5. Lexical/Syntactic Restriction on Locative Inversion

The analysis of locative inversion in Bantu presented here also offers a consistent account of an interesting observation by Bresnan (1994). She observes that locative inversion is blocked if there is an argument with a θ-role more highly ranked in the Thematic Hierarchy than Locative in the relevant clause.

(5.20) Bresnan's (1994) observation:

Locative inversion is blocked if there is an argument with a θ-role more highly ranked in the Thematic Hierarchy than Locative in the relevant clause.
(Thematic Hierarchy: Agent (≫ Goal) ≫ Locative ≫ Theme)

Now suppose that each thematic role is projected in accordance with the Thematic Hierarchy as illustrated in (5.21) (see §5.2.2 for details):

(5.21)

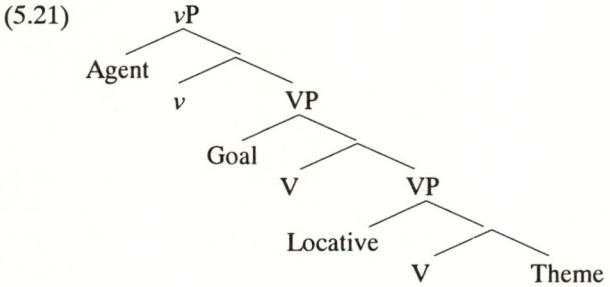

Then, neither Locative argument nor Theme argument can be attracted to the Spec of T unless Agent argument (or Goal, if any) is syntactically demoted. This is because Agent (or Goal) argument is always closer to Infl than Locative and Theme are, and, hence, Agent (or Goal) argument is always attracted by T unless it is syntactically demoted.

Furthermore, the analysis of locative inversion sketched above also gives a neat explanation of the well-known fact that locative inversion is possible only if the predicate involved is an unaccusative one. Following, essentially, Hale and Keyser's (1991, 1993) assumption, I hypothesize that the Agent argument of an (intransitive) unergative verb is generated at the Spec of *v* just like Agent of a transitive verb (cf. Chomsky 1995a). Thus, the underlying structure of an (intransitive) unergative verb looks like the following if Locative is also involved:

(5.22) (linear order irrelevant)

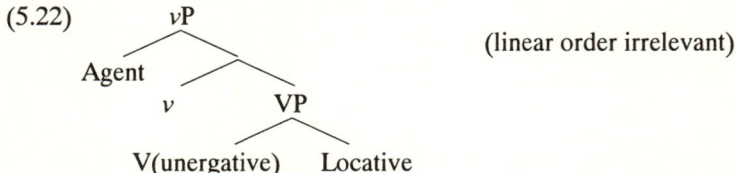

As is evident from (5.22), Locative cannot be attracted to a position higher than Agent, because Agent is always closer to the target than Locative.

5.1.6. Implications

5.1.6.1. Existential Constructions and Expletives

The locative inversion in Bantu just observed is somewhat similar to the impersonal existential construction with the expletive *there* in English and its equivalents in other languages, in that the Theme-DP of an (intransitive) unaccusative verb remains within VP before Spell-out in both constructions. Here it is interesting to note the difference between these constructions and its consequences.

As observed, the locative phrase in a clause with locative inversion induces subject agreement in Bantu. In other words, the Theme-DP has no ϕ-feature checking relation with Infl (= T) in this construction. In contrast, it is the Theme-DP in the English impersonal existential construction, but not the expletive *there*, that induces subject-agreement.

(5.23) *English*
    a.   There seem/*seems three men in that garden.
    b.   There *seem/seems a man in that garden.

According to Chomsky (1995a), the expletive *there* checks an EPP-feature of T in overt syntax, and it is deleted owing to the requirement of Full Interpretation. The associate of the expletive (i.e., Theme-DP), instead, moves onto T at LF and enters into a ϕ-feature checking relation and nominative Case-feature checking relation with T; therefrom, the fact shown in (5.23) naturally follows. Notice that the associate of the expletive (i.e., Theme-DP) is the only element that has a [+construable]-feature checking relation with T at LF in the English impersonal expletive construction.

Elsewhere in this book I argued that, from the hypothesis that only an element that has a [+construable]-feature checking relation with Infl (= T) bears the ability to control, it follows that the locative phrase gains that ability when it is preposed by locative inversion in Bantu. This hypothesis, thus, immediately leads to the prediction that it is the Theme-DP that has the ability to control in the English impersonal existential construction. According to Chomsky (1995a), this is borne out, as shown by the (somewhat marginally) well-formed examples in (5.24a):

(5.24) *English* (Chomsky 1995a: 284)
    a.   There arrived three men$_k$ (last night) [without PRO$_k$ identifying themselves].
    b.   *I met three men$_k$ (last night) [without PRO$_k$ identifying themselves].

The ill-formedness of (5.24b) clearly shows that an element without a [+construable]-feature checking relation with T has no ability to control the missing subject of the *without ...ing* construction. Besides, according to Chomsky (1995a), the same holds true in the Italian and German impersonal expletive constructions as well.[11]

Here it should be noted that in all the aforementioned languages, the associate of the expletive induces subject-agreement; that is, the associate has the φ-feature checking relation with Infl at LF. And the expletive, though checking off T's EPP-feature before Spell-out, is deleted (and erased) at LF where all the interpretation rules, including the interpretation concerning control-relation, take place. Hence, the hypothesis concerning GFs correctly predicts that the associate has the ability to control in those languages. In French, on the other hand, it is the expletive *il*, but not its associate, that induces subject-agreement (cf. Jaeggli 1981, Herschensohn 1982, and Burzio 1986). According to Chomsky (1995a), the expletive checks off all of T's nominal features in French. The hypothesis concerning GFs, therefore, predicts that the associate in the existential construction, having no [+construable]-feature checking relation with T throughout the derivation, does not have the ability to control the missing subject of the *without ...ing* construction in French. As Chomsky (1995a) points out, this prediction is also borne out:

(5.25) *French* (Chomsky 1995a: 284)

　　　　*Il　est entré　trois hommes [sans　　s'annoncer].
　　　　EXP is entered three men　　　without identifying themselves
　　　　Lit. 'It is entered three men [without PRO identifying themselves].'

In this regard the existential construction in French resembles the locative inversion in Bantu. And our theory prosperously accounts for all of the cases.[12]

5.1.6.2. Expletives and Long-Distance Agreement

In connection with the relation of the expletive and its associate, it is interesting to note the following fact, which comes from Icelandic.

In chapter 4 I claimed in depth that the dative subject in the Icelandic DSC (dative subject construction) plays the role of checking off the strong EPP-

---

[11] See Cardinaletti (1994) for more discussion. Cf., also, Perlmutter (1983) and Burzio (1986) for the Italian impersonal existential construction and Safir (1985) for the German one (and Vikner 1995 for existentials in Germanic languages). Takahashi (1997), incidentally, points out that the ill-formedness of (i)a needs explanation:

(i)　a.　　*There seems to be someone$_k$ in the bathroom [without PRO$_k$ seeming to be in the bedroom].

　　 b.　　Someone$_k$ seems to be in the bathroom [without PRO$_k$ seeming to be in the bedroom].

Notice, however, that, since the counterparts of (i)a in Italian and German are perfectly acceptable (cf. Cardinaletti 1994), I leave the ill-formedness of (i)a in English, though indeed problematic, as an exceptional case.

[12] See Bošković (1995) for an analysis of the feature-checking property of the *it*-type expletive.

feature of T but it has no other checking relation with T; for, its dative Case is inherent and, hence, it need not be checked. It is widely known that Icelandic allows the so-called transitive expletive construction (cf. Jonas and Bobaljik 1993; Chomsky 1994a, 1995a; Bobaljik and Jonas 1996; and, especially, Jonas 1996). According to Chomsky (1995a), the expletive merely plays the role of checking off the strong EPP-feature of T in Icelandic. Then, the analysis of the Icelandic DSC presented in §4.3 leads to the prediction that, if the expletive is included in the numeration of the derivation for a DSC, it is merged at the Spec of T, instead of the movement of the dative-marked EXP to that position. This prediction is borne out:

(5.26) *Icelamdic*

    a.   Mér   líka   ekki bílarnir.
           me(DAT) like(3PL) NEG the-cars(NOM)
           'I don't like the cars.' (Thráinsson 1979: 466)

    b.   Það líka   einhverjum/*mér   ekki bílarnir.
           EXP like(3PL) someone(DAT)/me(DAT) NEG the-cars(NOM)
           'Someone/*I do(es)n't like the cars.'

Here it is interesting to note that the so-called definiteness effect must be observed only by the dative-marked EXP. This is confirmed by the ill-formedness of (5.27), where the nominative-marked Theme is indefinite:

(5.27) *Icelandic*

        Það líka   einhverjum/*mér   ekki mys.
        EXP like(3PL) someone(DAT)/me(DAT) NEG mice(NOM)
        'Someone/I do(es)n't like mice.' (Schütze 1993: 355)

Furthermore, it should be noted that the subject-agreement in the well-formed examples in (5.26b) and (5.27) is induced by the nominative-marked Theme, regardless of whether it is indefinite or definite.

According to Chomsky (1995a), the N-feature of the expletive itself needs to be checked off by an indefinite NP at LF. In (5.27) the element with an N-feature that is closest to the expletive is the dative-marked EXP. The N-feature of the nominative-marked Theme cannot enter into a checking relation with the expletive because the dative-marked EXP, which has an N-feature, intervenes. Recall that the nominative Case-feature of T, as well as the φ-feature of T, is weak in Icelandic (see §4.3). Thus, in order to undergo a checking for its deletion at LF, the nominative Case-feature of T attracts the nominative Case-feature that is closest to it at LF. The nominative Case-feature of the nominative Theme is the closest one in (5.27); whence, it is attracted at LF to enter into a checking relation. But, notice that, as I claimed in §2.1.3 (cf., also, Chomsky's 1995 fall class lectures), the checking of T's nominative Case-feature must coincide with the checking of T's φ-feature in Icelandic. The LF movement of the nominative Case-feature of the nominative Theme must accompany the movement of its φ-feature by utilizing the FREE-RIDE STRATEGY with PIED-PIPING (cf. Chomsky 1995a);

therefrom, it naturally follows that the subject-agreement in (5.27) is induced by the nominative Theme, which is seemingly too remote from T.

Here it is noteworthy that the above explanation of the fact shown in (5.26b) and (5.27) cannot be possible without the theory of multiple feature checking in addition to Chomsky's (1995a) theory of expletives. Thus, as long as this explanation is valid, the fact lends strong support to the analysis of the DSC by means of the theory of multiple feature checking.

5.1.6.3. A Very Short Note on English Locative Inversion

As is well-known, English has a kind of locative inversion, in which a locative PP appears at the clause-initial position with a Theme (or, infrequently, Agent) lingering within VP in overt syntax (Levin 1985b, Coopmans 1989, Hoekstra and Mulder 1990, Rochemont and Culicover 1990, Bresnan 1994, Watanabe 1994b, and Levin and Rappaport Hovav 1995, to list a few).

(5.28)   *English* (Bresnan 1994: 75)
   a. i.   A lamp was in the corner.
      ii. In the corner was a lamp.
   b. i.   My friend Rose was sitting among the guests.
      ii. Among the guests was sitting my friend Rose.

According to Bresnan (1994) and Bresnan and Kanerva (1992), the preposed locative phrase in the English locative inversion construction, unlike the one in the Bantu locative inversion construction, shows equivocal subjecthood. Bresnan (1994), among many others, extensively examines how much the preposed locative phrase bears subjecthood in English. The following two of her arguments are decisive and crucial for our concern. First, it does not induce subject-agreement:

(5.29)   *English* (Bresnan 1994: 95)
   a.   In the swamp was/*were found a child.
   b.   In the swamp *was/were found two children.

This clearly shows that it is not the preposed locative phrase, but the postposed Theme argument that enters into a ϕ-feature checking relation with T.[13] Furthermore, the preposed locative phrase in English, unlike the one in Bantu, cannot control:

(5.30)   *English*
   a.   A woman$_k$ stood on the corner [without PRO$_k$ being near another woman].
   b.   *On the corner$_k$ stood a woman [without PRO$_k$ being another woman].

[13] Moreover, the word order tells us that this checking takes place at LF.

From this fact, the hypothesis concerning the ability to control leads to the conclusion that the preposed locative phrase in English has no [+construable]-feature checking relation with T at all. In contrast, the postposed Theme argument can control. This shows that it retains the ability to control even in the locative inversion construction, as shown in (5.31):

(5.31) *English*
?On the corner stood a woman$_k$ [without PRO$_k$ being near another woman].

Hence, I conclude that these facts should be interpreted as showing that the preposed locative phrase in English, just like the expletive *there*, has no subjecthood.[14]

5.2. Locative Inversion in Japanese

5.2.1. Basic Facts

The examples in (5.32) show the Japanese existential construction with a locative phrase marked by *-ni*:[15]

(5.32) *Japanese*
    a. Takusanno butuzoo-ga ano tera-ni ar-u.
        many statues-NOM that temple-LOC be-PRES
        'There are many statues in that temple.'
    b. Takusanno kanja-ga ano byooin-ni ir-u.
        many patients-NOM that hospital-LOC be-PRES
        'There are many patients in that hospital.'

By preposing the locative phrases in (5.32) to the clause-initial position, the well-formed examples in (5.33) are derived without changing their logical interpretations:[16]

---

[14] Obviously some (important) questions remain unsolved. What checks off the strong EPP-feature of T in a clause with locative inversion in English? Why is it that the preposed locative phrase can undergo raising, etc.? Perhaps the analysis of the English quotative inversion presented by Collins (1996) might be a key to these questions, though I leave them open here.

[15] The existential verb *ar/ir* alternates according to the animacy of the Theme-argument it selects: *Ir* is used when Theme is animate, and *ar* is used when Theme is non-animate. See Kishimoto (1996) for discussion.

[16] See Kuno (1973) and Shibatani (1978) for basic facts concerning existential sentences in Japanese. When the *-ni*-marked phrase in the clause with the existential predicate *ar/ir* is animate, the clause expresses possession. See Clark (1978), Freeze (1992), and references cited therein for discussion on the relation between existential constructions and possessive ones. In this section I will concentrate my attention on locative-existential constructions alone.

(5.33) *Japanese*

    a. Ano tera-ni takusanno butuzoo-ga ar-u.
       that temple-LOC many statues-NOM be-PRES
       'same as (5.32a)'

    b. Ano byooin-ni takusanno kanja-ga ir-u.
       that hospital-LOC many patients-NOM be-PRES
       'same as (5.32b)'

As is well-known, Japanese has scrambling, which may drastically change surface word orders. Thus, it looks as if the Locative-preposing illustrated in (5.33) is due to scrambling. On the contrary, I will claim that it looks much more like locative inversion found in Bantu, which accompanies GF-changing/splitting as observed in §5.1.

As has been established in the literature, scrambling is not a voice-changing/GF-changing operation (cf., among others, Saito 1985, 1989). Thus elements that are moved by scrambling never acquire new GFs. In contrast, the locative phrase preposed to the clause-initial position in the existential construction gains some subjecthood. First, it acquires the ability to bind a purely subject-oriented reflexive:

(5.34) *Japanese*

    Ano iinkai-ni$_k$ [[zibun-tati-zishin-no$_k$ rekishi-o hiteisita]
    that committee-LOC self-PL-self-GEN history-ACC denied
    zinbutu]-ga ir-u.
    person -NOM be-PAST
    Lit. 'In that committee$_k$ was [a person [who denied themselves's$_k$ history]].'

Note that a locative phrase cannot bind the purely subject-oriented reflexive *zibun-tati-zishin* unless it appears in the existential construction. This is illustrated in (5.35):

(5.35) *Japanese*

    *?John-ga ano iinkai-ni$_k$ [[zibun-tati-zishin-no$_k$ rekishi-o
      -NOM that committee-LOC self-PL-self-GEN history-ACC
    hiteisita] zinbutu]-o shoukaisi-ta.
    denied person -ACC introduce-PAST
    'John introduced [a person [who denied themselves's$_k$ history]] to that committee$_k$.'

    (cf. John-ga ano iinkai-ni$_k$ [[sore-no$_k$ rekishi-o hiteisita]
      -NOM that committee-LOC it-GEN history-ACC denied
    zinbutu]-o shoukaisi-ta.
    person -ACC introduce-PAST
    'John introduced [a person [who denied its$_k$ history]] to that committee$_k$.')

Second, the locative phrase preposed in the existential construction gains the ability to control the missing subject in a -*nagara*-clause:

(5.36) *Japanese*

[PRO$_k$ setubi-busoku de komat-tei-nagara], ano byooin-ni$_k$
　　　　facilities-lack due to suffer-PROG-while that hospital-LOC
takusanno kanja-ga ir-u.
many patients-NOM be-PRES
'[While PRO$_k$ being in trouble due to the lack of facilities], in that hospital$_k$ were many patients.'

On the other hand, the locative phrase cannot control the missing subject in a -*nagara*-clause if it appears in a construction other than an existential, as shown by the ill-formedness of (5.37):

(5.37) *Japanese*

*[PRO$_k$ setubi-busoku de komat-tei-nagara], ano byooin-ni$_k$
　　　　facilities-lack due to suffer-PROG-while that hospital-LOC
takusanno kanja-ga nyuuinsi-ta.
many patients-NOM enter-PAST
'[While PRO$_k$ being in trouble due to the lack of facilities], many patients went into that hospital$_k$.'

From these observation it is concluded that the locative phrase preposed in the existential construction gains some subjecthood.

Moreover, it is interesting to note that the nominative-marked Theme-argument in the existential construction has no ability to control the missing subject in a -*nagara*-clause:

(5.38) *Japanese*

*[PRO$_k$ kenkoo-o shimpaisi-tei-nagara], ano byooin-ni takusanno
　　　　health-ACC worry-PROG-while that hospital-LOC many
kanja-ga$_k$ ir-u.
patients-NOM be-PRES
'[While PRO$_k$ worrying about (their) health], there were many patients$_k$ in that hospital.'

(cf. [PRO$_k$ kenkoo-o shimpaisi-tei-nagara], ano byooin-ni
　　　　health-ACC worry-PROG-while that hospital-LOC
takusanno kanja-ga$_k$ nyuuinsi-ta.
many patients-NOM enter-PAST
'[While PRO$_k$ worrying about (their) health], many patients$_k$ went into that hospital.')

Given the hypothesis about GFs that has been developed so far, this indicates that the nominative-marked Theme in the Japanese existential construction has no [+construable]-feature checking relation with T. Furthermore, from the fact shown in (5.36), the hypothesis leads to the conclusion that the locative phrase preposed in the existential construction has a [+construable]-feature checking relation with T.

Keeping these conclusions in mind, let us see in the next section how the Japanese locative inversion is derived.

5.2.2. Deriving Japanese Locative Inversion

5.2.2.1. Proposals

In §5.1 I argued for the hypothesis that both Locative and Theme are projected within the maximal projection of an unaccusative verb. Given this hypothesis, the underlying structure for the Japanese existential construction looks like (5.39):

(5.39)

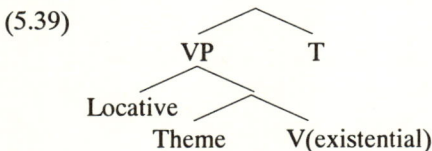

From this underlying structure the Theme(NOM)-LOC word order (as in (5.32)) is derived if the nominative-marked Theme is attracted by the strong EPP-feature of T to the Spec of T.[17] If the locative phrase is attracted to that position, then locative inversion results. But, it is necessary to figure out why it is possible for the locative phrase in the Japanese existential construction to be attracted to the Spec of T.

Here I propose to speculate that the -*ni*-marked locative phrase in Japanese is assigned an inherent Case by the existential verb *ar/ir*. Furthermore, I propose to assume that -*ni* is not a postposition, but merely a particle expressing its morphological Case-declension, just like -*ga* (nominative particle) or -*o* (accusative particle). This is opposite to what has sometimes been assumed in the literature with respect to the syntactic/morphological status of the locative -*ni*. Sadakane and Koizumi (1995) propose a diagnosis for the distinction between Case-particles and postpositions. According to them, Case-particles must, but postpositions must not, disappear if the element with them appears in the focus position in a cleft sentence:

(5.40) *Japanese*

a. [[t_k tegami-o Mary-kara morat-ta]-no]-wa John(*-ga) da.
          letter-ACC   -from received -NOMINL -TOP   -NOM is
'It is a letter that John received from Mary.'

b. [[John-ga t_k tegami-o morat-ta]-no]-wa Mary*(-kara) da.
          -NOM   letter-ACC received -NOMINL -TOP   -from is
'It is from Mary that John received a letter.'

---

[17] In chapter 4 I argued that T's EPP-feature and φ-feature in Japanese are strong.

c. [[John-ga t_k Mary-kara morat-ta]-no]-wa tegami(*-o) da.
     -NOM   -from received -NOMINL -TOP letter -ACC is
   'It is a letter that John received from Mary.'

Now (5.41) shows that the *-ni*-marker attached to the locative phrase in the existential construction must disappear if the locative phrase appears in the focus position in a cleft sentence:

(5.41) *Japanese*

[[takusanno ki-ga   ar-u   ]-no]-wa ano yama(*-ni)   da.
   many   trees-NOM be-PRES -NOMINL -TOP that mountain -LOC be
Lit. 'It is in that mountain that are lots of trees.'

Thus it is safe to conclude from this that the locative *-ni* in the existential construction is a Case-particle.[18]

Now that the locative phrase in the existential construction is merely a DP with a Case-particle, it can be attracted by the strong EPP-feature of T to the Spec of T before Spell-out. This process derives (5.42) from (5.39):

(5.42)
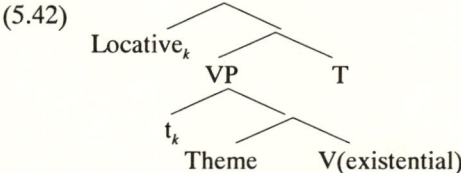

The diagram illustrated in (5.42) represents the surface structure of a clause with locative inversion in Japanese, such as (5.33), which are repeated here as (5.43):

---

[18] According to Sadakane and Koizumi (1995), a floating quantifier can be launched from an element with a Case-particle, but not from an element with a postposition. The sentence in (i) below sounds perfect to my ear, though there might be some native speakers who do not like it:

(i) ?[Kansai-no daigaku]-ni san-koo suupaa-kompyuutaa-ga ar-u.
       Kansai-in universities -LOC 3-CLASS super-computers-NOM be-PRES
    Lit. 'At three universities in the Kansai area are super-computers.'

Nonetheless, I believe that even those who dislike (i) judge (ii) much worse than (i):

(ii) *[Kansai-no daigaku]-kara san-koo gookaku-tuuchi-ga John-ni
        Kansai-in universities -from 3-CLASS admission-NOM   -to
     todoi-ta.
     was delivered-PRES
     Lit.'John was notified of admission from three universities in the Kansai area.'

I interpret this sharp contrast between (i) and (ii) to show the status of the locative *-ni* in the existential construction as a Case-particle.

(5.43)   *Japanese*

    a. Ano tera-ni   takusanno butuzoo-ga ar-u.
       that temple-LOC many   statues-NOM be-PRES
       'In that temple are many statues.'

    b. Ano byooin-ni   takusanno kanja-ga   ir-u.
       that hospital-LOC many   patients-NOM be-PRES
       'In that hospital are many patients.'

The derivation for locative inversion converges in the following fashion: The Case of the locative phrase need not be checked because of its inherent nature. T's strong EPP-feature and φ-feature are checked off before Spell-out by the locative phrase, which is a DP. The existential verb has no nominal features because of its unaccusative nature; thus, there is no need for worrying about their checking. The nominative-marked Theme can enter into a checking relation with the nominative Case-feature of T at LF.[19] Now all the features that require checking for convergence can be properly checked. As a consequence, the derivation converges.

5.2.2.2. GF-Splitting

As observed in §5.2.1, the locative phrase gains some subjecthood in the existential construction with locative inversion: More specifically, it gains the ability to control the missing subject in a *-nagara*-clause, and the ability to bind a purely subject-oriented reflexive.

In analyzing the dative subject construction in Japanese, I reached the conclusion that the ability to control the missing subject in a *-nagara*-clause results from a φ-feature checking relation with T and the ability to bind a purely subject-oriented reflexive results from an EPP-feature checking relation with T. Recall that under the analysis presented in §5.2.2.1, the locative phrase preposed in the existential construction has a φ-feature checking relation and an EPP-feature checking relation with T. Therefrom the fact naturally follows that the locative phrase preposed in the existential construction gains the ability to control the missing subject in a *-nagara*-clause, and the ability to bind a purely subject-oriented reflexive.

In addition, it was also observed in §5.2.1 that the nominative-marked Theme has no subjecthood. Given the hypothesis concerning GFs, this means that the nominative-marked Theme in the existential construction with locative inversion has no [+construable]-feature checking relation with T. Notice that this observation is perfectly consistent with my analysis of locative inversion, according to which only the checking relation the nominative-marked Theme has with T is a Case-feature checking one. Because Case-features are never [+construable], it is possible to correctly predict with the analysis presented in

---

[19] Recall that I am assuming that T's nominative feature in Japanese is weak. See chapter 4.

§5.2.2.1 that the nominative-marked Theme in the existential construction with locative inversion has no subjecthood.

5.2.3. Supporting Evidence

5.2.3.1. Scopal Interaction of LOC-NOM

Kuno (1973) observes that the locative phrase always takes its scope over the nominative-marked Theme in the existential construction with locative inversion, as shown in (5.44):[20]

(5.44) *Japanese*
    Dokoka-ni   daremo-ga   i-ta.
    somewhere-LOC everyone-NOM be-PAST
    Lit. 'Somewhere was everyone.'
    (interpretation: somewhere > everyone, *everyone > somewhere)

Given the proposed analysis of locative inversion in Japanese in addition to Kitahara's (1996) proposal that the feature-checking position of α counts as α's LF position relevant to its scopal interpretation, Kuno's observation can be fully explained.

According to the analysis of locative inversion, the feature checking of the locative phrase takes place at the Spec of T. Recall that the D-feature and ϕ-feature of the nominative-marked Theme do not have any checking relation. This is permitted because they are [+interpretable]. Thus, the checking relation the nominative-marked Theme has is the (nominative) feature-checking relation with T at LF. Where does this checking take place? At LF the nominative Case-feature of Theme moves up by feature-movement onto T to enter into a checking relation. Hence, the checking of the nominative feature of Theme takes place within T^{0max}. The situation is delineated as in (5.45):[21]

(5.45)
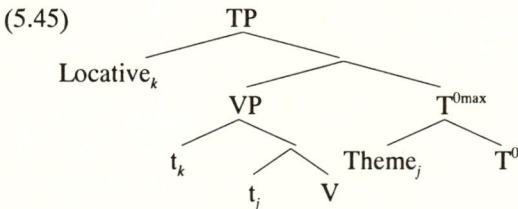

In (5.45) Locative asymmetrically c-commands Theme. Therefore, the scopal domain of the locative phrase contains that of Theme; as a consequence, the lo-

---

[20] See Yatsushiro (1996) for more minute observations concerning scopal interactions in the Japanese existential construction.

[21] For the sake of convenience for delineation alone, Theme in (5.45) represents the position of its Case-feature checking position. Precisely, the category of the Theme-DP does not raise at LF.

cative phrase always takes its scope over the nominative-marked Theme in the Japanese existential construction with locative inversion (cf. Aoun and Li 1994).

This, in turn, lends support to my analysis of locative inversion in Japanese.

5.2.3.2. Scopal Interaction of NEG-NOM

Under my analysis of Japanese locative inversion, the scopal domain of the nominative-marked Theme is equivalent to the domain that T^{0max} dominates. This leads to the prediction that the nominative-marked Theme can take its scope over the element whose scopal domain is contained in the domain that T^{0max} dominates at LF. To put it differently, if this prediction is borne out, then my analysis of locative inversion in Japanese gains strong support.

Now consider (5.46):

(5.46) *Japanese*
    a. Kono doobutuen-ni gorira-**dake**-ga i-**na**-i.
        this zoo-LOC gorilla-**only**-NOM be-**not**-PRES
    b. 'It is only a gorilla that does not exist in this zoo.' (only > not)
    c. '*It is not the case that only a gorilla exists in this zoo.'
       (*not > only)

The sentence in (5.46a) can be interpreted as illustrated in (5.46b), and it does not mean (5.46c).

As is evident from their word order, the neg-element *na* comes in between V and T. Thus the verbal complex at LF looks like the structure in (5.47):

(5.47)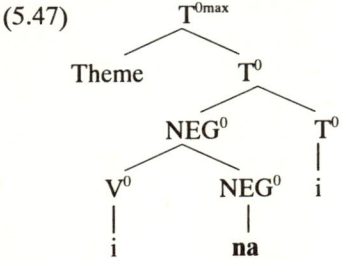

In (5.47) Theme asymmetrically c-commands the neg-element. Therefore, the neg-element never takes its scope over the nominative-marked Theme in the Japanese existential construction with locative inversion. This conforms to the above prediction, as expected.

On the other hand, the neg-element can take its scope over the accusative-marked Theme in a simple transitive clause, as in (5.47):

(5.47) *Japanese*
- a. Ano doobutuen-ga gorira-**dake**-o siikusitei-**na**-i.
   that zoo-NOM   gorilla-**only**-ACC feed-**not**-PRES
- b. 'It is not the case that this zoo feeds a gorilla.' (not > only)

It is expected that the accusative-marked element has a checking relation with the verb, and that the neg-element c-commands the verb at LF, as illustrated in (5.47) (see Ura 1995a, to appear c). Thus, the fact shown by (5.47) naturally follows. It is noteworthy here that the neg-element can take its scope over the element with a checking relation with the verb. The fact observed in (5.46), therefore, shows that the nominative-marked Theme in the existential construction with locative inversion does not have a checking relation with the verb (pace Yatsushiro 1996), and that the checking position of its nominative Case-feature is higher than the neg-element at LF.

Again, this points to the correctness of my analysis of locative inversion in Japanese, according to which the nominative-marked Theme enters into a nominative Case-feature checking relation with T (at LF).

5.3. Summary

In this chapter I argued that the locative phrase preposed in the existential construction in Bantu and in Japanese checks off T's strong EPP-feature and φ-feature, and that the Theme-argument in that construction has its nominative Case-feature checked off against T's weak nominative Case-feature at LF. It was demonstrated that these checking relations invoke some GF-splitting phenomena involved in locative inversion in Bantu and in Japanese.

6

Ergativity and Its Typological Variation

Ergativity has long been one of the hottest issues in the modern theory of linguistics, especially, within the framework of language/linguistic typology and that of Relational Grammar (RG). Under the framework of the PP-approach, there were several pieces of important work on the topic of ergativity in the GB era (e.g., among others, Marantz 1984 and B. Levin 1983), though the number of papers dealing directly with the topic in this framework was far less than that of papers written under the framework of language/linguistic typology and that of RG. This scarce concern about ergativity under the GB-framework may be due to the fact that the theory available in that era, which was being established mostly through the study of typical accusative languages like English and Japanese could hardly disentangle the intricate relations of the systems of case-marking, agreement, grammatical relations, and so forth found in ergative languages like Dyirbal, Georgian, and Basque. However, since Chomsky's (1992) invention of the Agr-based Case theory, which gives some clear vision concerning the relation between the system of case-marking and that of agreement by exploiting the Spec-head relation as the platform for both systems, many studies have appeared on ergativity and ergative languages under the Minimalist framework (e.g., Austin and López 1995; Belvin 1990b; Benua 1995; Bobaljik 1992, 1993; Laka 1993; Lyle 1995; Mahajan 1994, 1996; Manga 1996; Murasugi 1992, 1995; Nash 1996; and Phillips 1995, to list just a few).

In this vein, this chapter will offer a new approach to ergativity under the Agr-less checking theory of the Minimalist framework. In addition to its employment of the Agr-less checking theory, the theory of ergativity I will propose in this chapter is new in that it is expected to have rather broad coverage over empirical phenomena in various ergative languages. Furthermore, it will be demonstrated that ergative languages, though varying radically from each other in their morphological/syntactic behaviors, are all equivalent to each other, or even equivalent to accusative languages, in the sense that the mechanisms involved in their derivations are quite the same. In the literature, some propose that the ergative mechanism for Case-checking/assignment differs drastically from the accusative one, and others propose that DPs in the ergative system move through a course different from the course through which DPs move in the accusative system. The theory of ergativity to be advocated in this chapter needs nothing special for the ergative system with respect to its morphology/syntax: Case-checking in the ergative system takes place in the same way as in the accusative system, and DPs in the ergative system move in the same way as in the accusative system. Hence, this theory, with the aid of the theory of multiple feature checking, will give a consistent account of GF-splitting in both ergative and accusative languages.

6.1. Introduction: Ergativity

6.1.1. Morphological Ergativity

Traditionally, the notion **ergativity** has been considered to be connected with the coding properties of grammatical relations (GRs) such as case-marking of nominals, verb-agreement, and word order. Ergativity (or the ergative system), in this terminology, is merely a designation of the fact that SUBJ in an intransitive clause is *morphologically* coded in the same manner as OBJ in a transitive clause, and that SUBJ in a transitive clause is coded differently from SUBJ in an intransitive clause and OBJ in a transitive clause. This contrasts strikingly with **accusativity** (or the accusative system), in which SUBJ has the same morphological coding property regardless of whether it appears in an intransitive clause or a transitive one, and in which OBJ is morphologically coded in a manner different from SUBJ.

This can be delineated in the following fashion:

(6.1)
$$\begin{array}{ll} \text{NOMINATIVE} & \left\{ \begin{array}{l} \text{SUBJ(T)} \longrightarrow \text{ERGATIVE} \\ \text{SUBJ(I)} \\ \end{array} \right\} \\ \text{ACCUSATIVE} \longrightarrow \text{OBJ} & \left. \begin{array}{l} \\ \end{array} \right\} \text{ABSOLUTIVE} \\ \downarrow & \downarrow \\ \textit{Accusative System} & \textit{Ergative System} \end{array}$$

In (6.1) SUBJ(T) and SUBJ(I) stand for SUBJ in a transitive clause and SUBJ in an intransitive clause, respectively. To put it in a nutshell, a language L is said to be *morphologically ergative* if in L, SUBJ(I) is morphologically marked in the same way as OBJ in a transitive clause, and differently from SUBJ(T). Some instances of morphologically ergative languages are exemplified in (6.2):

(6.2) a. *Archi* (Van Valin 1981: 363)

   i. INTRANSITIVE

   Buwa-Ø   d-irxin.
   mother(II)-ABS IISG-work
   'Mother works.'

   ii. TRANSITIVE

   Buwa-mu   xalli-Ø   b-ar-ši   b-i.
   mother(II)-ERG bread(III)-ABS IIISG-bake-PROG IIISG-AUX
   'Mother is baking the bread.'

b. *Khinalug* (Comrie 1978: 344)

   i. INTRANSITIVE

   1. Ligɨld-Ø   sacaχ-Ø-q'iqomä.
      man-ABS   silent-M-be
      'The man is silent.'

   2. Xiñimk'ir-Ø   sacaχ-z-q'iqomä.
      woman-ABS   silent-F-be
      'The woman is silent.'

   ii. TRANSITIVE

   1. Bɨj-i   ši-Ø   tɨ-Ø-k'i.
      father-ERG son-ABS   awaken-M-T
      'The father awakened the son.'

   2. Bɨj-i   riši-Ø   tɨ-z-k'i.
      father-ERG daughter-ABS   awaken-F-T
      'The father awakened the daughter.'

c. *Yalarnnga* (Blake 1976: 283)

   i. INTRANSITIVE

   Manŋuru-Ø   ṭaŋa-mu.
   dog-ABS   run-PAST
   'A dog ran.'

   ii. TRANSITIVE

   Manŋuru-yu ŋia-Ø   ṭaca-mu.
   dog-ERG   I-ABS   bite-PAST
   'A dog bit me.'

d. *Yimas* (Phillips 1995: 342 and Phillips 1993: 186)

   i. INTRANSITIVE

   1. Pu-wa-t.   2. Na-wa-t.
      3PL.ABS-go-PERF   3SG.ABS-go-PERF
      'They went.'   'He went.'

ii. TRANSITIVE

1. Pu-n-tay.
   3PL.ABS-3SG.ERG-see
   'He saw them.'

2. Na-mpu-tay.
   3SG.ABS-3PL.ERG-see
   'They saw him.'

As shown by the examples in (6.2), morphological ergativity can be expressed by both case-marking on the arguments and agreement on the verb, or by either of them. As the examples in (6.2a) illustrate, Archi, a Daghestan language spoken in the Caucasus area, exhibits its morphological ergativity both in case-marking and verb agreement (see Kibrik 1979 and Van Valin 1981). In Khinalug, a Northwest Caucasian language, morphological ergativity is expressed even more clearly by case-marking and verb agreement (see Comrie 1978). On the other hand, there is no verb agreement in Yalarnnga, an Australian language spoken in western Queensland; however, its morphological ergativity can be expressed by case-marking on the arguments (see Blake 1976). In contrast, Yimas, a Papuan language of New Guinea (Foley 1991), expresses its morphological ergativity solely by means of verb agreement.[1]

Again, it is noteworthy that in a morphologically ergative language, SUBJ(I) and OBJ, excluding SUBJ(T), behave the same with respect to their morphological coding. But it is worthier to notice that it is not the case that all morphologically ergative languages treat SUBJ(I) and OBJ the same with respect to syntax. In other words, there are morphologically ergative languages in which their ergativity is merely morphological, but not syntactic. Hereafter I will call this type of language (i.e., morphologically ergative languages that are not syntactically ergative) *"Shallowly Ergative languages."*

6.1.2. Syntactic Ergativity

As mentioned in the previous section, in a syntactically ergative language, SUBJ(I) behaves the same as OBJ, differing from SUBJ(T), in syntactic respects. It is widely held in the literature that Dyirbal, an Australian language of North Queensland, is a typical language with syntactic ergativity (e.g., among many others, Dixon 1979, 1994; B. Levin 1983; Marantz 1984; and Bittner and Hale 1996a). Let us look at the syntactic ergativity that Dyirbal shows.

First, note that Dyirbal is morphologically ergative, too:

(6.3)   *Dyirbal* (Dixon 1994: 10)

a. INTRANSITIVE

Ŋuma-Ø   banaga-ɲu.
father-ABS return-NONFUT
'Father returned.'

---

[1] See Phillips (1993) for a detailed study on the system of verb agreement in Yimas.

b. TRANSITIVE
Ŋuma-Ø yabu-ŋgu bura-n.
father-ABS mother-ERG see-NONFUT
'Mother saw father.' ('*Father saw mother.')

As is evident from the examples in (6.3), SUBJ(I) and OBJ are marked as absolutive, and SUBJ(T) as ergative. In addition to the fact that SUBJ(I) and OBJ behave the same in morphological respects, they also behave the same in syntactic respects in Dyirbal; therefore, SUBJ(T) behaves differently from SUBJ(I) and OBJ in syntactic as well as morphological respects in Dyirbal.

The most-quoted evidence for the syntactic ergativity of Dyirbal is the fact concerning argument-omission involved in coordination. Argument-omission is a phenomenon found in the situation where two coordinated clauses share a DP, and the common DP can be omitted from the second clause. In syntactically accusative languages like English, argument-omission in coordination is possible only if the common DP functions as SUBJ in the first clause, as the examples in (6.4) illustrate:[2]

(6.4) *English*

a. [John$_k$ returned] and [Δ_k laughed].
b. [John$_k$ saw Mary$_j$] and [$\Delta_{k/*j}$ laughed].

These English examples show that OBJ cannot control the argument omitted in the second clause. Note, moreover, that only SUBJ in the first clause, irrespective of whether it is SUBJ(T) or SUBJ(I), has the ability to control the missing SUBJ in the second conjunct clause. It can therefore be concluded that in syntactically accusative languages like English, SUBJ(T) and SUBJ(I), excluding OBJ, behave the same in terms of argument-omission in coordination.

In contrast, SUBJ(I) and OBJ, excluding SUBJ(T), behave the same in terms of argument-omission in coordination in Dyirbal, as shown in (6.5):[3]

(6.5) *Dyirbal* (Dixon 1994: 161)

a. [Ŋuma-Ø$_k$ banaga-ɲu], [Δ_k miyanda-ɲu].
   father-ABS return-NONFUT laugh-NONFUT
   '[Father$_k$ returned] and [Δ_k laughed].'
b. [Ŋuma-Ø$_k$ yabu-ŋgu$_j$ bura-n], [$\Delta_{k/*j}$ banaga-ɲu].
   father-ABS mother-ERG see-NONFUT return-NONFUT
   '[Mother$_j$ saw father$_k$] and [$\Delta_{k/*j}$ returned].'

In (6.5b), *mother* (= SUBJ(T)) cannot control the omitted argument in the second intransitive clause, but *father* (= OBJ) can. Since SUBJ(I) can control the

---

[2] The Δ represents an argument omitted in a conjunct clause.

[3] In Dyirbal two clauses may be simply conjoined in a coordinate structure if they share a DP, according to Dixon (1972, 1994).

omitted argument in the second clause as shown in (6.5a), SUBJ(I) and OBJ behave the same in terms of argument-omission in coordination.

Elsewhere in this book I am utilizing the ability to control the missing argument in a subordinate-adjunct clause as a GF that is indicative of subjecthood. In syntactically accusative languages, this ability is typically possessed by SUBJ, but not by OBJ, as the following English examples show:[4]

(6.6) a. John$_k$ left here (together with Mary$_j$) [without PRO.$_{*j/k}$ speaking about *herself$_j$/himself$_k$].

b. They$_k$ hired John$_j$ [without PRO.$_{*j/k}$ having to commit themselves$_k$/*himself$_j$ to that salary].

In English, the missing subject of a *without*-clause can be controlled only by SUBJ. That is, SUBJ(T) and SUBJ(I) in syntactically accusative languages behave the same in that they have the ability to control.

In Dyirbal, on the other hand, the ability to control the missing argument in a subordinate-adjunct clause can be possessed by SUBJ(I) and OBJ, but not by SUBJ(T). According to Dixon (1994: 168), the purposive inflection *-ygu* is attached to the verb in the second conjunct clause and forms the purposive complement construction:

(6.7) *Dyirbal* (Dixon 1994: 168–169)

a. Ŋuma-Ø$_k$ banaga-ɲu [PRO$_k$ bural-ŋa-**ygu** yabu-gu].
    father-ABS return-NONFUT   see-ANT-PURP   mother-DAT
    'Father$_k$ returned [for the purpose of PRO$_k$ seeing mother].'

b. Yabu-Ø$_j$ ŋuma-ŋgu$_k$ giga-n [PRO.$_{*k/j}$ bural-ŋa-**ygu**
    mother-ABS father-ERG   tell-NONFUT   see-ANT-PURP
    jaja-gu].
    child-DAT
    'Father$_k$ told mother$_j$ [for the purpose of PRO.$_{*k/j}$ seeing child].'

In the intransitive clause in (6.7a), SUBJ(I) has the ability to control the missing argument of a *-ygu*-clause. Interestingly enough, the same ability is possessed by OBJ, but not SUBJ(T) in the transitive clause in (6.7b), contrary to the case in English, where SUBJ(T) has that ability in a transitive clause. The conclusion is that in Dyirbal, SUBJ(I) and OBJ, but not SUBJ(T), have the ability to control the missing argument in a subordinate-adjunct clause.[5]

Here it is interesting to note that SUBJ(I) syntactically behaves on a par not with OBJ but with SUBJ(T) in shallowly ergative languages (= morphologically ergative languages that show no syntactic ergativity). Warlpiri, a language spo-

---

[4] As I extensively argued elsewhere in this book, this ability to control may be possessed by an argument other than SUBJ even in syntactically accusative languages. Such a situation happens if some GF-splitting operation takes place.

[5] See B. Levin (1983), Marantz (1984), and Dixon (1994) for other pieces of evidence for the claim that Dyirbal is syntactically ergative (e.g., Equi-NP-deletion, relativization, etc.).

ken in Central Australia, counts as a morphologically ergative language, as is evident from its case-marking pattern illustrated by the examples in (6.8):

(6.8)   *Warlpiri* (B. Levin 1983: 141–142)

    a. INTRANSITIVE

        Ngarrka-Ø ka wangka-mi.
        man-ABS   PRES speak-NONFUT
        'The man is speaking.'

    b. TRANSITIVE

        Ngarrka-ngku ka marlu-Ø panti-mi.
        man-ERG   PRES kangaroo-ABS spear-NONFUT
        'The man is spearing the kangaroo.'

In spite of its morphological ergativity, Warlpiri shows syntactic accusativity (B. Levin 1983 and Bittner and Hale 1996a). This can be seen from the fact that the missing argument in a clause with the same-subject marker *-karra* can be controlled only by SUBJ (see Bittner and Hale 1996a for more detail). Consider the following:

(6.9)   *Warlpiri* (Bittner and Hale 1996a: 594–596)

    a. Ngarrka-Ø$_k$ ka wirnpirli-mi [PRO$_k$ karli-Ø
        man-ABS   PRES whistle-NONFUT   boomerang-ABS
        jarnti-rninja-**karra**].
        trim-INF-**SS**
        'The man$_k$ is whistling [while PRO$_k$ trimming a boomerang].'

    b. Ngarrka-ngku$_k$ karnta-Ø$_j$ nya-ngu [PRO$_{k/*j}$
        man-ERG   woman-ABS see-PAST
        yuka-nja-**karra**-rlu].
        enter-INF-**SS**-ERG
        Lit. 'The man$_k$ saw the woman$_j$ [while PRO$_{k/*j}$ entering].'

Compare the Warlpiri example in (6.9b) with the Dyirbal one in (6.7b). Whereas OBJ has the ability to control the missing argument in a subordinate-adjunct clause in syntactically ergative languages like Dyirbal, OBJ in shallowly ergative languages like Warlpiri does not; rather, SUBJ has the ability to control in those languages irrespective of the transitive/intransitive distinction of the clause. Put differently, in shallowly ergative languages, SUBJ(I) behaves the same as SUBJ(T), differing from OBJ, in syntactic respects, though SUBJ(I) behaves the same as OBJ, differing from SUBJ(T), in morphological respects.

In the literature, it has been revealed, since Anderson's (1976) seminal work, that shallowly ergative languages like Warlpiri include Kâte, Abkhazian (Anderson 1976), Khinalug (Comrie 1978), Enga (Li and Lang 1979), Walmatjari (Dixon 1979), Archi (Kibrik 1979), Jacaltec (Van Valin 1981), Basque (B. Levin 1983), Quiché (Larsen 1987), Hindi (Kachru 1987), Axvax (Kibrik 1985), Niuean (Wennevold Silva 1989), Nisgha (Belvin 1990a), Kabardian (Colarusso 1992), Lezgian (Haspelmath 1993), Kewa (Palmer 1994), Georgian (Lyle 1995),

Yimas (Phillips 1995), and many others, and syntactically ergative languages like Dyirbal include Hurrian (Anderson 1976), Sama (Foley and Van Valin 1984), Central Arctic Eskimo (Marantz 1984), Alutor (Kibrik 1985), Warrungu (Tsunoda 1988),[6] and (West Greenlandic) Inuit (Bittner and Hale 1996a).[7] As has been occasionally noted (Anderson 1976, Marantz 1984, and Palmer 1994), languages with syntactically pure ergativity are very infrequently found, though dozens of languages with some mixture of ergativity and accusativity in syntactic respects have been documented in the literature (including Kalkatung (Blake 1976), Yidiɲ (Dixon 1977), Chukchee (Comrie 1979), Tangut (Kepping 1979), Kalaw Lagaw Ya (Comrie 1981), Yup'ik (Payne 1982), and Tongan (Dixon 1994)). As will be evident later, these languages with a mixture of syntactic ergativity/accusativity pose interesting problems.

6.1.3. Split-Ergativity

When a language L shows some mixed properties of ergativity and accusativity in a certain respect R, L is said to be split-ergative with respect to R (cf. Comrie 1978, Dixon 1979, and DeLancey 1981). In a broader sense it may be plausible that L is said to be split-ergative if L shows ergativity in some respect R_1 but shows accusativity in another respect R_2. In this regard, shallowly ergative languages are split-ergative; for, they are ergative in morphological respects, but accusative in syntactic respects.

6.1.3.1. Morphological Split

In a variety of languages split-ergativity is found in their systems of morphological coding such as nominal case-marking and verb agreement. Georgian is well-known for its split-ergativity due to its tense/aspect distinction. In Georgian the aorist tense system demands ergativity and the present tense system demands accusativity:[8]

---

[6] Palmer (1994) states, based on Tsunoda's (1988) observations, that the syntax of Warrungu is largely, but not absolutely, ergative.

[7] As for West Greenlandic Inuit, some researchers (e.g., Kalmár 1979 and Manning 1996) argue that it does not show completely syntactic ergativity. In §6.1.3.2 I will touch on reflexive-binding in Inuit.

[8] Following Comrie (1978), I tentatively refer to *-i* as nominative if it appears in a present tense clause and as absolutive in an aorist tense clause. I will return directly to this point in §6.4.2.

(6.10) *Georgian* (Comrie 1978: 351–352)

    a. AORIST

        i. INTRANSITIVE

            Student-i   mivida.
            student-ABS go(AOR)
            'The student went.'

        ii. TRANSITIVE

            Student-ma ceril-i   dacera.
            student-ERG letter-ABS write(AOR)
            'The student wrote the letter.'

    b. PRESENT

        i. INTRANSITIVE

            Student-i   midis.
            student-NOM go(PRES)
            'The student goes.'

        ii. TRANSITIVE

            Student-i   ceril-s   cers.
            student-NOM letter-ACC write(PRES)
            'The student wrote the letter.'

Besides Georgian, Hindi, and many other Indo-Aryan languages, Burushaski, Tibetan, Nepali, Samoan, and so forth show similar split-ergativity due to the tense/aspect system (cf. Comrie 1978; Dixon 1979, 1994; Tsunoda 1981; and Palmer 1994).

Split-ergativity manifests itself in terms of the distinction between pronoun and full DP. The following examples come from Bidjara, an Australian language of Central Queensland:

(6.11) *Bidjara* (Blake 1976: 282)

    a. FULL DP (FULL NOMINAL)   b. PRONOMINAL

        i. INTRANSITIVE

            Ŋura-Ø wanguli-la.   Ŋaya-Ø barri-la.
            dog-ABS bark-PAST   I-NOM   cry-PAST
            'A dog barked.'   'I cried.'

        ii. TRANSITIVE

            Ŋura-ŋu munda-Ø bada-la. Ŋaya-Ø nuɲu-na bada-la.
            dog-ERG snake-ABS bite-PAST I-NOM him-ACC bite-PAST
            'A dog bit a snake.'   'I bit him.'

Other languages with this type of split-ergativity include Warrungu, Nepali, Dyirbal, and Yidiɲ (cf. Dixon 1979, 1994 and Palmer 1994).

Another interesting type of split-ergativity is found in Burushaski, the language isolate spoken in the area between Kashmir and Tibet. In this language the case-marking system is ergative but the system of verb agreement is accusative, as shown by the examples in (6.12):

(6.12) *Burushaski* (Palmer 1994: 57)

    a. INTRANSITIVE

        [Ne   hir]-Ø   yált-i.
        the(M) man -ABS yawn(PRET)-3SG.M
        'The man yawned.'

    b. TRANSITIVE

        i. [Ne   hir]-e   phaló-Ø   bók-i.
           the(M) man -ERG seed-ABS SOW(PRET)-3SG.M
           'The man planted the seeds.'

        ii. [Ne   hir]-e   ja-Ø a-yórtikin-i.
           the(M) man -ERG I-ABS 1SG-drag(PRET)-3SG.M
           'The man dragged me.'

As is evident from these examples, the verb-agreement, which appears in the final of the verbal complex, is controlled by SUBJ(I) in an intransitive clause and by SUBJ(T) in a transitive clause, despite the fact that SUBJ(I) has the same case-marking form as OBJ, but not as SUBJ(T). Of great concern to the topic in this book is the fact that this kind of disparity between case-marking and verb agreement clearly counts as GF-splitting, as was mentioned in chapter 1. Warlpiri (Hale 1972) and Avar (Givón 1984b) are languages that have ergative case-marking, but accusative verb agreement.

It is interesting to note, in passing, that some languages show more than one type of split-ergativity. In addition to the split-ergativity shown in (6.12), Burushaski shows the split-ergativity conditioned by the tense/aspect/mood distinction (Dixon 1979). Nepali shows the split-ergativity conditioned by the tense/aspect/mood distinction as well as the one conditioned by the pronominal/full nominal distinction (Palmer 1994).[9]

6.1.3.2. Syntactic Split

It was noted in §6.1.2 that it has been reported that there are languages with some mixture of ergativity and accusativity in syntactic respects (such as Kalkatung (Blake 1976), West Greenlandic Eskimo (Woodbury 1977), Yidiɲ (Dixon 1977), Chukchee (Comrie 1979), Tangut (Kepping 1979), Kalaw Lagaw Ya (Comrie 1981), Yup'ik (Payne 1982), and Tongan (Dixon 1994)). In the literature cited herein it has been held that SUBJ(I) behaves the same as SUBJ(T) in some syntactic respects and behaves the same as OBJ in others.

---

[9] For other types of morphological split-ergativity, see Dixon (1979, 1994), DeLancey (1981), Tsunoda (1981), and Givón (1984b).

Intriguingly, it is possible to find a syntactic split in languages with allegedly syntactic ergativity such as (West Greenlandic) Inuit. Consider (6.13):

(6.13) *West Greenlandic Inuit*
    a.   Juuna-p$_k$ Kaali-Ø$_j$ **immi**-nik$_{k/*j}$ uqaluttuup-p-a-a.
         -ERG   -ABS   self-INST   tell-IND-TRNS-3SG.3SG
       'Juuna$_k$ told Kaali$_j$ about self$_{k/*j}$.' (Bittner 1994: 146)
    b.   Juuna-Ø$_k$ **immi**-nut$_k$ tatigi-v-u-q.
         -ABS   self-DAT   trust-IND-INTR-3SG
       'Juuna$_k$ trusts in self$_k$.' (Bittner and Hale 1996a: 579)

Bittner (1994: chapter 4) argues, with ample examples, that the reflexive form *immi* in Inuit shows strong subject-orientation. Hence, the fact shown in (6.13) indicates that SUBJ(I) and SUBJ(T), excluding OBJ, behaves the same in terms of reflexive-binding in Inuit. Although Dyirbal has no overt reflexive pronoun, it employs reflexive-marking on the verbal complex. According to Dixon (1972, 1994), from the fact that OBJ is never construed as the binder of the reflexive-marker in Dyirbal, it can be concluded that SUBJ(I) and SUBJ(T) behave the same in reflexive-binding in Dyirbal, too, despite its syntactic ergativity.

Nonetheless, SUBJ(I) behaves the same as OBJ, differing from SUBJ(T), in other syntactic respects, in Inuit and Dyirbal. It was already noted that SUBJ(I) and OBJ, but not SUBJ(T), have the ability to control in Dyirbal. The following examples show that the same holds true in Inuit:

(6.14) *West Greenlandic Inuit* (Bittner 1994: 152–153)
    a.   [Juuna-Ø$_k$ isir-a-**mi**$_k$],   PRO$_k$ Kaali-Ø
         -ABS   enter-PAST-3SG.PROX   -ABS
       urnip-p-a-a.
       approach-IND-TRNS-3SG.3SG
       'When Juuna$_k$ entered, PRO$_k$ approached Kaali.'
    b.   [Juuna-p$_k$ Kaali-Ø$_j$ tatigi-mm-a-**ni**$_{*k/j}$],   PRO$_{*k/j}$
         -ERG   -ABS   trust-PAST-3SG.PROX
       tuqqissima-v-u-q.
       stay.calm-IND-INTR-3SG
       'Because Juuna$_k$ trusted Kaali$_j$, PRO$_{*k/j}$ stayed calm.'

Following the spirit of Hale (1992) (cf., also, Bittner 1994 and Bittner and Hale 1996a), I assume that the proximate suffix on an adjunct-clause is a kind of anaphor which is to be bound by an argument with subjecthood; as a result, the fact shown in (6.14) indicates that OBJ as well as SUBJ(I), but not SUBJ(T), has subjcthood in Inuit. Irrespective of subjecthood, this fact shows, at least, that SUBJ(I) and OBJ in Inuit behave the same in terms of the control involved in proximation.

Although I omit discussing any other arguments in favor of syntactic ergativity in Dyirbal and West Greenlandic Inuit,[10] it seems that even those syntacti-

---

[10] For more arguments, I refer the reader to Dixon (1994) for Dyirbal and Bittner and

cally ergative languages show accusativity in terms of reflexive binding (cf. Dixon 1979 and Manning 1996). In fact, Dixon (1994: 138–139) states:

> In every ergative language, as in every accusative language, the 'antecedent', i.e. the controller of reflexivity is A (or S, where it is extended to intransitives). This appears to be a universal and is related to the universal category of subject,[11] ...

If his intuition is correct, it has a big consequence for the study of ergativity in syntax. Since Anderson's (1976) study on syntactic ergativity, reflexive-binding is one of the most frequently used diagnoses for the purpose of showing a given language's syntactic accusativity/ergativity in syntax. Later in this chapter I will give a natural explanation of the question as to why even languages with "deepest" ergativity like Dyirbal show accusativity in terms of reflexive-binding. In any event, as many researchers have pointed out, syntactic ergativity is a matter of degree (cf. Blake 1976; Comrie 1979; B. Levin 1983; Givón 1984b; and, especially, Dixon 1979, 1994). I will also attempt to explain why syntactic ergativity varies from language to language.

6.1.3.3. Split Due to Shallow Ergativity

As stated in §6.1.2, shallowly ergative languages employ the ergative system in terms of their morphological coding, such as case-marking and verb agreement, but employ the accusative system in their syntactic respects. In other words, in these languages, SUBJ(I) and OBJ, excluding SUBJ(T), are treated equivalently in morphology, but SUBJ(I) and SUBJ(T), excluding OBJ, are treated equivalently in syntax. This may be viewed as a kind of split-ergativity in a broader sense, as mentioned above. I will show that, like other kinds of split-ergativity, this poses interesting problems to the Agr-based Case theory, which depends crucially on the structural definition of "checking."

6.2. Problems of Ergativity

Under the Case-theory in the GB era, Case is assigned under the structural condition *government* (Chomsky 1981): If a DP occupies the Spec of Infl, it is assigned a nominative Case by Infl under government, and it induces subject-agreement through the structurally defined notion *Spec-head agreement* between it and Infl. Under this theory of Case and agreement, the structural position of a DP is crucial for the DP's property in terms of Case and agreement.

The same holds true for the Agr-based Case theory. Under the Agr-based Case theory originating from Chomsky's (1989) introduction of Agr, the fundamental assumption is that the (structural) Case of a given DP and the agreement that the DP induces are determined by the structural position or relation that the

---

Hale (1996a) for West Greenlandic Inuit.

[11] A is almost corresponds to our SUBJ(T) and S to our SUBJ(I). See §1.4.3 for discussion.

DP holds in the derivation. Hence, a DP's occupation of the Spec of a tensed T (or AgrS) means that the DP has a nominative Case and induces subject-agreement. Notice that this is independent of the (in)transitivity of the clause: If DP occupies the Spec of T (or AgrS), DP has a nominative Case and induces subject agreement, regardless of whether the clause is transitive or intransitive.

It has been held that this tight relation between structure and Case/agreement explains two seemingly unrelated facts in accusative languages. First, it explains the fact that SUBJ(I) and SUBJ(T), excluding OBJ, in a tensed clause in accusative languages have the same case-marking and induce subject agreement. Second, it also explains the fact that SUBJ(I) and SUBJ(T) behave the same in syntactic respects in accusative languages. The explanation of the second fact presupposes that α in a clause C1 and β in another clause C2 in a given language show uniform behaviors in syntactic respects if the position of α is structurally equivalent to that of β. For example, SUBJ(I) and SUBJ(T) behave the same in syntactic respects because the position of SUBJ(I) is structurally equivalent to that of SUBJ(T) (they occupy the Spec of a tensed T, though the transitivity of the clause where SUBJ(I) appears is different from that of the clause where SUBJ(T) appears).

Returning to ergativity and the issues related to ergativity, however, we readily realize that this structure-based theory of Case and agreement encounters some problems. In what follows in this section I will sketch out what problems ergativity poses to the theory of Case and agreement.

6.2.1. Problems of Morphological Ergativity

Since the mid 1970s many articles have addressed their attention to the issues concerning SUBJECT, (or, more broadly, grammatical relations) in morphologically/syntactically ergative languages (e.g., among many others, George 1974, Johnson 1974b, Anderson 1976, Blake 1976, Woodbury 1977, Bechert 1979, Van Valin 1981, Marantz 1984, Comrie 1989, Murasugi 1992, Bobaljik 1993, Dixon 1994, Phillips 1995, and Manning 1996). Some of them go so far as to conclude that SUBJECT (or grammatical relations) cannot be detected or defined in ergative languages and, hence, is useless not only in those languages but also in universal grammar. Yet some others maintain that, given appropriate methods/modifications, they can be defined even in ergative languages, and are still useful in universal grammar. At any rate, ergativity is undoubtedly problematic in the theory of grammar.

As stated before, the structure-based theory of Case and agreement in the PP-approach is no exception in confronting problems of ergativity. To see this, consider the following Khinalug examples:

(6.15) *Khinalug*

    a. INTRANSITIVE

        Ligild-Ø sacaχ-Ø-q'iqomä.
        man-ABS silent-M-be
        'The man is silent.'

    b. TRANSITIVE

        Ligild-i riši-Ø ti- { *Ø / z } -k'i.
        man-ERG daughter-ABS awaken-*M/F -T
        'The man awakened the daughter.'

Khinalug is a morphologically ergative language with both ergative case-marking and ergative verb-agreement (Comrie 1978). *Ligild* 'the man' counts as SUBJ in (6.15a) and (6.15b); for, it is the argument with the highest θ-role in each clause. Nevertheless, it is marked as absolutive in (6.15a) but ergative in (6.15b). Moreover, whereas it induces agreement in (6.15a), it cannot in (6.15b).

These Khinalug examples sharply contrast with the following examples from Bhojpuri, an accusative language spoken in India (Shukla 1981):

(6.16) *Bhojpuri* (Shukla 1981: 65–66)

    a. INTRANSITIVE

        Ham-Ø su:t-**ab**.
        I-NOM sleep-1SG.FUT
        'I will sleep.'

    b. TRANSITIVE

        Ham-Ø manai:-ke de:k̑- { **ab** / *i } -k'i.
        I-NOM man-ACC see-1SG.FUT/*3SG.M.FUT
        'I will see a man.'

In accusative languages like Bhojpuri, SUBJ(I) and SUBJ(T) have the same case-marking and induce agreement, as shown in (6.16). The accusativity in morphology in those languages can be straightforwardly explained by the structure-based theory of Case and agreement in the PP-approach: Occupying the Spec of a tensed Infl (= T), SUBJ(I) and SUBJ(T) can have their nominative Case properly licensed by Infl and induce morphological agreement by the mediation of Infl. And the accusative Case of OBJ is licensed by a transitive verb, which has the ability to license (assign or check) an accusative Case. Hence, under the structure-based theory of case and agreement, the reason that SUBJ(I) and SUBJ(T) behave the same in terms of case-marking and verb-agreement in accusative languages naturally follows from the fact that they occupy the same structural position, the Spec of Infl. Likewise the morphological isolation of OBJ in accusative languages results from the dissimilarity of its position from the position of SUBJ(I) and SUBJ(T).

But the same explanation under the structure-based theory of case and agreement fails to be applied directly to morphologically ergative languages like Khinalug. This is simply because SUBJ(I) in morphologically ergative languages does not share its morphological property with SUBJ(T); as manifestly illustrated by the Khinalug examples in (6.15), it behaves the same as OBJ in terms of morphology. Thus, in order to explain the morphologically unitary behavior of SUBJ(I) and OBJ in ergative languages under the structure-based theory, it is necessary to hypothesize that it results from the fact that SUBJ(I) and OBJ occupy the same position in ergative languages, just as the morphologically unitary behavior of SUBJ(I) and SUBJ(T) results from the fact that SUBJ(I) and SUBJ(T) occupy the same position in accusative languages. As will be reviewed in §6.3, most solutions to the problems of ergativity ever proposed under the PP-approach have indeed advocated this hypothesis, with possible variations of implementation.

In fact, the structure-based theory of case and agreement reinforced with the aforementioned hypothesis can capture somehow the problem of ergativity with respect to morphology, but it still encounters problems if it is applied to broader phenomena involved in ergativity; it encounters problems involved in syntactic/shallow ergativity and split-ergativity.

6.2.2. Problems of Syntactic/Shallow Ergativity

If, as the above hypothesis stipulates, SUBJ(I) and OBJ occupy the same structural position in morphologically ergative languages, it leads to very strong predictions about the syntactic behaviors of SUBJ(I) and OBJ in those languages. This is because it is a fundamental assumption in the PP-approach that the syntactic structure in a given sentence is the sole source for the syntactic behaviors of the elements involved in the clause. Therefore, it is predicted under the structure-based theory of case and agreement that SUBJ(I) and OBJ in morphologically ergative languages behave the same in syntactic respects as well as in morphological respects.

This prediction is indeed borne out in syntactically ergative languages, which constitute one type of morphologically ergative languages; for, these languages are so-called just because SUBJ(I) and OBJ syntactically behave the same in those languages. Nevertheless, there are cases where this prediction is not realized. Recall that there are two types of morphologically ergative languages; syntactically ergative and shallowly ergative ones. In the latter type like Warlpiri, Basque, Niuean, and Archi (cf. §6.1.2), despite the fact that SUBJ(I) and OBJ behave the same in morphological respects, SUBJ(I) does not behave the same as OBJ in syntactic respects. Therefore, shallowly ergative languages offer much resistance to the hypothesis that SUBJ(I) and OBJ occupy the same structural position in morphologically ergative languages.

On the other hand, syntactic ergativity poses another kind of problem: In order to maintain the hypothesis that SUBJ(I) and OBJ occupy the same structural position in ergative languages, it is necessary to overcome a technical, theory-internal problem as to why the same situation is prohibited in accusative languages. The theory demands that the position of SUBJ(I), differing from that of

OBJ, corresponds to that of SUBJ(T) in accusative languages. Now the question is: What permits SUBJ(I) and OBJ to occupy the same position in ergative languages and, at the same time, prohibits them from occupying the same position in accusative languages. Several proposals have been made to this problem under the PP-approach, and the explanatory coverage of empirical phenomena depends largely upon how to implement the device to cope with this problem, as will be reviewed in §6.3.

6.2.3. Problems of Split-Ergativity

Another kind of problem arises if the structure-based theory of Case and agreement is applied to languages with split-ergativity. A relatively easy-to-deal-with problem is what causes the split according to tense/aspect/ mood and/or pronominal/full nominal (cf. §6.1.3.1). This kind of discrepancy in morphological marking can be occasionally detected also in accusative languages, and some technical expedient needs to be devised to cope with it under any kind of theory.[12]

A problem resistant to the structure-based theory of Case and agreement arises from the type of split-ergativity manifested in Warlpiri and Burushaski. It was observed in §6.1.3.1 that in these languages, the case-marking system is ergative but the system of verb-agreement is accusative, as shown by the Warlpiri examples in (6.17):

(6.17) *Warlpiri*

    a. INTRANSITIVE (B. Levin 1983: 143)

        i. Ŋatju-Ø ka-**na** wangka-mi.
           I-ABS   PRES-1SG speak-NON.PAST
           'I am speaking.'

        ii. Ɲuntu-Ø ka-**npa** wangka-mi.
           you-ABS PRES-2SG speak-NON.PAST
           'You are speaking.'

    b. TRANSITIVE

        i. Ŋatjulu-ḻu ka-**na** marlu-Ø ɲa-ɲi.
           I-ERG   TNS-1SG kangaroo-ABS see-NON.PAST
           'I see the kangaroo.'

        ii. Ɲuntulu-ḻu ka-**npa** marlu-Ø ɲa-ɲi.
           you-ERG   TNS-2SG kangaroo-ABS see-NON.PAST
           'You see the kangaroo.'

As is evident from these examples,[13] the verb-agreement, which is attached to the

---

[12] I will touch on this issue in §6.4.2.4.

[13] See Hale (1972) and Simpson (1991) for a detailed analysis of the agreement system in Warlpiri.

tense-marker *ka-*, is controlled by SUBJ(I) in an intransitive clause and by SUBJ(T) in a transitive clause, despite the fact that SUBJ(I) has the same case-marking form as OBJ, but not as SUBJ(T).

This morphological discrepancy between case-marking and agreement seriously challenges the structure-based theory of Case and agreement with the hypothesis that SUBJ(I) and OBJ occupy the same structural position in morphologically ergative languages. Under this theory, two DPs are expected to have the same morphological coding property if they occupy the same structural position. No matter what device may be implemented, this kind of split-ergativity necessitates differentiating the licensing mechanism for Case from the one for agreement.

6.2.4. Ergativity and GF-Splitting

As has been hinted thus far, GF-splitting phenomena abound in ergative languages. Representatively, shallow ergativity provokes GF-splitting. Let us consider the following examples from Archi:

(6.18)   *Archi* (Van Valin 1981: 364–365)

a. Bošor$_k$ [PRO$_k$ k'oaHan   soli   ]   weɪrʃu.
    man(ABS)   stick(ABS) hold(GER)   run-AOR
    'The man$_k$ ran, [PRO$_k$ holding the stick].'

b. Adamli$_k$ [PRO$_k$ k'aräši xit'boli]   č'ele   goɪroɪ-abti.
    man(ERG)   down   push(GER)   stone(ABS)   roll-AOR
    'The man$_k$ rolled the stone, [PRO$_k$ having pushed it down].'

It was observed in §6.1.1 that Archi is a morphologically ergative language, with SUBJ(I) and OBJ being marked as absolutive and SUBJ(T) as ergative (cf. (6.2a) in §6.1.1). As the above examples illustrate, SUBJ(I) shares the ability to control with SUBJ(T). As argued in §6.1.2, it is generally the case with shallowly ergative languages like Archi, that SUBJ(I) behaves the same as SUBJ(T), differing from OBJ, in syntactic respects, though SUBJ(I) behaves the same as OBJ, differing from SUBJ(T), in morphological respects. Obviously, this is a kind of GF-splitting. In an intransitive clause SUBJ(I) has the ability to stand in absolutive Case, to induce agreement, and to control the missing subject of a subordinate-adjunct clause. In a transitive clause, on the other hand, those GFs are split up into SUBJ(T) and OBJ.

Syntactic ergativity, too, provokes GF-splitting in some cases. It was observed in §6.1.3.2 that even in syntactically ergative languages like West Greenlandic Inuit and Dyirbal, in which SUBJ(I) and OBJ are expected to behave the same in syntactic respects in addition to morphological respects, SUBJ(I) shares the ability to bind a reflexive with SUBJ(T) (cf. (6.13)) despite the fact that SUBJ(I) shares other syntactic properties, like the ability to control, with OBJ, but not with SUBJ(T) (cf. (6.14)). This also counts as a kind of GF-splitting.

Besides the problems of ergativity described in the previous sections, ergativity therefore poses an interesting problem with respect to GF-splitting. Consequently, it is very interesting and important to the aim of this book to examine ergativity to elucidate the validity of the theory of GF-splitting developed and elaborated here.

6.2.5. Prospect under the Theory of Multiple Feature Checking

From chapter 2 to chapter 5 I demonstrated that the theory of multiple feature checking gives a congruous explanation to various kinds of GF-splitting phenomena found in a variety of languages. Given that ergative languages are very fertile in GF-splitting phenomena, it is natural to expect that the theory of multiple feature checking offers a consistent account of ergativity, too. Moreover, it might be possible to regard the contrast between ergativity and accusativity as a kind of broader GF-splitting astride between ergative and accusative languages. The ability to control, for example, may be split up into syntactically ergative languages and accusative ones; it is possessed by OBJ in the former languages and by SUBJ(T) in the latter. Then, it is expected that, if the theory of multiple feature checking is applied from this perspective, it will be possible to cope with the contrast between ergative and accusative languages just as with the contrast between active and inverse alternation in Apachean. Put differently, some parametric difference in terms of some feature checking derives a contrast between ergative languages and accusative ones in a certain syntactic respect, just like the difference between the active Infl and the inverse one in terms of the multiplicity of the checking ability of their EPP-feature results in the syntactic contrasts between active and inverse in Apachean (cf. §2.2).

It is worth noting that the system of multiple feature checking depends substantially upon the Agr-less checking theory reinforced with the theory of bare phrase structure (cf. §1.3). It is very important here to notice that, under the Agr-less checking theory reinforced with the theory of bare phrase structure, what determines a DP's property with respect to Case and agreement is not a structurally defined notion such as "government" or Spec-head agreement; it is determined solely by the DP's relation to a head in terms of feature checking. For example, unless it enters into a nominative Case-feature checking relation with T, the nominative Case of a DP cannot be formally licensed even though it occupies a Spec of T at a syntactically appropriate level. Accordingly, a DP's Case-property and its agreement-property are relationally determined in an independent manner, and the structural position of a DP per se does not play any role in the determination of these properties.

In this respect, the multiple feature checking theory, which presupposes the Agr-less checking theory, contrasts sharply with the structure-based theory of Case and agreement. As argued at the beginning of §6.2, the Case theory in the GB era and the Agr-based Case theory in the Minimalist program are variants of this structure-based theory of Case and agreement. Thus far it has been demonstrated that the structure-based theory of Case and agreement encounters several problems of ergativity largely because it treats Case and agreement as a unit that is defined structurally. On the other hand, the theory of multiple feature checking does not treat Case and agreement uniformly, nor does it define them by relating them to any structural notions or structural positions. Thus, it is expected to be free from most of the problems that the structure-based theory of Case and agreement encounters when it is applied to ergative languages.

Before entering into the discussion on ergativity under the theory of multiple feature checking, let us see, in order to spotlight the problems involved in ergativity, how they have been tackled by some previous studies in the PP-approach.

6.3. Approaches to Ergativity

In this section I will briefly review several major approaches to ergativity under the framework of the PP-approach,[14] and give some critiques of them from the viewpoint of the Minimalist assumptions advocated and vindicated in this book.

6.3.1. Marantz (1981, 1984) and B. Levin (1983)

Marantz (1981, 1984) proposes, under the "government-based" Case theory, that syntactic ergativity results from what he calls the "Ergative Hypothesis," according to which the Agent-role of a transitive verb, which is assigned to a position outside of VP in accusative languages, is assigned to a position within VP in syntactically ergative languages, and the Theme/Patient-role, which is assigned to a position internal to VP in accusative languages, is assigned to a position outside of VP in syntactically ergative languages. To put it in other words, the Ergative Hypothesis states that the external/internal argument distinction (Williams 1981) in ordinary accusative languages is reversed in syntactically ergative languages. And B. Levin (1983), examining Marantz's idea by applying it to other ergative languages, attempts to show its capacity for various phenomena involved in ergativity.

Besides empirical problems that might arise from Marantz's (1981, 1984) Ergative Hypothesis,[15] I would like to point out its theoretical inconsistency with the Minimalist assumptions presupposed in this book. First and most crucially, the Ergative Hypothesis is fundamentally inconsistent with the hypothesis concerning the syntactic mapping of argument structure advocated throughout this book (cf. §1.4.2), according to which each θ-role of a given predicate is structurally discharged in accordance with its rank in the Thematic Hierarchy: The higher a θ-role is ranked in the Thematic Hierarchy, the higher it is discharged in the

---

[14] For a concise summary of approaches to ergativity in other frameworks, see Dixon (1994: appendix).

[15] For some of those empirical problems, see Johns (1987), Wennevold Silva (1989), Bok-Bennema (1991), and, especially, Manning (1996).

syntactic structure. This hypothesis thus insists that the mapping of argument structure purported to happen in syntactically ergative languages under the Ergative Hypothesis should be nonexistent in those languages.

In fact, Manning (1996) shows that the mapping of argument structure in syntactically ergative languages is quite the same as in accusative ones; he discovers (1) that idioms in Dyirbal, a syntactically ergative language, are in general absolutive-verb compound idioms and no ergative-verb idioms have been found, and (2) that it is only a Theme/Patient argument that can be incorporated into V by noun-incorporation in Central Arctic Eskimo, a language alleged to be syntactically ergative by Marantz (1984). According to the theory of idioms Marantz (1981, 1984) advocates, it is always the case that V and its internal argument (i.e., argument whose θ-role is assigned to a position internal to VP) pair up into an idiom. As a consequence, fact (1) gives a flat contradiction to the Ergative Hypothesis. Moreover, fact (2) is also contradictory to the Ergative Hypothesis; for, Baker's (1988) theory of incorporation requires that external arguments should not be incorporated into V. These facts, however, are never inconsistent with the hypothesis concerning the syntactic mapping of argument structure assumed in this book, according to which the positions where Agent and Theme/Patient are syntactically discharged in a transitive clause are invariant regardless of ergativity/accusativity.

Furthermore, the Ergative Hypothesis is not only inconsistent with the Minimalist assumption about the nature of parameters, which states that all parametric variations must stem from the morphology of lexical items (Chomsky 1992, 1995a), but also highly implausible as a possible parameter in natural language because the trigger of the parameter that determines whether a given language is ergative or accusative is not straightforward at all; it is by no means clear, under the Ergative Hypothesis, with what clue a child comes to realize whether his/her language is ergative or accusative.[16]

6.3.2. Other Pre-Minimalist Approaches

There have been some other influential approaches proposed under the pre-Minimalist framework which assume a structure-based theory of Case without recourse to feature checking. They include Bok-Bennema (1991), Johns (1992), Bittner (1994), and Bittner and Hale (1996a). Naturally, each of them has its own theory of ergativity, which has some advantage on empirical grounds. Excepting Bittner and Hale (1996a), the other three are of one accord both in basically embracing the "government-based" Case theory for accusative languages and in regarding ergative languages as peculiar in that they are not subject to the canonical application of the "government-based" Case theory.

---

[16] In addition, Marantz's (1984) treatment of shallowly ergative languages is inconsistent with the "government-based" Case theory: It is necessary to admit that the mechanism of Case-assignment for those languages is totally different from the one for ordinary accusative languages, in which Case is assigned by government. See B. Levin (1983) for discussion.

On the other hand, Bittner and Hale (1996a) assume the Case theory proposed by Bittner and Hale (1996b), which counts as a variant of the structure-based Case theory, and attempt to account for the cross-linguistic differences in terms of the typology of case-marking. According to them, given an appropriate parameter, the difference between ergative languages and accusative ones in terms of their case-marking patterns can be uniformly accounted for by their Case theory.[17]

It is noteworthy that, apart from the differences in their implementations and the differences in their empirical coverage, they have in common the basic assumption that Case should be assigned/licensed in a structurally dependent fashion. Therefore, they are more or less liable to the problems involved with the structure-based theory of Case which I described in §6.2.

6.3.3. Two Minimalist Approaches

In this subsection I will review Murasugi's (1992, 1995) approach and Bobaljik's (1992, 1993), both of which assume the checking theory of the Minimalist program. These two approaches to ergativity are particularly important because most of the approaches proposed thereafter under the Minimalist framework lay the foundation of their analysis on one of these approaches. Nevertheless, I will argue that, without appropriate modifications, these approaches encounter both theoretical and empirical problems.

6.3.3.1. *Murasugi (1992, 1995)*

Under the checking theory proposed by Chomsky (1992), each of the two argument-DPs in a transitive clause must move to an appropriate position where it has its Case-feature properly checked off. According to Chomsky (1992), the crossing paths necessarily emerge in a transitive clause because OBJ moves from the V-complement position to the Spec of AgrO and SUBJ moves from the Spec of V to the Spec of Infl, as illustrated in (6.19):

---

[17] I will not go into detail about their Case theory, referring the reader to Bittner and Hale (1996b). For some comments on their Case theory from the Minimalist point of view, see Ura (to appear a).

(6.19) *Crossing Paths (transitive clause in accusative languages)*

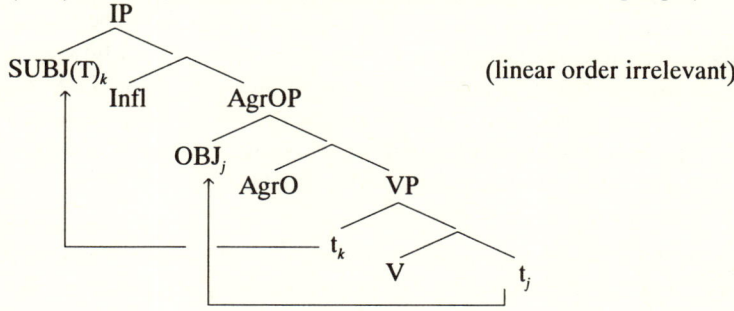

(linear order irrelevant)

Notice that OBJ obligatorily moves to the Spec of AgrO in a transitive clause because V alone has the ability to check off OBJ's Case-feature and the Spec of AgrO is the only position where V can execute the checking of OBJ's Case-feature (see Chomsky 1992). It should be noted here that in this story, a transitive V and OBJ are predetermined to be linked in terms of Case-feature checking.

Exploiting this prescribed link between a transitive V and OBJ in terms of Case-feature, Murasugi (1992, 1995) claims, under the checking theory of Chomsky (1992), that another type of path may be created in a transitive clause if a transitive V happens to be free from its obligation to check OBJ's Case-feature. According to Murasugi, if this happens, then SUBJ moves from the Spec of V to the Spec of AgrO (which is called Tr (= Transitive) in Murasugi 1992, 1995) and OBJ moves from the V-complement to the Spec of Infl, resulting in the nested paths illustrated in (6.20):

(6.20) *Nested Paths (transitive clause in ergative languages)*

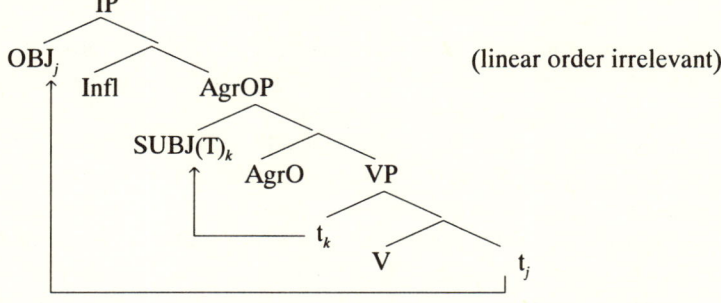

(linear order irrelevant)

Murasugi (1992, 1995) argues that, if a transitive V does not have the obligation to check OBJ's Case-feature, the Shortest Move Requirement of Chomsky (1992), an alleged economy condition, requires that SUBJ should be moved to the Spec of AgrO; for, SUBJ is the argument closest to the Spec of AgrO.

Let us suppose, as Murasugi (1992, 1995) does, that the Case-feature that V checks off through the mediation of AgrO (or Tr) is accusative/ergative and the Case-feature that T (or Infl) checks off is nominative/absolutive. Then, (6.19) represents a transitive clause in accusative languages and (6.20) a transitive clause in morphologically ergative languages. It is now evident that whether a transitive V is obligatorily linked to OBJ's Case or not counts as the parameter that distinguishes ergative languages from accusative ones under Murasugi's theory. It is noteworthy that this parameter is more plausible than Marantz's (1984) parameter for the distinction of ergative/accusative languages, because it is dependent on the lexical property of transitive Vs. As Murasugi (1992) claims, many empirical facts (mainly concerning syntactic ergativity) can be captured by postulating (6.20) as the transitive structure for ergative languages.

Murasugi's (1992, 1995) theory of ergativity, although sophisticated and fairly pertinent to the checking theory of the Minimalist program, does not conform, without an appropriate modification, to the Minimalist assumptions developed by Chomsky (1995a) and advocated in this book. Above all, it is inconsistent with the concept of Attract in the Agr-less checking theory. Recall that this book, following Chomsky (1995a), rejects Chomsky's (1992) stipulation that the domain of a head α is extended to the domain of β if α head-moves onto β. Thus, for example, there is no way for OBJ to be attracted to the Spec of Infl in (6.20).

Besides, Murasugi (1992, 1995) argues on a par with most of the traditional approaches[18] that ergative Case in ergative languages is merely a morphological allonym of accusative Case in accusative languages. But under her theory, transitive Vs that assign ergative are syntactically different from ones that assign accusative; for, while the latter Vs are bound to OBJ in terms of Case-feature checking, the former are free in that respect. Notice that this difference of the syntactic property of transitive Vs results in the syntactic differences between ergative languages and accusative ones. Here it is important to note that under Murasugi's theory of ergativity, an (active) transitive clause in morphologically ergative languages always has the structural shape of (6.20). This poses an empirical problem, however. As has been observed so far, there are two types in morphologically ergative languages: One is syntactically ergative and the other is shallowly ergative. It was observed in §6.1 that in languages of the latter type, the syntactic behaviors of SUBJ(T) are the same as the ones in ordinary accusative languages. Since the syntactic structure of a transitive clause in shallowly ergative languages (which is illustrated in (6.20)) differs radically from the one in accusative languages (illustrated in (6.19)) under Murasugi's theory, it is quite hard, though not impossible, for the theory to give a uniform account of the facts concerning shallowly ergative languages, as some authors (e.g., Bobaljik 1993) point out. For example, it is rather difficult, without some ad hoc stipulation, to explain why SUBJ(T) in some shallowly ergative languages, which is supposed to be located at a position lower than OBJ at LF under Murasugi's theory, can bind OBJ (cf. Anderson 1976 and Bobaljik 1992, 1993).

---

[18] According to Manning (1996), this tradition goes back to Trubetzkoy (1939) or even earlier.

6.3.3.2. Bobaljik (1992, 1993)

One of the crucial assumptions of Murasugi's (1992, 1995) theory of ergativity is that ergative Case and absolutive Case in ergative languages are morphologically identified with accusative Case and nominative Case in accusative languages, respectively. This assumption, which is a very traditional one (cf. footnote 18), is also maintained by recent approaches such as Marantz (1984), B. Levin (1983), Bok-Bennema (1991), Johns (1992), Bittner (1994), and others.

Bobaljik (1992, 1993), contra this traditional assumption, proposes that ergative should correspond to nominative while absolutive corresponds to accusative. This is a resurrection of J. Levin and Massam's (1985) idea, and several authors vote for it (e.g., Marantz 1991, Chomsky 1992, and Laka 1993). Babaljik guarantees these correspondences in terms of case-marking by proposing what he calls the "Obligatory Case Parameter," which states:

(6.21) *Obligatory Case Parameter* (Bobaljik 1993: 50)

    a. In accusative languages, nominative (= ergative) Case is obligatorily checked.

    b. In ergative languages, absolutive (= accusative) Case is obligatorily checked.

Since absolutive is identified with accusative in Bobaljik's theory, (6.21b) means that SUBJ(I) in an intransitive clause in ergative languages must enter into a Case-feature checking relation with the element that checks an accusative Case-feature in an intransitive clause in accusative languages. Examples (6.22) and (6.23) illustrate the transitive structure and the intransitive one for ergative languages under Bobaljik's theory of ergativity:

(6.22) *Transitive clause in ergative (and accusative) languages*

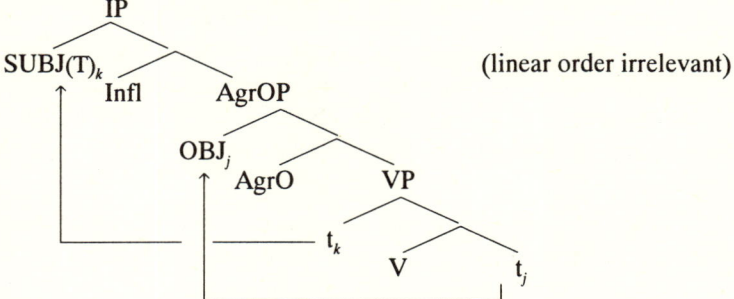

(6.23) *Intransitive clause in ergative languages*

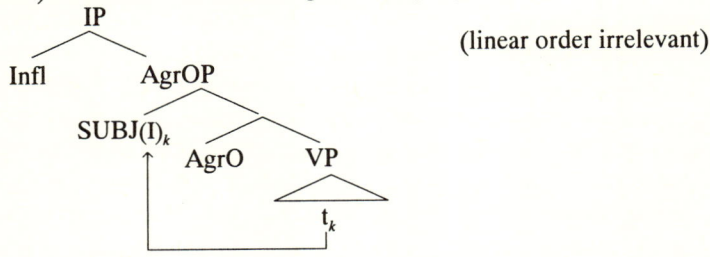

(linear order irrelevant)

Notice that, whereas the transitive clause in accusative languages looks the same as (6.22), the intransitive clause in accusative languages looks like (6.24) below:

(6.24) *Intransitive clause in accusative languages*

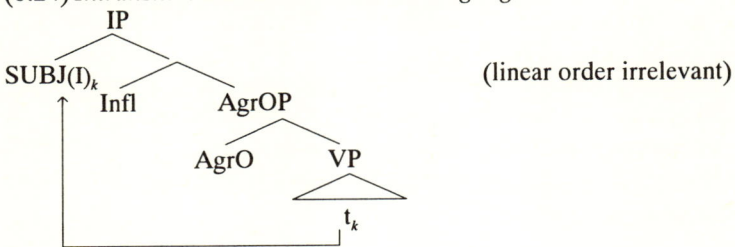

(linear order irrelevant)

In short, under Bobaljik's theory of ergativity, the Case-feature that is checked at the Spec of AgrO is morphologically realized as accusative/absolutive, and the one that is checked at the Spec of Infl is morphologically realized as nominative/ergative. This contrasts sharply with Murasugi's theory of ergativity not only in terms of the pairing of the ergative/absolutive Case-marking pattern with the nominative/accusative one, but also in terms of the source of the parametric difference between ergative and accusative languages. Recall that the difference lies in V's Case-related property in a *transitive clause* under Murasugi's theory. Under Bobaljik's theory, on the other hand, it lies in AgrO's Case-related property in an *intransitive clause*: If AgrO in an intransitive clause is active (i.e., can help V check off Case-feature), then an intransitive clause with absolutive SUBJ(I) appears (= (6.23)), and an intransitive clause with nominative SUBJ(I) appears (= (6.24)) if it is inactive.

Like Murasugi's (1992) theory of ergativity, Bobaljik's (1992, 1993) is so elaborate under the Agr-based checking theory of the Minimalist program that it can explain an array of facts concerning ergativity. It is, however, not immune to some technical as well as empirical problems. First, it is important to note, again, that, under Bobaljik's theory, the syntactic structure of a transitive clause is invariant regardless of the distinction between ergative and accusative languages. Then, it leads immediately to the prediction that syntactic behaviors of a transitive clause basically do not differ between ergative and accusative languages. In fact, this prediction is very pertinent to the facts observed in shallowly ergative languages, in which SUBJ(T) behaves (almost) the same as SUBJ(T) in accusative languages. But it is totally irreconcilable with the facts observed in syntactically ergative languages like Dyirbal, in which SUBJ(T) behaves like OBJ in accusative languages. Empirically, this may be most problematic for Bobaljik's (1992, 1993) theory of ergativity.[19]

In addition to empirical problems, the Obligatory Case Parameter (OCP) has a very serious technical problem in the light of the Minimalist theory of formal features and their checking. The OCP states that absolutive (= accusative) Case must be checked off in ergative languages, resulting in the intransitive structure illustrated in (6.23). Even if it is admitted that an intransitive V (or AgrO) has the ability to check off SUBJ(I)'s Case feature in an intransitive clause in ergative languages, it is by no means clear what checks off the ergative (= nominative) Case-feature of Infl (= tensed T) that is obviously [–interpretable]. Since Infl has the ergative (= nominative) Case-feature available for checking when it appears at a transitive clause, it must be checked off even in an intransitive clause; otherwise, the derivation crashes. Thus, unless some ad hoc stipulation is provided (for example, to stipulate that a tensed T (= Infl) has no Case only when it appears in an intransitive clause in ergative languages, or that some phonologically invisible element like *pro* appears only in an intransitive clause in ergative languages to check off the ergative Case-feature of Infl), the OCP cannot be maintained in the Minimalist theory of formal features and their checking assumed in this book.

6.4. Theory of Ergativity and Multiple Feature Checking

In this section I will propose a Minimalist approach to ergativity under the theory of multiple feature checking, which depends crucially upon the Agr-less checking theory reinforced with the bare phrase structure theory of Chomsky (1994a). Elsewhere in this book I showed that under this theory, only the checking relations that a given DP holds determine the DP's properties in terms of Case and agreement in addition to its GFs. Thus, the approach to ergativity that lays its foundations upon the theory of multiple feature checking together with the Agr-less checking theory is expected to be free from the aforementioned problems, which are resistant to any structure-based theory of case and agreement, as stated in §6.2.5. Furthermore, I will demonstrate that the application of the theory of multiple feature checking opens up the possibility of coping conspicuously with typological variations of ergative languages in terms of GF-splitting phenomena by resorting to a limited set of plausible parameters, just as it provides a consistent way to deal with typological variations of accusative languages in terms of GF-splitting, as extensively argued thus far in this book.

---

[19] See Murasugi (1992) and Manning (1996) for further empirical problems for Bobaljik's theory of ergativity.

6.4.1. Parameter for the Ergativity/Accusativity Distinction

The theory of ergativity that I am proposing here requires no special stipulation peculiar to ergative languages or ergativity, excepting only one simple parameter. The parameter, which I call the "Theta-Position Checking parameter" (hereafter, ΘPC-parameter), states that elements can enter into a formal feature-checking relation at their θ-position in a language L only if the value of L's ΘPC-parameter is set as [+ΘPC]. This idea parametrizes Chomsky's (1995a: §4.5.6) stipulation that an element introduced (base-generated) by Merge in its θ-position cannot undergo feature checking unless it moves somewhere other than its base-generated position. Notice that Chomsky draws this stipulation from empirical observations (on accusative languages) and, hence, it is merely a stipulation that is not derived on purely conceptual grounds (that is, it has no conceptual necessity). Thus, it is not unnatural to speculate that there are some languages that are not subject to this stipulation (see §1.4.7.2 for more on the ΘPC-parameter).

Now let us see how this parameter works to derive the distinction between ergative and accusative languages. First, let us consider what effects it brings to a simple transitive clause with Agent-argument and Theme-argument. The diagram in (6.25) represents the (universal) base-structure for a transitive clause:

(6.25) *Base-structure for a transitive clause*

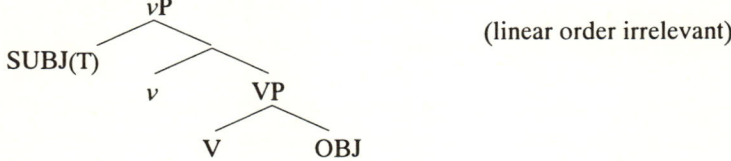

(linear order irrelevant)

Suppose that (6.25) occurs in a language whose ΘPC-parameter is [–ΘPC]. Then, the derivation cannot converge unless SUBJ(T) moves from the Spec of *v* to somewhere else where its Case-feature can be properly checked off, because, thanks to the parameter-setting, SUBJ(T) cannot enter into any formal feature-checking relation if it lingers there. Suppose, instead, that the parameter concerned is [+ΘPC]. Then, SUBJ(T) at the Spec of *v* can enter into a Case-feature checking relation with *v* without moving anywhere else if the Case-feature of SUBJ(T) and that of *v* match (Ura 1994b,e, 1995c; Chomsky 1995a). I will argue later in this chapter that the former case happens in accusative languages and the latter in ergative languages, assuming on a par with Murasugi (1992, 1994) and most of the traditional approaches that nominative and absolutive, on one hand, and accusative and ergative, on the other, pair up in morphological respects; that is, *v* assigns/checks accusative/ergative and (tensed) T assigns/checks nominative/absolutive. If SUBJ(T) and *v* enter into a Case-feature checking relation in a transitive clause, OBJ must enter into a Case-feature checking relation with T somehow; otherwise, OBJ's Case remains unchecked at LF, resulting in an LF crash.[20] Therefore, if a language L allows *v* and SUBJ(T) at the Spec of *v* to enter

---

[20] Later in this section I will discuss the issue of how OBJ enters into a Case-feature

into a Case-feature checking relation in a transitive clause (that is, if L is [+ΘPC]), L counts as a morphologically ergative language because SUBJ(T)'s Case is morphologically realized as ergative (= accusative) and OBJ's as absolutive (= nominative) in L.

Next let us turn to a simple intransitive clause. The diagram in (6.26) represents the base-structure for an intransitive clause:[21]

(6.26) *Base-structure for an intransitive (unergative) clause*

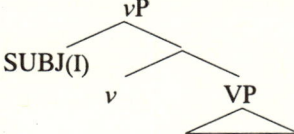

Let us suppose (tentatively) that *v* in an intransitive unergative clause has no Case-feature. Then, the Case-feature of SUBJ(I) cannot be checked off at the Spec of *v* regardless of the value of the ΘPC-parameter. As a consequence, SUBJ(I) obligatorily moves up to the Spec of T, where its Case-feature can be checked off by the Case-feature of T. It is important to note that this movement is required irrespective of the value of the ΘPC-parameter. It can therefore be concluded that, provided that *v* in an intransitive clause does not have any Case-feature available for SUBJ(I)'s Case, SUBJ(I) moves up to the Spec of T to enter into a Case-feature checking relation with T regardless of whether the ΘPC-parameter is set as [+ΘPC] or [-ΘPC]. Given the hypothesis that nominative in accusative languages is morphologically the same as absolutive in ergative languages, this answers the question of why, in general, the Case of SUBJ(I) in an intransitive clause is morphologically realized as nominative/absolutive regardless of whether the language at issue is accusative or ergative.[22]

6.4.2. Typological Varieties of Ergative Languages

In the previous section it was shown how the basic structure of morphologically ergative languages is derived under the theory of multiple feature checking with the ΘPC-parameter. Naturally, several syntactic differences among morphologically ergative languages are expected to be derived by some parametric variations, just as syntactic differences between languages with the active/inverse alternation and languages without it, or between languages with DSCs (dative subject constructions) and languages without them, can be derived by some parametric variations. In this section I will demonstrate how the theory of multiple

---

checking relation with T in ergative languages.

[21] Here I tentatively ignore the so-called intransitive unaccusative, the construction to which I will return directly in §6.4.4.

[22] As has been pointed out in the literature, in some ergative languages the Case of SUBJ(I) can be realized as ergative if the predicate of the clause is unergative, while it cannot if the predicate is unaccusative. I will return directly to this issue in §6.4.4.

feature checking can capture the typological variations of ergative languages in their syntactic respects with possible parametric differences.

6.4.2.1. Shallow Ergativity

Let us, first, consider how the principal distinction between shallowly ergative languages and syntactically ergative ones can be derived under the theory of multiple feature checking. As argued in §6.4.1, in morphologically ergative languages SUBJ generated at the Spec of v can enter into a Case-feature checking relation with v regardless of whether the clause is intransitive or transitive. First, consider what happens in a transitive clause. Exampl (6.27) is the basic structure of a transitive clause:

(6.27) [$_{vP}$ SUBJ(T) v [$_{VP}$ V OBJ]] (linear order irrelevant)

Now suppose (1) that SUBJ(T) has an ergative/accusative Case-feature, and (2) that v's Case-feature, which is ergative/accusative by definition,[23] is strong. Then, SUBJ(T) actually enters into an ergative Case-feature checking relation with v at this stage in the derivation if this situation obtains in a language whose ΘPC-parameter is set as [+ΘPC], as illustrated in (6.28):

(6.28) [$_{vP}$ SUBJ(T) v [$_{VP}$ V OBJ]] (before Spell-out)
                       ergative Case-checking

At the next step in the derivation, T is introduced by Merge, deriving (6.29) from (6.28):

(6.29) [$_{TP}$ T [$_{vP}$ SUBJ(T) v [$_{VP}$ V OBJ]]] (before Spell-out)
                       ergative Case-checking

What happens at the next step in the derivation depends solely on the properties of T's formal features. In English, for example, T's EPP-feature is strong, though its other nominal features (i.e., nominative Case-feature and φ-feature) are weak (Chomsky 1995a). Obviously, English is [−ΘPC]. But, it is quite natural to presume that there are some [+ΘPC] languages in which T has a strong EPP-feature, but weak Case- and φ-features, just as in English. If T in (6.29) has such a property, SUBJ(T), but not OBJ, is attracted to the Spec of T to check off T's strong EPP-feature, because SUBJ(T) is the DP closest to T in (6.29). Then, (6.30) is derived from (6.29):

---

[23] Recall that v counts as a transitive morpheme in the two-layered VP-shell of Chomsky (1995a): It may select an unaccusative V, forming a transitive VP-shell, and it discharges an Agent-role to its Spec and it assigns an accusative (= ergative) Case (i.e., Buruzio's generalization). For more discussion, see Chomsky (1992, 1995a) and, especially, Hale and Keyser (1991, 1993).

Ergativity and Its Typological Variation

(6.30) [$_{TP}$ SUBJ(T)$_k$ T [$_{vP}$ t$_k$ v [$_{VP}$ V OBJ]]] (before Spell-out)

            EPP-checking   ergative Case-checking

Since all the strong features involved in this derivation are checked off in (6.30), the pre-Spell-out derivation ends at this stage. Here it should be noted that SUBJ(T) lost its Case-feature when it entered into a Case-feature checking relation with v at the stage illustrated in (6.28); therefore, it can no longer check off any Case-feature. Consequently, the Case-feature of OBJ must be attracted to T at LF to check off the weak absolutive/nominative Case-feature of T; otherwise, the derivation crashes at LF.

(6.31)   absolutive Case-checking

        [$_{TP}$ SUBJ(T)$_k$ T [$_{vP}$ t$_k$ v [$_{VP}$ V OBJ]]] (at LF)

            EPP-checking   ergative Case-checking

Now the question is: What checks off the weak φ-feature of T in (6.31)? It is possible that OBJ's φ-feature checks it off at LF, just as OBJ's Case-feature checks off T's weak Case-feature at LF. Or, it could be checked off by SUBJ(T)'s φ-feature by moving it onto SUBJ(T) at LF, as illustrated in (6.32):

(6.32)

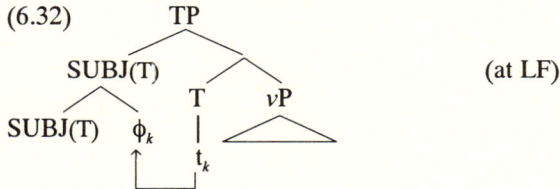

(at LF)

In chapter 3 (§3.2.3) it was argued that, in order for the two matching features α and β to enter into a checking relation at LF, an LF feature-movement must occur even in the case where either of them has already located a position within the other's checking domain. Note that in (6.31), SUBJ(T)'s φ-feature, being [+interpretable], can enter into multiple checking relations even if it has already entered into a φ-feature checking relation. Note also that SUBJ(T)'s φ-feature in (6.31) cannot move onto T at LF because this would be an illicit downward movement, causing a violation of LF cyclicity (Watanabe 1995a). Thus, unless, as illustrated in (6.32), T's φ-feature moves onto SUBJ(T) at LF, SUBJ(T)'s φ-feature and T's weak φ-feature can never enter into a checking relation (see §3.2.3 for more details).

Nevertheless, under the assumption that T's φ-feature is weak, the checking of it by SUBJ(T)'s φ-feature is blocked by the general economy condition. As illustrated in (6.32), it must involve a movement and, hence, it has a cost from the viewpoint of the economy condition. In contrast, the checking of T's weak φ-feature at LF by OBJ can be executed with no cost, because OBJ's φ-feature can be carried freely together with the movement of OBJ's Case-feature onto T by exploiting the strategy of Generalized Pied-Piping. Thus, the general economy condition prefers that OBJ's φ-feature check off T's weak φ-feature in (6.31). The final stage of the derivation, hence, looks like (6.33):

(6.33)

$$[_{TP} \text{ SUBJ(T)}_k \underbrace{\text{T}}_{\text{EPP-checking}} [_{vP} \underbrace{t_k \quad v}_{\text{ergative Case-checking}} [_{VP} \text{ V OBJ }]]] \text{ (at LF)}$$

with brackets indicating f- and absolutive Case-checking between T and OBJ.

Since all the formal features that need to be checked off are checked off in (6.33) as required, the derivation converges.

What kind of language has the derivation sketched above? First, it is [+ΘPC]. Second, *v*'s Case-feature is strong. Third, T's EPP-feature is strong, while its Case-feature and φ-feature are weak. Next, what morphological properties result from this derivation? First, SUBJ(T)'s Case is realized as ergative because it enters into a Case-feature checking relation with *v*. Second, OBJ induces the verb-agreement because it enters into a φ-feature checking relation with T at LF. Third, OBJ's Case is realized as absolutive because it enters into a Case-feature checking relation with T at LF. It is evident from these morphological properties that the language in question is morphologically ergative. To tell whether this language is shallowly ergative or syntactically ergative, it is necessary to consider what syntactic properties result from this derivation.

Elsewhere in this book I extensively argued that the following hypothesis about GFs cross-linguistically holds good: The so-called subject-properties result from a [+construable]-feature checking relation with T; more precisely, the ability to bind a subject-oriented reflexive results from an EPP-feature checking relation with T, and the ability to control the missing argument in a subordinate-adjunct clause results from a [+construable]-feature checking relation with T upon the condition that, if there is more than one argument with a [+construable]-feature checking relation with T in a single clause, the ability to control is possessed by the argument which is ranked as the highest according to the following hierarchy: argument with a φ-feature checking relation with T before Spell-out ≫ argument with an EPP-feature checking relation with T before Spell-out ≫ argument with a φ-feature checking relation with T at LF ≫ argument with an EPP-feature checking relation with T at LF.

Given this hypothesis, it can be predicted that SUBJ(T) has both the ability to control and the ability to bind a reflexive in this type of morphologically ergative language, because only SUBJ(T) has a [+construable]-feature checking relation with T before Spell-out in the above derivation. As observed in §6.1.2, this prediction is borne out: SUBJ(T) has the subject-properties in shallowly ergative languages like Archi. In Archi, for example, SUBJ(T), but not OBJ, has the ability to control the missing argument in a subordinate-adjunct clause, as shown in (6.34):

(6.34) *Archi* (Van Valin 1981: 364-365)

a. Bošor$_k$ [PRO$_k$ k'oaHan soli] weırʃu.
man(ABS)　　　　　stick(ABS) hold(GER) run-AOR
'The man$_k$ ran, [PRO$_k$ holding the stick].'

b. Adamli$_k$ [PRO$_k$ k'aräši xit'boli] č'ele　　goıroı-abti.
man(ERG)　　　　down push(GER)　stone(ABS) roll-AOR
'The man$_k$ rolled the stone, [PRO$_k$ having pushed it down].'

And Kibrik (1979) shows that SUBJ(T), but not OBJ, has the ability to bind a reflexive in Archi. It has been revealed in the literature that this typical class of shallowly ergative languages, where the absolutive-marked OBJ induces the verb-agreement and SUBJ(T) has those so-called subject-properties, includes Kâte, Abkhazian (Anderson 1976), Enga (Li and Lang 1979), Walmatjari (Dixon 1979), Jacaltec (Van Valin 1981), Basque (B. Levin 1983), Quiché (Larsen 1987), Hindi (Kachru 1987), Axvax (Kibrik 1985), Niuean (Wennevold Silva 1989), Nisgha (Belvin 1990a), Lezgian (Haspelmath 1993), Kewa (Palmer 1994), Georgian (Lyle 1995), and Yimas (Phillips 1995). Example (6.33) thus represents the derivation for ergative transitive clauses in those languages.

Notice, again, that this class results from the interaction of the following parameters: (1) it is [+ΘPC]; (2) v's Case-feature is strong; (3) T's EPP-feature is strong; (4) T's Case-feature is weak; and (5) T's φ-feature is weak. It was argued in the preceding passage that it is owing to parameter (5) that OBJ but not SUBJ(T) checks off T's φ-feature in (6.31). Now consider what happens in the derivation if T's φ-feature is strong with the other parameters intact.

The derivation proceeds in the same fashion until it arrives to the stage illustrated in (6.30). Now that the φ-feature of T in (6.30) is strong, it is checked off by SUBJ(T) at the same time that SUBJ(T) is attracted to the Spec of T. This is because a strong feature must be checked off as soon as possible (see §1.4.1):

(6.35)　　[$_{TP}$ SUBJ(T)$_k$　T [$_{vP}$ t$_k$　　v [$_{VP}$ V OBJ]]]　(before Spell-out)
　　　　　　　　　　└──────┘　　└─────┘
　　　　　　φ- and EPP-checking　ergative Case-checking

This derivation converges if OBJ's Case-feature moves up onto T at LF to check off T's weak Case-feature, as illustrated in (6.36):

(6.36)　　　　　　　　　absolutive Case-checking
　　　　　　　　　┌──────────────────┐
　　　　[$_{TP}$ SUBJ(T)$_k$　T [$_{vP}$ t$_k$　　v [$_{VP}$ V OBJ]]]　(at LF)
　　　　　　　└──────┘　　└─────┘
　　　　　φ- and EPP-checking　ergative Case-checking

In the languages with those parameters that allow this derivation, SUBJ(T)'s Case is realized as ergative because it enters into a Case-feature checking relation with v, SUBJ(T) induces the verb-agreement because it enters into a φ-feature checking relation with T, and OBJ's Case is realized as absolutive because it enters into a Case-feature checking relation with T. As a result, this type of language shows a morphological split in ergativity: Case-marking is ergative but verb agreement is accusative. In fact, it was observed in §6.1.3.1 that this kind of split-ergativity is found in Burushaski, Warlpiri, and Avar. Example (6.37) comes from Warlpiri:

(6.37) *Warlpiri* (= (6.17b))

    a. Ŋatjulu-ḻu ka-**na** marlu-Ø ɲa-ɲi.
        I-ERG   TNS-1SG   kangaroo-ABS   see-NON.PAST
        'I see the kangaroo.'

    b. Ɲuntulu-ḻu ka-**npa** marlu-Ø ɲa-ɲi.
        you-ERG   TNS-2SG   kangaroo-ABS   see-NON.PAST
        'You see the kangaroo.'

It is important to note that our hypothesis about GFs correctly predicts that in this type of shallowly ergative language, too, SUBJ(T) has the ability to control the missing argument in a subordinate-adjunct clause and the ability to bind a subject-oriented reflexive; for, only SUBJ(T) has a [+construable]-feature checking relation with T. As observed in §6.1.2, it is SUBJ(T), but not OBJ, that controls the missing argument in a subordinate-adjunct clause in Warlpiri (cf. (6.9)). In addition, Bittner and Hale (1996a) show that in Warlpiri, SUBJ(T) binds a subject-oriented reflexive in a transitive clause with the proximate affix.

To sum up, the difference in terms of parameter (5) results in the difference between the ordinary type of shallowly ergative language in which case-marking and verb agreement are both ergative-based and the Warlpiri type of shallowly ergative language in which only case-marking is ergative-based. Aside from this difference, the following parameters derive the shallow ergativity: (1) [+ΘPC]; (2) *v*'s Case-feature is strong; (3) T's EPP-feature is strong; (4) T's Case-feature is weak; and (5) T's φ-feature is weak (ordinary type of shallowly ergative languages), or (5') strong (Warlpiri-type of shallowly ergative languages).

6.4.2.2. Syntactic Ergativity

Now let us consider what kind of ergativity is derived from the following parameters: (1) [+ΘPC]; (2) *v*'s Case-feature is strong; (3) T's EPP-feature is strong; (4) T's Case-feature is strong; and (5) T's φ-feature is weak/strong. Note that these parameters differ in terms of (4) from the parameters that derive shallowly ergative languages.

Owing to parameters (1) and (2), SUBJ(T) at the Spec of *v* enters into an ergative Case-feature checking relation with *v*, as illustrated in (6.38):

(6.38)   [$_{vP}$ SUBJ(T)   *v* [$_{VP}$ V OBJ]]   (before Spell-out)
                    └─────────┘
                     ergative Case-checking

After T is introduced to (6.38), deriving (6.39), what is required to happen at the next step?

(6.39)　　[$_{TP}$ T [$_{vP}$ SUBJ(T)　v [$_{VP}$ V OBJ]]]　(before Spell-out)
　　　　　　　　　|_____|
　　　　　　　　　ergative Case-checking

Now that T has a strong EPP-feature and strong (absolutive) Case-feature, neither of them is allowed to escape being checked off before Spell-out. In (6.39) SUBJ(T) has been deprived of its Case-feature by entering into a Case-feature checking relation with v, but it has the ability to enter into an EPP-feature checking relation with T. OBJ in (6.39), on the other hand, has the ability to enter into a Case-feature checking relation with T in addition to the ability to enter into an EPP-feature checking relation with T. Which of them is actually attracted to the (canonical) Spec of T in (6.39)?

If OBJ in (6.39) would be moved from the V-complement position to the canonical Spec of T, then it could check both of T's strong features at one time. But it causes a violation of the MLC, because the movement passes over SUBJ(T). Although the DP that holds a Case-feature closest to T is OBJ, the DP that holds a D-feature closest to T is SUBJ(T) in (6.39). Note that even if T's strong Case-feature tries to attract the Case-feature of OBJ before Spell-out, the Case-feature of OBJ alone cannot be attracted but OBJ as a whole category must be moved over SUBJ(T) to the Spec of T, deviating from the MLC part of the definition of *Attract*.[24] In contrast, SUBJ(T) in (6.39) is safely attracted, without deviating from the definition of *Attract*, to the canonical Spec of T for the purpose of checking off T's strong EPP-feature. This derives (6.40) from (6.39):

(6.40)　　[$_{TP}$ SUBJ(T)$_k$　T [$_{vP}$ t$_k$　v [$_{VP}$ V OBJ]]]　(before Spell-out)
　　　　　　|_____|　　　　|_____|
　　　　　　EPP-checking　　　　ergative Case-checking

Here notice that SUBJ(T) in (6.40) has been deprived of its Case-feature. Thus, T's strong Case-feature remains unchecked in (6.40), so that something with Case-feature must be attracted to an outer Spec of T before Spell-out. Now that in (6.40), there is nothing structurally intervening between T and OBJ, OBJ can be safely attracted to an outer Spec of T without deviating from the MLC part of the definition of *Attract*, as illustrated in (6.41):

(6.41)　　　　　　　absolutive Case-checking
　　　　　　┌─────────────────────┐
　　　[$_{TP}$ OBJ$_j$ [$_{TP}$ SUBJ(T)$_k$　T [$_{vP}$ t$_k$　v [$_{VP}$ V t$_j$]]]]　(before Spell-out)
　　　　　　　　　　|_____|　　　|_____|
　　　　　　　　　　EPP-checking　　　ergative Case-checking

---

[24] See Ferguson (1996), Ueda (to appear), and Ura (1996a) for arguments in favor of the claim that γ blocks α's attraction of β if all of them share an identical formal feature and γ structurally intervenes between α and β.

Except for T's φ-feature, all the formal features that need to be checked off are properly checked off in (6.41); as a result, the derivation converges if T's φ-feature is properly checked off somehow.[25]

Note that, since the φ-feature of SUBJ(T) and that of OBJ are both [+interpretable], either SUBJ(T) or OBJ can enter into a φ-feature checking relation with T in (6.41). If T's φ-feature is weak, OBJ always checks it off at LF. In §3.2.3 I claimed that the general economy condition requires that the element in an outer Spec must check off a weak feature of a head H at LF when more than one element, each of which is able to check it off, occupies H's multiple Specs. Therefore, if T's φ-feature is weak in (6.41), the general economy condition prohibits SUBJ(T) from entering into a φ-feature checking relation with T, forcing OBJ to enter into a φ-feature checking relation with T at LF. If T's φ-feature is strong, which argument checks it off? Now suppose that Procrastinate is so strong that it requires that later operations are always selected by the general economy condition. Under this strong version of Procrastinate, a syntactic operation α is selected over another syntactic operation β which is to be applicable earlier than α even if α and β are applicable at the same level. Then, from the hypothesis that Checking is a syntactic operation that is subject to the general economy condition (see §1.4.6), it follows that the checking of T's strong φ-feature by OBJ is always selected over the checking of it by SUBJ(T) by the demand of the strong version of Procrastinate for the reason that the former operation is later than the latter. To summarize, regardless of the strength of T's φ-feature, OBJ checks it off in (6.41), though the checking is executed before Spell-out if T's φ-feature is strong, and at LF if T's φ-feature is weak.

Now let us see what languages whose transitive clause is derived in the manner sketched above look like in morphological respects. They must be morphologically ergative languages because SUBJ(T) is marked as ergative and OBJ is marked as absolutive, and verb agreement is induced by OBJ independently of the strength of T's φ-feature, as argued above. Moreover, given our hypothesis about GFs, these languages are expected to have the following syntactic properties: Regardless of whether T's φ-feature is checked before Spell-out or at LF, the ability to bind a subject-oriented reflexive is possessed only by SUBJ(T) because SUBJ(T) is the only element that enters into an EPP-feature checking relation with T. As for the ability to control, it is predicted that it is possessed by SUBJ(T) if T's φ-feature is weak (i.e., OBJ checks it off at LF); for, SUBJ(T) is the only element that holds a [+construable]-feature checking relation with T before Spell-out in this case. If T's φ-feature is strong, then the ability to control is possessed by OBJ, because only OBJ checks off T's φ-feature before Spell-out (see §6.4.2.1).

---

[25] It is true that global economy blocks the series of steps in the derivation illustrated here because two operations are invoked to check off T's strong features despite the fact that they could be checked by a single operation (namely, movement of OBJ to the canonical Spec of T). But, recall that I am assuming, throughout this book, the local/strictly stepwise economy. See §1.4.5.3 and references cited there.

Recall that the languages at issue have the following parameters: (1) [+ΘPC]; (2) v's Case-feature is strong; (3) T's EPP-feature is strong; (4) T's Case-feature is strong; and (5) T's φ-feature is weak, or (5') strong. The languages with (1), (2), (3), (4), and (5') are well known; they correspond to the Dyirbal type of syntactically ergative language. It was already observed in §6.1.2 that, in addition to their morphologically ergative encoding on case and agreement, these languages, unlike shallowly ergative ones, have the following syntactic properties: OBJ, but not SUBJ(T), has the ability to control the missing argument in a subordinate-adjunct clause. The following examples come from Dyirbal and West Greenlandic Inuit:

(6.42) *Dyirbal* (Dixon 1994: 168)

    a.   Ŋuma-Ø$_k$ banaga-ɲu [PRO$_k$ bural-ŋa-**ygu** yabu-gu].
        father-ABS   return-NONFUT   see-ANT-**PURP** mother-DAT
        'Father$_k$ returned [for the purpose of PRO$_k$ seeing mother].'

    b.   Yabu-Ø$_l$ ŋuma-ŋgu$_k$ giga-n   [PRO$_{*k/j}$ bural-ŋa-**ygu**
        mother-ABS father-ABS tell-NONFUT   see-ANT-**PURP**
        jaja-gu].
        child-DAT
        'Father$_k$ told mother$_j$ [for the purpose of PRO$_{*k/j}$ seeing mother].'

(6.43) *West Greenlandic Inuit* (Bittner 1994: 152–153)

    a.   [Juuna-Ø$_k$ isir-a-**mi**$_k$],   PRO$_k$ Kaali-Ø
          -ABS   enter-PAST-3SG.PROX   -ABS
        urnip-p-a-a.
        approach-IND-TRNS-3SG.3SG
        'When Juuna$_k$ entered, PRO$_k$ approached Kaali.'

    b.   [Juuna-p$_k$ Kaali-Ø$_j$ tatigi-mm-a-**ni**$_{*k/j}$], PRO$_{*k/j}$
          -ERG   -ABS   trust-PAST-3SG.PROX
        tuqqissima-v-u-q.
        stay.calm-IND-INTR-3SG
        'Because Juuna$_k$ trusted Kaali$_j$, PRO$_{*k/j}$ stayed calm.'

Furthermore, it was pointed out in §6.1.4.2 that, despite this ability of OBJ, which is suggestive of its subjecthood, OBJ has no ability to bind a reflexive even in those syntactically ergative languages like Dyirbal (Dixon 1994) and West Greenlandic Inuit (Bittner 1994); rather, it is SUBJ(T) that has that ability (see Dixon 1994 for Dyirbal and Bittner 1994 for West Greenlandic Inuit). This rather surprising fact about syntactically ergative languages naturally follows: Under our analysis of this type of syntactically ergative language, it is SUBJ(T) that has the ability to bind a reflexive, as argued above. Thus, all the facts observed for syntactically ergative languages conform to the languages with the above parameters (i.e., (1), (2), (3), (4), and (5')).

As for the languages with the parameters (1), (2), (3), (4), and (5), it happens that they correspond to the typical kind of shallowly ergative language:

Morphologically, SUBJ(T) is marked as ergative and OBJ is marked as absolutive, and OBJ induces verb agreement; and, syntactically, SUBJ(T) has the ability to control the missing argument of a subordinate-adjunct clause and the ability to bind a reflexive. In the previous subsection there is another derivation for the typical type of shallowly ergative language. So there are two possible derivations for this type of shallowly ergative language.[26]

To recapitulate, it was argued that the following parameter-settings result in a syntactically ergative language: (1) [+ΘPC]; (2) v's Case-feature is strong; (3) T's EPP-feature is strong; (4) T's Case-feature is strong; and (5) T's φ-feature is strong. It was also argued in this subsection and the previous one that shallowly ergative languages emerge if the value of parameter (5) is altered, or if that of (4) is altered.

Here it should be emphasized that, as argued thus far, the theory of multiple feature checking makes it fairly easy to derive the distinction between shallowly ergative languages and syntactically ergative ones as well as several more minute differences found in various ergative languages. This is a major advantage of our approach over Murasugi's (1992, 1995) approach and Bobaljik's (1992, 1993), both of which have some difficulty in uniformly explaining the difference between these two types of ergativity without ad hoc stipulations, as pointed out in §6.3.3.

6.4.2.3. Other Parameter-Settings

Thus far I argued (I) that the shallow ergativity results from the parameters (1) [+ΘPC]; (2) v's Case-feature is strong; (3) T's EPP-feature is strong; (4) T's Case-feature is weak; and (5) T's φ-feature is strong/weak, and (II) that the syntactic ergativity results from the parameters (1) [+ΘPC]; (2) v's Case-feature is strong; (3) T's EPP-feature is strong; (4) T's Case-feature is strong; and (5) T's φ-feature is strong. That is to say, the difference in terms of the strength of T's Case-feature is the decisive factor of the distinction between the shallowly ergative languages and the syntactically ergative ones. Now let us consider what differences emerge if the relevant values of the other parameters are altered.

As argued in §6.4.1, a language L counts as morphologically accusative if L is a [−ΘPC] language. In L, SUBJ(T) at the Spec of v is prohibited from entering into a Case-feature checking relation with the light verb (= v) that assigns a θ-role to SUBJ(T). This means that OBJ, the other DP with a Case-feature in a transitive clause, must enter into a Case-feature checking relation with v to check off v's Case-feature. It follows that OBJ always has a Case-feature checking relation with v in L; that is, it is always the case that OBJ's case is morphologically realized as accusative/ergative in L. As a consequence, SUBJ(T) must check off

---

[26] Note, however, that it was suggested in §2.1.3 that many languages have the parameter that does not allow T's Case-feature and its φ-feature to be separately checked off. If this is true, the derivation for shallowly ergative languages sketched in this subsection is far rarer than the one sketched in the previous subsection.

T's Case-feature whenever T has a Case-feature. It follows that SUBJ(T)'s case is morphologically realized as nominative/absolutive in L. It is therefore concluded that L is a morphologically accusative language.

Next, let us examine what happens if the value of parameter (2) is altered; that is, if the language in question has the following parameter-setting for (2): v's Case-feature is weak. Elsewhere in this book I argued that two cases are possible when v's Case-feature is weak. One case emerges when it is weak and never tolerates any unforced violation of Procrastinate, and the other case emerges when it is weak and tolerates an unforced violation of Procrastinate. The first case leads to the cancellation of the effect of parameter (1): Irrespective of whether the value of parameter (1) is set as [+ΘPC] or [−ΘPC], the language in question counts as morphologically accusative if v's Case-feature is weak and never tolerates any unforced violation of Procrastinate. This is so because SUBJ at the Spec of v is not forced to enter into a Case-feature checking relation with v before Spell-out, and, hence, Procrastinate requires SUBJ not to enter into that relation with v before Spell-out. Accordingly, SUBJ is attracted to the Spec of T to check off T's strong EPP-feature before Spell-out because of parameter (3), which states that T's EPP-feature is strong. Once SUBJ occupies the Spec of T, another head that has a Case-feature, there is no possibility for SUBJ to enter into a Case-feature checking relation with v later in the derivation.

Now consider the case in which v's Case-feature is weak and tolerates an unforced violation of Procrastinate. I have claimed so far in this book that if v's Case-feature tolerates an unforced violation of Procrastinate in accusative languages, OBJ base-generated at the V-complement position may move to a Spec of v before Spell-out. Let us consider, then, what happens in a language with [+ΘPC] when v's Case-feature in the language is weak and tolerates an unforced violation of Procrastinate. Elsewhere in this book I suggested that Procrastinate requires the execution of Checking, a syntactic operation, to be deferred as late as possible. Under this interpretation of Checking, it is possible for SUBJ(T) base-generated at the Spec of v to check off the weak Case-feature of v if [+ΘPC] is operative in this situation. This derives (6.45) from the underlying transitive structure (6.44):

(6.44)   [$_{vP}$ SUBJ(T) v [$_{VP}$ V OBJ]] (before Spell-out)

(6.45)   [$_{vP}$ SUBJ(T) v [$_{VP}$ V OBJ]] (before Spell-out)
               └─────────┘
            ergative/accusative Case-checking

In spite of the weakness of v's Case-feature, this *Checking* operation before Spell-out is permissible because v tolerates an unforced violation of Procrastinate. Or, it is possible for OBJ to be attracted overtly to an outer Spec of v in (6.44) to check off the weak Case-feature of v before Spell-out. This derives (6.46) from (6.44):

(6.46)   [$_{vP}$ OBJ$_k$ [$_{vP}$ SUBJ(T) v [$_{VP}$ V t$_k$]]]   (before Spell-out)

ergative/accusative Case-checking

This derivation is permissible; for, SUBJ(T) can escape checking v's Case-feature because it is weak, and OBJ may be attracted to check it off before Spell-out because v tolerates an unforced violation of Procrastinate.

Here it should be noted that in a [+ΘPC] language whose v is weak and tolerates an unforced violation of Procrastinate, either (6.45) or (6.46) may be derived from the underlying transitive structure (6.44) without any morphological mediation, just as the Bantu active/inverse alternation (cf. chapter 2) has nothing with any morphological mediation. Furthermore, it is evident that a convergent derivation derivable from (6.45) results in a morphologically ergative language and a convergent derivation derivable from (6.46) results in a morphologically accusative one. Therefore, it is expected that in the language in question, morphological ergativity and morphological accusativity freely alternate without any morphological sign. Very surprising though it is, it is possible to discover such a language in the world. The examples in (6.47) come from Kabardian, a Northwest Caucasian language:[27]

(6.47)   *Kabardian* (Catford 1976: 45)

    a.   Jeʁedʒaḳe-r   ʃale-m   jewɨʃɨjaʃ.
        teacher-NOM   youth-ACC   admonished
        'The teacher admonished the youth.'

    b.   Jeʁedʒaḳe-m   ʃale-r   jewɨʃɨjaʃ.
        teacher-ERG   youth-ABS   admonished

6.4.2.4. Deriving Split-Ergativity

Thus far it has been argued that some parametric differences yield a few types of split-ergativity such as the Case/agreement disparity found in Warlpiri and Burushaski and the control/binding disparity found in Dyirbal and West Greenlandic Inuit. In §6.1.3.1 it was observed that there are two major types of morphological split of ergativity: One type of split-ergativity is due to the tense/aspect/mood distinction, and the other is due to the pronominal/full nominal distinction. In this section I will show how these two types of split ergativity are derived.

As is well-known, the split-ergativity due to the tense/aspect/mood distinction is found in many ergative languages such as Georgian, many Indo-Aryan languages including Hindi, Burushaski, some Tibetan-languages, Samoan, and so forth (cf. Comrie 1978 and Dixon 1979, 1994). The examples in (6.48) come from Kalaw Lagaw Ya, a language spoken by Torres Strait Islanders (cf. Comrie 1981):

---

[27] Colarusso (1992) argues, incidentally, that Kabardian is syntactically accusative despite its ergative morphology.

(6.48) *Kalaw Lagaw Ya* (Mel'čuk 1992: 122)

    a. Garkaz-in galas-Ø palgapal-an.
        man-ERG glass-ABS break-AUX
        'The man breaks the glass.'

    b. Garkaz-Ø galas-in palgapal-i.
        man-NOM glass-ACC break-AUX
        The man breaks all the glass.'

According to the theory of ergativity I proposed thus far, morphological ergativity stems solely from the parameter-setting of [+ΘPC]. Thus, in order to derive the Hindi type of split-ergativity, it is necessary to postulate that a clause with the tense/aspect/mood system that provokes the morphologically ergative encoding in those languages assumes [+ΘPC] in spite of its [−ΘPC] property in the tense/aspect/mood system that does not provoke ergativity. Then, how can we implement this postulation? Recall that the parameter concerning [±ΘPC] stipulates that *v*'s formal features can be checked off by SUBJ at the Spec of *v*. In this regard it is plausible that the [±ΘPC]-ness lies in *v*'s lexical properties. In fact, Watanabe (1996) proposes that the head responsible for the aspect/mood distinction is closely related to the formal feature-checking property of *v* (which he calls Agr).[28] Exploiting this idea, I propose that *v*'s property concerning formal feature checking depends upon the aspectual-head that selects *v* as its complement. Accordingly, it is possible to say that in some languages, some type of aspectual-head selects *v* whose checking property is set as [+ΘPC] and the other types select *v* whose property is set as [−ΘPC]. If this situation obtains in a language L, then the morphological ergativity emerges in a clause with the former type of aspectual-head in L.

The other type of split-ergativity, which is due to the pronominal/full nominal distinction, exemplified by (6.49) below, can be captured by positing a proviso concerning the checking of pronominals.

(6.49) *Bidjara* (Blake 1976: 282)

    a. INTRANSITIVE

        i. FULL DP (FULL NOMINAL)   ii. PRONOMINAL
           Ŋura-Ø wanguli-la.   Ŋaya-Ø barri-la.
           dog-ABS bark-PAST   I-NOM cry-PAST
           'A dog barked.'   'I cried.'

    b. TRANSITIVE

        i. FULL DP (FULL NOMINAL)   ii. PRONOMINAL
           Ŋura-ŋu munda-Ø bada-la.   Ŋaya-Ø nuŋu-na bada-la.
           dog-ERG snake-ABS bite-PAST   I-NOM him-ACC bite-PAST
           'A dog bit a snake.'   'I bit him.'

---

[28] Apparently, it is a promising idea to relate Watanabe's (1996) idea to the idea of Mahajan (1994, 1996) on the extension of the so-called *have-be* alternation to split ergativity due to the tense/aspect/mood distinction (cf. Nash 1994 and Lyle 1995), though I leave it to future research to pursue it.

It is a widely attested phenomenon that a pronominal is morphosyntactically related closely to the verb that selects it as its internal argument: In many languages with rich incorporation, a pronominal object is obligatorily incorporated into the verb (cf. Baker 1988), and a pronominal object obligatorily undergoes object shift in Scandinavian languages (cf. Holmberg and Platzack 1995, Jonas 1996, and Vikner 1994). It is possible to conjecture that the reason for this morphosyntactically tight relation between a verb and its pronominal object might be due to the obligatory checking relation between them; that is, a pronominal object must enter into a nominal feature-checking relation with the verb for some reason. If this conjecture is on the right track, then a pronominal object, even in a language with the [+ΘPC] parameter-setting, does not fail to check off v's nominal feature. Now that v's nominal feature, including Case-feature, is checked off by the pronominal object, there is no possibility for SUBJ(T) to enter into a Case-feature checking relation with v although it has the potential to do so because of the [+ΘPC] parameter-setting. Accordingly, SUBJ(T) is forced to check off T's Case-feature, the only remaining Case-feature in a transitive clause, resulting in its nominative manifestation in a transitive clause.

6.4.3. Intransitives and Case-marking of SUBJ(I)

Thus far I have concentrated my attention on the derivations of transitive clauses in the ergative system. In this section let us examine how intransitive clauses are derived in the ergative system.

There are two structures conceivable for the underlying structure of an intransitive clause. When an intransitive verb involved in the clause is unergative, the underlying structure looks like (6.50), and it looks like (6.51) when an intransitive unaccusative verb is involved (cf. Hale and Keyser 1991, 1993 and Chomsky 1992, 1995a):

(6.50)   *Intransitive unergative clause*

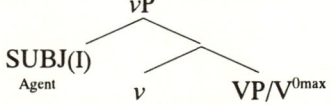

(6.51)   *Intransitive unaccusative clause*

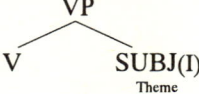

It should be noted that an intransitive unaccusative verb, unlike an intransitive unergative one, does not form a two-layered VP-shell with the light verb (= v) that bears Agent-role to be discharged to its Spec. This is so because an intransitive unaccusative verb has no Agent-role.

The stage in the derivation after T is introduced by *Merge* looks like the following:

(6.52) a. *Intransitive unergative*

[$_{TP}$ T [$_{vP}$ SUBJ(I) *v*]] (before Spell-out)

b. *Intransitive unaccusative*

[$_{TP}$ T [$_{VP}$ V SUBJ(I)]] (before Spell-out)

T has a nominative/absolutive Case-feature to be checked off, at the latest, at LF. Since there is only one argument, SUBJ(I), in (6.52), SUBJ(I) is forced to check it off to save the derivation from crash; as a result, SUBJ(I) enters into a nominative/absolutive Case-feature checking relation with T. Consequently, SUBJ(I) stands in absolutive in an intransitive clause in the ergative system, regardless of whether the intransitive clause is unaccusative or unergative.

It is, in passing, noteworthy that it has been sometimes pointed out that intransitive unergative verbs, unlike intransitive unaccusative ones, may have an accusative Case in accusative languages. This can be seen from examples like the following:

(6.53) *Resultatives*
    a. John laughed himself silly. (unergative)
    b. John sang himself hoarse. (unergative)
    c. *John arrived himself breathless. (unaccusative)

(6.54) *Cognate objects*
    a. John smiled a charming smile. (unergative)
    b. John sang a song. (unergative)
    c. *John arrived a glamorous arrival. (unaccusative)

Whereas the postverbal nominals in (6.53a,b) and (6.54a,b) can be provided with an accusative Case by each unergative verb, the ones in (6.53c) and (6.54c) cannot; whence, the ill-formedness of the (c)-examples results.

Given that unergative verbs can provide an accusative/ergative Case despite its intransitivity,[29] it leads to the prediction that in some ergative languages, there is a case where SUBJ(I) at the Spec of *v* in an intransitive unergative clause can check off *v*'s possible accusative/ergative Case-feature; for, it is theoretically possible, thanks to the [+ΘPC] parameter-setting, that SUBJ(I) enters into a checking relation with *v* without SUBJ(I) moving anywhere. This prediction is, indeed, borne out in several ergative languages including Hindi (Mahajan 1990), Georgian (Harris 1981), Tsova-Tush (Holisky 1987), Basque (B. Levin 1983), Bandjalang (Austin 1982), Kalkatungu (Blake 1982), and Burushaski (Morin

---

[29] This is compatible with the assumption that the light verb *v* is the locus of an accusative/ergative Case-feature (cf. Chomsky 1995a).

and Tiffou 1988)[30] as has been pointed out in the literature (e.g., Marantz 1991, Laka 1993, and Bobaljik 1993, among others):

(6.55) a. *Hindi* (Mahajan 1996: 46)

Kuttō-ne bhɔkaa.
dogs-ERG barked(PERF.M.SG)
'Dogs barked.'

b. *Georgian* (Nash 1996: 203)

Kac-ma iTira.
man-ERG cry(AOR)
'The man cried.'

c. *Basque* (Ortiz de Urbina 1989: 54)

Kotxe-ak ondo funtzionatzen du.
car-ERG well work AUX
'The car works well.'

Even in these languages, however, SUBJ(I) is obligatorily marked as ergative if an intransitive verb involved in the clause is unaccusative (Bobaljik 1993 dubs it Marantz's generalization):

(6.56) a. *Hindi* (Mahajan 1996: 46)

Raam-Ø/*-ne gir gəyaa.
Ram-ABS/-ERG fall(PERF)
'Ram fell down.'

b. *Georgian* (cf. Nash 1996: 203, and Harris 1981)

Kac-i/*-ma movida.
man-ABS/-ERG come(AOR)
'The man came.'

c. *Basque* (cf. Ortiz de Urbina 1989: 54, and B. Levin 1983)

Jon-Ø/*-ak heldu da.
John-ABS/-ERG arrive AUX
'John has arrived.'

Under the analysis of intransitive clauses in ergative languages developed in this section, the fact shown by the examples in (6.56), just like the one shown in (6.55), straightforwardly follows: The clause with an intransitive unaccusative verb has no *v* and, hence, there is no accusative/ergative Case available; therefore, it is impossible for SUBJ(I) to stand in ergative in this environment.

Here it is worth considering the reason why it is not the case that SUBJ(I) in an intransitive unergative clause is always able to be marked as ergative in all ergative languages. In fact, SUBJ(I) is always marked as absolutive in many ergative languages, such as Warlpiri and Samoan (cf. Bittner and Hale 1996b and Dixon 1994). The reason is simple: It is due to a parameter-setting, which al-

---

[30] For a list of those languages, see Dixon (1994: chapter 4).

lows/disallows the failure of T's Case-feature to be checked off. Let us return to the derivation of an intransitive unergative clause in which SUBJ(I) is marked as ergative. The derivation starts from the underlying structure (6.57):

(6.57)   [$_{vP}$ SUBJ(I) v] (before Spell-out)

In (6.57), SUBJ(I) can enter into an accusative/ergative Case-feature checking relation with v thanks to the [+ΘPC] parameter. After SUBJ(I) checks it off, T is introduced by *Merge*, deriving (6.58):

(6.58)   [$_{TP}$ T [$_{vP}$ SUBJ(I) v]] (before Spell-out)
                         └──────────┘
                         ergative checking

Whether it is strong or weak, T's nominative/absolutive Case-feature, being [−interpretable], must be checked off in (6.58); otherwise, the derivation crashes. But in (6.58), there remains no argument that bears a Case-feature available for checking it off; for, SUBJ(I)'s Case-feature has been deleted and erased after SUBJ(I) entered into a Case-feature checking relation with v. Now that there is no Case available for checking T's Case-feature in (6.58), there is no saving the derivation from crash unless T's Case-feature may escape being checked off. Elsewhere in this book I argued that there are languages with T whose Case-feature may escape being checked off (*The Impersonal Parameter*, see §1.4.7.1). Given this parameter, the derivation at issue can converge only if the Impersonal Parameter for the language is active; that is, the language allows T's Case-feature to fail to be checked off. To put it differently, even though a language L is [+ΘPC], SUBJ(I) in an intransitive unergative clause in L cannot stand in ergative unless L has the active value for the Impersonal Parameter. This is the reason why it is not the case that all ergative languages allow SUBJ(I) in an intransitive unergative clause in L to be marked as ergative.

Finally, a comment on the nonexistence of accusative/ergative SUBJ(I) in accusative languages is in order. To the best of my knowledge, it has not been reported in the literature that SUBJ(I) in an intransitive unergative clause can be marked as accusative in accusative languages, as hypothetically illustrated by the following English example:

(6.59)   *Him laughed/danced/sat.

Even in accusative languages with the active value for the Impersonal Parameter like German, Icelandic, or Tamil, sentences such as (6.59) are ill-formed, too. The reason for their nonexistence in accusative languages is simple, again: There is no way for SUBJ(I) of an intransitive unergative verb to enter into a Case-feature checking relation with v in accusative languages, because accusative languages are all [−ΘPC].

6.4.4. Anti-Passive

Anti-passive is regarded as the reverse counterpart of passive in the sense that in an anti-passive clause, it is OBJ that is syntactically demoted and it is SUBJ(T) that is syntactically promoted. OBJ is syntactically demoted from the characteristic direct-object case-marking by a more conventionalized grammatical device, placing it in an oblique case-marking such as dative, instrumental, locative, and so forth. According to OBJ's syntactic demotion, SUBJ(T), which is marked as ergative in an active clause, is marked as absolutive in an anti-passive clause. Thus, anti-passive, like passive, shares with active-intransitive in the morphological case-marking: SUBJ is marked as nominative/absolutive. Some anti-passive examples are:

(6.60) *Dyirbal* (Palmer 1994: 18)

    a. ACTIVE

        Yabu-Ø   ŋuma-ŋgu bura-n.
        mother-ABS father-ERG see-PAST
        'Father saw mother.'

    b. ANTI-PASSIVE

        Ŋuma-Ø buṛal-ŋa-ɲu (yabu-gu).
        father-ABS see-ANT-PAST mother-DAT

(6.61) *West Greenlandic Inuit* (Bittener and Hale 1996b: 36)

    a. ACTIVE

        Juuna-p   Anna-Ø   kunip-p-a-a.
        Juuna-ERG Anna-ABS kiss-IND-TRNS-3SG.3SG
        'Juuna kissed Anna.'

    b. ANTI-PASSIVE

        Juuna-Ø   (Anna-mik) kunis-si-v-u-q.
        Juuna-ABS Anna-INST   kiss-ANT-IND-INTR-3SG

(6.62) *Chukchee* (Palmer 1994: 177)

    a. ACTIVE

        Ətləg-e   keyŋ-ən penrə-nen.
        father-ERG bear-ABS attack-3SG.3SG.AOR
        'Father attacked the bear.'

    b. ANTI-PASSIVE

        Ətləg-en penrə-tko-gʔe   (keyŋ-etə).
        father-ABS attack-ANT-3SG.AOR bear-DAT

(6.63) *Chamorro* (Cooreman 1988: 578)

    a. ACTIVE

        Un-patek   i   ga'lagu.
        2SG(ERG)-kick the dog
        'You kicked the dog.'

    b. ANTI-PASSIVE

        Mam-atek hao   gi   ga'lagu.
        ANT-kick 2SG(ABS) LOC dog
        'You kicked at the dog.'

Now let us look at the derivation for anti-passive.

As for the passive formation in accusative languages, thus far I have simply assumed, following, basically, Baker, Johnson, and Roberts (1989), that the passive morpheme absorbs the accusative Case-feature of v.[31] Here I propose to assume that the anti-passive morpheme behaves the same as the passive morpheme with respect to its Case-related property; that is, it absorbs the ergative (= accusative) Case-feature of v. Moreover, I assume, extending, again, the idea of Baker, Johnson and Roberts (1989), that the anti-passive morpheme, just like its passive counterpart, is a DP that needs a θ-role. But I propose to speculate that the anti-passive morpheme, unlike its passive counterpart, absorbs the internal θ-role of the verb to which it is attached.[32]

With these assumptions in mind, let us see how anti-passive is derived in a transitive clause in ergative languages. Example (6.64) represents the stage in the derivation where the anti-passive morpheme is attached to v in the underlying structure for a transitive clause (=(6.44) above):

(6.64)   [$_{vP}$ SUBJ(T) v-ANT [$_{VP}$ V OBJ]] (before Spell-out)

Notice that OBJ in (6.64) should not be base-generated at the V-complement position (this state of affairs is represented in (6.64) by marking OBJ with a special font), because the verb involved must discharge its internal θ-role to the anti-passive morpheme. Recall that we reached the conclusion (see §6.4.2) that morphologically ergative languages have the following parameter-setting, irrespective of whether they are shallowly or syntactically ergative: (1) [+ΘPC]; (2) v's Case-feature is strong; (3) T's EPP-feature is strong; (4) T's Case-feature is weak/strong; and (5) T's φ-feature is weak/strong.

---

[31] Again, I refer the reader to Watanabe (1996) for extensive discussions on the mechanism of passive under the theory of Minimalist feature checking. I believe that the analysis of anti-passive presented here as well as the analysis of passive presented elsewhere in this book can be recast, without any loss, by Watanabe's (1996) Minimalist extension of the idea of Baker, Johnson, and Roberts (1989).

[32] Obviously, this causes a deviation from Burzio's generalization. In fact, however, some authors have argued that Burzio's generalization holds true only in accusative languages (e.g., B. Levin 1983, Laka 1993). I will return directly to this issue in §6.4.5.

Due to the above assumption, v's strong (ergative) Case-feature is absorbed by the anti-passive morpheme. Then, without entering into a Case-checking relation with v, SUBJ(T) in (6.64) is attracted to the Spec of T by T's strong EPP-feature due to parameter (3), because it is the DP closest to T at that stage in the derivation. (6.65) is thereby derived:

(6.65) $[_{TP}$ SUBJ(T)$_k$ T $[_{vP}$ t$_k$ v-ANT $[_{VP}$ V $]$ $]$ $]$ (before Spell-out)

Since SUBJ(T) is the sole DP in this derivation, it is imperative for the derivation's convergence that SUBJ(T) should check off all of T's nominal features (i.e., EPP-, ϕ-, and Case-features). Accordingly, SUBJ(T) is marked as absolutive in an anti-passive clause, as T's Case-feature is absolutive (= nominative). If OBJ is to be introduced in this derivation with its morphophonologically overt manifestation, it is necessary for OBJ to be introduced as an oblique argument, to which the anti-passive morpheme transmits its θ-role in some way (see Roberts 1986 and Baker, Johnson, and Roberts 1989 for a proposal about the mechanics of the transmission from the (anti-)passive morpheme to the oblique argument). Finally, (6.66) is derived, which corresponds to the anti-passive clause in ergative languages:

(6.66)   ANTI-PASSIVE

                                                    internal θ-role

         $[_{TP}$ SUBJ(T)$_k$ T $[_{vP}$ t$_k$ v-ANT $[_{VP}$ V (OBJ-OBL) $]$ $]$ $]$

         absolutive-, ϕ-, EPP-checking

This derivation converges, because SUBJ(T)'s Case-features are checked against T's and T's other [−interpretable] nominal features are checked off by SUBJ(T). (OBJ's Case-features do not have to be checked off because it is oblique (i.e., it is an inherent Case).)

In the analysis of the anti-passive formation presented above I exploited the speculation that the anti-passive morpheme, which behaves the same as the passive morpheme in that it absorbs the Case-feature of v and one of the θ-roles of the transitive verb to which it is attached, differs from the passive morpheme in that while the θ-role the passive morpheme absorbs is the external one, the one the anti-passive morpheme absorbs is the internal one. Then, what happens if the passive morpheme is employed in place of the anti-passive morpheme in (6.64), which represents the underlying transitive clause in a morphologically ergative language with the parameter-setting: (1) [+ΘPC]; (2) v's Case-feature is strong; (3) T's EPP-feature is strong; (4) T's Case-feature is weak/strong; and (5) T's ϕ-feature is weak/strong? This situation is represented in (6.67):

(6.67) $[_{vP}$ SUBJ(T) v-PASS $[_{VP}$ V OBJ $]$ $]$ (before Spell-out)

Since SUBJ(T) is deprived of its θ-role by the passive morpheme, it is not base-generated at the Spec of v, where it would be introduced by *Merge* if the external θ-role of the transitive verb were available. After T is introduced by *Merge* into (6.67), OBJ is attracted to the Spec of T by T's strong EPP-feature due to parameter (3), because it is the DP closest to T at that stage in the derivation. The step in (6.68) is thereby derived:

(6.68) $[_{TP}$ OBJ$_k$ T $[_{vP}$ v-PASS $[_{VP}$ V t_k]]] (before Spell-out)

In (6.68) OBJ checks off all of T's nominal features (i.e., EPP-, φ-, and Case-features). Accordingly, OBJ is marked as absolutive in a passive clause, as T's Case-feature is called absolutive in ergative languages. If SUBJ(T) is to be introduced in this derivation with its morphophonologically overt manifestation, it is necessary to be introduced as an oblique argument, to which the passive morpheme transmits its θ-role in some way (see Roberts 1986 and Baker, Johnson, and Roberts 1989). Finally, (6.69) is derived, which corresponds to the passive clause in ergative languages:

(6.69) PASSIVE

$[_{TP}$ OBJ$_k$ T $[_{vP}$ v-PASS $[_{VP}$ V t_k (SUBJ(T)-OBL)]]]

absolutive-, φ-, EPP-checking ; external θ-role

Here it is important to notice that, just as in the derivation for anti-passive, the [+ΘPC] parameter plays no role in the derivation for passive in ergative languages. Recall that the [+ΘPC]-parameter is decisively crucial for ergative languages. Hence, the derivation for passive in ergative languages sketched above is quite the same as the derivation for passive in accusative languages. Indeed, there are many ergative languages which have passive voice as well as anti-passive voice; they include Nisgha (Belvin 1990a), Quiché (Larsen 1987), Mam (England 1988), Nez Perce (Rude 1988), Chamorro (Cooreman 1988), Päri (Andersen 1988), Inuit (Johns 1992), Halkomelem Salish (Gerdts 1988), Yup'ik (Payne 1982), Chinookan (Van Valin 1980), Basque (Van Valin 1980), and many others.

(6.70) *Inuktitut* (Legendre 1995: 300)

    a. ACTIVE

        Arna-up   angut-Ø kunik-paa.
        woman-ERG man-ABS kiss-3SG.3SG
        'The woman kissed the man.'

    b. PASSIVE

        Angut-Ø arna-mit   kunik-tau-vuq.
        man-ABS woman-ABL kiss-PASS-3SG

    c. ANT-PASSIVE

        Arna-Ø   angum-mik kunik-si-vuq.
        woman-ABS man-COM   kiss-ANT-3SG

6.4.5. Nonexistence of Anti-Passive in Accusative Languages

In the previous section I showed that passive and anti-passive, in principle, coincide in a single ergative language. The other logical possibility is that anti-passive coincides with passive in a single accusative language. As has sometimes been pointed out in the literature (e.g., Bok-Bennema 1991, Dixon 1994, Palmer 1994, and Manning 1996), however, it seems universally true that there is no accusative language that has anti-passive voice.[33] Then, why is it that anti-passive is found only in ergative languages?

Recall that the anti-passive morpheme absorbs the Case-feature of v and the internal θ-role of the transitive verb to which it is attached. This yields the stage in the derivation illustrated in (6.64). As already noted in footnote 32, (6.64) causes a deviation from so-called Burzio's generalization, which states that a verb discharges its structural Case if and only if it discharges its external θ-role. In (6.64) the verbal complex (= the amalgam of v + the anti-passive morpheme + V) discharges its external θ-role to SUBJ(T) despite the fact that its structural Case is not discharged, resulting in a deviation from Burzio's generalization. On the other hand, the derivation for passive obeys Burzio's generalization. The diagram in (6.67) represents the passive counterpart of (6.64). In (6.67) the verbal complex (= the amalgam of v + the passive morpheme + V) does not discharge its structural Case, nor does it discharge its external θ-role; whence, Burzio's generalization is trivially fulfilled here.

Therefore the conclusion is that the fact that anti-passive is impossible in accusative languages indicates that anti-passive is blocked in accusative languages just because Burzio's generalization is observable only in accusative languages, but not in ergative languages. This conforms with the view held by the authors such as B. Levin (1983) and Laka (1993), who explicitly state that Burzio's generalization holds only in accusative languages.[34]

6.5. Summary

In this chapter I studied ergativity and its typological variations, and examined how ergativity is derived under the theory of multiple feature checking. It was argued that any approach to ergativity that employs the structure-based theory of Case and agreement is more or less problematic on empirical grounds. Exploiting the theory of multiple feature checking, which is free from the problems the

---

[33] Occasionally, the existence of anti-passive in some accusative language has been reported (e.g., Postal 1977 and Heath 1976), though it seems that the construction alleged to be an anti-passive is very limited or construction-specific or should be analyzed as Unspecified Object Deletion such as the following English example: *John ate (an egg)*, or as the conative alternation like *Mary kicked the ball* → *Mary kicked at the ball* (cf. Dixon 1994 and Manning 1996).

[34] The next question to be answered is: Why is it that Burzio's generalization is observable only in accusative languages? I will leave it to future research, referring the reader to Mahajan (to appear) and references cited therein.

structure-based theory of Case and agreement encounters, I argued that shallowly ergative languages result from the parameter-setting: (1) [+ΘPC]; (2) *v*'s Case-feature is strong; (3) T's EPP-feature is strong; (4) T's Case-feature is weak; and (5) T's ϕ-feature is weak (→the ordinary type of shallowly ergative language), or (5') strong (→the Warlpiri-type of shallowly ergative language), and syntactically ergative languages result from the parameter-setting: (1) [+ΘPC]; (2) *v*'s Case-feature is strong; (3) T's EPP-feature is strong; (4) T's Case-feature is strong; and (5) T's ϕ-feature is strong. Moreover it was demonstrated that some GF-splitting phenomena due to several types of ergativity are fully accounted for by the theory of multiple feature checking.

7

Double Object Constructions

In chapter 7 and chapter 8, through studying phenomena not directly connected to GF-splitting, I will explore some of the consequences of the theory of multiple feature checking advocated in this book. In this chapter I will try to investigate the structure of the so-called double object construction (DOC) under the Agr-less feature-checking theory reinforced with the theory of multiple feature checking. It will be demonstrated that some parametric variations as well as their interesting correlation with optional object shift can be naturally accounted for.

7.1. Larsonian VP-Shell in Agr-Based Case Theory

The so-called Larsonian VP-shell was first introduced by Larson (1988) in order to capture the structural asymmetry between double objects, which was originally pointed out by Barss and Lasnik (1986). Recently several proposals have been made to accommodate the VP-shell analysis of the double object construction to the Agr-based Case theory, under which the structural cases such as nominative and accusative are not assigned, but checked by an appropriate functional head at the Spec of that head (namely, Agr) (cf. Chomsky 1992, 1994a; Lasnik 1993; and Watanabe 1993). As proponents for the proposals correctly point out, it is necessary to make the following two assumptions: (1) It is necessary to split up the Larsonian VP-shell by inserting a projection of Agr between the two VP projections; and (2) it is necessary to assume another Agr projection immediately higher than the higher VP projection in the VP-shell.[1] The underlying structure for the double object construction with these assumptions, thus, looks like (7.1):

---

[1] See Bures (1993) and, especially, Collins and Thráinsson (1993: 137–141) for detailed discussions on this point. I omit repeating them for the sake of space.

(7.1) 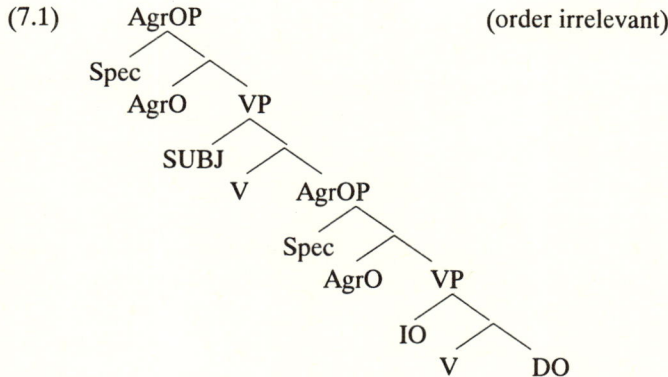 (order irrelevant)

In fact, lots of recent work (e.g., Hoffman 1991, Bures 1993, Cheng and Demirdache 1993, Murasugi 1994, Ura 1994c, Fujita 1996, inter alia) have adopted this "neo-Larsonian VP-shell" for the underlying structure of the double object construction.

As is evident from the delineation in (7.1), the "neo-Larsonian VP-shell", in which the direct object (DO) is generated at the complement of the lower V, the indirect object (IO) at the Spec of the lower V, and the Agent-argument (SUBJ) at the Spec of the higher V (Larson 1988), is split up by an Agr-head and its projection. However, the neo-Larsonian VP-shell delineated in (7.1), as it is, has a theory-internal problem under the minimalist theory of movement proposed by Chomsky (1992), as Bures (1993), Koizumi (1993), Collins and Thráinsson (1993, 1996), Ura (1994c), and Bobaljik (1995b) point out.[2] In this theory two sequential Specs cannot be skipped over by a single step of movement; consequently, IO cannot move up to the position where its Case-feature is properly checked off (i.e., the Spec of the higher AgrO in (7.1)) after the Spec of the lower AgrO is filled with DO.

With this in mind, consider the following Icelandic examples:

(7.2) *Icelandic* (Collins and Thráinsson 1993: 142–143)

   a. Ég lána Maríu ekki bækurnar.
      I lend Maria not the books
      'I do not lend Maria the books.'

   b. ?Ég lána Maríu bækurnar ekki.
      I lend Maria the books not

Assuming that the Scandinavian negative elements like *inte* in Swedish, *ekki* in Icelandic, and *ikke* in Danish are adjoined to VP (cf. Collins and Thráinsson 1993, Bobaljik 1995b, Holmberg and Platzak 1995), it can be inferred from (7.2b) that both objects may overtly move up out of a VP in Icelandic. Thus, it is very reasonable to make out, following Bobaljik (1995b), that both objects in (7.2b) undergo the so-called "object shift," which is analyzed in the Agr-based

---

[2] See Bobaljik (1995b) for empirical arguments against the neo-Larsonian VP-shell, no matter how it may be constructed.

Case theory as an operation by which an object is overtly moved to the Spec of AgrO (Chomsky 1992; Collins and Thráinsson 1993, 1996; Watanabe 1993; Jonas 1996; inter alia). Hence, the conclusion is that there is a case, in Icelandic, where IO overtly moves to the Spec of the higher AgrO in addition to the overt DO movement to the Spec of the lower AgrO, a case that poses a serious problem to the underlying structure for double objects illustrated in (7.1).

To overcome this theory-internal problem, several proposals have been made under the Agr-based Case theory: Bures (1993) stipulates that there are two cycles; Collins and Thráinsson (1993) (cf., also, Koizumi 1993, 1995) introduce another projection between the lower AgrOP and the higher VP in (7.1) for the purpose of providing an escape-hatch for IO's movement beyond the two sequential Specs in question; and Ura (1994c) postulates that in languages like Icelandic, there is a parameter such that the lower AgrO may provide an extra Spec for an escape-hatch for the movement of IO at issue.[3]

In this chapter, I will attempt, without recourse to the Agr-based Case theory, to establish the theory of the double object construction under the Agr-less checking theory. At the same time I will provide very strong support in favor of the theory advocated here, by demonstrating that it offers a natural account of the differences in the passivizability of DO in a DOC between Norwegian (and Swedish) vs. Danish, on the one hand, and between British vs. American English, on the other, in addition to a very simple account of a generalization concerning the passivizability of IO and DO universally detected in the world's languages.

7.2. Underlying Structure for DOC

Chomsky (1995a: §10) proposes to discard the Agr-systems for Case-checking. Instead, he suggests that SUBJ's nominal feature checking and OBJ's, if taking place before Spell-out, are executed at a Spec of T (= Infl) and a Spec of v, respectively, where v stands for the higher verb in the two layered VP-shell for a transitive verb (see §1.3.1.4). This can be delineated as in (7.3):

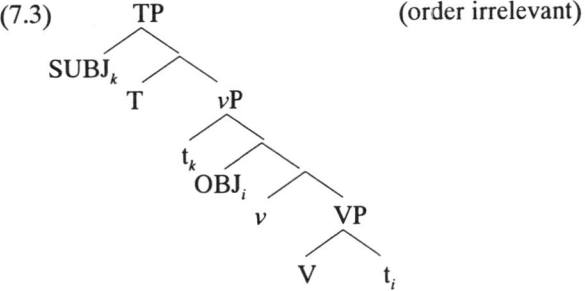

(7.3)   (order irrelevant)

---

[3] See Bobaljik (1995b) for some empirical arguments against these proposals under the neo-Larsonian VP-shell. In appendix A of this chapter other problems for the neo-Larsonian VP-shell will be examined.

In (7.3), the nominal feature of OBJ is checked off at the innermost (i.e., canonical) Spec of v, and SUBJ, which is base-generated at the outer Spec of v,[4] has its nominal feature checked off at the Spec of T.

As is evident from (7.3), the Agr-less checking theory of Chomsky (1995a) assumes a kind of Larsonian VP-shell for the underlying structure of a transitive verb. In this respect, he follows Hale and Keyser's (1991, 1993) approach to the mapping of argument structure to syntactic structure. Following this direction, it is naturally postulated that the underlying structure of a ditransitive verb consists of a Larsonian VP-shell that has three layers of VP, as illustrated in (7.4a):

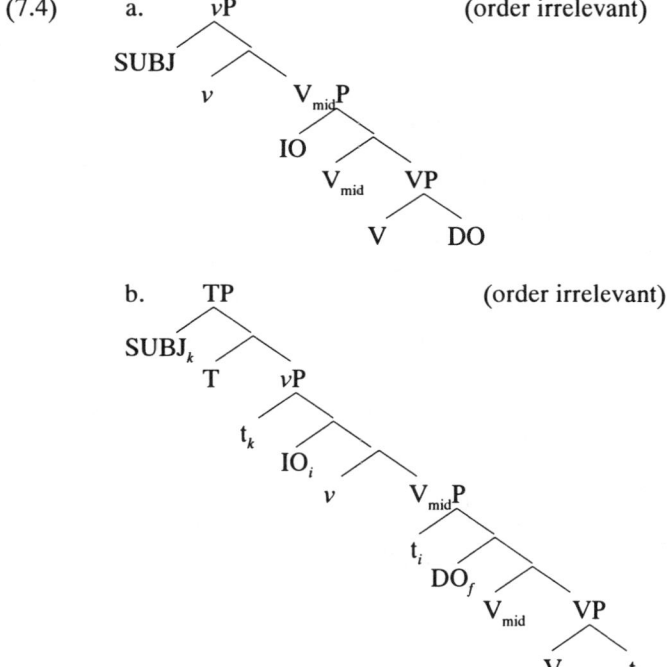

That is to say, DO is generated within the lowest V (V in (7.4)), IO is generated at a Spec of the mid V (V_{mid}), and SUBJ is generated at a Spec of v. Now I propose that the nominal feature checking of DO and that of IO in an active clause are executed at a Spec of V_{mid} and at a Spec of v, respectively, if these checkings take place before Spell-out. This is illustrated in (7.4b).[5] This can be viewed as a translation of the neo-Larsonian VP-shell for the DOC under the Agr-based checking theory into the Agr-less checking theory à la Chomsky (1995a: §10).[6] It is plausible that the intermediate V (V_{mid} in (7.4)) has a meaning

---

[4] The structure delineated in (7.3), in which OBJ comes in the innermost Spec of v, is derived only if v's nominal feature is strong. See §1.4.1 for detail.

[5] Whether the overtly shifted object comes to the innermost Spec or an outer one depends on the strength of the head that attracts the object. See §1.4.1 for discussion.

[6] I owe the idea about (7.4b) to Bobaljik (1995b), who proposes a structure for the DOC

of aspect or something like that, as Collins and Thráinsson (1993, 1996) suggest for their T appearing between the two V projections in the neo-Larsonian VP-shell. Indeed, there are languages that have an overt realization of V_{mid} (see appendix A of this chapter).

It is important to note that in (7.4b), there is no crossing of the paths created by the overt movements of the arguments involved: DO does not cross over IO on its way to its checking position, and IO does not cross over SUBJ on its way to its checking position. This is achieved by postulating that Move (XP) to a Spec of H may precede Merge (YP) with HP as a base-generation of YP. As Bobaljik (1995b) emphasizes, this brings a big advantage; it overcomes the problem that the neo-Larsonian VP-shell for the DOC encounters. As pointed out previously, the neo-Larsonian VP-shell needs a stipulation for an escape-hatch for the overt movement of IO to the Spec of AgrIO beyond the Spec of AgrDO and the Spec of the higher V in the Larsonian VP-shell (see §7.1). The structure (7.4b) is free from this problem because there is no path crossing of argument movement. See Bobaljik (1995b) for various empirical arguments for this "stacking" hypothesis for the checking position of the object(s). It is true that, as was noted in footnote 6, (7.4) is different from Bobaljik's (1995b) structure for the DOC in that it does not assume the Agr-based Case theory, but it seems that there is no difference between those two structures for the DOC in terms of the points Bobaljik (1995b) notices. So at this moment, it is safe to say that (7.4) has the same advantage as Bobaljik's (1995b) structure for the DOC.

In the next section I will turn to the issue concerning typological/dialectal differences of the DOC in terms of the passivizability of each object. It will be demonstrated that, given some parametric differences in terms of multiple Specs for the heads responsible for the feature-checking of each object in a DOC, the proposed underlying structure for DOCs, which is illustrated in (7.4), offers a natural explanation of the typological/dialectal differences of the DOC in natural language.

7.3. Deriving Typological/Dialectal Differences in DOC

In the literature it has often been pointed out that between two dialects of a given language or between two languages very closely related to each other, there may be a difference in terms of the passivizability of DO in a DOC. For example, in Norwegian and Swedish, DO as well as IO can be promoted to the subject position by passivization, but in Danish, DO cannot be promoted by passivization

---

almost similar to (7.4a); however, he (partially) maintains the Agr-based Case theory. Thus, it is more precise to say that (7.4b) should be viewed as a translation of Bobaljik's (1995b) underlying structure for the DOC into the Agr-less checking theory of Chomsky (1995a). My assumption concerning the position of SUBJ and the overt checking position of OBJ at Specs of v crucially differs from Bobaljik's (1995b) in that Bobaljik does not maintain the claim that Move (OBJ) must be prior to Merge (SUBJ) because the derivation would otherwise crash due to the unchecked strong feature of v. See §7.3.1 for details. I will return this issue later in this section.

(cf. Holmberg and Platzak 1995); or in Bantu languages, some languages allow DO to be passivized, but others do not (cf. Bresnan and Moshi 1990).

Moreover, it has sometimes been noted in the literature on language typology, that there is no language that allows only DO, but not IO, to be passivized, where both objects are marked with the same morphological device (Johnson 1974a,b, 1977; Keenan 1975; Faltz 1978; Givón 1979, 1984b).

In this section I will show that these typological/dialectal variations of the DOC in terms of the passivizability of DO can be accounted for with the Agr-less checking theory reinforced with the theory of multiple feature checking.

7.3.1. Norwegian/Swedish vs. Danish

It is commonly held that Norwegian (plus Swedish) and Danish are very similar to each other in syntactic respects. But, as mentioned above, there is a clear and remarkable difference between them in terms of the passivizability of DO in the DOC: In Norwegian (and Swedish) either DO or IO in a DOC can be passivized as shown in (7.5), while in Danish, only IO, but not DO, can be passivized, as shown in (7.6):[7]

(7.5)　*Norwegian* (Holmberg and Platzak 1995: 215)

    a.　Jon ble gitt boken.
       Jon was given the-book
       'John was given the book.'

    b.　Boken ble gitt Jon.
       the-book was given Jon
       'The book was given (to) John.'

(7.6)　*Danish* (Holmberg and Platzak 1995: 215)

    a.　Jens blev givet bogen.
       Jens was given the-book
       'John was given the book.'

    b.　*Bogen blev givet Jens.
       the-book was given Jens
       'The book was given (to) John.'

Now the question is: How and why do Norwegian (plus Swedish) and Danish differ in this respect? I will postulate a very simple parametric difference between them. It will be demonstrated that there is a piece of empirical evidence in favor of this parametric difference.

---

[7] For the relevant fact in Swedish, see Falk (1990) and Holmberg and Platzak (1995). For the passive formation in Scandinavian, see Åfarli (1992), Holmberg and Platzak (1995), and references cited therein.

Before considering how to implement a parameter that can derive the difference at issue, however, let us look at the interaction between the underlying structure of the DOC and the parameter that (dis)allows object shift in the DOC.

7.3.1.1. The Parameter for Multiple Specs

Chomsky (1995a: §10) proposes that a head H may have such a parameter-setting that it may tolerate a single (or arbitrarily many) unforced violation(s) of Procrastinate. On the other hand, according to Collins's (1995a) elaboration of the theory of multiple feature checking of Ura (1994e), it is a formal feature F, but not a head H, that has a parameter-setting concerning multiple/single feature checking (see §1.3.2).

Let us return to the structure (7.4b), which illustrates the checking position of each object of DOC. Now I propose that the following parametric difference exists between Norwegian (plus Swedish) and Danish:

(7.7) **Parametric difference between Norwegian (Swedish) and Danish**

Whereas in Norwegian and Swedish, v in DOC tolerates arbitrarily many violations of Procrastinate, in Danish it does not tolerate any violation of Procrastinate.

Recall that I am assuming that, as illustrated in (7.4b) above, IO has its nominal features checked off at the innermost Spec of v if the checking is induced by a strong feature. Here I propose that the nominal features of v for the DOC in those languages are weak. Then, as I argued in §1.4.1, IO is attracted to an outer Spec of v if it is overtly attracted by v. Given (7.7), the prediction is that there is a case where IO in Norwegian and Swedish may move overtly to an outer Spec of v before Spell-out, violating Procrastinate. This prediction is indeed borne out, as Holmberg and Platzak (1995: chapter 6) report:

(7.8)   *Norwegian* (Holmberg and Platzak 1995: 172)

De ga Marit ikke blomstene.
they gave Marit not the-flowers
'They did not give Marit the folowers.'

If VP-adverbials such as *ikke* 'not' in Norwegian can be adjoined to either vP or V_{mid}P, but not to VP, in a DOC,[8] the well-formedness of (7.8) indicates that IO moves up overtly to a Spec of v. One might be tempted to conjecture that this overt movement of IO is induced by a strong nominal feature of v. If this were the case, IO would be always required to move up overtly in Swedish and Norwegian, regardless of whether IO is a full NP or a pronoun; however, the fact is that IO may stay in situ if it is a full NP in Norwegian and Swedish, as the well-formedness of (7.9) shows (cf. Holmberg and Platzak 1995: chapter 6):

---

[8] I will discuss this issue later in this subsection.

(7.9) *Norwegian*

De ga [$_{vP/VmidP}$ ikke [$_{VmidP}$ Marit blomstene]].
they gave   not   Marit the-flowers
'same meaning as (7.8)' (Holmberg 1991, Holmberg and Platzak 1995)

So it must be the case that the nominal feature of v in a DOC is weak in Norwegian and Swedish.[9]

Here it is noteworthy that full NPs may not undergo object shift in Norwegian and Swedish (and Danish, as well) in a simple transitive clause (see Vikner 1994, Bobaljik 1995b, and Holmberg and Platzak 1995). In Norwegian and Swedish, full NPs may undergo object shift only if they appear as an IO in a DOC.[10] This fact can be captured by assuming that only v in the verbal complex of ditransitive verbs, but not v in the verbal complex of ordinary transitive verbs, tolerates unforced violations of Procrastinate in Norwegian and Swedish.[11]

On the other hand, our claim that v in DOC does not tolerate any unforced violation of Procrastinate in Danish leads to the prediction that a full-NP IO in Danish, unlike in Norwegian and Swedish, may not undergo object shift. This

---

[9] Later in this subsection I will dispute a possible claim that the word order of IO and the VP-adverbial in (7.8) results from the base-position of IO at a Spec of V_{mid} on the outside of the VP-adverbial, as in (i):

(i)
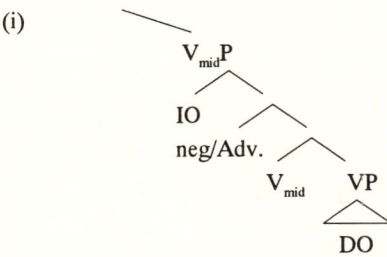

If (i) were a possible analysis of (7.8), there would be no object shift of IO involved in (7.8).

[10] DO in a DOC, if it is a full NP, may not undergo object shift even in Norwegian and Swedish let alone in Danish (Holmberg 1991, Bobaljik 1995b, Allan, Holmes, and Lundskær-Nielsen 1995, and, especially, Holmberg and Platzak 1995). I will return to this issue in §7.3.1.3.

[11] Along this line of analysis, it might be possible to say that pronouns in Norwegian (and Swedish and Danish, as well) undergo object shift because they have a strong feature in themselves, though it has been suggested in the literature that the "pronoun shift" in Mainland Scandinavian is not a real object shift (cf. Jonas and Bobaljik 1993). As is well known, even full NPs may undergo object shift in transitive clauses in Icelandic and Faroese (see, for example, Vikner 1994, Bobaljik 1995b, and Jonas 1996). This fact can be captured by saying that v in the verbal complex of both transitive and ditransitive verbs tolerates violations of Procrastinate. There are other possible explanations of these facts, however. Here I leave it open to investigate the theory of object shift in general, because it is far beyond our scope. See Vikner (1994), Bobaljik (1995b), Jonas (1996), and Holmberg and Platzak (1995) for extensive discussions on the issue.

prediction is also borne out by the following contrast (cf. Holmberg and Platzak 1995: chapter 6):

(7.10) *Danish*

a. *Peter viste [$_{vP}$ Marie$_k$ [$_{vP/VmidP}$ {ikke/jo} [$_{VmidP}$ t$_k$ bogen]]]]
   Peter showed Marie   not/indeed   the book
   'Peter {didn't show/indeed showed} Marie the book.' (cf. (7.8))

b. Peter viste [$_{vP/VmidP}$ {ikke/jo} [$_{VmidP}$ Marie bogen]]]
   Peter showed   not/indeed   Marie the book
      (cf. Vikner 1989, Allan, Holmes, and Lundskær-Nielsen 1995)

It is interesting to note, in passing, that the overt movement of IO to a Spec of v in the Norwegian example in (7.8) is alleged to have taken place beyond the VP-adverbial that is alleged to be adjoined to vP or V$_{mid}$P. If the VP-adverbial in (7.8) is adjoined to vP,[12] the Spec of v where IO lands must be in the outside of an adjunct to vP. This is clearly disallowed by the "conventional" X-bar theory, but it is allowed under the bare phrase structure theory (Chomsky 1994a and Ura 1994e) if a Spec of a head H is defined in the manner described in §1.3.2.1.[13]

(7.11) α is located in a Spec of X^0 iff (i) and (ii):

(i) α is excluded by X^0 (i.e., α is not dominated by X^{0max})

(ii) (a) α enters into a feature-checking relation with X^0, or

(b) α is assigned an external θ-role by X^0.

Given this, XP is regarded as being in a Spec of H, regardless of its position relative to H, if its feature enters into a checking relation with H. Returning to (7.8), it is therefore possible to say that IO is in a Spec of v even if the VP-adverbial, which is adjoined to vP, occurs on the inside of the VP-adverbial.

If the VP-adverbial is adjoined to V$_{mid}$P in (7.8), it is necessary to assume, in order to ensure that IO undergoes object shift in (7.8), that the VP-adverbials never come on the inside of the base-position of IO. This assumption seems inconsistent with the above conclusion that a Spec of H may come on the outside of adjuncts to HP. It is true that from the viewpoint of the phrase structure, there may be a case where adjuncts to HP are allowed to come on the inside of a Spec of H, as argued previously. But I would like to propose that no adjunct to HP be allowed to occur on the inside of a Spec of H if the Spec has no feature-checking relation with H. Note that there is a case where XP is regarded as being in a Spec of H even though XP has no feature-checking relation with H. When XP is assigned an external θ-role by H, XP is regarded as a Spec of H (cf. (7.11(ii(b)))). The reason that no adjunct to HP is allowed to occur on the inside of a Spec of H

---

[12] This means that VP-adverbials are adjoined to vP when they are introduced by Merge. In the final representation, the node that immediately dominates them is no longer regarded as vP under Chomsky's (1994a) definition of the maximal projection.

[13] For discussion on the definition of Specs, see Ura (1993b) and the one in Ura (1994e). The one given in (7.11) is an updated and more sophisticated definition of Specs, which can cover the older one.

when the Spec has no feature-checking relation with H is that the linkage of a θ-relation between H and H's Spec is affected (or blocked) by the intervention of adjuncts. It is often claimed that a θ-relation is not really a relation between a head and XP, but it is a relation between XP and XP (Marantz 1984; Williams 1980, 1994). Thus it is not unnatural to assume that the thematic relation between WP and X in (7.12a) differs from the one in (7.12b), because the category XP before Merge (WP) in (7.12a) differs from XP before Merge (WP) in (7.12b):

(7.12)

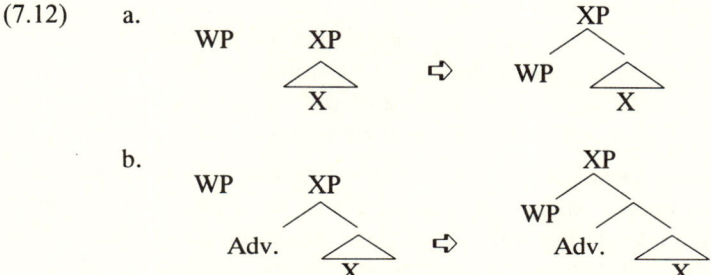

In other words, I am proposing that attachment of adverbials to XP should affect the semantic interpretation of XP.

In contrast, feature checking under the Minimalist program is a relation between X^0 and X^0 (head-head agreement), or between X^0 and XP (head-Spec agreement); hence, the intervention of adverbials has no effect on feature checking. Moreover, the intervention of some elements with a checking relation with X^0 does not disallow X^0's θ-assignment to an outer Spec, because checking has no effect on the interpretation of XP.

Recall that I am relying crucially on the assumption that VP-adverbials such as 'not' or 'often' are never adjoined to VP. Contrary to this assumption, it is sometimes held that VP-adverbials can be adjoined to any maximal projection of V in a given VP-shell (cf. Bobaljik 1995b). According to this view, the Icelandic example in (7.13a) and the Swedish one in (7.13b) do not necessarily indicate that IO in these examples undergoes object shift.

(7.13) a. *Icelandic* (Collins and Thráinsson 1993: 142)

Ég lána Maríu ekki bækurnar.
I   lend Maria not the books
'I do not lend Maria the books.'

b. *Swedish* (Dikken 1995: 141)

?Han gav Sara$_k$ inte boken.
he   gave Sara   not the book
'He didn't give Sara the book.'

Under this view, the word order of IO and the neg-element in these examples can be explained by simply saying that the neg-element is adjoined to VP in the

DOC. In fact, this explanation seems to hold in these languages, but it encounters a problem in explaining the ill-formedness of the Danish counterpart:

(7.14)   *Danish* (Allan, Holmes, and Lundskær-Nielsen 1995: 513)

    *Jeg gav Peter ikke bogen.
    I gave Peter not the book
    'I didn't give Peter the book.'

To explain the difference, it must be stipulated that the Danish neg-element *ikke* differs from the other Scandinavian equivalents in that it cannot be adjoined to VP in a DOC. In light of the fact that the neg-elements in all Scandinavian languages behave the same in other syntactic respects, this stipulation is highly ad hoc. Rather, it is more natural to stipulate that the neg-element cannot be adjoined to VP in a DOC in all Scandinavian languages, as I assume here.

To recapitulate, I made the hypothesis that in Swedish and Norwegian, v in a DOC tolerates arbitrarily many unforced violations of Procrastinate, while in Danish it does not tolerate any violation of Procrastinate. This hypothesis is confirmed by the fact that, whereas in Swedish and Norwegian, a full-NP IO may undergo object shift, it may not in Danish. Keeping this in mind, let us turn to the main concern about the difference between Swedish/Norwegian and Danish in terms of the passivizability of DO in the DOC.

7.3.1.2. Passivizability of DO in DOC

Now that v in the DOC tolerates arbitrarily many unforced violations of Procrastinate in Norwegian and Swedish, it can be concluded that IO may move overtly to an outer Spec of v before Spell-out even in a passive clause. The overt movement of IO to a Spec of v in a Norwegian or Swedish passive clause derives (7.16) from (7.15), which is the core underlying structure of a passivized DOC:

(7.15)   (*Swedish/Norwegian*)

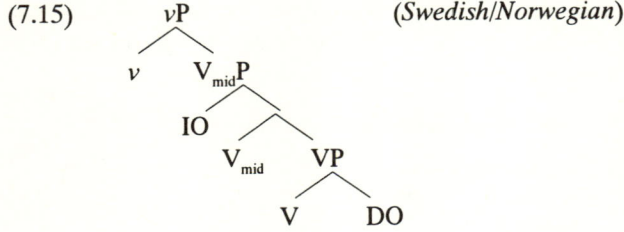

(7.16) 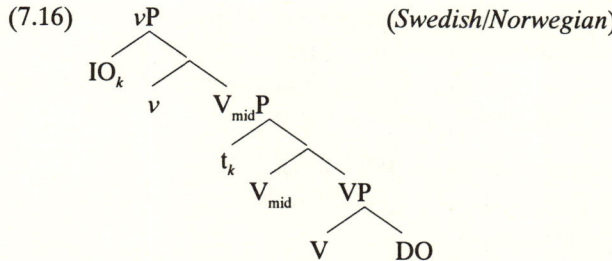 (*Swedish/Norwegian*)

One should notice that in (7.15) DO, instead of IO, may not be attracted to a Spec of v beyond IO; for, IO is closer to v than DO is. In (7.16), as a result of IO's movement to a Spec of v, DO becomes closest to v. (Traces are invisible to Attract/Move (Chomsky 1995a).)

Now, thanks to the hypothesis that v in Norwegian and Swedish tolerates arbitrarily many unforced violations of Procrastinate, DO in (7.16) may move up overtly to an outer Spec of v and enter into a checking relation with v; thereby, (7.17) is derived from (7.16):

(7.17) 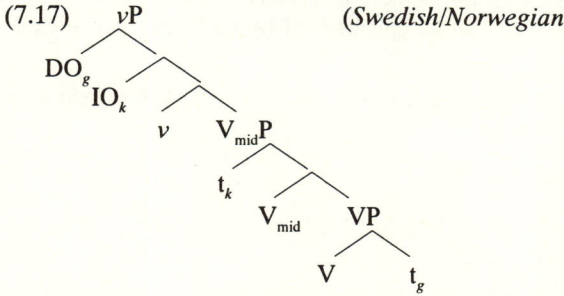 (*Swedish/Norwegian*)

Since this is a passive clause, SUBJ is demoted. Now T is introduced by Merge, deriving (7.18) from (7.17):

(7.18) 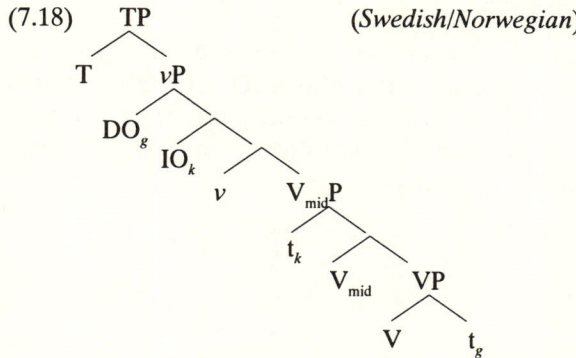 (*Swedish/Norwegian*)

Here, it is important to note that DO and IO in (7.18) are in the same minimal domain of v; that is, they are equidistant from T. This gives rise to a situation where either of them can be equally attracted by T, which is naturally supposed to have a strong EPP-feature (i.e., D-feature) in Norwegian and Swedish because of the existence of the expletive in those languages (cf. Vikner 1995). If DO is attracted by T in (7.18), then a sentence like (7.5b) (repeated here as (7.19b) together with (7.5a) (repeated as (7.19a))), where DO is promoted to the subject with IO still being marked as accusative, is derived.

(7.19) *Norwegian* (Holmberg and Platzak 1995: 235)

    a. Jon ble gitt boken.
       Jon was given the-book
       'John was given the book.'

    b. Boken ble gitt Jon.
       the-book was given Jon
       'The book was given (to) John.'

In this case IO's accusative Case-feature can be checked off by the verbal complex (i.e., the amalgam of v, V_{mid}, and V), though the verbal complex is deprived of one of its two accusative Case-features by the passive morpheme.[14]

If IO is attracted by T in (7.18), then a sentence like (7.19a), where IO is promoted to the subject with DO being marked as accusative, is derived. In this case DO's accusative Case-feature can be checked off by the verbal complex at the outer Spec of v in (7.18).

Now let us return to the DOC examples in Danish (i.e., (7.6), repeated here as (7.20)):

(7.20) *Danish* (Falk 1990: 86)

    a. Han blev tilbudt en stilling.
       he was offered a job
       'He was offered a job.'

    b. *En stilling blev tilbudt ham.
        a job was offered him
       'A job was offered him.'

The hypothesis is that v in Danish does not allow any unforced violation of Procrastinate. From this hypothesis, it follows that neither IO nor DO in the core underlying structure of DOC, which is illustrated in (7.15), may move to a Spec of v or anywhere before the introduction of T. The structure in (7.21) is derived from (7.15) by the introduction of T by Merge:

---

[14] Here I simply assume that the passive morpheme absorbs an accusative Case (feature) of the verb to which it is attached (cf. Baker, Johnson, and Roberts 1989). See Watanabe (1993, 1996) for more discussion on this issue under the Minimalist framework.

(7.21)   *(Danish)*

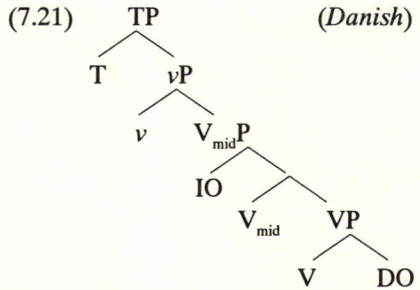

Since T in Danish has a strong EPP-feature (cf. Vikner 1995), the element with a D-feature that is closest to T is attracted by T to the Spec of T before Spell-out. In (7.21) IO is the element with a D-feature that is closest to T. Thus, IO moves up overtly to the Spec of T, resulting in the passive clause in which IO is promoted (i.e., (7.6a)). DO's accusative Case-features can be checked at LF in such a way that it moves up to the verbal complex at LF, entering into a checking relation with the verbal complex, which retains one accusative Case-feature, though being deprived of one of its two accusative Case-features by the passive morpheme.

One should notice here that in (7.21), DO cannot be attracted by T anyway, because IO is closer to T than DO is. This is the reason why DO cannot be promoted by passivization in Danish.

7.3.1.3. Parameter for V_{mid} in DOC

Given the account of the difference between Norwegian/Swedish and Danish in terms of the passivizability of DO in the DOC, one might suspect that if V_{mid} in Norwegian and Swedish, but not in Danish, tolerates an unforced violation of Procrastinate, it could give rise to a situation where DO can pass over IO through an extra Spec of V_{mid} as an escape-hatch in Norwegian and Swedish, regardless of whether *v* in those languages tolerates arbitrarily many unforced violations of Procrastinate. Thus, to maintain the account presented in the preceding subsection, it is necessary to ensure that both in Norwegian/Swedish and in Danish, V_{mid} does not tolerate any unforced violation of Procrastinate.

There is a piece of empirical evidence which shows that V_{mid} in Norwegian/Swedish and Danish does not tolerate any unforced violation of Procrastinate. Recall that I argued that in those languages, a full-NP may undergo object shift if the head of its target tolerates an unforced violation of Procrastinate. Hence, if V_{mid} in those languages tolerates an unforced violation of Procrastinate, then it leads to the prediction that DO may undergo object shift, moving overtly beyond a VP-adverbial. Recall that we are assuming that VP-adverbials in those languages can be adjoined to *v*P or V_{mid}P, but not to VP. As the ill-formedness of the examples in (7.22) shows, neither in Swedish nor in Danish is this prediction borne out:

(7.22) a. *Swedish* (cf. Holmes and Hinchiffe 1994: 520–524)

*Jag gav [$_{\nu P}$ honom$_i$ [$_{\nu P/VmidP}$ **ofta** [$_{VmidP}$ boken$_k$ [$_{VmidP}$ **aldreg** [$_{VmidP}$ t$_i$
I gave him often the-book never

[$_{VP}$ t$_k$]]]]]].

(cf. Jag gav honom ofta den aldreg.
 I gave him often it never)

b. *Danish* (cf. Allan, Holmes, and Lundskær-Nielsen: 502–503)

*Peter viste [$_{\nu P}$ hende$_i$ [$_{\nu P/VmidP}$ **jo** [$_{VmidP}$ bogen$_k$ [$_{VmidP}$ **aldrig** [$_{VmidP}$ t$_i$
Peter showed her indeed the-book never

[$_{VP}$ t$_k$]]]]]].

(cf. Peter viste hende jo den aldrig.
 Peter showed her indeed it never)

Under the proposed theory of the object shift of full NPs in (Mainland) Scandinavian, the examples in (7.22) should be well-formed if it were the case that V_{mid} tolerates an unforced violation of Procrastinate (or if V_{mid} were strong); hence, both in Swedish/Norwegian and in Danish V_{mid} does not tolerate any unforced violation of Procrastinate (and it must be weak).

7.3.2. British vs. American English

In the preceding section I argued that the difference between Swedish/ Norwegian and Danish in terms of the passivizability of DO in the DOC results from the parametric difference between those languages in terms of the property of v in the underlying structure of the DOC. More specifically, I claimed that, whereas DO in a DOC can be promoted by passivization in Swedish and Norwegian because v in those languages tolerates unforced violations of Procrastinate, it cannot be promoted by passivization in Danish because v in this language does not tolerate any unforced violation of Procrastinate at all. In this section it will be shown that the same parametric difference of v in the DOC results in the same difference between British English and American English in the passivizability of DO in a DOC.

It has been frequently pointed out in the literature (Jespersen 1927, Czepluch 1982, McCawley 1988, and many others) that DO in a DOC may be promoted by passivization in British English (hereafter, BE), whereas it may not in American English (AE), as shown in (7.23):[15]

(7.23) a. The book was given Mary (by John). (OK:BE, *:AE)
 (cf. The book was given to Mary. (OK: BE and AE))

---

[15] It has sometimes been reported in the literature (e.g., Oehrle 1976 and Quirk et al. 1985) that these examples are extremely improved if IO is replaced by a pronoun. I will return to this issue later in this section.

b. These letters were sent Mary (by John). (OK:BE, *:AE)
(cf. These letters were sent to Mary. (OK: BE and AE))

Since this corresponds exactly to the difference detected between Swedish/ Norwegian and Danish, it is natural to expect that the same parametric difference between Swedish/Norwegian and Danish in terms of the violability of Procrastinate is involved with the above contrast between BE and AE; that is to say, the expectation is that, while v in a DOC tolerates arbitrarily many unforced violations of Procrastinate in BE, it does not tolerate any unforced violation of Procrastinate in AE.

Recall that the ability of IO to undergo object shift in Swedish/Norwegian is regarded as evidence that v in a DOC tolerates an unforced violation of Procrastinate in those languages. This leads one to expect that IO may undergo object shift in BE, but not in AE. This expectation is indeed realized by the fact that the examples in (7.24) are fairly acceptable in BE, but totally unacceptable in AE (Dikken 1995: 142 for BE, attributing the judgments to Ouhalla 1991; and Koizumi 1993 for AE):[16]

(7.24) a. I gave Bill reluctantly the keys. (OK/?:BE, *:AE)
b. I sent Mary immediately the parcel. (OK/?:BE, *:AE)

It can therefore be concluded from this that v in a DOC in BE, just as in Swedish/Norwegian, tolerates arbitrarily many unforced violations of Procrastinate, and that v in a DOC in AE, just as in Danish, does not tolerate any unforced violation of Procrastinate.

Given this conclusion, it is possible to account for the contrast between BE and AE found in (7.23) in the same way as in the case of the contrast between Swedish (plus Norwegian) and Danish. Now that v in DOC tolerates arbitrarily many violations of Procrastinate in BE, it is possible to infer that IO may move overtly to a Spec of v before Spell-out even in a passive clause in BE. The overt movement of IO to a Spec of v in a BE passive clause derives (7.26) from (7.25), which is the core underlying structure of a passivized DOC:

(7.25)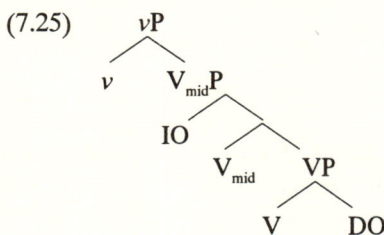

---

[16] In BE or AE, the neg-element *not* cannot come at the same position at which the VP-adverbial in (7.24) is located, although the neg-element in Swedish/Norwegian can, as observed in the preceding section. This results from the difference in the status of the neg-element between Swedish/Norwegian (or Scandinavian in general) and English: In Scandinavian, the neg-element may behave syntactically like a VP-adverbial, but it behaves like a (functional) head in English (cf. Pollock 1989).

(7.26) 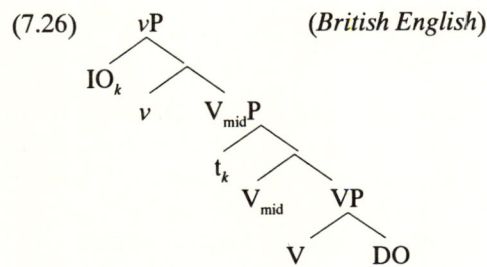 (*British English*)

Since IO has moved to a Spec of v in (7.26), DO in (7.26) becomes the closest to v. Thanks to the hypothesis that v in BE tolerates arbitrarily many unforced violations of Procrastinate, DO in (7.26) may move up overtly to an outer Spec of v; thereby, (7.27) is derived from (7.26):

(7.27) 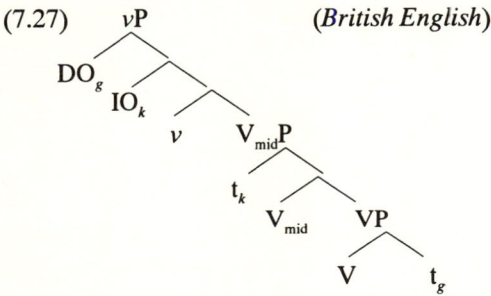 (*British English*)

Now T is introduced by Merge, deriving (7.28) from (7.27):

(7.28) 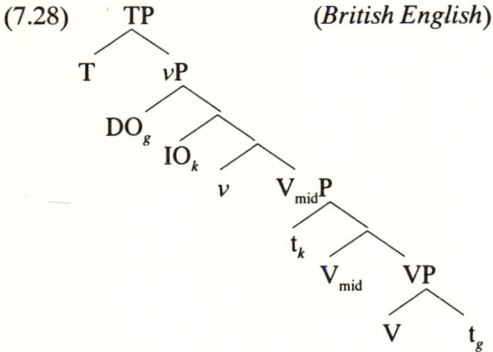 (*British English*)

Since DO and IO in (7.28) are in the same minimal domain of v, either of them can be attracted by T, whose EPP-feature is strong in English (Chomsky 1995a). If DO is attracted by T in (7.28), then a sentence like (7.23), where DO is promoted to the subject with IO still marked as accusative, is safely derived in BE. In (7.23) IO's accusative Case-feature can be checked off by the verbal complex (i.e., the amalgam of v, V_{mid}, and V), though it is deprived of one of its two accusative Case-features by passivization.

If IO is attracted by T in (7.28), then a sentence like (7.29), where IO is promoted to the subject with DO marked as accusative, is derived.

(7.29) a. Mary was given the book (by John).
    b. Mary was sent these letters (by John).

In this case DO's accusative Case-feature can be checked off by the verbal complex at the outer Spec of v in (7.28).

Now let us turn to AE. Since v in AE does not allow any unforced violation of Procrastinate, neither IO nor DO in the core underlying structure of a DOC, which is illustrated in (7.25), may move to a Spec of v or anywhere before the introduction of T. The structure in (7.30) is derived from (7.25) by the introduction of T by Merge:

(7.30)   *(American English)*

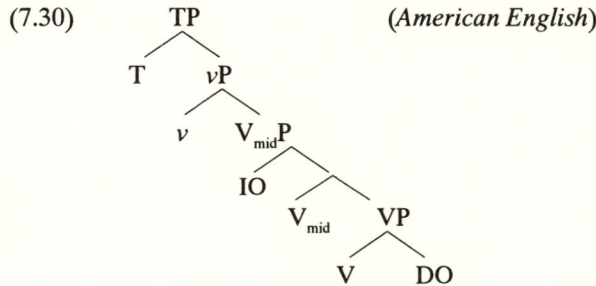

In (7.30) it is IO that is the element with a D-feature that is closest to T. Hence, it is attracted by T to the Spec of T before Spell-out. DO's accusative Case-feature can be checked at LF in such a way that it moves up to the verbal complex at LF, entering into a checking relation with the verbal complex, which retains one nominal feature, though it is deprived of one of its two nominal features by passivization. The sentence derived in this way corresponds to (7.29).

It should be noticed that in (7.30), DO cannot be attracted by T anyway, because IO is closer to T than DO is. This is the reason why DO cannot be promoted by passivization in AE.

Here it is interesting to note that DO in a DOC can be promoted by passivization even in AE if IO is a pronoun (see footnote 15), as illustrated in (7.31). Compare (7.31a,b) with (7.23), repeated here as (7.31c,d):[17]

(7.31) a. The book was given her (by John).   (OK: BE and AE)
    b. These letters were sent her (by John).   (OK: BE and AE)

    c. The book was given Mary (by John).   (OK:BE, *:AE)
    d. These letters were sent Mary (by John).   (OK:BE, *:AE)

Let us assume, essentially following Oehrle (1976), that an unstressed pronoun in English behaves as a clitic in syntax. Then, it is natural to say that the pronominal IO in (7.31) head-moves onto v (i.e., incorporates into v) before Spell-

---

[17] Jonathan Bobaljik (personal communication) reported to me that there are some American English speakers who do not accept (7.31) let alone (7.23). Those who do not accept (7.31) also do not like (7.33). See footnote 20.

out (Baker 1988; Chomsky 1995a). Suppose that this incorporation of pronominal IO into *v* happens in a passive clause in AE; then the structure after Merge(T) looks like (7.32):

(7.32) 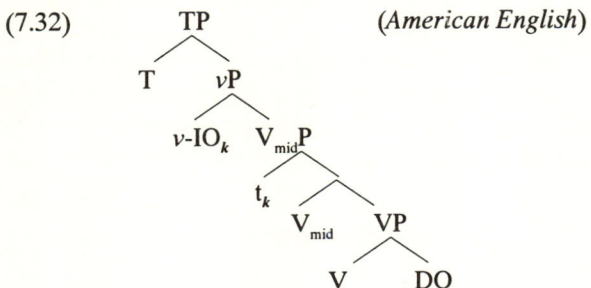 (*American English*)

Here I would like to propose that the element with a D-feature closest to T in (7.32) is DO, stipulating à la Rizzi (1990) that, once ω incorporates into a head, it never induces a kind of minimality effect on XP because ω now counts as an X^0. Recall that I argued that DO cannot be passivized in AE because IO is always closer to T than DO in AE and there is no way to make both objects equidistant from T due to the inability of *v* in AE to tolerate any unforced violation of Procrastinate. In (7.32) IO's incorporation into *v* gives rise to a situation where DO counts as the element with a D-feature that is closest to T. This opens up the possibility for DO to be promoted to the Spec of T by passivization in AE. The conclusion is that DO can be safely promoted to the subject position by passivization in AE only if IO is a pronoun and incorporates into *v* before Spell-out.

This account of the well-formedness of (7.31) in AE leads to the prediction that sentences like those in (7.33) should be acceptable even in AE; for, I am assuming that a pronominal IO may incorporate into *v* before Spell-out:[18]

(7.33) a. I gave him reluctantly the keys. (OK:BE, ?:AE)   (cf. (7.24a))
       b. I sent her immediately the parcel. (OK:BE, ?:AE)   (cf. (7.24b))

The fact is that even in AE, the examples in (7.33), where a pronominal IO precedes a VP-adverbial, though not perfectly acceptable, are far better than the examples in (7.24), where a full-NP IO precedes a VP-adverbial. Therefore these facts are consistent with the analysis presented here for the difference between BE and AE in terms of the passivizability of DO in the DOC. This, in turn, points to the validity of the theory of the DOC advocated in this chapter.

---

[18] As mentioned in footnote 17, those who do not accept (7.33) do not accept (7.31). This can be captured by saying that pronouns do not act as clitics for those speakers. Howard Lasnik (personal communication) reported to me that the sentences sound worse if the pronouns in (7.33) are stressed. Since it is natural that a stressed pronoun cannot act like a clitic, this fact is pertinent to the analysis presented here.

7.3.3. Explanation of the Crosslinguistic Generalization

As was mentioned at the beginning of §7.3, it has sometimes been noted in the literature on language typology that IO is always passivizable in a language L if DO is also passivizable in L under the condition where both objects have the morphologically same case-marking. Furthermore, there is no language that allows only DO, but not IO, to be passivized, where both objects are marked with the same morphological device (cf. Johnson 1974a,b, 1977; Keenan 1975, 1985; Faltz 1978; and Givón 1979, 1984a).

Given the theory of the DOC developed in this chapter, this generalization can be given a very simple explanation. In the core underlying structure of a DOC illustrated in (7.4a), repeated here as (7.34), IO is always closest to T if SUBJ is demoted by passivization. It follows that IO is always passivizable (as long as the "passive" operation exists in the language under consideration).

(7.34) a. (order irrelevant)

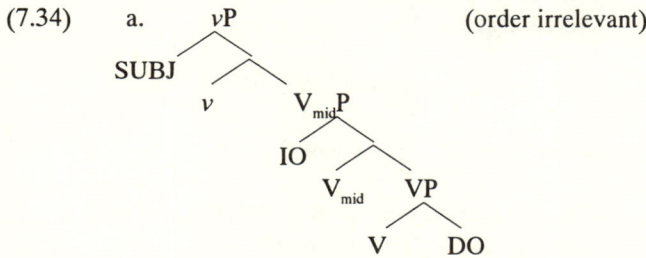

In order for DO to be eligible for the promotion to the subject position by passivization (i.e., in order for it to be attracted by T), it must enter the same minimal domain where IO is located before Spell-out. There are two ways for DO to enter such a domain before Spell-out; by moving up overtly to a Spec of V_{mid} or by moving up overtly to a Spec of v along with IO's overt movement to a Spec of v. To sum up, IO can always be passivized in a language L if L has the active/passive alternation, but DO cannot be passivized unless DO is allowed to enter the same minimal domain where IO is located before Spell-out in L. In other words, DO's passivizability means that there must be a stage in the derivation where DO and IO are in the same minimal domain before Spell-out. Therefore, IO is passivizable wherever DO is passivizable; hence, the aforementioned generalization concerning the passivizability of DO naturally follows.

7.4. Summary

In this chapter I presented an approach to the structure of the DOC under the theory of multiple feature checking. I demonstrated (1) that it is free from the problems that have annoyed those who advocate the Larsonian VP-shell for the DOC under the Minimalist theory of Case and movement (§7.1 and §7.2); (2) that it provides a systematic account of the typological differences in terms of the passivizability of DO in a ditransitive clause between Swedish/Norwegian and

Danish, on the one hand, and British English and American English, on the other; and (3) that the crosslinguistic generalization concerning the passivizability of IO and DO naturally follows.

Appendix
Typological Variety of DOC

In this appendix I will sketch out the typological variety of the DOC in the languages of the world. Limiting my concern to the constructions in which both objects of a ditransitive verb have the same Case-morphology, I recognize that it is the logical possibility that there are four types of DOC with respect to the passivizability of each object in the DOC, as illustrated in the following list:

Type A languages: Korean (Shibatani 1977, O'Grady 1991)
*passive of IO, *passive of DO

Type B languages: Chichewa (Bresnan and Moshi 1990), English, Swahili (Vitale 1981), German (Czepluch 1988), etc.
✓passive of IO, *passive of DO

Type C languages: *There is no language of this type in the world.*
*passive of IO, ✓passive of DO

Type D languages: Kinyarwanda (Kimenyi 1980), Swedish (Falk 1990), Indonesian (Givón 1984a), etc.
✓passive of IO, ✓passive of DO

As shown in this table, crosslinguistic surveys (e.g., Faltz 1978; Givón 1979, 1990; and, especially, Johnson 1974b) have revealed that in terms of the passivizability of each object in a DOC, there are actually three types of DOCs in the natural languages in the world (the existence of Type C languages has never been reported in the literature), notwithstanding the fact that there are logically four types.

In these four types of language, it is possible to find a double accusative construction,[19] in which both objects can be morphologically marked in the same way as the typical transitive objects in those languages. So the languages in these types have in common this property in terms of the morphological marking of the double objects. But they differ in terms of the passivizability of each of the

---

[19] I use "Acc(usative)" rather sketchily. Here it is simply used to refer to the morphological Case form of a noun phrase that typically acts as the transitive direct object in a given language, irrespective of whether the language is a so-called "nominative-accusative" language or "ergative-absolutive" language. Moreover, my use of "indirect object" here is limited to refer to the argument with the thematic role other than Theme in the DOC; so, it may refer to the Goal, Benefactor, or Instrument argument in the DOC. The Theme argument in the DOC is referred to as "direct object" in this appendix.

double objects. To the best of my knowledge, Korean is the sole language belonging to Type A languages; it allows the passivization of neither object (Shibatani 1977; Postal 1986), as shown by the ill-formedness of (7.35b,c).[20]

(7.35) *Korean* (O'Grady 1991: 62)

    a. Nay-ka   John-ul   yenphil-ul cwu-ess-ta.
        I-NOM   -ACC   pencil-ACC give-PAST-IND
       'I gave John a pencil.'

    b. *Yenphil-i   John-ul cwu-eci-ess-ta.
         pencil-NOM   -ACC   give-PASS-PAST-IND
       'The pencil was given John.'

    c. *John-i   yenphil-ul cwu-eci-ess-ta.
         -NOM   -ACC   give-PASS-PAST-IND
       'John was given a pencil.'

In Type B languages, which include American English, many Bantu languages like Chichewa (Bresnan and Moshi 1990), Swahili (Vitale 1981), Fula (Sylla 1979), Runyambo (Rugemalira 1993), and Chi-Mwi:-ni (Kisseberth and Abasheikh 1977), HiBena (Hodges and Stucky 1979), German (Czepluch 1988),[21] Danish (Vikner 1989), Latin (Woolford 1993), Modern Greek (Joseph and Philippaki-Warburton 1987), Maltese (Borg and Comrie 1984), Arabic, Punjabi (Bhatia 1993), Mandarin Chinese (Lin 1985), Ojibwa (Rhodes 1990), Tzotzil (Aissen 1983), Southern Tiwa (Allen and Frantz 1983), Yaqui (Escalante 1990), Nez Perce (Rude 1982), Huichol (Comrie 1982), Nahuatle (Faltz 1978), Imbabura Quechua (Jake 1985), Yindjibarndi (Dryer 1986), Saramaccan (Byrne 1987), and so forth, the passivization of IO is allowed, but not that of DO. In Yindjibarndi and German, for example, there are constructions in which the two objects of a ditransitive predicate are marked as accusative; nevertheless, the Theme argument (i.e., DO) of the predicate cannot be passivized in spite of the fact that IO can be passivized.

(7.36) *Yindjibarndi* (Dryer 1986: 829–830)

    a. Ngaarta   yungku-nha ngayu   murla-yi.
         man(NOM) give-PAST   me(OBJ)   meat-OBJ
       'A man gave me the meat.'

    b. Ngayi   yungku-nguli-nha murla-yi ngaarta-lu.
         I(NOM)   give-PASS-PAST   meat-OBJ man-INST
       'I was gaven the meat by a man.'

---

[20] See the discussion at the end of this appendix for a speculation on the total lack of Korean passive in the DOC.

[21] Note that this holds good only in the case where both objects are marked as accusative. When IO is dative and DO is accusative, the promotion of DO by passivization is possible in German. See §4.3.3 for discussion on the passive clause with the dative-marked IO in Germanic languages.

c. *Murla   yungku-nguli-nha ngayu ngaarta-lu.
   meat(NOM) give-PASS-PAST   me(OBJ) man-INST
   'The meat was gaven me by a man.'

(7.37) *German* (Czepluch 1988: 83)[22]

a. Sie   haben den Jungen   das Lied   gelehrt.
   they(NOM) have the boy(ACC) the song(ACC) taught
   'They have taught the boy the song.'

b. dann ist der Jungen   das Lid   gelehrt worden.
   then is the boy(NOM) the song(ACC) taught been
   'then the boy was taught the song'

c. *dann ist den Jungen   das Lid   gelehrt worden.
   then is   the boy(NOM) the song(NOM) taught been
   'then the song was taught the boy'

Skipping over Type C languages for a while, let us look at Type D languages: In Type D languages either IO or DO in a DOC can be passivized. Many Bantu languages, such as Kinyarwanda (Kimenyi 1980), Kitharaka (Harford 1993), Kichaga (Bresnan and Moshi 1990), Kikuyu (Masunaga 1983), KiRimi (Hualde 1989), Kinande (Hualde 1989), Mashi (Gary 1977), Haya (Duranti and Byarushengo 1977), Runyoro (Keach and Rochemont 1992), and Xhosa (Du Plessis and Visser 1992), and British English (Jespersen 1927), Swedish (Falk 1990), Norwegian (Åfarli 1992), Indonesian (Chung 1983, Givón 1984a), Malagasy (Keenan 1976a), Shoshone (Dayley 1989), Mapuche (Cartrileo 1972), Hausa (Smirnova 1982), Tigrinya (Palmer 1994), Oromo (Owens 1985), and so forth, fall into this type.

(7.38) *Kinyarwanda* (Kimenyi 1980: 127)

a. Umugabo y-a-haa-ye   umugóre igitabo.
   man   HE-PAST-give-ASP woman   book
   'The man gave the woman the book.'

b. Igitabo cy-a-haa-w-e   umugóre n'ûmugabo.
   book   IT-PAST-give-PASS-ASP woman   by man
   'The book was given the woman by the man.'

c. Umugóre y-a-haa-w-e   igitabo n'ûmugabo.
   book   SHE-PAST-give-PASS-ASP book   by man
   'The woman was given the book by the man.'

---

[22] In German, passivization of DO in a DOC is acceptable if the special passive auxiliary *bekommen* is used instead of the normal *werden*. See Wilkinson (1983) for discussion.

(7.39) *Malagasy*[23] (Keenan 1976a: 251, 278)

    a. Manome azy   an-dRakoto aho.
         give-ACT it(ACC) ACC-Rakoto I(NOM)
         'I am giving Rakoto it.'

    b. Omena-ko   azy   Rakoto.
         give-PASS-me(INST) it(ACC) Rakoto
         'Rakoto was given it by me.'

    c. Omena-ko   an-dRakoto izy.
         give-PASS-me(INST) ACC-Rakoto it(NOM)
         'It was given Rakoto by me.'

(7.40) *Oromo* (Owens 1985: 169)

    a. Innii na   gaafii   gaafat-e.
         he(NOM) me(ABS) question(ABS) ask-PAST
         'He asked me a question.'

    b. An   gaafii   gaafat-am-e.
         I(NOM) question(ABS) ask-PASS-PAST
         'I was asked a question.'

    c. Gaafii-n   na   gaafat-am-t-e.
         question-NOM me(ABS) ask-PASS-FEM-PAST
         'A question was asked me.'

Returning to Type C languages, an examination of the literature reveals the typological generalization that this type cannot be found in natural language; that is, there is no language in which the passivization of DO is allowed, but that of IO is not.[24] Needless to say, Type C is logically possible. In §7.3.3 of this chapter the explanation for the total lack of this type in the world's languages was provided.

A comment on the lack of the passive of DO let alone that of IO in Korean is in order. Korean has the active/passive alternation for ordinary transitive clauses.[25] Thus, it is inevitable to say that Korean ditransitive verbs resist the at-

---

[23] Note that Malagasy is a VOS language.

[24] One might suspect that Dutch and Frisian would count as counterexamples in this respect. In fact, it looks as if DO, but not IO, in a DOC can be promoted by passivization in these languages (cf. Evereart 1990, Mulder 1992, and Dikken 1995 for Dutch and Tiersma 1985 for Frisian). But they have no morphological distinction between accusative and dative; hence, it is impossible to tell whether IO is marked as accusative or dative in a DOC. If it is marked as (morphophonologically invisible) dative, then this fact does not contradict the above generalization concerning the typology of a DOC. Cf. Hoekstra (1980) for relevant discussion.

[25] Thanks to Akira Watanabe (personal communication) for reminding me of this fact in Korean.

tachment of the passive morpheme, though ordinary transitive verbs allow it.[26] This is a highly ad hoc speculation, but the fact that Korean is the only detected language of Type A suggests that something idiosyncratic happens in Korean DOC.

---

[26] In Korean possessor-raising from OBJ in an ordinary transitive clause is possible (see Ura 1996b and references cited therein). This gives rise to a situation where two arguments with accusative Case appear in an ordinary transitive clause. According to Cho (1996), passivization is possible in this situation; that is, passivization of (derived) double objects is possible if the verb to which the passive morpheme is attached is a simple transitive one, but not a ditransitive one. See Cho (1996) for interesting treatment of relevant facts under the theory of multiple feature checking.

8

Object Shift in Japanese

Since Chomsky (1992) gave an appealing account of the so-called Holmberg's generalization by means of the MLC under the Agr-based Case theory, "object shift" has been one of the hottest subjects in the minimalist theory. But, in the literature, many discussions on this topic have been made in connection with Germanic, especially Scandinavian languages (e.g., Holmberg 1986, Johnson 1991, Collins and Thráinsson 1993, Vikner 1994, and Bobaljik 1995b, to list only a few), though object shift in other languages has occasionally been discussed (Branigan 1992, Mahajan 1990, and Déprez 1994, among others). In this chapter I will address my attention to Japanese, providing evidence in favor of the claim that Japanese has overt object shift only in ditransitive clauses.

The aim of this chapter is twofold: First, I will argue that Japanese has an *optional* object shift, as has been hinted in some recent literature such as Koizumi (1993), Nemoto (1993), Miyagawa (1996, 1997), and Takano (1996), but I will further claim that object shift, even though optional, is allowed in ditransitive, but not in transitive clauses in Japanese. I will defend this claim by analyzing word order variations in simple transitive and ditransitive clauses in Japanese. My conclusion differs somewhat from the ones proposed by the aforementioned authors. For all of them make little mention of the possibility of object shift (what most of them call S-scrambling) in transitive clauses in Japanese. Watanabe (1993), on the other hand, explicitly states that object shift in a transitive clause is impossible in Japanese; however, he makes no reference to the existence of optional object shift in ditransitive clauses in Japanese and its relevance to the nonexistence of object shift in transitive clauses.

In this respect Japanese resembles Swedish and Norwegian. In chapter 7 it was observed that a full NP in Swedish or Norwegian cannot undergo object shift in a transitive clause, but it may in a ditransitive clause. There I claimed that optional object shift in a ditransitive clause in Swedish and Norwegian results from the fact that the highest verbal projection of the three-layered VP-shell for the underlying structure of a ditransitive verb tolerates unforced violations of Procrastinate. Thus I will claim in this chapter that, whereas the intermediate verbal projection of the three-layered VP-shell for the underlying structure of a ditransitive verb in Japanese also tolerates unforced violations of Procrastinate, the higher verbal projection of the two-layered VP-shell for the underlying structure of a transitive verb in Japanese does not tolerate any unforced violation of Procrastinate. It will be shown that this results in the difference between ditransitive and transitive clauses in Japanese with respect to the possibility of optional overt object shift. To put it differently, my claim is that the optionality of Japanese object shift in ditransitive clauses comes from the fact that the head that checks the formal features of DO in a ditransitive clause tolerates an unforced violation of Procrastinate.

8.1. Word Order in Japanese Ditransitive Clauses

In this section the behavior of object shift in Japanese ditransitive clauses will be examined. First let us take a closer look at the basic word order of ditransitive clauses in Japanese. In Japanese, because of the effect of what Tada (1993) calls S(hort)-scrambling, which permutes an element within VP, the double object construction has two possible surface word orders:

(8.1)   *Japanese*
   a.   John-ga   Mary-ni   hon-o   ageta/okutta/miseta. (S-IO-DO-V)
        -NOM   -DAT   book-ACC   gave/sent/showed
        'John gave/sent/showed a book to Mary.'
   b.   John-ga   hon-o   Mary-ni   ageta/okutta/miseta. (S-DO-IO-V)
        -NOM   book-ACC   -DAT   gave/sent/showed

Given the hypothesis that scrambling is a syntactic movement operation (see Saito 1985, among others), the question is which of the above two forms represents the basic word order of the construction.

Hoji (1985) extensively argues that the S-DO-IO-V order is derived from the S-IO-DO-V order by the S-scrambling of DO from the post-IO position to the pre-IO position. His arguments in favor of this claim are based mainly on two phenomena: pronominal variable binding and scope interaction. To briefly sum up his arguments, he points out the following facts with respect to pronominal variable binding: (1) A pronominal variable contained within the accusative-marked DO at the post-IO position can be bound by the dative-marked IO (cf. (8.2a)); (2) a pronominal variable contained within IO cannot be bound by DO if the variable is located at the post-IO position (cf. (8.2b)); and (3) a pronominal variable within IO, however, can be bound by DO if the operator is located at the pre-IO position (cf. (8.2c)):

(8.2) a. SUBJ DP$_i$-DAT [$_{DP}$ ... vbl_i ...]-ACC V

b. *SUBJ [$_{DP}$ ... vbl_i ...]-DAT DP$_i$-ACC V

c. SUBJ [$_{DP}$ ... vbl_i ...]-ACC$_k$ DP$_i$-DAT t_k V

Hoji (1985) argues that these facts indicate that IO is base-generated at a higher position than DO: If the base-position of IO were as high as that of DO (i.e., the base-position of IO and that of DO mutually c-command each other), or if the base-position of IO were lower than that of DO, then (8.2b) would be acceptable.[1]

As for scope interaction, Hoji (1985) maintains that scope interaction is found in (8.3b), but not (8.3a):

(8.3) *Japanese*

a. Mary-ga dareka-ni [subete-no hon]-o ageta.
 -NON someone-DAT every-GEN book -ACC gave
 'Mary gave every book to someone.' (IO>DO, *IO<DO)

b. Mary-ga [subete-no hon]-o$_k$ dareka-ni t_k ageta.
 -NOM every-GEN book -ACC someone-DAT gave
 'Mary gave every book to someone.' (IO>DO, IO<DO)

If it is the case that the base-position of IO precedes that of DO, it is possible to infer that, because of the rigidity condition on quantifier scope (Huang 1982, Lasnik and Saito 1992), (8.3a) is unambiguous, allowing only the wide-scope reading of IO; nevertheless, (8.3b) is ambiguous. This is reminiscent of the well-known fact about scrambling: QP at the object position in a simple transitive clause in Japanese cannot take its scope over QP at the subject position, but it can if it is scrambled over QP-SUBJ to the clause-initial position (cf. Hoji 1985; Aoun and Li 1994).

In addition to these arguments of Hoji (1985), K. Fujita (1994) and Takano (1996) independently add one more argument in favor of the claim that the IO-DO order reflects the base structure of the double object construction in Japanese. Consider the examples in (8.4):

(8.4) *Japanese*

a. Mary-ga [John to Bill]-ni$_k$ [otagai-no$_k$ sensei]-o
 -NOM and -DAT each other-GEN teacher -ACC
 syookaisita.
 introduced
 '??Mary introduced each other's teachers to John and Bill.'

---

[1] The well-formedness of (8.2c) is due to the so-called connectivity effect on binding. See Barss (1986) for this effect, and Abe (1993) and Uchibori (1996) for a Minimalist approach to it.

b. *Mary-ga [otagai-no$_k$ sensei]-ni [John to Bill]-o$_k$
      -NOM   each other-GEN teacher -DAT   and   -ACC
   syookaisita.
   intoduced
   'Mary introduced John and Bill to each other's teachers.'

If the base-position of IO were as high as that of DO, or if the former position were lower than the latter, then the conjoined DP in (8.4b) (i.e., DO) could bind the reciprocal contained within IO; however, this is not the case. This shows that the base-position of IO is higher than that of DO in Japanese.[2]

Now that the IO is generated at a position higher than DO is generated, I assume that the underlying structure of a Japanese ditransitive clause is the same as the underlying structure of the double object construction that I proposed and defended in chapter 7, except for word order. It is delineated as in the following:

(8.5)   (underlying structure of a Japanese ditransitive clause)

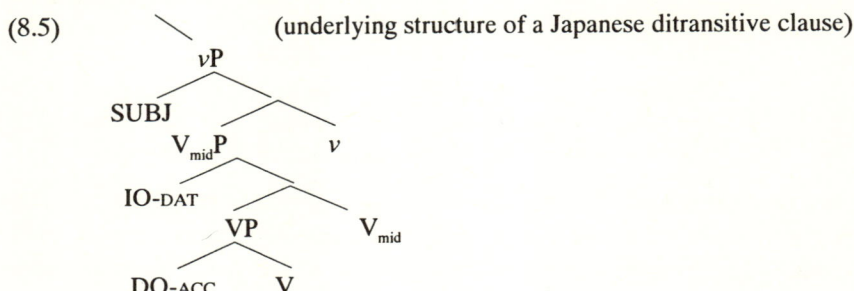

With this underlying structure of a Japanese ditransitive clause in mind, let us proceed to the investigation of optional object shift in ditransitive clauses in Japanese.

8.2. Object Shift in Ditransitive Clauses

8.2.1. Object Shift to an A-Position

In the literature on object shift/S(hort)-scrambling in Japanese (Nemoto 1993, Saito 1994, Miyagawa 1996, Takano 1996, and, especially, Tada 1993), it has been established that the shifted (S-scrambled) DO is moved to an A-position. The strongest evidence for this claim comes from the fact concerning reciprocal binding.

As observed in (8.4b), repeated below as (8.6), DO cannot bind a reciprocal contained within IO if it is located at the post-IO position (i.e., its base-position). As the well-formedness of (8.7) shows, a reciprocal within IO can be bound by DO if DO is shifted/S-scrambled to the pre-IO position:

---

[2] See Fukuhara (1993) and Takano (1996) for additional arguments for Hoji's (1985) conclusion. From the contrast shown in (8.4), K. Fujita (1994) draws the conclusion that Japanese has an (optional) object shift.

(8.6) *Japanese*

*Mary-ga [otagai-no$_k$ sensei]-ni [John to Bill]-o$_k$
-NOM   each other-GEN teacher -DAT   and   -ACC
syookaisita.
introduced
'Mary introduced John and Bill to each other's teachers.'

(8.7) *Japanese*

Mary-ga [John to Bill]-o$_k$ [otagai-no$_k$ sensei]-ni t$_k$
-NOM   and   -ACC   each other-GEN teacher -DAT
syookaisita.
introduced

As the contrast shown by the English examples in (8.8) indicates, only elements occupying an A-position can bind reciprocals.

(8.8) *English*
   a. *[John and Bill]$_k$, I told to each other$_k$ that Mary loved t$_k$.
   b. [John and Bill]$_k$ seem to each other$_k$ [to t$_k$ have proposed to her].

The well-formedness of (8.7), thus, shows that the shifted/S-scrambled DO is located at an A-position.

Skipping over other possible arguments in favor of the claim that the S-scrambled/shifted DO occupies an A-position, I conclude, following those previous studies,[3] that object shift/S-scrambling moves DO to an A-position.

8.2.2. Whither Is the Object Shifted?

Now it is concluded that the shifted/S-scrambled DO in Japanese occupies an A-position, the next question is where the position is in the clause structure. In this section I will explore this question. Now, let us take a much closer look at object shift in ditransitive clauses in Japanese.

8.2.2.1. Floating Quantifiers and Adverbials

In this section, in order to detect the movement involved in each example, I utilize a floating numeral quantifier as the marker of the base-position of the moved element. As is often claimed, it seems almost certain that a floating (numeral) quantifier in Japanese marks the position where its associate is base-generated (Miyagawa 1989; Koizumi 1993, 1995):[4] It can mark the original position of the

---

[3] Cf. Nemoto (1993), Saito (1994), Miyagawa (1996), Takano (1996), and, especially, Tada (1993).

[4] It might be possible, contrary to Sportiche (1988), that floating quantifiers in English and other European languages do not mark these positions, as Bobaljik (1995b) claims.

surface subject of a passive clause or of an unaccusative clause, as Miyagawa (1989) suggested.

(8.9) *Japanese*

a. **Gakusei-ga**$_k$ [$_{vP}$ kinoo [$_{vP}$ ano otoko-ni(yotte) [$_{VP}$ **san-nin**$_k$]]]
   students-NOM   yesterday   that man-by   three-CL
   koros-are-ta.
   kill-PASS-PAST
   Lit. '*Students$_k$ were killed three$_k$ by that man yesterday.'

b. **Doa-ga**$_k$ [$_{VP}$ yukkuri [$_{VP}$ **futa-tsu**$_k$]] ai-ta.
   door-NOM   slowly   two-CL   open-PAST
   Lit. '*Doors$_k$ slowly opened two$_k$.'

Hence, I take it for granted throughout this chapter that a floating (numeral) quantifier marks the base-position of its associate in Japanese.

The placement of adverbials in a given clause is the other important diagnosis to be used for showing the surface positions of DPs involved in the clause. In chapter 7 I made a stipulation that adverbials cannot hierarchically intervene between a head and its Spec if the head assigns its θ-role to the Spec. With this stipulation in mind, let us consider the following examples (cf. Miyagawa 1989 and N. Fujita 1993):

(8.10) *Japanese*

a. Gakusei-ga$_k$ [$_{vP}$ **kinoo** [$_{vP}$ futa-ri$_k$ [$_{VP}$ sakana-o]]] kut-ta.
   students-NOM   yesterday   two-CL   fish-ACC   eat-PAST
   'Two students ate fish yesterday.'

b. *Gakusei-ga$_k$ [$_{vP}$ **yukkuri/naifu-de** [$_{vP}$ futa-ri$_k$ [$_{VP}$ sakana-o]]]
   students-NOM   slowly/knife-with   two-CL   fish-ACC
   kut-ta.
   eat-PAST
   'Two students ate fish slowly/with a knife.'

c. Gakusei-ga$_k$ [$_{vP}$ kinoo [$_{vP}$ futa-ri$_k$ [$_{VP}$ **yukkuri/naifu-de** [$_{VP}$ sakana-o
   students-NOM   yesterday   two-CL   slowly/knife-with   fish-ACC
   ]]] kut-ta.
           eat-PAST
   'Yesterday two students ate fish slowly/with a knife.'

Given that a floating quantifier marks the base-position of its associate, the well-formedness of (8.10a) indicates both that time-adverbials like *kinoo* 'yesterday' are adjoined to the outer projection of the VP-shell,[5] and that SUBJ overtly moves up to a Spec of T in Japanese.[6] The ill-formedness of (8.10b) and the well-formedness of (8.10c), on the other hand, indicate that manner adverbs like

---

[5] See Miyagawa (1989) and N. Fujita (1993) for the same point.

[6] Watanabe (1993) reached the same conclusion, though he claims that the target of SUBJ's movement is the Spec of AgrS under the Agr-based Case theory, which is virtually equivalent to the Spec of T under the Agr-less checking theory.

yukkuri 'slowly' and instrumental ones like *naifu-de* 'knife-with' are adjoined only to the inner projection of the VP-shell, as N. Fujita (1993) suggests. These facts can be delineated as in the following:

(8.11) (transitive clauses)

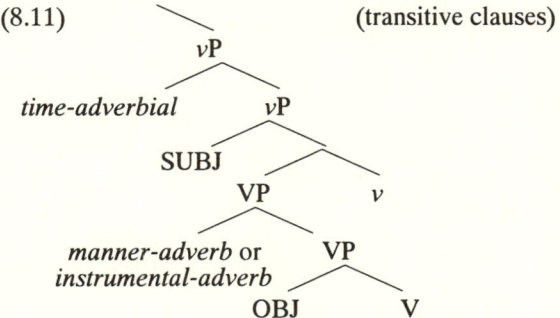

As for the adverbial placement in ditransitive clauses, the fact that time-adverbials like *kinoo* 'yesterday' come at a position higher than the base-position of SUBJ (cf. (8.12a) below) indicates that they are attached to the highest projection of the three-layered VP-shell for a ditransitive predicate. Manner-adverbs such as *kossori* 'secretly', on the other hand, cannot appear before the base-position of SUBJ, as the ill-formedness of (8.12b) shows.

(8.12) *Japanese*

a. Gakusei-ga$_k$ [$_{vP}$ **kinoo** [$_{vP}$ san-nin$_k$ [$_{VmidP}$ Mary-ni [$_{VP}$ hon-o]]]]
students-NOM yesterday three-CL -DAT book-ACC
age-ta.
give-PAST
'Three students gave a book to Mary yesterday.'

b. *Gakusei-ga$_k$ [$_{vP}$ **kossori** [$_{vP}$ san-nin$_k$ [$_{VmidP}$ Mary-ni [$_{VP}$ hon-o]]]]
students-NOM secretly three-CL -DAT book-ACC
age-ta.
give-PAST
'Three students secretly gave a book to Mary.'

c. Gakusei-ga$_k$ [$_{vP}$ kinoo [$_{vP}$ san-nin$_k$ [$_{VmidP}$ **kossori** [$_{VmidP}$ Mary-ni [$_{VP}$
students-NOM yesterday three-CL secretly -DAT
hon-o]]]] age-ta.
book-ACC give-PAST
'Three students secretly gave a book to Mary yesterday.'

d. Gakusei-ga$_k$ [$_{vP}$ kinoo [$_{vP}$ san-nin$_k$ [$_{VmidP}$ Mary-ni [$_{VP}$ **kossori** [$_{VP}$
students-NOM yesterday three-CL -DAT secretly
hon-o]]]] age-ta.
book-ACC give-PAST
'same meaning as (8.12c)'

The well-formedness of (8.12c,d) shows that manner-adverbs can be adjoined either to the intermediate projection or to the lowest projection of the three-layered

VP-shell for a ditransitive predicate. These facts can be delineated as in the following:

(8.13) (ditransitive clauses)

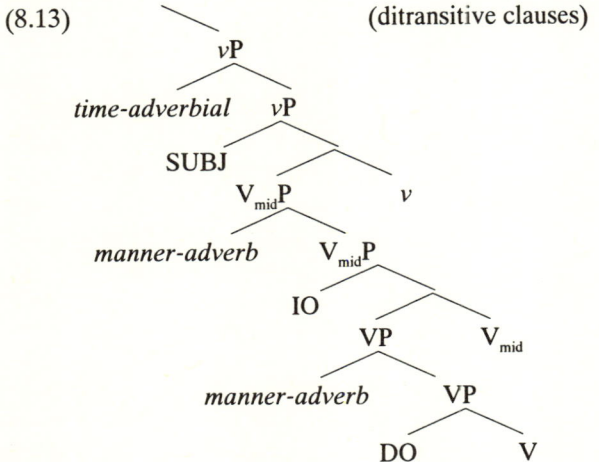

Keeping in mind this underlying structure of a ditransitive clause, let us proceed to discussion on object shift in ditransitive clauses in Japanese.

8.2.2.2. Object Shift of IO?

Before probing into object shift of DO in ditransitive clauses in Japanese, it is necessary to examine the movability of IO before Spell-out, because the position of IO plays the role of pivot in the surface order.

1. **IO may not move over the base-position of SUBJ.**

As the ill-formedness of the following example shows, IO may not move up beyond the base-position of SUBJ before Spell-out.

(8.14) *Japanese*

  *Gakusei-ga$_j$ Mari-ni$_k$ [$_{vP}$ san-nin$_j$ [$_{VmidP}$ t$_k$ hon-o]] ageta.
   -NOM -DAT three-CL   book-ACC gave
  'Three students gave a book to Mary.'

2. **IO may not move up even out of V$_{mid}$P.**

Now consider the example in (8.15):

(8.15) *Japanese*

  *Gakusei-ga$_j$ [$_{vP}$ kinoo [$_{vP}$ san-nin$_j$ hana-ni$_k$ [$_{VmidP}$ kossori [$_{VmidP}$
   -NOM yesterday three-CL flowers-DAT secretly
  jup-pon$_k$ [$_{VP}$ mizu-o]]]] ageta.
  ten-CL water-ACC gave
  'Three students gave water to ten flowers yesterday.'

(cf. (?)Gakusei-ga$_j$ [$_{\nu P}$ kinoo [$_{\nu P}$ san-nin$_j$ [$_{VmidP}$ kossori [$_{VmidP}$ hana-ni
-NOM   yesterday three-CL   secretly   flowers-DAT
jup-pon [$_{VP}$ mizu-o]]]]] ageta.
ten-CL   water-ACC   gave   )

In (8.15), the position of the manner-adverb and that of the floated quantifier associated with IO prove that IO is moved out of the $V_{mid}P$; consequently, the ill-formedness of (8.15) shows that IO cannot move even out of $V_{mid}P$ before Spell-out. From the facts (1) and (2), I therefore conclude that IO may not undergo object shift/S-scrambling (before Spell-out).

8.2.2.3. Object Shift of DO

Now let us take a much closer look at DO's object shift in ditransitive clauses in Japanese.

1.   DO may move over IO.

As was observed in the previous section, DO may move over IO in an active ditransitive clause in Japanese:

(8.16) *Japanese* (Koizumi 1993: 137)
  a. John-ga [$_{VmidP}$ Mary-ni [$_{VP}$ hon-o]] ageta.
     -NOM   -DAT   book-ACC gave
     'John gave a book to Mary.'
  b. John-ga hon-o$_k$ [$_{VmidP}$ Mary-ni [$_{VP}$ t$_k$]] ageta.
     -NOM   book-ACC   -DAT   gave

(8.17) *Japanese*
  John-ga   hon-o$_k$ [$_{VmidP}$ Mary-ni [$_{VP}$ san-satsu$_k$]] ageta.
  -NOM   book-ACC   -DAT   three-CL   gave
  'John gave three books to Mary.'

The well-formedness of (8.17) more clearly shows that DO may move up beyond IO before Spell-out.

2.   DO may not move over the base-position of SUBJ.

Watanabe (1993), observing that the object in a simple transitive clause may not move up beyond the base-position of SUBJ before Spell-out, arrived at the conclusion that the object in a transitive clause does not move before Spell-out in Japanese. DO in a ditransitive clause, too, cannot move up overtly beyond the base-position of SUBJ, which is marked by a floated quantifier associated with SUBJ.

(8.18) *Japanese* (Koizumi 1993: 138)

*Gakusei-ga$_j$ hon-o$_k$ [$_{vP}$ san-nin$_j$ Mary-ni t$_k$] ageta.
   -NOM   book-ACC   three-CL   -DAT   gave
'Three students gave a book to Mary.'

The facts (1) and (2) lead to the conclusion that DO in a ditransitive clause may move up beyond IO, but not beyond the base-position of SUBJ. Now that IO always stays at the innermost Spec of V_{mid} before Spell-out, it follows from the above conclusion, that DO may move to an outer Spec of V_{mid}, but not to an outer Spec of v, if DO's movement targets a Spec.

3. DO may move up to a position in between the base-position of SUBJ and IO.

Now it is expected that DO may come in between IO and the base-position of SUBJ. Indeed, this is the case, as shown by the well-formedness of (8.19):

(8.19) *Japanese*

  a. Gakusei-ga$_j$ kinoo [$_{vP}$ san-nin$_j$ hon-o$_k$ [$_{VmidP}$ Mari-ni [$_{VP}$ t$_k$
      -NOM yesterday three-CL book-ACC   -DAT
]]] ageta.
       gave
'Three students gave a book to Mary yesterday.'

  b. Gakusei-ga$_j$ kinoo [$_{vP}$ san-nin$_j$ hon-o$_k$ [$_{VmidP}$ Mari-ni [$_{VP}$
      -NOM yesterday three-CL book-ACC   -DAT
go-satsu$_k$]]] ageta.
five-CL   gave
'Three students gave five books to Mary yesterday.'

4. DO may stay in situ.

As is emphasized by Tada (1993) as the most peculiar property of S(hort)-scrambling/object shift in Japanese, DO in a ditransitive clause is allowed not to undergo S-scrambling/object shift, despite the fact that S-scrambling/object shift is a kind of A-movement.

(8.20) *Japanese*

John-ga Mary-ni [$_{VP}$ kossori [$_{VP}$ hon-o$_k$ (san-satsu$_k$)]] ageta.
 -NOM   -DAT   secretly   book-ACC three-CL   gave
'John secretly gave three books to Mary.'

This optionality seems very peculiar because it is commonly assumed that an element to be A-moved is required to be A-moved before Spell-out if the feature relevant to that movement is strong; otherwise, the element is required to stay in situ owing to Procrastinate.

    To recapitulate the properties of the object shifts of IO and DO in ditransitive clauses in Japanese, the following were observed:

IO: IO may not undergo object shift. (It always stays at a Spec of V_{mid} before Spell-out.)

DO: (i) DO may move overtly to a position in between the innermost Spec of V_{mid} and the innermost Spec of v, or

(ii) DO may stay in situ before Spell-out.

➡ *DO optionally undergoes object shift in a ditransitive clause.*

Now the question is what kind of position DO is moved to by object shift, besides the question as to where the optionality of object shift in Japanese comes from. In what follows in this section, I will explore these questions.

8.2.2.4. Feature-Checking of Double Objects

In chapter 7 I argued that it holds universally true that the formal features of DO and those of IO in an active ditransitive clause, if both DO and IO have a structural Case to be checked off before Spell-out, are checked off at a Spec of V_{mid} and at a Spec of v, respectively, as illustrated in (8.21):

(8.21) vP (order irrelevant)

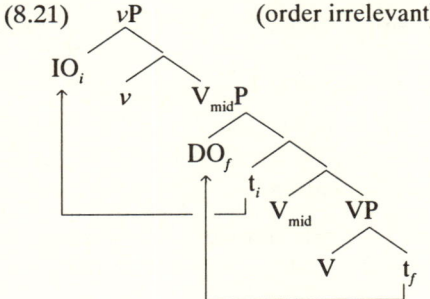

In Japanese ditransitive clauses, DO stands in accusative, which invariantly marks OBJ in transitive clauses, but IO stands in dative. Even though the accusative Case of DO naturally counts as a structural Case, it is not straightforwardly clear whether the dative Case of IO counts as a structural or inherent Case.

If it turns out that the Case of IO in Japanese is structural, it becomes possible to extend the structure in (8.21) to Japanese ditransitive clauses. Let us, then, examine the nature of the dative Case of IO in Japanese.

8.2.2.5. Checking of IO

In their broad study on dative Case in Japanese, Sadakane and Koizumi (1995) provide two pieces of subsidiary evidence that the dative Case of IO in Japanese is a structural Case. First, they claim that IO can launch numeral quantifier floating, as in (8.22a):

(8.22) *Japanese*

    a. John-ga   tomodati-ni$_k$ san-nin$_k$ tegami-o okut-ta.
         -NOM   friends-DAT three-CL letters-ACC sent
        'John sent letters to three of his friends.'

    b. *John-ga   tomodati-kara$_k$ san-nin$_k$ tegami-o   morat-ta.
         -NOM   friends-from   three-CL letters-ACC received
        'John received letters from three of his friends.'

In general, DP with an inherent Case cannot launch numeral quantifier floating in Japanese, as the ill-formedness of (8.22b) shows. But, as observed in the previous subsections, DP with a structural Case can.

Second, Sadakane and Koizumi (1995) claim that the dative Case-particle *-ni* of IO must disappear if IO appears in the focus position of cleft sentences, as shown by (8.23a):

(8.23) *Japanese*

    a. [[John-ga t$_k$ tegami-o okut-ta]-no   ]-wa Mary(*-ni) da.
            -NOM   letter-ACC sent   -NOMINL -TOP   -DAT   is
        'It is to Mary that John sent a letter.'

    b. [[John-ga t$_k$ tegami-o morat-ta]-no   ]-wa Mary*(-kara) da.
            -NOM   letter-ACC received -NOMINL -TOP   -from is
        'It is from Mary that John received a letter.'

    c. [[John-ga t$_k$ Mary-kara morat-ta]-no   ]-wa tegami(*-o) da.
            -NOM   -from received -NOMINL -TOP letter -ACC is
        'It is a letter that John received from Mary.'

Structural Case-particles must, but inherent Case-particles must not, disappear in the same environment, as the ill-formedness of (8.23b) and the well-formedness of (8.23c), respectively, show.

From these data, in which IO behaves the same as SUBJ or OBJ, I infer that IO's dative Case is of the same types as the Cases of SUBJ and OBJ in Japanese. That is, I conclude from the above data that the dative Case of IO is a structural Case in Japanese. From the conclusion that IO *always* stays in situ (i.e., the innermost Spec of V_{mid}), it thus follows that the structural dative Case-feature of IO moves at LF for checking. This, in turn, means that the dative Case-feature of *v* in a Japanese ditransitive clause is weak and does not tolerate any unforced violation of Procrastinate.

Now that IO in a ditransitive clause in Japanese, though being marked as dative, has a structural Case, it is natural to assume that the underlying structure of the double object construction shown in (8.21), repeated as (8.24) with a modification to accommodate the word order of Japanese, is also applicable to Japanese ditransitive clauses.

(8.24)

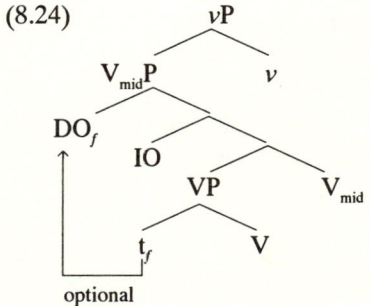

8.2.2.6. Checking of DO

In §8.2.2.3 I reached the conclusion that DO may move up overtly to a position in between the base-position of IO (i.e., the innermost Spec of V_{mid}) and the base-position of SUBJ (i.e., the innermost Spec of v). Elsewhere in this chapter I implied that the (ultimate) landing site of the S-scrambled/shifted DO in an active ditransitive clause is a Spec of V_{mid}, where the formal features of DO are properly checked off (cf. (8.24)).

This idea sounds very natural because it offers a simple account of the fact that the S-scrambled/shifted DO has exclusively A-type properties, as observed in §8.2.1: An element is in an A-position if it has a feature-checking relation with an L-head (Ura 1993b, 1994e). In fact, Nemoto (1993) proposes, under the Agr-based Case theory, that the S-scrambled/shifted DO is located at the Spec of AgrO.

As pointed out in Tada (1993), the problem involved in this view lies in its difficulty to give a consistent explanation of the optionality of S-scrambling/object shift. As mentioned before, one might be tempted to surmise that every Case- (or feature-)driven movement before Spell-out is obligatory. If this were correct, then it would be almost impossible to maintain that what is called object shift in Japanese (which is called S-scrambling by Tada 1993) is an object shift in its ordinary sense; object shift is commonly considered to be an A-movement targeting the position where the formal features of the element to be shifted are properly checked off.[7]

On the other hand, Tada (1993) and some subsequent work, including that of Saito (1994), Takano (1996), and Fukui and Saito (to appear), propose that DO is permuted by S-scrambling to a position adjoined to some maximal projection of V. By dissociating S-scrambling/object shift in Japanese from a Case- (or feature-)driven movement and by assimilating it with heavy NP-shift in English

---

[7] In chapter 7, however, I claimed that the object shift of DO in Swedish and Norwegian is optional, and I further argued that its optionality is totally derivable under the view that it is a feature-driven movement. Later in this section, I will make the same proposal for Japanese object shift/S-scrambling.

or long-distance scrambling in Japanese, they try to ensure that S-scrambling/ object shift is totally optional in Japanese.

However, I will maintain, pace these authors, that S-scrambling/object shift in Japanese is a feature-driven movement.[8] It will be demonstrated in the next section that, admitting that it is a feature-driven movement, its optionality in Japanese can be offered a consistent explanation.

8.2.3. Optionality of Object Shift and Violability of Procrastinate

8.2.3.1. Fukui (1993) on Optionality of Movement/Scrambling

Since Saito (1985) argued at length that scrambling in Japanese is a syntactic movement, its optionality has been a big problem in the literature on the topic. Fukui (1993) hypothesizes that any movement operation is costless and, hence, freely applicable as an optional movement in a language L if (1) the movement is to be directed in the opposite direction from the head-parameter of L, and (2) no deriving force such as Case Filter or Spec-head agreement is involved with the movement (i.e., the movement is not motivated by any "Last Resort" kind of force). In Japanese, the head-parameter is fixed as head-final. Therefore, according to Fukui's (1993) hypothesis, we can conclude that S-scrambling/object shift in Japanese is freely applicable without any cost, resulting in its optionality in Japanese, if S-scrambling/object shift in Japanese is not derived by any Case- (or feature-checking) theoretic reason.

Fukui's (1993) hypothesis, though attractive thanks to both its simplicity and its ample consequences (cf. Fukui and Saito to appear), is hard to extend to S-scrambling/object shift in Japanese.[9] For it seems probable that it bears some empirical inadequacy in light of Sarma's (1994) extensive investigation on Tamil scrambling. According to Sarma, in Tamil in which scrambling is allowed to take place either rightward or leftward (cf., also, Herring 1994), scrambling can be undone at LF in the sense of Saito (1992) regardless of whether it is a rightward scrambling or a leftward one. For Fukui (1993), LF undoing is a property of an optional movement. Hence, Tamil scrambling seriously challenges Fukui's hypothesis, irrespective of the head-parameter of Tamil (though it is almost certain that Tamil is a head-final language like Japanese (cf. Lehmann 1993)).

A more directly relevant case comes from the fact concerning the optional object shift of full NPs in Icelandic ditransitive clauses. According to Collins

---

[8] Miyagawa (1997) reached the same conclusion from a viewpoint different from mine, though he makes little mention of optionality.

[9] I have no commitment to the issue as to whether Fukui's hypothesis is applicable to M- and L-scrambling. See Miyagawa (1997) and Fukui and Saito (to appear) for discussion. For M-scrambling and L-scrambling and their A/A-bar properties in Japanese, see Saito (1992), Tada (1993), Abe (1993), Miyagawa (1997), and Takano (1994, 1996), among many others. Cf., also, Mahajan (1990) and Jones (1993) for Hindi, Sarma (1994) for Tamil, and Y.-S. Lee (1993) and R. Lee (1995) for Korean.

and Thráinsson (1993, 1996), DO in a ditransitive clause in Icelandic, if it is a full NP, may undergo optional overt object shift, as shown in (8.25):

(8.25) *Icelandic* (Collins and Thráinsson 1993: 34)

a. Hann   gaf konunginum   ambáttina.
    he(NOM) gave the-king(DAT) the-maidservant(ACC)
    'He gave the king the maidservant.'

b. Hann   gaf ambáttina$_k$ konunginum t$_k$.
    he(NOM) gave the-maidservant(ACC) the-king(DAT)

DO's overt object shift in Icelandic, hence, shows striking similarities to the Japanese one in terms of its optionality as well as the position of the shifted IO.[10] Despite these similarities, we cannot apply Fukui's (1993) hypothesis to the Icelandic case, because Icelandic is clearly head-initial (cf. Rohrbacher 1994). Thus, in addition to admitting Fukui's (1993) hypothesis about optionality, it is necessary to postulate another hypothesis in order to explain the optionality of DO's overt object shift in Icelandic. To put it differently, the Icelandic optional overt object shift of DO provides a case where an optional movement does exist even if the movement is induced for a Case- (or feature-checking) theoretic reason.

The most serious problem for the application of Fukui's (1993) hypothesis about optionality of S-scrambling/object shift in Japanese is the fact that it fails to account for the lack of S-scrambling/object shift in transitive clauses in Japanese. In §8.4 I will show that S-scrambling/object shift does not exist in simple transitive clauses in Japanese (cf., also, Watanabe 1993). According to Fukui's hypothesis, however, there is no reason to prohibit S-scrambling/object shift in a transitive clause in Japanese: Applying Fukui's hypothesis to S-scrambling/object shift in Japanese leads to the prediction that S-scrambling/object shift is allowed to take place no matter in what type of clauses; for, according to Fukui's hypothesis, S-scrambling/object shift is totally costless in Japanese. Thus, as long as the claim is correct that S-scrambling/object shift is impossible in transitive clauses in Japanese, it is impossible to apply Fukui's (1993) hypothesis to S-scrambling/object shift in Japanese.

8.2.3.2. Optionality and Modification of the Last Resort Condition

As for the optionality of Japanese scrambling and, in particular, S-scrambling, Tada (1993), Saito (1994), and Takano (1996) independently try to offer an explanation of it. They have one thing in common: They try to derive the optionality at issue by modifying the Last Resort Condition (of the definition of Attract/Move).

Let us cast a quick glance over their proposals. Tada (1993) proposes a dynamic definition of the Last Resort Condition (Tada 1993: 52):

---

[10] See Collins and Thráinsson (1993, 1996) and Holmberg and Platzak (1995) for more discussion on object shift in Icelandic ditransitive clauses.

The Last Resort Condition allows movement of α without checking motivation only if for any β, checking of β never takes place because of the movement.

According to this definition of the Last Resort Condition, scrambling in general counts as an optional movement if there is no checking involved in scrambling. For Saito (1994), on the other hand, S-scrambling/object shift is an adjunction operation (cf. Fukui and Saito to appear). It leads him to conclude that S-scrambling/object shift may freely apply without being subject to the Last Resort Condition, since only those operations that create a new category (i.e., substitution) are subject to the Last Resort Condition under his theory of phrase structure. Lastly, Takano (1996) maintains, basically following Fukui's (1986) idea, that movement of α is cost-free if α moves within the same minimal domain and the movement is exempted from the Last Resort Condition and the Shortest Move Condition (of the definition of Attract/Move). By assuming that S-scrambling/object shift takes place within a minimal domain and that it is irrelevant to feature checking, Takano (1996) derives the optionality of S-scrambling/object shift in Japanese.

Here it is noteworthy that, in order to derive the optionality of S-scrambling/object shift in Japanese, they all propose both that S-scrambling/object shift in Japanese is not Case- (or feature-)driven and that some modification of the Last Resort condition (of the definition of Attract/Move) proposed by Chomsky (1995a) should be necessary.

8.2.3.3. Proposal: Violability of Procrastinate

My proposal about object shift (S-scrambling) in Japanese ditransitive clauses is very simple; nothing special is involved with it. More specifically, I propose that object shift in Japanese has nothing different from optional object shift of full NPs in Icelandic, or optional object shift of a full-NP IO in Norwegian and Swedish (see chapter 7). Therefore, it is induced by feature checking and, hence, its landing site is a Spec of an L-head. In this sense I am proposing that scrambling is not a special phenomenon that requires some special device or explanation for it; rather, it is a subcase of (optional) object shift, which is abound in natural languages. Moreover, it is totally unnecessary for me to modify the Last Resort Condition of the definition of Attract/Move, keeping Chomsky's (1995a) definition intact.

Furthermore, the optionality of object shift/S-scrambling in Japanese can be satisfactorily explained in spite of the fact that object shift/S-scrambling is induced by feature checking. In chapter 7 it was attested that the optionality of IO's object shift in Swedish and Norwegian, which is motivated by feature checking, is fully derivable by assuming that the feature of the head relevant to IO's feature checking is weak, but the head tolerates an unforced violation of Procrastinate. Exploiting the idea about the violability of Procrastinate in the case of Japanese object shift makes it possible to explain why the overt object shift of DO in a Japanese ditransitive clause is optional despite its feature-driven motivation: In Japanese, the feature of the head relevant to DO's feature checking is weak, but the head tolerates a violation of Procrastinate; thereby, the overt movement of DO to its checking position is not required, but is allowed to take place.

To summarize, I propose (1) that DO's object shift (S-scrambling) in a Japanese ditransitive clause is induced by feature checking and, hence, its landing site is a Spec of an L-head; and (2) that the feature of the head relevant to DO's feature checking is weak, but the head tolerates a violation of Procrastinate in Japanese. (1) explains why object shift (S-scrambling) shows A-movement properties, and (2) explains where the optionality of object shift comes from. Thereby the miseries involved in Japanese S-scrambling noted by Tada (1993) are naturally resolved.

To make the story more concrete, let us return to (8.24), repeated here as (8.26), in which the underlying structure of a Japanese ditransitive clause is delineated:

(8.26)

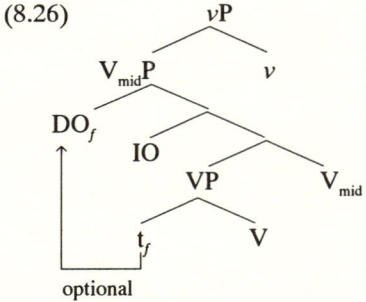

In §8.2.2.5, I concluded that IO stays at the innermost Spec of V_{mid} before Spell-out. This is due to the fact that the nominal feature of v in Japanese ditransitive clauses is weak and v does not tolerate any unforced violation of Procrastinate. Moreover, I have just proposed that the movement of DO in (8.26) may take place before Spell-out owing to the fact that the nominal feature of V_{mid} is weak, but V_{mid} tolerates an unforced violation of Procrastinate in Japanese ditransitive clauses.

In the next section it will be shown that a seemingly unrelated phenomenon can be accounted for by the claim that V_{mid} in the underlying structure of a ditransitive predicate in Japanese tolerates a violation of Procrastinate.

8.2.4. Passivizability of DO and Violability of Procrastinate

In chapter 7 I demonstrated that in a ditransitive clause, DO cannot be promoted to the Spec of IP beyond IO by passivization, unless it first enters the minimal domain in which IO is located. This is because IO would otherwise be closer to the surface subject position (i.e., the Spec of IP) than DO would be; therefore,

IO, but not DO, would be attracted to the subject position by passivization. (See chapter 7 for detailed discussion.)

Now that, thanks to the assumption that V_{mid} tolerates an unforced violation of Procrastinate, DO in a Japanese ditransitive clause may move up to a Spec of V_{mid}, where DO is in the same minimal domain as IO is, it is predicted that DO in Japanese, like DO in Norwegian or Icelandic, may be passivized. This prediction is borne out by the well-formedness of the following example:

(8.27) *Japanese*

[Ano kitanai mizu]-ga$_k$ Mary-niyotte Hana-ni t$_k$ yar-are-ta.
that dirty water -NOM -by flowers-DAT give-PASS-PAST
'That dirty water$_k$ was given to the flowers by Mary.'

In (8.27) the promoted DO is a non-human/non-animate DP, and, hence, it is certain that the passivization in (8.27) is a syntactic passive that involves syntactic movement of OBJ to the Spec of T (cf. Kitagawa and Kuroda 1992, Kubo 1992, and Hoshi 1994).

This fact lends support to my analysis of object shift in Japanese ditransitive clauses, and it also points to the consistency of my analysis of object shift in general.

8.3. Object Shift out of Desiderative Complements

Thus far I have claimed that the optional overt object shift of DO in Japanese is due to the fact that the head relevant to DO's feature checking tolerates an unforced violation of Procrastinate. And I further argued that this claim is supported by the correlation of the passivizability of DO and the optionality of DO's optional overt shift. In this section I will demonstrate that this correlation of passivizability and violability of Procrastinate can also be found in another place in Japanese syntax.

8.3.1. Desiderative Complement in Japanese

The Japanese desiderative form is made by attaching the suffix *-tagar* to the verb (Kageyama 1982, 1993; Sugioka 1985; Nishigauchi 1993):[11]

---

[11] The suffix *-tagar* can be divided into *-ta(i)* and *-gar*, the former of which expresses the meaning of desiderative, and changes the verb into an adjective when attached to a verb. The suffix *-gar* is a verbalizer of an adjective (Kuroda 1965). See Kageyama (1993), Nishigauchi (1993), and, especially, Sugioka (1985) for discussion on this topic and related matters. And see Kubo (1992) for the syntactic nature of *-ta(i)*.

(8.28) *Japanese*

    a. John-ga   sakana-o tabe-ta.
          -NOM   fish-ACC   eat-PAST
        'John eats fish.'

    b. [$_{TP}$ John-ga$_i$ [$_{VP}$ [$_{AP}$ PRO$_i$ [$_{vP}$ PRO$_i$ [$_{VP}$ sakana-o tabe]]-**ta**]-**gar**
         -NOM   fish-ACC eat   -DES -VERBL
       ]-ta].
       -PAST
       'John wanted to eat fish.'

Nishigauchi (1993) argues that two PROs are involved in a desiderative complement of *-tagar*. The lower PRO and the higher one in (8.28b) are assigned their θ-role by the embedded verb *tabe* 'eat' and the desiderative morpheme *-ta(i)*, respectively.

Of particular concern here is the fact that overt object shift out of a desiderative complement is blocked. This fact stands in contrast to the fact that overt object shift out of a control complement, which syntactically resembles a desiderative complement, is possible. The sentence in (8.29) exemplifies a Japanese control complement construction:[12]

(8.29) *Japanese*

    John-ga$_i$ [$_{VP}$ [$_{vP}$ PRO$_i$ [$_{VP}$ sakana-o tabe]]-**oe**]-ta.
    -NOM   fish-ACC eat   -**finish** -PRES
    'John finished eating fish.'

See Nishigauchi (1993) and Kageyama (1993) for extensive discussion on the control complement embedded by the morpheme *-oer* 'finish'.

Given that even PRO can launch floating quantifier (Kitagawa and Kuroda 1992), the ill-formedness of (8.30b) indicates that OBJ generated in a desiderative complement clause cannot move up beyond the lower PRO in the desiderative complement, which occupies the (innermost) Spec of *v* in the two-layered VP-shell of the embedded predicate:

(8.30) *Japanese*

    a. Gakusei-ga$_i$ [$_{VP}$ [$_{AP}$ PRO$_i$ [$_{vP}$ kinoo [$_{vP}$ PRO$_i$ san-nin$_i$ [$_{VP}$ sakana-o
        -NOM   yesterday   three-CL   fish-ACC
       tabe]]]-**ta**]-**gar**]-ta.
       eat   -DES -VERBL -PAST
       'Three students wanted to eat fish yesterday.'

---

[12] For the syntactic behaviors of Japanese control complements in general, see Sakaguchi (1990), Nemoto (1993), and Watanabe (1995b).

b. *Gakusei-ga$_i$ [$_{VP}$ [$_{AP}$ PRO$_i$ [$_{vP}$ sakana-o$_k$ [$_{vP}$ PRO$_i$ san-nin$_i$ [$_{VP}$ t$_k$ tabe
      -NOM   fish-ACC   three-CL   eat
]]]-**ta**]-**gar**]-ta.
     -DES -VERBL -PAST
'Three students wanted to eat fish.'

In contrast, OBJ generated in a control complement clause can move up beyond PRO in the control complement clause, as the well-formedness of (8.31b) shows:

(8.31) *Japanese*

    a. Gakusei-ga$_i$ [$_{VP}$ [$_{vP}$ sono toki [$_{vP}$ PRO$_i$ san-nin$_i$ [$_{VP}$ sakana-o tabe
            -NOM   that time   three-CL   fish-ACC eat
]]]-**oe**]-ta.
     -**finish** -PAST
'Three students finished eating fish at that time.'

    b. Gakusei-ga$_i$ [$_{VP}$ [$_{vP}$ sakana-o$_k$ [$_{vP}$ PRO$_i$ san-nin$_i$ [$_{VP}$ t$_k$ tabe]]]-**oe**
            -NOM   fish-ACC   three-CL   eat   -**finish**
]-ta.
 -PAST
'Three students finished eating fish.'

Moreover, OBJ generated in a desiderative complement clause cannot move up even beyond an instrumental-adverb, which is supposed to be attached to the lower projection of the two-layered VP-shell as argued in §8.2.2.1.

(8.32) *Japanese*

    a. John-ga$_i$ [$_{VP}$ [$_{AP}$ PRO$_i$ [$_{vP}$ PRO$_i$ [$_{VP}$ naifu-de [$_{VP}$ sakana-o$_k$ san-biki$_k$
           -NOM   knife-with   fish-ACC   three-CL
tabe]]]-ta]-gar]-ta.
eat   -DES -VERBL -PAST
'John wanted to eat three fish with a knife.'

    b. *?John-ga$_i$ [$_{VP}$ [$_{AP}$ PRO$_i$ [$_{vP}$ sakana-o$_k$ [$_{vP}$ PRO$_i$ [$_{VP}$ naifu-de [$_{VP}$ t$_k$
           -NOM   fish-ACC   knife-with
san-biki$_k$ tabe]]]]-ta]-gar]-ta.
three-CL eat   -DES -VERBL -PAST

In contrast, OBJ generated in a control complement clause can move up beyond a manner-adverb:

(8.33) *Japanese*

    a. John-ga$_i$ [$_{VP}$ [$_{vP}$ PRO$_i$ naifu-de [$_{VP}$ sakana-o$_k$ san-biki$_k$ tabe]]-**oe**
           -NOM   knife-with   fish-ACC   three-CL   eat   -**finish**
]-ta.
 -PAST
'John finished eating three fish with a knife.'

b. John-ga$_i$ [$_{VP}$ [$_{vP}$ sakana-o$_k$ [$_{vP}$ PRO$_i$ naifu-de [$_{VP}$ t$_k$ san-biki$_k$ tabe
    -NOM   fish-ACC   knife-with   three-CL eat
]]]-oe]-ta.
-finish -PAST

To conclude, these facts indicate that, whereas OBJ in a control complement clause can be moved up overtly by S-scrambling as Nemoto (1993) pointed out, OBJ in a desiderative complement clause cannot be moved up overtly out of the clause by S-scrambling. Under the hypothesis presented in §8.2 it is natural to interpret these facts to show that OBJ generated in a control complement clause, but not OBJ generated in a desiderative complement clause, may undergo object shift. Incidentally, this object shift, too, is optional, as is shown by the linear ordering of the manner-adverb and the object in a control complement clause in (8.33a).

8.3.2. Violability of Procrastinate

Now I propose that the contrast between Japanese control clauses and desiderative ones in terms of the possibility of optional object shift should be accounted for by assuming that, whereas v in the VP-shell of the predicate embedded by a control morpheme tolerates an unforced violation of Procrastinate, v in the VP-shell of the predicate embedded by a desiderative morpheme does not tolerate any violation of Procrastinate.

Given this, it is possible to explain the optionality of the shift (S-scrambling) of OBJ in a control complement clause in just the same way as in the case of DO's object shift in Japanese ditransitive clauses. Also it is possible to preclude overt object shift of OBJ in a desiderative complement clause, as required: It violates Procrastinate, resulting in ill-formedness.

(8.34)

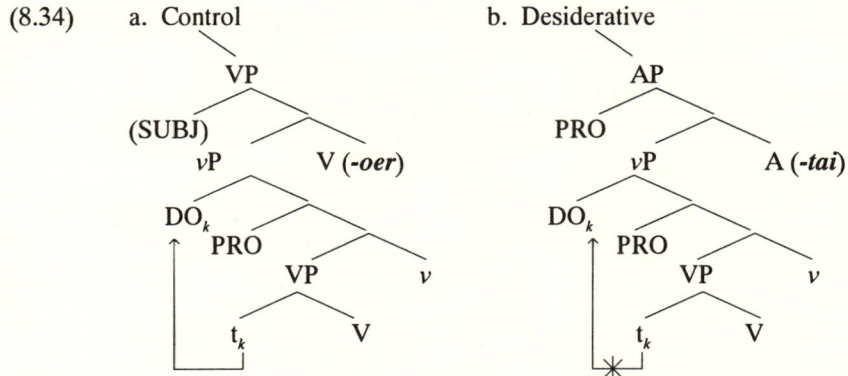

Here one should recall the correlation of passivizability and violability of Procrastinate, which was noted in chapter 7. Then, the prediction is that, while the object in a control complement can undergo passivization, the object in a desiderative complement cannot. Sugioka (1985) and Nishigauchi (1993) report that this prediction is, indeed, borne out:

(8.35) *Japanese*

    a. Control

        Sakana-ga$_k$ [$_{VP}$ John$_i$-niyotte [$_{vP}$ PRO$_i$ [$_{VP}$ naifu-de [$_{VP}$ t$_k$ san-biki$_k$
        fish-NOM   -by   knife-with   three-CL
        tabe]]]-oe]-rare-ta.
        eat   -finish -PASS-PAST
        Lit. '*Three fish$_k$ were tried to eat t$_k$ with a knife by John.'

    b. Desiderative

        *Sakana-ga$_k$ [$_{VP}$ John$_i$-niyotte [$_{AP}$ PRO$_i$ [$_{vP}$ PRO$_i$ [$_{VP}$ naifu-de [$_{VP}$ t$_k$
        fish-NOM   -by   knife-with
        san-biki$_k$ tabe]]]-ta]-gar]-are-ta.
        three-CL eat   -DES -VERBL -PASS-PAST
        Lit. '*Three fish were wanted to eat t$_k$ with a knife by John.'

These facts concerning the contrast between control complements and desiderative complements in Japanese in terms of the passivizability of their object lend further support in favor of my analysis of (optional) object shift in Japanese.

8.4. Object Shift in Transitive Clauses

8.4.1. Impossibility of Object Shift in Transitive Clauses

In §8.2 I showed that DO in a Japanese ditransitive clause optionally undergoes object shift. In this section I will try to demonstrate that OBJ in a Japanese simple transitive clause never undergoes object shift.

Watanabe (1993), following Ueda's (1990) observation that time adverbs or locative adverbs can intervene between SUBJ and a floating quantifier associated with it, concludes that SUBJ overtly moves from its base-position (i.e., the Spec of *v*P) to its checking position (i.e., the Spec of IP).

(8.36) *Japanese*

    a. [$_{IP}$ Gakusei-ga$_k$ [$_{vP}$ kinoo [$_{vP}$ t$_k$ san-nin [$_{VP}$ hon-o]]] kat-ta].
           students-NOM   yesterday   three-CL   book-ACC buy-PAST
        'Three students bought a book yesterday.'

    b. [$_{IP}$ Inu-ga$_k$ [$_{vP}$ soko-de [$_{vP}$ t$_k$ san-biki]] hoe-teir-ta].
           dog-NOM   there-at   three-CL   bark-PROG-PAST
        'Three dogs were barking there.'

On the other hand, Kuroda (1983) and Miyagawa (1989) observe that OBJ cannot be permuted to a position in between the surface position of SUBJ and its base-position:

(8.37) *Japanese*

*[$_{IP}$ Gakusei-ga$_k$ hon-o$_j$ [$_{vP}$ t$_k$ san-nin [$_{VP}$ t$_j$]] kat-ta].
    students-NOM book-ACC   three-CL   buy-PAST
'Three students bought a book.'

Watanabe (1993) concludes that the ill-formedness of (8.37) shows the impossibility of the overt movement of OBJ to the Spec of AgrO under the Agr-based Case theory. Under the Agr-less checking theory, in which OBJ's formal features are supposed to be checked off at an outer Spec of v in the two-layered VP-shell for a transitive predicate, it is possible to interpret this fact to show that OBJ in a simple transitive clause is not allowed to move up overtly to its checking position (i.e., a Spec of vP). This, in turn, indicates that the nominal features of v in a transitive clause in Japanese are weak and do not tolerate any unforced violation of Procrastinate.[13]

If correct, this is a somewhat surprising fact, because I showed in §8.2 that DO in a ditransitive clause may undergo object shift. Let us thus more closely examine whether OBJ in a Japanese transitive clause may not undergo object shift. One might suspect that the above claim is simply incorrect, by pointing out that the following sentence is clearly acceptable:

(8.38) *Japanese*

a. John-ga   hon-o   kossori kat-ta.
      -NOM   book-ACC secretly buy-PAST
    'John secretly bought a book.'

b. John-ga [$_{vP}$ hon-o$_j$ [$_{VP}$ kossori [$_{VP}$ t$_j$]]] kat-ta.
      -NOM   book-ACC   secretly   buy-PAST

In §8.2.2.1 I illustrated that manner-adverbs like *kossori* 'secretly' are adjoined to the lower projection of the two-layered VP-shell. Given this, one might be tempted to assign the structure illustrated in (8.38b) to the sentence in (8.38a). But (8.38b) is not the only structure derivable from (8.38a); unless Kayne's (1994) theory of word order is assumed, there is no reason to prevent manner-adverbs from being adjoined to the right side of VP. Then, it is possible to assign the structure illustrated in (8.39) to (8.38a):

(8.39) John-ga [$_{vP}$ [$_{VP}$ [$_{VP}$ hon-o]   kossori]] kat-ta.
          -NOM   book-ACC secretly   buy-PAST

In (8.39) OBJ does not move; whence, it is impossible to conclude only from the well-formedness of (8.38a), that OBJ in a transitive clause may undergo object shift.

---

[13] In Ura (1996b), through studying possessor-raising in Japanese, I also reached the same conclusion that the nominal features of v in a transitive clause in Japanese are weak and do not tolerate any unforced violation of Procrastinate.

Since a floating quantifier marks the base-position of its associate in Japanese (cf. §8.2.2.1), it is possible to disambiguate the structural ambiguity of (8.38a) by introducing a floating quantifier associated with OBJ.

(8.40) *Japanese*

a. John-ga hon-o$_j$ kossori san-satsu$_j$ kat-ta.
-NOM book-ACC secretly three-CL buy-PAST
'John secretly bought three books.'

b. John-ga hon-o$_j$ [$_{VP}$ kossori [$_{VP}$ t$_j$ san-satsu$_j$]] kat-ta.
-NOM book-ACC secretly three-CL buy-PAST

Now that the floating quantifier in (8.40a) marks the base-position of OBJ, there is no way to assign any structure other than (8.40b) to the sentence in (8.40a); in other words, the well-formedness of (8.40a) shows without doubt that OBJ may move out of VP (i.e., the lower projection of the two-layered VP-shell) before Spell-out.

Now does this fact count as evidence against the claim that OBJ may not undergo object shift in transitive clauses in Japanese? No, it does not, because there is a way to analyze OBJ's movement in (8.40) other than to attribute it to OBJ's object shift. Japanese has a syntactic operation that Tada (1993) calls "M(iddle)-scrambling," by which OBJ is permuted to a position adjoined to IP (cf. Saito 1985, 1992, and Miyagawa 1997). Putting aside the important issue as to what motivates M-scrambling in Japanese (see Fukui and Saito to appear and Miyagawa 1997 for discussion), it is possible to attribute OBJ's movement in (8.40) to M-scrambling; for, the nominative-marked DP *John-ga* in (8.40) can be regarded as a MAJOR SUBJECT (see Kuroda 1986, Ueda 1990, and Tateishi 1991 for discussion on MAJOR SUBJECTS in Japanese). That is to say, it is possible to assign a more minutely illustrated structure (shown in (8.41)) to the sentence in (8.40a):

(8.41) John-ga$_k$ [$_{IP}$ hon-o$_j$ [$_{IP}$ (pro$_k$) [$_{VP}$ kossori [$_{VP}$ t$_j$ san-satsu$_j$]] kat-ta]].
-NOM book-ACC secretly three-CL buy-PAST

Following, essentially, Ueda (1990), I assume that a MAJOR SUBJECT is in a Spec of an L-related functional category higher than T (= Infl). (It might be possible that a null NP, which is assigned an AGENT-role by the predicate and controlled by the MAJOR SUBJECT, occupies the canonical (i.e., innermost) Spec of T (or stays at the Spec of *v*).) In any event, the object *hon-o* in (8.41) is moved by M-scrambling to a position adjoined to IP.

To sum up, there is no doubt that the well-formedness of (8.40a) shows that OBJ may move out of VP (i.e., the lower projection of the two-layered VP-shell) before Spell-out, but it is still not clear whether (8.40a) has the structure shown in (8.41) or the structure shown in (8.41) in which OBJ is moved by object shift to a Spec of *v*P:

(8.41) John-ga [$_{vP}$ hon-o$_j$ [$_{VP}$ kossori [$_{VP}$ t$_j$ san-satsu$_j$]]] kat-ta.
-NOM book-ACC secretly three-CL buy-PAST

Now, if there is a way to detect whether a given element is moved by M-scrambling or by object shift, it is possible to tell whether or not (8.40a) shows that OBJ may undergo object shift in a transitive clause in Japanese.

In fact, there is a diagnosis available for distinguishing object shift from M-scrambling. Saito (1983) claims that the accusative Case-particle cannot be dropped from an M-scrambled element, as the ill-formedness of (8.42) shows:

(8.42) *Japanese*[14]

[$_{IP}$ Hon-*(o)$_j$ [$_{IP}$ John-ga [$_{vP}$ [$_{VP}$ kossori [$_{VP}$ t$_j$ san-satsu$_j$]]]
　　　 book-ACC 　　 -NOM 　 secretly 　　　 three-CL
kat-ta]] (yo).
buy-PAST PART
'Three books$_j$ John secretly bought t$_j$.'

On the other hand, the accusative Case-particle can be dropped from a DP that has undergone object shift, as the well-formedness of (8.43) shows:

(8.43) *Japanese*

[$_{IP}$ John-ga [$_{vP}$ kinoo [$_{VmidP}$ hon-(o)$_j$ [$_{VmidP}$ Mary-ni [$_{VP}$ t$_j$ san-satsu]]]]
　　　 -NOM yesterday 　 book-ACC 　　　 -DAT 　　 three-CL
age-ta] (yo).
give-PAST PART
'John gave three books to Mary yesterday.'

Thus, the generalization is that the accusative Case-particle can be dropped from an element that has undergone object shift, but it cannot be dropped from an M-scrambled element.[15]

Now let us see what happens if the accusative Case-particle is dropped from the permuted OBJ in (8.40a).

(8.44) ?*John-ga hon-Ø$_j$ kossori san-satsu$_j$ kat-ta (yo).
　　　　 -NOM book 　 secretly three-CL 　 buy-PAST PART
'John secretly bought three books.'

The ill-formedness of (8.44) shows two things: First it shows that the permuted OBJ in (8.40a) is not moved by object shift to a Spec of *v*P, but that it is moved by M-scrambling to a position adjoined to IP; for, if it were moved to a Spec of *v*P by object shift, (8.44) would be acceptable just as is (8.43). This leads to the

---

[14] In (8.42) the nominative-marked DP *John-ga* is not a MAJOR SUBJECT, but a real subject, as is evident from its linear order. Recall that M-scrambling moves an element to a position adjoined to IP (Saito 1985, 1992; Tada 1993) and that a MAJOR SUBJECT is in the Spec of a functional category higher than Infl (= T) (Ueda 1990). As for the particle *-yo* in the sentence-final position and its relevance to Case-particle drop in Japanese, see Masunaga (1988). When this particle is attached to the sentence-final position, Case-particle drop becomes more acceptable. Notice that (8.42) is still terrible even though *-yo* is attached to its sentence-final position.

[15] At present I have no idea about why this should be so. See Ura (1994d, 1995a) for relevant discussion and a possible solution.

conclusion that it is the structure illustrated in (8.41) that expresses the real structure of (8.40a). This means that the well-formedness of (8.40a) does not at all show that OBJ may undergo object shift (S-scrambling) in a transitive clause in Japanese.

Furthermore, the ill-formedness of (8.44) shows a more substantial thing: As long as the aforementioned generalization that the accusative Case-particle can be dropped from an element that has undergone object shift is correct, it directly shows the nonexistence of object shift in transitive clauses in Japanese.

Thus far I claimed (1) that OBJ in a Japanese simple transitive clause cannot move up beyond the base-position of SUBJ (cf. (8.37)), (2) that seemingly possible counterexamples against (1) are all illusory, and (3) that the accusative Case-particle cannot be dropped from a permuted OBJ in a transitive clause. From these facts I would like to draw the conclusion that OBJ may not undergo object shift in a transitive clause in Japanese.

8.4.2. Lexical Difference in Violability of Procrastinate

In §8.2 I arrived at the conclusion that object shift is possible in ditransitive clauses in Japanese. Now, the question is where the difference between transitive and ditransitive clauses in Japanese in terms of the possibility of object shift comes from.

Under the theory of formal feature checking advocated in this book, the impossibility of (overt) object shift of OBJ in transitive clauses in Japanese means both that the nominal feature of v in the two-layered VP-shell for a simple transitive predicate in Japanese is weak, and that it does not tolerate any unforced violation of Procrastinate; thereby, OBJ in a transitive clause cannot undergo object shift thanks to Procrastinate. On the other hand, the optionality of object shift in ditransitive clauses means that V_{mid} in the three-layered VP-shell for a ditransitive predicate in Japanese is weak and tolerates an unforced violation of Procrastinate.

This parametric difference between transitive predicates and ditransitive ones in terms of violability of Procrastinate is quite plausible, because it stems from lexical properties (cf. Borer 1984; Manzini and Wexler 1987).

8.5. Summary

In this chapter I examined overt object shift in Japanese. Through various syntactic tests, it was concluded (1) that DO, but not IO, in ditransitive clauses may undergo overt object shift, (2) that OBJ in a control complement, but not OBJ in a desiderative complement, may undergo overt object shift out of the complement clause, and (3) that OBJ in transitive clauses may not undergo overt object shift. Furthermore, I claimed that the optionality of object shift (S-scrambling), which has been a problem in Japanese syntax, can be provided a natural account, given the notion "violability of Procrastinate." In addition, it was observed that the introduction of "violability of Procrastinate" explains its correlation with passivizability of a certain argument, which is seemingly unrelated to it.

Appendix
Optional vs. Obligatory Object Shift

In this chapter I argued that optional object shift of DO in Japanese results from the property of V_{mid} to tolerate an unforced violation of Procrastinate. Recall that I argued that optionality of object shift indicates the weakness of the nominal feature of V_{mid} in Japanese. As I claimed in §1.4.1, overt movement that is induced by a feature of H targets an outer Spec of H only if (1) the feature is weak, and (2) H tolerates an unforced violation of Procrastinate. If the feature is strong, then overt movement (of XP) always targets the canonical (i.e., innermost) Spec of H owing to the condition on strong features (see §1.4.1 for details).

Now that V_{mid} is weak (but may tolerate an unforced violation of Procrastinate) in Japanese, DO may be moved to an outer Spec of V_{mid} with IO generated at its canonical Spec. Here it is important to note, again, that, under this theory of object shift, the shifted object may be in an outer Spec of the head responsible for its checking if and only if (1) (the nominal feature of) the head is weak and (2) it tolerates an unforced violation of Procrastinate.

Jonas (1996) has found the case to be very pertinent to this theory of object shift in Icelandic. She showed that the shifted OBJ is always in a position higher than the base-position of SUBJ in Icelandic.[16] Interestingly enough, object shift in Icelandic is optional (unless OBJ is a weak pronoun). My theory of object shift consistently explains these facts: In Icelandic, v is weak, but it tolerates an unforced violation of Procrastinate. This straightforwardly explains the optionality of object shift. If v has such a property, my theory also leads to the correct prediction that the shifted object always targets an outer Spec of v, as required.

Koizumi (1995), on the other hand, showed that object shift is obligatory in Zarma, a Nilo-Saharan language spoken in Niger. More interestingly, he argued that the base-position of SUBJ in this language is always higher than the position of the shifted object. If he is correct, then both facts in Zarma naturally follow under my theory of object shift: If object shift is obligatory, then the shifted object always targets the innermost Spec of v with SUBJ being generated at an outer Spec of v.

Furthermore, Chris Collins (personal communication) reported to me that in languages like Ewe and Mande, this correlation holds true: In those languages, object shift is obligatory and the shifted object is always in a position lower than the base-position of SUBJ.

---

[16] Jonas and Bobaljik (1993), Bobaljik (1995b), and Bobaljik and Jonas (1996) tried to show the opposite in Icelandic, but if Jonas (1996) is correct, all the examples they cite are irrelevant in that regard. See Jonas (1996) for details.

To conclude, my theory of object shift makes the following strong predictions, with the aid of the condition on strong features (see §1.4.1): (1) If object shift is optional, then the shifted object is always in a position higher than the base-position of SUBJ; and (2) if object shift is obligatory, then the shifted object is always in a position lower than the base-position of SUBJ. In this appendix, I showed that both predictions are empirically borne out.[17]

---

[17] See chapter 2 for some relevant facts found in Bantu languages.

9

Conclusion and Further Issues

In this book, through examining varieties of grammatical function splitting phenomena found in various languages, I devoted myself to elucidating the significance of the theory of multiple feature checking, which is a conceptually natural extension of Chomsky's (1995a) theory of formal features and their checking. In the course of the discussions, I established the hypothesis about grammatical functions (GFs) in a structure-independent fashion under the bare phrase structure theory of Chomsky (1994a). The hypothesis I finally reached is that the so-called subject-oriented GFs like the ability to control (the missing argument in a subordinate-adjunct clause), the ability to bind a (purely) subject-oriented reflexive, and the ability to induce subject-agreement result from a [+construable]-feature checking relation with Infl (= T). By studying various kinds of phenomena, I demonstrated that this hypothesis is well substantiated on empirical grounds. To implement the hypothesis, I utilized (1) the theory of multiple feature checking, under which each feature of a single head may be independently allowed to enter into more than one checking relation, and (2) the Agr-less checking theory proposed in Chomsky (1995a: §10).

A comment on the notion Grammatical Relation (GR) and its relevance to the above hypothesis about GFs is in order. GRs have been traditionally regarded as intermediary abstract entities that fill the role of relating semantic roles such as "Agent," "Patient," and so forth. with their surface representations (cf. Marantz 1984, Andrews 1985, and Müller-Gotama 1994). It has been commonly held that they are formally encoded by means of case-marking or word order. There have been two big questions concerning GRs: The first question is whether they are necessary (or how useful they are) in the theory of grammar, and the second one is, assuming that the answer to the first question is yes, how we can define them. In this connection, it is a widely held view, under most syntactic theories, that GRs are necessary in order to discern what GFs a given argument assumes in the clause. The presupposition behind this is that an argument with a particular GR assumes a certain set of GFs (most notably, under the framework of Relational Grammar; cf. Johnson 1974a,b, 1977; Perlmutter and Postal 1983; and Perlmutter 1984). The argument with the GR SUBJECT, for example, is believed to assume the "subject properties" such as the abilities to induce subject-agreement, to bind a (subject-oriented) reflexive, to control, and so forth (cf. Keenan 1976a; Schachter 1977; Perlmutter 1984; Foley and Van Valin 1984; Andrews 1985; Comrie 1988, 1989; Dixon 1989, inter alia).[1] As has been extensively observed throughout this book, however, this alleged correlation between GRs and GFs is not universal at all and frequently collapse even in a single language. This leads some researchers to go so far as to conclude that the notion GR is useless and, hence, not necessary in the theory of grammar at all (e.g., Bhat 1991). Leaving open the answer to the first question above,[2] the theory of GFs developed in this book enables us to (functionally) define the GR SUBJECT: Now that the theory of GFs decides that an argument with a [+construable]-feature checking relation with Infl bears GFs associated with the so-called subject-properties, the GR SUBJECT should be assumed by an argument with a [+construable]-feature checking relation with Infl.

This definition of SUBJECT has some merits. First, it is perfectly immune from the aforementioned problems for the universality of the links between GRs and GFs. Under the theory of formal feature checking advocated in this book, the internal properties of Infl's [+construable]-features concerned may vary from language to language as possible parametric differences;[3] accordingly, it is very natural that the checking of each of Infl's [+construable]-features in some language may be executed in a manner different from the one executed in another language. Moreover, it is free from the problem for the uniformity of the links between GRs and GFs. With the aid of the theory of multiple feature checking, it guarantees that there may be multiple arguments with the GR SUBJECT in a single clause, because it is totally possible under this theory that there are multiple arguments with a [+construable]-feature checking relation with Infl in a single clause.

Before concluding this book, I would like to sketch out some possible applications/extensions of the theory presented here. One possibility is to apply the theory to the issues concerning (non-)configurationality. Since Hale (1983), there has long been a controversy as to whether the so-called free word order languages like Japanese and Warlpiri are configurational or not. Miyagawa (1996) suggests that an extensive use of multiple Specs results in non-

---

[1] See Harley (1995b) for discussion on the subject-properties and a survey of the other approaches to them from the viewpoint of the recent PP-approach.

[2] From a functional point of view, it is possible to say that using GRs as a coverterm to refer to a particular element in the clause in a theory of grammar has an advantage: It is very inconvenient for us not to refer to an argument in the clause without its alleged GR. Of course, this has no theoretical or conceptual significance, though.

[3] For instance, T's ϕ-feature may have the property [+multiple, −strong] in some languages, while it may have the property [−multiple, +strong] in others (see §1.3.1.3).

configurationality. Whether it finally succeeds or not, the pursuit along this line will have big consequences for the theory of configurationality and word order in general. Another possibility is to apply the theory to the issues concerning the polysynthesis parameter of Baker (1995). According to Baker, arguments can be base-generated at a position adjoined to some maximal projection, a position that is remote from the positions where they are expected to be assigned their θ-role (i.e., their base-position). As Chomsky (1995a) envisaged, the theory of multiple feature checking is expected to provide a more principled account of the phenomena that Baker (1995) tries to capture by invoking the above parameter

Promising and worth pursuing though they are, I leave it to future research to explore these possibilities.

References

Abbi, A. 1990. Experiental constructions and the "subjecthood" of the experiencer NPs in South Asian languages. In *Experiencer subjects in South Asian languages*, ed. M. Verma and K. P. Mohanan, 253–267. Stanford, Calif.: CSLI.

Abe, J. 1993. Binding conditions and scrambling without A/A-bar distinction. Ph.D dissertation, University of Connecticut.

Åfarli, T. 1992. *The syntax of Norwegian passive constructions*. Philadelphia: John Benjamins

Aissen, J. 1983. Indirect advancement in Tzotzil. In *Studies in relational grammar*, vol. 1, ed. David Perlmutter, 272–302. Chicago: University of Chicago Press.

Allan, R., P. Holmes, and T. Lundskær-Nielsen. 1995. *Danish: A comprehensive grammar*. London: Routledge.

Allen, B., and D. Frantz. 1983. Advancements and verb agreement in Southern Tiwa. In *Studies in relational grammar*, vol. 1, ed. David Perlmutter, 303-314. Chicago: University of Chicago Press.

Allen, C. 1995. *Case marking and reanalysis: Grammatical relations from Old to Early Modern English*. Oxford: Oxford University Press.

Andersen, P. K. 1991. *A new look at the passive*. Frankfurt am Main: Peter Lang.

Andersen, T. 1988. Ergativity in Päri, a Nilotic OVS language. *Lingua* 75, 289–324.

Andersen, T. 1991. Subject and topic in Dinka. *Studies in Language* 15, 265–294.

Anderson, S. 1976. On the notion of subject in ergative languages. In *Subject and topic*, ed. C. Li, 1–23. New York: Academic Press.

Anderson, S. 1986. The typology of anaphoric dependencies: Icelandic (and other) reflexives. In *Topics in Scandinavian synax*, ed. L. Hellan and K. K. Christensen, 65–88. Dordrecht: Kluwer.

Andrews, A. 1982. The representation of case in Modern Icelandic. In *The mental representation of grammatical relations*, ed. J. Bresnan, 427–503. Cambridge, Mass.: MIT Press.

Andrews, A. 1985. The major functions of the noun phrases. In *Language typology and syntactic description I: Clause structure*, ed. T. Shopen, 62–154. Cambridge: Cambridge University Press.

Andrews, A. 1990. Case structures and control in Modern Icelandic. In *Modern Icelandic syntax: Syntax and semantics*, vol. 24, ed. J. Maling and A. Zaenen, 187–234. New York: Academic Press.

Aoun, J., and Y.-H. A. Li. 1994. *Syntax of scope*. Cambridge, Mass.: MIT Press.

Arnold, J. 1994. Inverse voice marking in Mapudungun. In *Proceedings of BLS* 20, 28–41.
Austin, J. 1982. Transitivity and cognate objects in Australian languages. In *Studies in transitivity: Syntax and semantics*, vol. 15, ed. P. Hopper and S. Thompson, 37–47. New York: Academic Press.
Austin, J., and L. López. 1995. Nominative, absolutive, and dative languages. In *Proceedings of ConSole* 3, 1–16.
Awbery, G. M. 1976. *The syntax of Welsh: A transformational study of the passive*. Cambridge: Cambridge University Press.
Bailyn, J. 1991. The configurationality of Case assignment in Russian. In *Cornell working papers in linguistics* 9, 57–98. Ithaca, N.Y.: DMLL Publications.
Baker, M. 1988. *Incorporation: A theory of grammatical function changing*. Chicago: University of Chicago Press.
Baker, M. 1995. *The polysynthesis parameter*. Oxford: Oxford University Press.
Baker, M., K. Johnson, and I. Roberts. 1989. Passive argument raised. *Linguistic Inquiry* 20, 219–251.
Bamgbose, A. 1974. On serial verbs and verbal status. *Journal of West African Languages* 9, 17–48.
Barss, A. 1986. Chains and anaphoric dependence: On reconstruction and its implications. Ph.D. dissertation, MIT.
Barss, A., and H. Lasnik. 1986. A note on anaphora and double objects. *Linguistic Inquiry* 17, 347–354.
Bechert, J. 1979. Ergativity and the constitution of grammatical relations. In *Ergativity: Towards a theory of grammatical relations*, ed. F. Plank, 45–59. New York: Academic Press.
Belletti, A., and L. Rizzi. 1988. Psych-verbs and q-theory. *Natural Language & Linguistic Theory* 6, 291–352.
Belvin, R. 1990a. Ergativity and accusativity in Nisgha syntax. In *Proceedings of BLS 16: Special session on general topics in American Indian linguistics*, 3–18.
Belvin, R. 1990b. Person marking and patterns of Case assignment in Nisgha. In *Proceedings of Student Conference in Linguistics 2: MIT working papers in linguistics* 12, 14–30. Cambridge, Mass.: MITWPL.
Benua, L. 1995. Yupi'ik antipassive. In *Proceedings of CLS 31: Main session*, 28–44.
Besten, H. den. 1981. A case filter for passives. In *Theory of markedness in generative grammar*, ed. A. Belletti et al., 65–122. Pisa: Scuola Normale Superiore.
Bhat, D. N. S. 1991. *Grammatical relations: The evidence against their necessity and universality*. London: Routledge.
Bhatia, T. 1993. *Punjabi*. New York: Routledge.
Bhatt, R. 1993. The case of quirky constructions. In *Proceedings of FLSM* 4, 20–34. Department of Linguistics, University of Iowa.
Bittner, M. 1994. *Case, scope, and binding*. Dordrecht: Kluwer.
Bittner, M., and K. Hale. 1996a. Ergativity: Towards a theory of a heterogeneous class. *Linguistic Inquiry* 27, 531–601.
Bittner, M., and K. Hale. 1996b. The structural determination of case and agreement. *Linguistic Inquiry* 27, 1–68.
Blake, B. 1976. On ergativity and the notion of subject: Some Australian cases. *Lingua* 39, 281–300.
Blake, B. 1982. The absolutive: Its scope in English and Kalkatungu. In *Studies in transitivity: Syntax and semantics*, vol. 15, ed. P. Hopper and S. Thompson, 71–94. New York: Academic Press.
Blake, B. 1990. *Relational grammar*. London: Routledge.

Bobaljik, J. 1992. Nominally absolutive is not absolutely nominative. In *Proceedings of WCCFL* 11, 44–60. Stanford, Calif.: CSLI.

Bobaljik, J. 1993. On ergativity and ergative unergatives. In *Papers on Case & agreement II: MIT working papers in linguistics* 19, 45–88. Cambridge, Mass.: MITWPL.

Bobaljik, J. 1995a. In terms of merger: Single output syntax and the strict cycle. In *Papers on minimalist syntax: MIT working papers in linguistics* 27, 41–64. Cambridge, Mass.: MITWPL.

Bobaljik, J. 1995b. Morphosyntax: The syntax of verbal inflection. Ph.D. dissertation, MIT.

Bobaljik, J., and D. Jonas. 1996. Subject positions and the roles of TP. *Linguistic Inquiry* 27, 195–236.

Bok-Bennema, R. 1991. *Case and agreement in Inuit*. Dordrecht: Foris.

Bokamba, E. 1976. Question formation in some Bantu languages. Ph.D. dissertation, Indiana University, Bloomington.

Bokamba, E. 1979. Inversions as grammatical relation changing rules in Bantu languages. *Studies in the Linguistic Sciences* 9, 1–24.

Borer, H. 1984. *Parametric syntax*. Dordrecht: Foris.

Borer, H. 1989. Anaphoric AGR. In *The null subject parameter*, ed. O. Jaeggli and K. Safir, 69–109. Dordrecht: Kluwer.

Borg, A., and B. Comrie. 1984. Object diffuseness in Maltese. In *Objects: Towards a theory of grammatical relations*, ed. F. Plank, 109–126. Orlando, Fla.: Academic Press.

Bošković, Š. 1994. ECP, Spec-head agreement, and multiple wh-movement in overt syntax. In *Formal approaches to Slavic linguistics* 1993, ed. S. Averutin et al., 119–143. Ann Arbor, Mich.: Michigan Slavic Publications.

Bošković, Š. 1995. Principles of economy in nonfinite complementation. Ph.D. dissertation, University of Connecticut.

Bouchard, D. 1995. *The semantics of syntax*. Chicago: University of Chicago Press.

Branigan, P. 1992. Subjects and complementzers. Ph.D. dissertation, MIT.

Branigan, P., and C. Collins. 1993. Verb movement and the quotative construction in English. In *Papers on Case and agreement I: MIT working papers in linguistics* 18, 1–13. Cambridge, Mass.: MITWPL.

Bresnan, J. 1994. Locative inversion and the architecture of Universal Grammar. *Language* 70, 72–131.

Bresnan, J., and J. Kanerva. 1989. Locative inversion in Chichewa: A case study of factorization in grammar. *Linguistic Inquiry* 20, 1–50.

Bresnan, J., and J. Kanerva. 1992. The thematic hierarchy and locative inversion in UG: A reply to Schachter's comments. In *Syntax and lexicon: Syntax and semantics*, vol. 26, ed. T. Stowell and E. Wehrli, 111–125. New York: Academic Press.

Bresnan, J., and S. Mchombo. 1985. On topic, pronoun, and agreement in Chichewa. In *Proceedings of ESCOL '85*, 276–312. Ithaca, N.Y.: DMLL Publications.

Bresnan, J., and S. Mchombo. 1995. The lexical integrity principle: Evidence from Bantu. *Natural Language & Linguistic Theory* 13, 181–254.

Bresnan, J., and L. Moshi. 1990. Object asymmetries in comparative Bantu syntax. *Linguistic Inquiry* 21, 147–185.

Brody, M. 1995. *Lixico-logical form: A radically minimalist theory*. Cambridge, Mass.: MIT Press.

Broekhuis, H. 1992. *Chain-government: Issues in Dutch syntax*. Dordrecht: Holland Institute of Generative Grammar.

Bures, A. 1993. There is an argument for a cycle at LF, here. In *Proceedings of CLS* 29-II, 14–35.

Burzio, L. 1986. *Italian syntax: A government and binding approach*. Dordrecht: Kluwer.

Byrne, F. 1987. *Grammatical relations in a radical creole*. Philadelphia: John Benjamins.

Calabrese, A. 1986. Pronomina: Some properties of the Italian pronominal system. In *MIT working papers in linguistics* 8, 1–46. Cambridge, Mass.: MITWPL.

Cardinaletti, A. 1994. Agreement and control in expletive constructions. Ms., University of Venice and MIT.

Carrier-Duncan, J. 1985. Linking of thematic roles in derivational word formation. *Linguistic Inquiry* 16, 1–34.

Carstens, V. 1991. The morphology and syntax of determiner phrases in Kswahili. Ph.D. dissertation, UCLA.

Carstens, V. 1993. On nominal morphology and DP structure. *Theoretical aspects of Bantu grammar* 1, ed. S. Mchombo, 151–180. Stanford, Calif.: CSLI.

Catford, J. C. 1976. Ergativity in Caucasian languages. In *Proceedings of NELS* 6, 37–48.

Catrileo, C. 1972. A tagmemic sketch of Mapuche grammar. M.A. thesis, University of Texas at El Paso.

Cheng, L. L.-S. 1991. On the typology of wh-questions. Ph.D. dissertation, MIT.

Cheng, L. L.-S., and H. Demirdache. 1993. External arguments in Basque. In *Generative studies in Basque linguistics*, ed. José Hualde and Jon Ortiz de Urbina, 71–87.

Cho, E. 1996. Multiple feature checking and accusative Case on the passives. In *Morphosyntax in generative grammar*, ed. H.-D. Ahn et al., 113–122. Seoul, Korea: Hankuk Publishing.

Chomsky, N. 1965. *Aspects of the theory of syntax*. Cambridge, Mass.: MIT Press.

Chomsky, N. 1966. *Cartesian linguistics*. New York: Harper and Row.

Chomsky, N. 1970. Remarks on nominalization. In *Readings in English transformational grammar*, ed. R. Jocabs and P. Rosenbaum, 184–221. Waltham, Mass.: Ginn and Company.

Chomsky, N. 1975. *Reflections on language*. New York: Pantheon.

Chomsky, N. 1981. *Lectures on government and binding*. Dordrecht: Foris.

Chomsky, N. 1986a. *Barriers*. Cambridge, Mass.: MIT Press.

Chomsky, N. 1986b. *Knowledge of language: Its nature, origin, and use*. New York: Praeger.

Chomsky, N. 1989. Some notes on economy of derivation and representation. In *MIT working papers in linguistics* 10, 43–74. Cambridge, Mass.: MITWPL.

Chomsky, N. 1991a. Linguistics and adjacent fields: A personal view. In *The Chomskyan turn*, ed. A. Kasher, 3–25. Cambridge, Mass.: Basil Blackwell.

Chomsky, N. 1991b. Linguistics and cognitive science: Problems and mysteries. In *The Chomskyan turn*, ed. A. Kasher, 26–53. Cambridge, Mass.: Basil Blackwell.

Chomsky, N. 1992. *A minimalist program for linguistic theory*. MIT occasional papers in linguistics no. 1. Cambridge, Mass.: MITWPL.

Chomsky, N. 1994a. *Bare phrase structure*. MIT occasional papers in linguistics no. 5, Cambridge, Mass.: MITWPL.

Chomsky, N. 1994b. *Language and thought*. Wakefield, R.I.: Moyer Bell.

Chomsky, N. 1995a. Categories and transformations. In *The minimalist program*, 219–394. Cambridge, Mass.: MIT Press.

Chomsky, N. 1995b. Language and nature. *Mind* 104, no. 413, 1–61.

Chomsky, N. 1996. Some observations on economy in generative grammar. Ms., MIT, Cambridge, Mass.

Chomsky, N., and H. Lasnik. 1993. The theory of principles and parameters. In *Syntax: An international handbook of contemporary research*, ed. J. Jacobs et al., 506–569. Berlin: Walter de Gruyter.

Chung, S. 1976. On the subject of two passives in Indonesian. In *Subject and topic*, ed. C. Li, 57–98. New York: Academic Press.

Chung, S. 1983. An object-creating rule in Bahasa Indonesian. In *Studies in Relational Grammar*, vol. 1, ed. D. Perlmutter, 219–271. Chicago: University of Chicago Press.

Clark, E. 1978. Locationals: Existential, locative, and possessive constructions. In *Universals of human language*, vol. 4: *Syntax*, ed. J. Greenberg, 85–126. Stanford, Calif.: Stanford University Press.

Colarusso, J. 1992. *A grammar of the Kabardian language*. Calgary: University of Calgary Press.

Cole, P. 1982. *Imbabura Quechua*. Amsterdam: North Holland Publishing.

Cole, P., and J. Jake. 1978. Accusative subjects in Imbabura Quechua. *Studies in the Linguistic Sciences* 8, 72–96.

Collins, C. 1993. Topics in Ewe syntax. Ph.D. dissertation, MIT.

Collins, C. 1994b. Argument sharing in serial verb constructions. Ms., Cornell University, Ithaca, New York.

Collins, C. 1995a. Serial verb constructions and the theory of multiple feature chekcing. Ms., Cornell University, Ithaca, New York.

Collins, C. 1995b. Toward a theory of optimal derivations. In *Papers on minimalist syntax: MIT working papers in linguistics* 27, 65–103. Cambridge, Mass.: MITWPL.

Collins, C. 1996. *Local economy*. Cambridge, Mass.: MIT Press.

Collins, C., and P. Branigan. 1995. Quotative inversion. Ms., Cornell University, Ithaca, New York, and Memorial University of Newfoundland, St. John's, Canada.

Collins, C., and H. Thráinsson. 1993. Object shift in double object constructions and the theory of Case. In *Papers on Case and agreement II: MIT working papers in linguistics* 19, 131–174. Cambridge, Mass.: MITWPL.

Collins, C., and H. Thráinsson. 1996. VP internal structure and object shift in Icelandic. *Linguistic Inquiry* 27, 391–444.

Comrie, B. 1977. In defense of spontaneous demotion: The impersonal passive. In *Grammatical relations: Syntax and semantics*, vol. 8, ed. P. Cole and J. Sadock, 47–58. New York: Academic Press.

Comrie, B. 1978. Ergativity. In *Syntactic typology*, ed. W. P. Lehman, 329–394. Austin: University of Texas Press.

Comrie, B. 1979. Degrees of ergativity: Some Chukchee evidence. In *Ergativity: Towards a theory of grammatical relations*, ed. F. Plank, 219–240. New York: Academic Press.

Comrie, B. 1981. Ergativity and grammatical relations in Kalaw Lagaw Ya (Saibai Dialect). *Australian Journal of Linguistics* 1, 1–42.

Comrie, B. 1982. Grammatical relations in Huichol. In *Studies in transitivity: Syntax and semantics*, vol. 15, ed. Paul Hopper and Sandra Thompson, 95–115. New York: Academic Press.

Comrie, B. 1989. *Language universals and linguistic typology*, 2nd ed. Oxford: Basil Blackwell.

Coopmans, P. 1989. Where stylstic and syntactic processes meet: Locative inversion in English. *Language* 65, 728–751.

Cooreman, A. 1984. A functional analysis of passives in Chamorro narrative discourse. *Papers in Linguistics* 17, 395–428.

Cooreman, A. 1988. The antipassive in Chamorro: Variations on the theme of transitivity. In *Passive and voice*, ed. M. Shibatani, 561–593. Philadelphia: John Benjamins.

Cowper, E. 1988. Non-nominative subjects in Icelandic. In *Proceedings of NELS* 18, 94–108. Amherst, Mass.: GLSA.

Creamer, M. 1974. Ranking in Navajo nouns. *Diné Bizaard Nánil' íih (Navajo language Review)* 1, 29–38.

Croft, W. 1990. *Typology and universals*. Cambridge: Cambridge University Press.

Czepluch, H. 1982. Case theory and the dative construction. *The Linguistic Review* 2, 1–38.

Czepluch, H. 1988. Case patterns in German: Some implications for the theory of abstract Case. *McGill working papers in linguistics, special issue on comparative German syntax*, 79–122.

Dahlstrom, A. 1991. *Plains Cree morphosyntax*. New York: Garland.

Davies, W. 1993. Javanese subjects and topics and psych verbs. *Linguistics* 31, 239–277.

Davies, W. 1995. Javanese adversatives, passives and mapping theory. *Journal of Linguistics* 31, 15–51.

Davison, A. 1985. Experiencers and patients as subjects in Hindi-Urdu. In *Proeedings of the conference on participant roles: South Asia and adjacent areas*, ed. A. Zide et al., 160–178. Bloomington, Ind.: IULC.

Dayley, J. 1989. *Tümpisa (Panamint) Shoshone grammar*. Berkeley: University of California Press.

DeLancey, S. 1981. An interpretation of split ergativity and related patters. *Language* 57, 626–657.

den Besten, H. 1984. The ergative hypothesis and free word order in Dutch and German. In *Studies in German grammar*, ed. J. Torman, 23–64. Dordrecht: Foris.

Denison, D. 1993. *English historical syntax*. London: Longman.

Déprez, V. 1990. Two ways of moving the verbs in French. In *Papers on wh-movement: MIT working papers in linguistics* 13, 47–85. Cambridge, Mass.: MITWPL.

Déprez, V. 1994. Parameters of object movement. In *Studies on scrambling*, ed. N. Corver and H. van Riemsdijk, 101–152. Berlin: Mouton de Gruyter.

Dikken, M. den. 1995. *Particles*. Oxford: Oxford University Press.

Dixon, R. M. W. 1972. *The Dyirbal language of North Queensland*. Cambridge: Cambridge University Press.

Dixon, R. M. W. 1977. *A grammar of YidiÇ*. Cambridge: Cambridge University Press.

Dixon, R. M. W. 1979. Ergativity. *Language* 55, 59–138.

Dixon, R. M. W. 1987. Studies in ergativity: Introduction. *Lingua* 71, 1–16.

Dixon, R. M. W. 1989. Subject and object in universal grammar. In *Essays on grammatical theory and universal grammar*, ed. D. Arnold et al., 91–118. Oxford: Oxford University Press.

Dixon, R. M. W. 1994. *Ergativity*. Cambridge: Cambridge University Press.

Dryer, M. 1982. Passive and inversion in Kannada. In *Proceedings of BLS* 8, 311–321.

Dryer, M. 1986. Promary objects, secondary objects, and antidative. *Language* 62, 808–845.

Du Plessis, J. A., and M. Visser. 1992. *Xhosa syntax*. Hatfield: Via Africa.

Duranti, A. & E. R. Byarushengo. 1977. On the notion of "direct object." In *Haya grammatical structure: Southern California occasional papers in linguistics* no. 6, 45–71.

Dziwirek, K. 1994. *Polish subjects*. New York: Garland.

Einarsson, S. 1945. *Icelandic: Grammar, texts, glossary*. Baltimore: Johns Hopkins University Press.

Elmer, W. 1981. *Diachronic grammar: The history of Old and Middle English subjectless constructions*. Tübingen: Niemeyer.
England, N. 1988. Mam voice. In *Passive and voice*, ed. M. Shibatani, 525–545. Philadelphia: John Benjamins.
Epstein, S. D., H. Thráinsson, and J.-W. Zwart. 1996. Introduction. In *Minimal ideas*, ed. Abrahan et al., 1–66. Philadelphia: John Benjamins.
Escalante, F. 1990. Voice and argument structure in Yaqui. Ph.D. dissertation, University of Arizona, Tucson.
Everaert, M. 1990. NP-movement 'across' secondary objects. In *Grammar in progress*, ed. Joan Mascaró and Marina Nespor, 125–136. Dordrecht: Foris.
Faarlund, J. T. 1990. *Syntactic change: Toward a theory of historical syntax*. Berlin: Mouton de Gruyter.
Falk, C. 1990. On double object constructions. *Working papers in Scandinavian syntax* 46, 53–100.
Falk, Y. N. 1991. Case: Abstract and morphological. *Linguistics* 29, 197–230.
Faltz, L. 1978. On indirect objects in universal syntax. In *Proceedings of CLS* 14, 76–87.
Farrell, P. 1994. *Thematic relations and relational grammar*. New York: Garland.
Ferguson, S. 1996. A feature-relativized shortest move requirement. Ph.D. dissertation, Harvard University.
Fischer, O., and F. van der Leek. 1983. The demise of the Old English impersonal construction. *Journal of Linguistics* 19, 337–368.
Foley, W. 1991. *The Yimas language of New Guinea*. Stanford, Calif.: Stanford University Press.
Foley, W., and R. Van Valin. 1977. On the viability of the notion of "subject" in universal grammar. In *Proceedings of BLS* 3, 293–320.
Foley, W., and R. Van Valin. 1984. *Functional syntax and universal grammar*. Cambridge: Cambridge University Press.
Fox, B., and P. Hopper. 1994. Introduction. In *Voice: Form and function*, ed. B. Fox and P. Hopper, ix–xiii. Philadelphia: John Benjamins.
Fox, D. 1995. Economy and scope. *Natural Language Semantics* 3, 283–341.
Frampton, J. 1996. Expletive insertion. In *The role of economy principles in linguistic theory*, ed. C. Wilder et al., 36–57. Berlin: Akademie Verlag.
Franks, S. 1995. *Parameters of Slavic morphosyntax*. Oxford: Oxford University Press.
Franks, S., and G. Greenberg. 1988. Agreement, tense, and the case of subjects in Russian. In *Proceedings of CLS* 24, part 2, 71–86.
Freeze, R. 1992. Existentials and other locatives. *Language* 68, 553–595.
Freidin, R., and R. Sprouse. 1991. Lexical case phenomena. In *Principles and parameters in comparative grammar*, ed. R. Freidin, 392–416. Cambridge, Mass.: MIT Press.
Fried, M. 1994. Grammatical functions in case languages: Subjecthood in Czech. In *Proceedings of BLS* 20, 184–193.
Frishberg, N. 1972. Navaho object markers and the great chain of being. In *Syntax and semantics*, vol. 1, ed. J. Kimball, 259–266. New York: Academic Press.
Fujita, K. 1994. Case checking and a theory of LF binding. *Studies in English Literature* 70, 149–170.
Fujita, K. 1996. Double objects, causatives, and derivational economy. *Linguistic Inquiry* 27, 146–173.
Fujita, N. 1993. Floating quantifiers and adverbs in Japanese. In *Proceedings of FLSM* IV, 90–103. Iowa City: Department of Linguistics, University of Iowa.
Fukuhara, M. 1993. Case-checking in Japanese. M.A. thesis, University of Connecticut.
Fukui, N. 1986. A theory of category projection and its applications. Ph.D. dissertation, MIT.

Fukui, N. 1993. Parameters and optionality. *Linguistic Inquiry* 24, 399–420.
Fukui, N. 1995. The principles-and-parameters approach: A comparative syntax of English and Japanese. In *Approaches to language typology*, ed. M. Shibatani and T. Bynon, 327–372. Oxford: Oxford University Press.
Fukui, N. 1996. On the nature of economy in language. *Cognitive Studies: Bulletin of The Japanese Cognitive Science Society* 3 (1), 51–71.
Fukui, N. 1997. Attract and A-over-A principle. Ms., University of California, Irvine.
Fukui, N., and M. Saito. To appear. Order in phrase structure and movement. *Linguistic Inquiry*.
Gair, J. W., and K. Wali. 1989. Hindi agreement as anaphor. *Linguistics* 27, 45–70.
Gary, J. 1977. Object-formation rules in several Bantu languages: Questions and implications for universal grammar. In *Proceedings of CLS 13*, 125–136.
George, L. 1974. Ergativity and relational grammar. In *Proceedings of NELS 5*, 265–275.
Gerdts, D. 1988. *Object and absolutive in Halkomelem Salish*. New York: Garland.
Gerdts, D., and C. Youn. 1988. Korean psych construction: Advancement or retreat? In *Proceedings of CLS* 24:1, 155–175.
Givón, T. 1972. Pronoun attraction and subject postposing in Bantu. In *The Chicago which hunt: Papers from the relative clause festival*, ed. P. Peranteau et al., 190–197. Chicago: CLS.
Givón, T. 1975. Promotion, accessibility and case marking: Toward understanding grammar. *Working papers on language universals* 19, 55–125.
Givón, T. 1979. *On understanding grammar*. Orlando, Fla.: Academic Press.
Givón, T. 1984a. Direct object and dative shifting: Semantic and pragmatic case. In *Objects: Towards a theory of grammatical relations*, ed. F. Plank, 151–182. Orlando, Fla.: Academic Press.
Givón, T. 1984b. *Syntax: A functional-typological introduction*, vol. 1. Philadelphia: John Benjamins.
Givón, T. 1990. *Syntax: A functional-typological introduction*, vol. 2. Philadelphia: John Benjamins.
Givón, T., ed. 1994. *Voice and inversion*. Philadelphia: John Benjamins.
Gjerlow-Johnson, K., and E. Ayom. 1986. The passive in Bor Dinka. In *Current approaches to African linguistics*, vol.3, ed. G. Dimmendaal, 171–178. Dordrecht: Foris.
Goodall, G. 1993. On Case and the passive morphology. *Natural Language & Linguistic Theory* 11, 31–44.
Greenberg, J. 1966. Some universals of grammar with particular reference to the order of meaningful elements. In *Universals of grammar*, ed. J. Greenberg, 73–113. Cambridge, Mass.: MIT Press.
Grewendorf, G. 1989. *Ergativity in German*. Dordrecht: Foris.
Grimshaw, J. 1990. *Argument structure*. Cambridge, Mass.: MIT Press.
Grønbech, K. 1936. *Die türkische Sprachau*. Copenhagen: Levin and Munksgaard.
Guéron, J. 1994. Beyond predication: The inverse copular construction in English. In *Paths towards Universal Grammar*, ed. G. Cinque et al., 173–187. Washington D.C.: Georgetown University Press.
Haider, H. 1984. The case of German. In *Studies in German grammar*, ed. J. Torman, 65–101. Dordrecht: Foris.
Hale, K. 1970. Passive and ergative in language change: The Australian case. In *Pacific linguistic studies in honour of Arthur Capell*, ed. S. A. Wurm and D. C. Laycock, 757–781. Canberra: Linguistics Circle of Canberra.
Hale, K. 1972. Person marking in Walbiri. In *A festshrift for Morris Halle*, ed. S. Anderson and P. Kiparsky, 308–344. New York: Holt, Rinehart, and Winston.

Hale, K. 1973. A note on subject-object inversion in Navajo. In *Issues in linguistics: Papers in honor of Henry and Renée Kahane*, ed. Y. Kachru et al., 300–309. Urbana: University of Illinois Press.
Hale, K. 1983. Walpiri and the grammar of non-configurational languages. *Natural Languages & Linguistic Theory* 1, 5–47.
Hale, K. 1992. Subject obviation, switch reference, and control. In *Control and grammar*, ed. R. Larson et al., 51–77. Dordrecht: Kluwer.
Hale, K., and J. Keyser. 1991. *On the syntax of argument strutcure*. Lexicon project working papers no. 34. Cambridge, Mass.: MITWPL.
Hale, K., and J. Keyser. 1993. On argument structure and the lexical expression of syntactic relations. In *The view from Building 20*, ed. by K. Hale and J. Keyser, 53–109. Cambridge, Mass.: MIT Press.
Hale, K., E. Tsosie-Perkins, R. Demers, and D. Shank. 1977. *Structure of Navajo*. Ms., University of Arizona, Tucson.
Harada, S.-I. 1976. Honorifics. In *Japanese generative grammar: Syntax and semantics*, vol. 5, ed. M. Shibatani, 499–561. New York: Academic Press.
Harbert, W., and A. Toribio. 1991. Nominative objects. In *Cornell working papers in linguistics* 9, 127–192.
Harford, C. 1993. Object asymmetries in Kitharaka. In *Proceedings of BLS 17: Special session on African lnaguage structures*, 98–106
Harley, H. 1995a. Abstracting away from abstract case. In *Proceedings of NELS 25*, 207–221. Amherst, Mass.: GLSA.
Harley, H. 1995b. Subjects, events, and licensing. Ph.D. dissertation, MIT.
Harris, A. 1981. *Georgian syntax: A study in relational grammar*. Cambridge: Cambridge University Press.
Harris, A. 1984. Inversion as a rule of universal grammar: Georgian evidence. In *Studies in relational grammar*, vol. 2, ed. D. Perlmutter and C. Rosen, 259–291. Chicago: University of Chicago Press.
Haspelmath, M. 1993. *A grammar of Lezgian*. Berlin: Mouton de Gruyter.
Hawkins, J. 1986. *A comparative typology of English and German*. London: Croom Helm.
Heath, J. 1976. Antipassivization: A functional typology. In *Proceedings of BLS 2*, 202–211.
Hermon, G. 1984. *Syntactic modularity*. Dordrecht: Foris.
Herring, S. 1994. Postverbal position in Tamil. In *Theoretical perspectives on word order in South Asian languages*, ed. M. Butt, et al., 119–152. Stanford, Calif.: CSLI.
Herschensohn, J. 1982. The French presentative as a base-generated structure. *Studies in Language* 6, 193–219.
Hestvik, A. 1986. Case theory and Norwegian impersonal constructions: Subject-object alternations in active and passive verbs. *Nordic Journal of Linguistics* 9, 181–197.
Hewitt, B. G. 1995. *Georgian: A structural reference grammar*. Philadelphia: John Benjamins.
Heycock, C. 1994. *Layers of predication*. New York: Garland.
Heycock, C. 1995. The internal structure of small clauses: New evidence from inversion. In *Proceedings of NELS 25*, vol. 1, 223–238. Amherst, Mass.: GLSA.
Higginbotham, J., and R. May. 1981. Questions, quantifiers, and crossing. *The Linguistic Review* 1, 41–80.
Hodges, K. S., and S. Stucky. 1979. On the inadequacy of a grammatical relation referring rule in Bantu. *Studies in the Linguistic Sciences* 9, 91–99.
Hoekstra, T. 1980. The status of the indirect object. In *Linguistics in the Netherlands 1977–1979*, ed. J. Kooiji, 152–169. Dordrecht: Foris.

Hoekstra, T. 1984. *Transitivity: Grammatical relations in government-binding theory*. Dordrecht: Foris.

Hoekstra, T., and R. Mulder. 1990. Unergatives as copular verbs: Locational and existential predication. *The Linguistic Review* 7, 1–79.

Hoffman, M. 1991. The syntax of argument-structure-changing morphology. Ph.D. dissertation, MIT.

Hoji, H. 1985. Logical form constraints and configurational structures in Japanese. Ph.D. dissertation, University of Washington.

Holisky, D. 1987. The case of intransitive subject in Tsova-Tush (Batsbi). *Lingua* 71, 103–132.

Holmberg, A. 1986. Word order and syntactic features in the Scandinavian languages and English. Ph.D. dissertation, University of Stockholm.

Holmberg, A. 1991. The distribution of Scandinavian weak pronouns. In *Clitics and their hosts*, ed. H. van Riemsdijk and L. Rizzi, 155–174.

Holmberg, A. 1994. The pros and cons of agreement in Scandinavian impersonals. In *Paths towards Universal Grammar*, ed. G. Cinque et al., 217–236. Washington, D.C.: Georgetown University Press.

Holmberg, A., and C. Platzak. 1995. *The role of inflection in Scandinavian syntax*. Oxford: Oxford University Press.

Holmes, P., and Ian Hinchiffe. 1994. *Swedish: A comprehensive grammar*. New York: Routledge.

Hoshi, H. 1994. Passive, causative, and light verbs: A study on theta role assignment. Ph.D. dissertation, University of Connecticut.

Hualde, J. 1989. Double object constructions in Kinande and Case theory. In *Current approaches to African linguistics*, vol.6, ed. I. Häik, 239–257. Dordrecht: Foris.

Huang, J. 1982. Logical relations in Chinese and the theory of grammar. Ph.D. dissertation, MIT.

Inoue, K. 1976. *Henkei bumpoo to Nihon-go [Transformational grammar and Japanese]*. Tokyo: Taishyuu-kan.

Jackendoff, R. 1972. *Semantic interpretation in generative grammar*. Cambridge, Mass.: MIT Press.

Jaeggli, O. 1981. *Topics in Romance syntax*. Dordrecht: Foris.

Jake, J. 1985. *Grammatical relations in Imbabura Quechua*. New York: Garland.

Jayaseelan, K. A. 1983. Case-marking and q-marking in Malayalam: Implications for the projection principle. In *Proceednigs of BLS* 9, 104–115.

Jelinek, E. 1990. Grammatical relations and coindexing in inverse system. In *Grammatical relations: A cross-theoretical perspective*, ed. K. Dziwirek et al., 227–246. Stanford, Calif.: SLA.

Jespersen, O. 1927. *A Modern English grammar on historical principles*, pt. 3. Copenhargen: Ejnar Munksgaard.

Johns, A. 1987. Transitivity and grammatical relations in Inuktitut. Ph.D. dissertation, University of Ottawa.

Johns, A. 1992. Deriving ergativity. *Linguistic Inquiry* 23, 57–87.

Johnson, D. 1974a. On the role of grammatical relations in linguistic theory. In *Proceedings of CLS* 10, 269–283.

Johnson, D. 1974b. Toward a theory of relationally-based grammar. Ph.D. dissertation, University of Illinois, Urbana.

Johnson, D. 1977. On relational constraint on grammar. In *Grammatical relations: Syntax and semantics*, vol. 8, ed. P. Cole and J. Sadock, 151–178. New York: Academic Press.

Johnson, K. 1991. Object positions. *Natural Language & Linguistic Theory* 9, 577–636.

Jonas, D. 1992. Case theory and nominative case in Icelandic. In *Harvard working papers in linguistics* 1, 175–195.
Jonas, D. 1996. Clause strutcure and verb syntax in Scandinavian and English. Ph.D. dissertation, Harvard University.
Jonas, D., and J. Bobaljik. 1993. Specs for subjects: The role of TP in Icelandic. *MIT working papers in linguistics* 18, 59–98. Cambridge, Mass.: MITWPL.
Jones, C. 1992. *Purpose clauses*. Dordrecht: Kluwer.
Jones, D. 1993. Binding as an interface condition: An investigation of Hindi scrambling. Ph.D. dissertation, MIT.
Jónsson, J. 1994. On case and agreement in Icelandic. In *UMass occasional papers in linguistics* 17, 85–101. Amherst, Mass.: GLSA.
Joseph, B., and I. Philippaki-Warburton. 1987. *Modern Greek*. London: Routledge.
Kachru, Y. 1987. Ergativity, subjecthood, and topicality in Hindi-Urdu. *Lingua* 71, 223–238.
Kachru, Y. 1990. Experiencer and other oblique subjects in Hindi. In *Experiencer subjects in South Asian languages*, ed. M. Verma and K. P. Mohanan, 59–75. Stanford, Calif.: CSLI.
Kageyama, T. 1978. On identifying grammatical relations. *Gengo Kenkyu* 73, 43–61.
Kageyama, T. 1982. Word formation in Japanese. *Lingua* 57, 215–258.
Kageyama, T. 1993. *Bumpoo to gokeisei [Grammar and word formation]*. Tokyo: Hituzi Syobo.
Kalmár, I. 1979. The antipassive and grammatical relations in Eskimo. In *Ergativity: Towards a theory of grammatical relations*, ed. F. Plank, 117–143. New York: Academic Press.
Katada, F. 1991. The LF representation of anaphors. *Linguistic Inquiry* 22, 287–313.
Kato, Y. 1985. *Negative sentences in Japanese*. Sophia Linguistica 19. Tokyo: Sophia University.
Katz, J., and T. Bever. 1976. The fall and rise of empiricism. In *An integrated theory of linguistic ability*, ed. T. Bever et al., 11–30. New York: Thomas Y. Crowell.
Katz, J., and P. Postal. 1964. *An integrated theory of linguistic descriptions*. Cambridge, Mass.: MIT Press.
Kayne, R. 1984. *Connectedness and binary branching*. Dordrecht: Foris.
Kayne, R. 1994. *The antisymmetry of syntax*. Cambridge, Mass.: MIT Press.
Kayne, R. 1996. Microparametric syntax: Some introductory remarks. In *Microparametric syntax and dialect variation*, ed. J. R. Black and V. Motapanyane, ix–xviii. Philadelphia: John Benjamins.
Kayne, R., and J.-Y. Pollock. 1978. Stylistic inversion, successive cyclicity, and move NP in French. *Linguistic Inquiry* 9, 595–621.
Keach, C., and M. Rochemont. 1992. On the syntax of possessor raising in Swahili. *Studies in African Linguistics* 23, 81–106.
Keenan, E. 1974. The functional principles: Generalizing the notion of "subject of," In *Proceedings of CLS* 10, 298–309.
Keenan, E. 1975. Some universals of passive in relational grammar. In *Proceedings of CLS* 11, 340–352.
Keenan, E. 1976a. Remarkable subjects in Malagasy. In *Subject and topic*, ed. C. Li, 247–301. New York: Academic Press.
Keenan, E. 1976b. Towards a universal definition of "subject," In *Subject and topic*, ed. C. Li, 303–333. New York: Academic Press.
Keenan, E. 1985. Passive in the world's languages. In *Language typology and syntactic description*, vol. 1: *Clause Structure*. ed. T. Shopen, 243–281. Cambridge: Cambridge University Press.
Keenan, E. 1987. *Universal grammar: 15 essays*. London: Croom Helm.

Kemenade, A. van. 1987. *Syntactic case and morphological case in the history of English*. Dordrecht: Foris.
Kepping, K. B. 1979. Elements of ergativity and nominativity in Tangut. In *Ergativity: Towards a theory of grammatical relations*, ed. F. Plank, 263–2289. New York: Academic Press.
Kibrik, A. E. 1979. Canonical ergativity and Daghestan languages. In *Ergativity: Towards a theory of grammatical relations*, ed. F. Plank, 61–78. New York: Academic Press.
Kibrik, A. E. 1985. Toward a typology of ergativity. In *Grammar inside and outside the clause*, ed. J. Nichols and A. Woodbury, 268–323. Cambridge: Cambridge University Press.
Kikuchi, A., and D. Takahashi. 1991. Agreement and small clauses. In *Topics in small clauses*, ed. H. Nakajima and S. Tonoike, 75–105. Tokyo: Kurosio.
Kim, H. 1996. Subjecthood in impersonal constructions in Early English. In *Proceedings of CLS 32: The main session*, 165–178.
Kim, Y.-J. 1990. The syntax and semantics of Korean case: The interpretation between lexical and semantic levels of representation. Ph.D. dissertation, Harvard University.
Kimenyi, A. 1980. *A relational grammar of Kinyarwanda*. Berkeley: University of California Press.
Kimenyi, A. 1988. Passives in Kinyarwanda. In *Passive and voice*, ed. M. Shibatani, 355–386. Philadelphia: John Benjamins.
King, T. H. 1994. SpecAgrP and Case: Evidence from Georgian. In *The morphology-syntax connection: MIT working papers in linguistics* 22, 91–110. Cambridge, Mass.: MITWPL.
Kinyalolo, K. 1991. Syntactic dependencies and the SPEC-head agreement hypothesis in KiLega. Ph.D. dissertation, UCLA.
Kishimoto, H. 1996. Agr and agreement in Japanese. In *Proceedings of FSJL 2: MIT working papers in linguistics* 29, 41–60. Cambridge, Mass.: MITWPL.
Kisseberth, C., and Mohannad Imam Abasheikh. 1977. The object relationship in Chi-Mwi:-ni, a Bantu language. In *Syntax and semantics*, vol. 8, ed. P. Cole and J. Sadock, 179–218. New York: Academic Press.
Kitagawa, Y., and S.-Y. Kuroda. 1992. Passive in Japanese. Ms., University of Rochester, NY, and UC, San Diego.
Kitahara, H. 1994. Target a: A unified theory of movement and structure building. Ph.D. dissertation, Harvard University.
Kitahara, H. 1996. Raising quantifiers without quantifier raising. In *Minimal ideas*, ed. W. Abraham et al., 189–198. Philadelphia: John Benjamins.
Klaiman, M. H. 1981. *Volitionality and subject in Bengali*. Bloomington, Ind.: IULC.
Klaiman, M. H. 1989. Inverse voice and head-marking in Tanoan languages. In *Proceedings of CLS* 25, 258–271.
Klaiman, M. H. 1991. *Grammatical voice*. Cambridge: Cambridge University Press.
Klaiman, M. H. 1993. The relationship of inverse voice and head-marking in Arizona Tewa and other Tanoan languages. *Studies in Language* 17, 3–370.
Knecht, L. E. 1986. Subject and object in Turkish. Ph.D. dissertation, MIT.
Koizumi, M. 1993. Object agreement phrases and the split VP-hypothesis. In *Papers on Case & agreement I: MIT working paper in linguistics* 18, 99–148. Cambridge, Mass.: MITWPL.
Koizumi, M. 1994a. Layered specifiers. In *Proceedings of NELS* 24, 255–269. Amherst, Mass.: GLSA.
Koizumi, M. 1994b. Nominative objects: The role of TP in Japanese. In *Proceedings of FAJL 1: MIT working papers in linguistics* 24, 211–230. Cambridge, Mass.: MITWPL.

References

Koizumi, M. 1995. Phrase structure in minimalist syntax. Ph.D. dissertation, MIT.

Kondrashova, N. 1993. Dative subjects in Russian. In *Proceedings of FLSM* 4, 200–219. Department of Linguistics, University of Iowa.

Koopman, H., and D. Sportiche. 1991. The position of subjects. *Lingua* 85, 211–258.

Koster, J. 1978. *Locality principles in syntax.* Dordrecht: Foris.

Kubo, M. 1992. Japanese syntactic stuctures and their constructional meanings. Ph.D. dissertation, MIT.

Kuno, S. 1973. *The structure of the Japanese language.* Cambridge, Mass.: MIT Press.

Kuroda, S.-Y. 1965. Generative grammatical studies in the Japanese language. Ph.D. dissertation, MIT.

Kuroda, S.-Y. 1983. What can Japanese say about government and binding? In *Proceedings of WCCFL* 2, 153–164. Stanford, Calif.: SLA.

Kuroda, S.-Y. 1986. Movement of noun phrases in Japanese. In *Issues in Japanese linguistics*, ed. T. Imai and M. Saito, 229–271. Dordrecht: Foris.

Laka, I. 1993. Unergatives that assign ergative, unaccusatives that assign accusative. In *Papers on Case & agreement I: MIT working papers in linguistics* 18, 149–172. Cambridge, Mass.: MITWPL.

Langacker, R. 1976. *Non-distinct arguments in Uto-Aztecan.* Berkeley: University of California Press.

Larsen, T. W. 1987. The syntactic status of ergativity in Quiché. *Lingua* 71, 33–59.

Larson, R. 1988. On the double object construction. *Linguistic Inquiry* 19, 335–391.

Lasnik, H. 1988. Subjects and the θ-criterion. *Natural Language & Linguistic Theory* 6, 1–17.

Lasnik, H. 1992. Two notes on control and binding. In *Control and grammar*, ed. R. Larson et al., 235–252. Dordrecht: Kluwer.

Lasnik, H. 1993. *Lectures on minimalist syntax.* UConn occasional papers in linguistics no. 1, Cambridge, Mass.: MITWPL.

Lasnik, H., and M. Saito. 1992. *Move a.* Cambridge, Mass.: MIT Press.

Law, P., and T. Veenstra. 1992. On empty operators in serial verb constructions. In *MIT working papers in linguistics* 17, 183–203. Cambridge, Mass.: MITWPL.

Lederer, H. 1969. *Reference grammar of the German language.* New York: Scribner's.

Lee, E.-J. 1992. On the extended projection principle. Ph.D. dissertation, University of Connecticut.

Lee, R. 1995. Economy of representation. Ph.D. dissertation, University of Connecticut.

Lee, Y.-S. 1993. Scrambling as Case-driven obligatory movement. Ph.D. dissertation, UPenn, Philadelphia.

Lefebvre, C., and P. Muysken. 1982. Raising as Move Case. *The Linguistic Review* 2, 161–210.

Lefebvre, C., and P. Muysken. 1988. *Mixed categories: Nominalizations in Quechua.* Dordrecht: Kluwer.

Legendre, G. 1995. Causee prominence constraints in French and elsewhere. In *Grammatical relations: Theoretical approaches to empirical questions*, ed. C. Burgess et al., 291–308. Stanford, Calif.: CSLI.

Lehmann, T. 1993. *A grammar of Modern Tamil.* Pondicherry, India: Pondicherry Institute of Linguistics and Culture.

Levin, B. 1983. On the nature of ergativity. Ph.D. dissertation, MIT.

Levin, B., and M. Rappaport. 1986. The formation of adjectival passives. *Linguistic Inquiry* 17, 623–661.

Levin, B., and M. Rappaport Hovav. 1995. *Unaccusativity.* Cambridge, Mass.: MIT Press.

Levin, J., and D. Massam. 1985. Surface ergativity: Case/theta relations reexamined. In *Proceedings of NELS* 15, 286–301.

Levin, L. 1985a. Identifying non-nominative subjects in LFG. In *Proceedings of ESCOL '85*, 313–324. Ithaca, N.Y.: DMLL Publications.

Levin, L. 1985b. Operations in lexical forms: Unaccusative rules in Germanic languages. Ph.D. dissertation, MIT.

Levin, L., and J. Simpson. 1981. Quirky case and lexical representations of Icelandic verbs. In *Proceedings of CLS* 17, 185–196.

Li, C. N., and R. Lang. 1979. The syntactic irrelevance of an ergative case in Enga and other Papuan languages. In *Ergativity: Towards a theory of grammatical relations*, ed. F. Plank, 307–324. New York: Academic Press.

Lightfoot, D. 1979. *Principles of diachronic syntax*. Cambridge: Cambridge University Press.

Lightfoot, D. 1991. *How to set parameters*. Cambridge, Mass.: MIT Press.

Lin, Z.-y. 1985. Some advancement phenomena in Mandarin Chinese: The enlightment from relational grammar. In *Proceedings of ESCOL '85*, 144–155. Ithaca, N.Y.: DMLL Publications.

Lockwood, W. B. 1977. *An introduction to Modern Faroese*. Tórshavn: Føroya Skúlabókagrunnur.

Lyle, J. 1995. Split ergativity and NP-movement. In *Proceedings of WCCFL* 14, 587–601.

Mahajan, A. 1989. Agreement and agreement phrases. In *MIT working papers in linguistics* 10, 217–252. Cambridge, Mass.: MITWPL.

Mahajan, A. 1990. The A/A-bar distinction and movement theory. Ph.D. dissertation, MIT.

Mahajan, A. 1994. The ergative parameter: Have-be alternation, word order, and split ergativity. In *Proceedings of NELS* 24, 317–331. Amherst, Mass.: GSLA.

Mahajan, A. 1995. ACTIVE passives. In *Proceedings of WCCFL* 13, 286–301. Stanford, Calif.: SLA.

Mahajan, A. 1996. Universal grammar and the typology of ergative languages. In *Universal Grammar and typological variation*, ed. A. Alexiadou and T. A. Hall, 35–57. Philadelphia: John Benjamins.

Mahajan, A. To appear. Oblique subjects and Burzio's generalization. In *Burzio's generalization*, ed. E. Reuland.

Maki, H. 1995. The syntax of particles. Ph.D. dissertation, University of Connecticut.

Maling, J. 1986. Clause-bounded reflexives in Modern Icelandic. In *Topics in Scandinavian synax*, ed. L. Hellan and K. K. Christensen, 53–63. Dordrecht: Kluwer.

Manga, L. 1996. A minimalist account of accusative vs. ergative languages. In *Morphosyntax in generative grammar*, ed. H.-D. Ahn et al., 345–356. Seoul: Hankuk Publishing.

Manning, C. 1996. *Ergativity: Argument structures and grammatical relations*. Stanford, Calif.: CSLI.

Manzini, R., and K. Wexler. 1987. Parameters, binding theory, and learnability. *Linguistic Inquiry* 18, 413–444.

Marantz, A. 1981. On the nature of grammatical relations. Ph.D. dissertation, MIT.

Marantz, A. 1984. *On the nature of grammatical relations*. Cambridge, Mass.: MIT Press.

Marantz, A. 1988. Apparent exceptions to the projection principle. In *Morphology and modularity*, ed. M. Everaert et al., 217–232. Dordrecht: Foris.

Marantz, A. 1989. Relations and configurations in Georgian. Ms., University of North Carolina, Chapel Hill.

Marantz, A. 1991. Case and licensing. In *Proceednigs of ESCOL '91*, 234–253. Ithaca, N.Y.: DMLL Publications.

Marantz, A. 1995. The minimalist program. In *Government and binding theory and the minimalist program*, ed. G. Webelhuth, 349–382. Cambridge, Mass.: Blackwell.
Martin, J. 1991. The determination of grammatical relations. Ph.D. dissertation, UCLA.
Martin, R. 1992. On the distribution and Case features of PRO. Ms., University of Connecticut.
Masica, C. 1976. *Defining a linguistic area*. Chicago: University of Chicago Press.
Masullo, P. J. 1992. Quirky datives in Spanish and the non-nominative subject parameter. In *Papers from SCIL 4: MIT working papers in linguistics* 16, 89–103. Cambridge, Mass.: MITWPL.
Masullo, P. J. 1993. Two types of quirky subjects: Spanish versus Icelandic. In *Proceedings of NELS* 23, 303–317. Amherst, Mass.: GLSA.
Masunaga, K. 1983. The applied suffix in Kikuyu. In *Current approaches to African linguistics*, vol.2, ed. J. Kaye et al., 283–295.
Masunaga, K. 1988. Case deletion and discourse context. In *Japanese syntax*, ed. W. Poser, 145–156. Stanford, Calif.: CSLI.
McCarthy, J., and A. Prince. 1993. Prosodic morphology I: Constraint interaction and satisfaction. Ms., University of Massachusetts, Amherst, and Rutgers University.
McCawley, J. 1988. *The syntactic phenomena in English*. Chicago: University of Chicago Press.
McClosky, J. 1996. Subjecthood and subject positions. In *The syntax of the Celtic languages*, ed. R. Borsley and I. Roberts, 241–283. Cambridge: Cambridge University Press.
McDonough, J. 1990. Topics in the phonology and morphology of Navajo verbs. Ph.D. dissertation, University of Massachusetts, Amherst.
McGinnis, M. 1995. Fission as feature-movement. In *Papers on minimalist syntax: MIT working papers in linguistics* 27, 165–187. Cambridge, Mass.: MITWPL.
McGinnis, M. To appear. Projection and position: Evidence from Georgian. In *Proceedings of ConSole* 4.
Meeussen, A. E. 1971. Relative clauses in Bantu. *Studies in African Linguistics, Suppliment* 2, 3–10.
Mel'čuk, I. 1992. Toward a logical analysis of the notion "ergative construction," *Studies in Language* 16, 91–138.
Miyagawa, S. 1989. *Structure and case marking in Japanese: Syntax and semantics*, vol. 22. New York: Academic Press.
Miyagawa, S. 1993. LF Case checking and minimal link condition. In *Papers on Case & agreement II: MIT working papers in linguistics* 19, 213–254.
Miyagawa, S. 1996. Word order restrictions and nonconfigurationality. In *Formal approaches to Japanese linguistics 2: MIT working papers in linguistics* 29, 117–141.
Miyagawa, S. 1997. Against optional scrambling. *Linguistics Inquiry* 28, 1–25.
Mohanan, K. P. 1982. Grammatical relations and clause structure in Malayalam. In *The mental representation of grammatical relations*, ed. J. Bresnan, 504–589. Cambridge, Mass.: MIT Press.
Mohanan, T. 1994. *Argument structure in Hindi*. Stanford, Calif.: CSLI.
Morikawa, M. 1993. *A parametric approach to Case alternation phenomena in Japanese*. Tokyo: Hituzi Syobo.
Morin, Y.-C., and É. Tiffou. 1988. Passive in Burushaski. In *Passive and voice*, ed. M. Shibatani, 493–524. Philadelphia: John Benjamins.
Moro, A. 1991. The raising of predicates: Copular, expletives, and existence. In *More papers on wh-movement: MIT working papers in linguistics* 15, 119–181. Cambridge, Mass.: MITWPL.
Mulder, R. 1992. *The aspectual nature of syntactic complementation*. Dordrecht: Holland Institute of Generative Grammar.

Müller, G. 1995. *A-bar syntax: A study in movement types.* Berlin: Mouton de Gruyter.

Müller-Gotama, F. 1994. *Grammatical relations: A cross-linguistic perspective on their syntax and semantics.* Berlin: Mouton de Gruyter.

Munro, P., and L. Gordon. 1982. Syntactic relations in Western Muskogean: A typological perspective. *Language* 58, 81–115.

Murasugi, K. 1992. Crossing and nested paths: NP movement in accusative and ergative languages. Ph.D. dissertation, MIT.

Murasugi, K. 1994. A constraint on the feature-specification on Agr. In *The morphology-syntax connection: MIT working papers in linguistics* 22. 131–152.

Murasugi, K. 1995. Lexical case and NP raising. In *Grammatical relations: Theoretical approaches to empirical questions*, ed. C. Burgess et al., 309–320. Stanford, Calif.: CSLI.

Muysken, P. 1982. Parametrizing the notion "head." *Journal of Linguistic Research* 2, 57–75.

Myers, S. 1987. Tone and the structure of words in Shona. Ph.D. dissertation, University of Massachusetts, Amherst.

Nash, L. 1994. On BE and HAVE in Georgian. In *The morphlogy-syntax connection: MIT working papers in linguistics* 22, 153–171. Cambridge, Mass.: MITWPL.

Nash, L. 1996, The internal ergative subject hypothesis. In *Proceedings of NELS* 26, 195–209. Amherst, Mass.: GLSA.

Ndayiragije, J. 1996. Case checking and OVS in Kirundi. In *Configurations: Essays on structure and interpretation*, ed. A.-M. di Sciullo, 267–292. Somerville, Mass.: Cascadilla Press.

Nebel, A. 1947. *A Dinka grammar.* Verona: Museum Combonianum 2.

Neeleman, A. 1994. Scrambling as a D-structure phenomenon. In *Studies on scrambling*, ed. N. Corbert and H. van Riemsdijk, 387–429. Berlin: Mouton de Gruyter.

Nemoto, N. 1993. Chains and Case positions: A study from scrambling in Japanese. Ph.D. dissertation, University of Connecticut.

Nerbonne, J. 1982. Some passives not characterized by universal rules: Subjectless impersonals. In *Grammatical relations and relational grammar: Working papers in linguistics* 26, ed. B. Joseph, 59–92. Columbus: Ohio State University.

Nichols, J. 1993. Ergative and linguistic geography. *Australian Journal of Linguistics* 13, 39–89.

Nichols, L. 1995. Referential hierarchies and c-command in Northern Tiwa. Ms., Harvard University.

Nishigauchi, T. 1993. Long distance passive. In *Japanese syntax in comparative grammar*, ed. N. Hasegawa, 79–114. Tokyo: Kuroshio.

Noonan, M. 1981. Lango syntax. Ph.D. dissertation, UCLA.

Noonan, M. 1992. *A grammar of Lango.* Berlin: Mouton de Gruyter.

Noonan, M., and E. Bavin Woock. 1978. The passive analog in Lango. In *Proceedings of BLS* 4, 128–139. Berkeley, Calif.: BLS.

Noonan, M., and E. Bavin. 1981. Parataxis in Lango. *Studies in African Linguistics* 12, 45–69.

O'Connor, M. C. 1992. *Topics in Northern Pomo grammar.* New York: Garland.

Oehrle, R. 1976. The grammatical status of the English dative alternation. Ph.D. dissertation, MIT.

O'Grady, W. 1991. *Categories and case.* Philadelphia: John Benjamins.

Oka, T. 1993a. Minimalism in syntactic derivation. Ph.D. dissertation, MIT.

Oka, T. 1993b. Shallowness. In *Papers on Case & agreement II: MIT working papers in linguistics* 19, 255–320. Cambridge, Mass.: MITWPL.

Oka, T. 1995. Fewest steps and island sensitivity. In *Papers on minimalist syntax: MIT working papers in linguistics* 27, 189–208. Cambridge, Mass.: MITWPL.

Okutsu, K.-I. 1978. *"Boku-wa unagi-da" no bumpoo [The grammar of "boku-wa unagi-da"]*. Tokyo: Kurosio.

Onions, C. T. 1905. *Modern English syntax*. London: Routledge and Kegan Paul.

Ortiz de Urbina, J. 1989. *Parameters in the grammar of Basque*. Dordrecht: Foris.

Ostler, N. 1979. Case linking: A theory of case and verb diathesis applied to Classical Sanskrit. Ph.D. dissertation, MIT.

Ouhalla, J. 1991. *Functional categories and parametric variation*. London: Routledge.

Owens, J. 1985. *A grammar of Harar Omoro*. Hamburg: Buske.

Palmer, F. R. 1994. *Grammatical roles and relations*. Cambridge: Cambridge University Press.

Pandharipande, R. 1990. Experiencer (dative) NPs in Marathi. In *Experiencer subjects in South Asian languages*, ed. M. Verma and K. P. Mohanan, 161–179. Stanford, Calif.: CSLI.

Park, Y.-M. 1991. Head movement: Inflectional morphology and complex predicates in Korean. Ph.D. dissertation, University of Wisconsin, Madison.

Partee, B. H. 1965. Subject and object in Modern English. Ph.D. dissertation, MIT.

Payne, D. 1993. The Tupí-Guaraní inverse. In *Voice: Form and function*, ed. B. Fox and P. Hopper, 313–340. Philadelphia: John Benjamins.

Payne, T. 1982. Role and reference related subject properties and ergativity in Yup'ik Eskimo and Ragalog. *Studies in Language* 6, 75–106.

Perkins, E. T. 1978. The role of word order and scope in the interpretation of Navajo sentences. Ph.D. dissertation, University of Arizona. Tucson.

Perlmutter, D. 1978. Impersonal passives and the unaccusative hypothesis. In *Proceedings of BLS* 4, 157–189. Berkeley, Calif.: BLS.

Perlmutter, D. 1982. Syntactic representation, syntactic levels, and the notion of subject. In *The nature of syntactic representation*, ed. P. Jacobson and G. Pullum, 283–340. Dordrecht: Reidel.

Perlmutter, D. 1983. Personal vs. impersonal constructions. *Natural Language & Linguistic Theory* 1, 141–200.

Perlmutter, D. 1984. Working 1s and inversion in Italian, Japanese, and Quechua. In *Studies in relational grammar*, vol. 2, ed. D. Perlmutter and C. Rosen, 292–330. Chicago: University of Chicago Press.

Perlmutter, D., and P. Postal. 1983. Toward a universal characterization of passivization. In *Studies in relational grammar*, vol. 1, ed. D. Perlmutter, 3–29. Chicago: University of Chicago Press.

Perlmutter, D., and P. Postal. 1984. Impersonal passives and some relational laws. In *Studies in relational grammar*, vol. 2, ed. D. Perlmutter and C. Rosen, 126–170. Chicago: University of Chicago Press.

Pesetsky, D. 1995. *Zero syntax*. Cambridge, Mass.: MIT Press.

Phillips, C. 1993. Conditions on agreement in Yimas. In *Papers on Case & agreement I: MIT working papers in linguistics* 18, 173–213. Cambridge, Mass.: MITWPL.

Phillips, C. 1995. Ergative subjects. In *Grammatical relations: Theoretical approaches to empirical questions*, ed. C. Burgess et al., 341–357. Stanford, Calif.: CSLI.

Polinsky, M. 1993. Subject inversion and intransitive subject incorporation. In *Proceedings of CLS* 29, 343–361.

Pollock, J.-Y. 1989. Verb-movement, Universal Grammar, and the structure of IP, *Linguistic Inquiry* 20, 356–424.

Poole, G. 1996. Transformations across components. Ph.D. dissertation, Harvard University.

Postal, P. 1971. *Crossover phenomena*. New York: Holt, Rinehart and Winston.

Postal, P. 1977. Antipassive in French. *Linguisticæ Investigationes* 1, 333–374.

Postal. P. 1986. *Studies on passive clauses*. Albany: SUNY Press.

Postal, P. 1990. Some unexpected English restrictions. In *Grammatical relations: A cross-theoretical perspective*, ed. K. Dziwirek et al., 365–385. Stanford, Calif.: CSLI.

Preslar, R. M. 1994. The syntax of Russian impersonal sentences. Ph.D. dissertation, University of Washington.

Prince, A., and P. Smolensky. 1993. *Optimality theory: Constraint interaction in generative grammar*. Ms., Rutgers University, and University of Colorado, Boulder.

Quirk, R., S. Greenbaum, G. Leech, and J. Svartvik. 1985. *A comprehensive grammar of the English language*. London: Longman.

Rappaport, G. 1986. On anaphor binding in Russian. *Natural Language & Linguistic Theory* 4, 97–120.

Reinhart, T. 1995. Quantifier scope. Ms., Utrecht University.

Rhodes, R. 1990. Ojibwa secondary objects. In *Grammatical relations*, ed. K. Dziwirek et al., 401–414. Stanford, Calif.: CSLI.

Rhodes, R. 1994. Agency, inversion, and thematic alignment in Ojibwe. In *Proceedings of BLS* 20, 431–447.

Rizzi, L. 1990. *Relativized minimality*. Cambridge, Mass.: MIT Press.

Roberts, I. 1986. *The representation of implicit and dethematized subjects*. Dordrecht: Foris.

Rochemont, M., and P. Culicover. 1990. *English focus constructions and the theory of grammar*. Cambridge: Cambridge University Press.

Rögnvaldsson, E. 1986. Some comments on reflexivization in Icelandic. In *Topics in Scandinavian synax*, ed. L. Hellan and K. K. Christensen, 89–102. Dordrecht: Kluwer.

Rohrbacher, B. 1994. The Germanic VO languages and the full paragigm: A theory of V to I raising. Ph.D. dissertation, University of Massachusetts, Amherst.

Rosenbaum, P. 1967. *The grammar of English predicate complement constructions*. Cambridge, Mass.: MIT Press.

Rothstein, S. 1987. Three forms of English *Be*. In *MIT working papers in linguistics* 9, 225–238. Cambridge, Mass.: MITWPL.

Rude, N. 1982. Promotion and topicality of Nez Perce objects. In *Proceedings of BLS* 8, 463–483.

Rude, N. 1988. Ergative, passive, and antipassive in Nez Perce: A discourse perspective. In *Passive and voice*, ed. M. Shibatani, 547–560. Philadelphia: John Benjamins.

Rudin, C. 1988. On multiple questions and multiple wh fronting. *Natural Language & Linguistic Theory* 6, 445–501.

Rugemalira, J. 1993. Bantu multiple "object" constructions. *Linguistic Analysis* 23, 226–252.

Sadakane, K., and M. Koizumi. 1995. On the nature of the "dative" particle *ni* in Japanese. *Linguistics* 33, 5–33.

Safir, K. 1984. Missing subjects in German. In *Studies in German grammar*, ed. J. Torman, 193–229. Dordrecht: Foris.

Safir, K. 1985. *Syntactic chains*. Cambridge: Cambridge University Press.

Saito, M. 1982. Case-marking in Japanese: A preliminary study. Ms., MIT.

Saito, M. 1983. Case and government in Japanese. In *Proceedings of WCCFL* 2, 247–259. Stanford, Calif: SLA.

Saito, M. 1985. Some asymmetries in Japanese and their theoretical implications. Ph.D. dissertation, MIT.

Saito, M. 1989. Scrambling as semantically vacuous A'-movement. In *Alternative conceptions of phrase strutcure*, ed. M. Baker and A. Kroch, 182–200. Chicago: University of Chicago Press.

Saito, M. 1992. Long distance scrambling in Japanese. *Journal of East Asian Linguistics* 1, 69–118.

Saito, M. 1994. Improper adjunction. In *Formal approaches to Japanese linguistics 1: MIT working papers in linguistics* 24, 263–293. Cambridge, Mass.: MITWPL.

Sakaguchi, M. 1990. Control structures in Japanese. In *Proceedings of Japanese/Korean linguistics* 1, 303–317. Stanford, Calif.: CSLI.

Sapir, E., and H. Hoijer. 1967. *The phonology and morphology in the Navajo language*. Berkeley: University of California Press.

Sarma, V. 1994. [Title unknown], Syntax generals paper, MIT.

Schachter, P. 1976. The subject in Philippine languages: Topic, actor, acto-rtopic, or none of the above? In *Subject and topic*, ed. C. Li, 491–518. New York: Academic Press.

Schachter, P. 1977. Reference-related and role-related properties of subjects. In *Grammatical relations: Syntax and semantics*, vol. 8, ed. P. Cole and J. Sadock, 279–306. New York: Academic Press.

Schachter, P. 1992. Comments on Bresnan and Kanerva's "locative inversion in Chichewa: A case study of factorization in grammar". In *Syntax and lexicon: Syntax and semantics*, vol. 26, ed. T. Stowell and E. Wehrli, 103–110. New York: Academic Press.

Schütze, C. 1993. Towards a minimalist account of quirky case and licensing in Icelandic. In *Papers on Case and agreement II: MIT working papers in linguistics* 19, 321–375. Cambridge, Mass.: MITWPL.

Schütze, C. 1996. A note on Ura 1996 and the analysis of Icelandic. Ms., MIT.

Shayne, J.-A. 1982. Some semantic aspects of *Yi-* and *Bi-* in San Carlos Apache. In *Studies in transitivity: Syntax and semantics*, vol. 15, ed. P. Hopper and S. Thompson, 379–407. New York: Academic Press.

Shibatani, M. 1977. Grammatical relations and surface cases. *Language* 53, 789–809.

Shibatani, M. 1978. *Nihongo-no bunseki [Analyses of Japanese]*. Tokyo: Taisyukan.

Shibatani, M. ed. 1988. *Passives and voice*. Philadelphia: John Benjamins.

Shibatani, M., and T. Bynon. 1995. Approaches to language typology: A conspectus. In *Approaches to language typology*, ed. M. Shibatani and T. Bynon, 1–25. Oxford: Oxford University Press.

Shibatani, M., and E. G. Cotton. 1976. Remarks on double-nominative sentences. *Papers in Japanese Linguistics* 5, 261–277.

Shukla, S. 1981. *Bhojpuri grammar*. Washington, D.C.: Georgetown University Press.

Siewierska, A. 1984. *The passive: A comparative linguistic analysis*. London: Croom Helm.

Sigurðsson, H. A. 1989. Verbal syntax and case in Icelandic: In a comparative GB approach. Ph.D. dissertation, University of Lund.

Silverstein, M. 1976. Hierarchy of features and ergativity. In *Grammatical categories in Australian languages*, ed. R. M. W. Dixon, 112–171. Canberra: Australian Institute of Aboriginal Studies.

Simpson, J. 1991. *Warlpiri morpho-syntax*. Dordrecht: Kluwer.

Smirnova, M. 1982. *The Hausa language*. London: Routledge.

Smith, H. 1994. 'Dative sickness' in Germanic. *Natural Language & Linguistic Theory* 12, 675–736.

Smith, N. 1987. Universals and typology. In *Noam Chomsky: Consensus and controversy*, ed. S. Modgil and C. Modgil, 57–66. New York: Falmer Press.

Sobin, N. 1985. Case assignment in Ukranian morphological passive constructions. *Linguistic Inquiry* 16, 649–662.

Sohn, H.-M. 1994. *Korean*. London: Routledge.

Speas, M. 1990. *Phrase structure in natural language*. Dordrecht: Kluwer.

Sportiche, D. 1988. A theory of floating quantifiers and its corollaries for constituent structure. *Linguistic Inquiry* 19, 425–449.
Sprouse, R. 1989. On the syntax of the double object construction in selected Germanic languages. Ph.D. dissertation, Princeton University.
Sridhar, S. N. 1976. Dative subjects. In *Proceedings of CLS* 12, 582–593.
Sridhar, S. N. 1979. Dative subjects and the notion of subject. *Lingua* 49, 99–125.
Stowell, T. 1981. Origins of phrase structure. Ph.D. dissertation, MIT.
Stowell, T. 1988. As *so*, not so *as*. Ms., UCLA.
Stowell, T. 1989. Subjects, specifiers, and X-bar theory. In *Alternative conceptions of phrase structure*, ed. M. Baltin and A. Kroch, 232–262. Chicago: University of Chicago Press.
Sugioka, Y. 1985. *Interaction of derivational morphology and syntax in Japanese and English*. New York: Garland.
Sylla, Y. 1979. Grammatical relations and Fula syntax. Ph.D. dissertation, UCLA.
Tada, H. 1992. Nominative objects in Japanese. *Journal of Japanese Linguistics* 14, 91–108.
Tada, H. 1993. A/A-bar partition in derivation. Ph.D. dissertation, MIT.
Takahashi, D. 1994. Minimality of movement. Ph.D. dissertation, University of Connecticut.
Takahashi, D. 1995. Move-F and null operator movement. Ms., Tohoku University, Sendai, Japan.
Takahashi, D. 1997. On feature movement. Talk presented at Kanda University of International Studies.
Takano, Y. 1994. Scrambling, relativized minimality, and economy of derivation. In *Proceedings of WCCFL* 13, 385–399. Stanford, Calif.: CSLI.
Takano, Y. 1996. Movement and parametric variation in syntax. Ph.D. dissertation, University of California, Irvine.
Takezawa, K. 1987. A configurational approach to Japanese Case-marking. Ph.D. dissertation, University of Washington.
Taraldsen, T. 1995. On agreement and nominative objects in Icelandic. In *Studies in comparative Germanic syntax*, ed. H. Haider et al., 307–327. Dordrecht: Kluwer.
Tateishi, K. 1991. The syntax of "subjects". Ph.D. dissertation, University of Massachusetts, Amherst.
Thompson, C. 1990. On the treatment of topical objects in Chepang: Passive or inverse? *Studies in Language* 14, 405–427.
Thompson, C. 1994. Passives and inverse constructions. In *Voice and inversion*, ed. T. Givón, 47–63. Philadelphia: John Benjamins.
Thráinsson, H. 1976/1990. A semantic reflexive in Icelandic. In *Modern Icelandic syntax: Syntax and semantics*, vol. 24, ed. J. Maling and A. Zaenen, 289–307. New York Academic Press.
Thráinsson, H. 1979. *On complementation in Icelandic*. New York: Garland.
Tiersma, P. 1985. *Frisian reference grammar*. Dordrecht: Foris.
Tonoike, S. 1979. Complementation and case particles in Japanese. Ph.D. dissertation, University of Hawaii, Honolulu.
Toribio, A. J. 1990. Specifier-head agreement in Japanese. In *Proceedings of WCCFL* 9, 535–548. Stanford, Calif.: SLA.
Toribio, A. J. 1993. Lexical subjects in finite and non-finite clauses. In *Cornell working papers in linguistics* 11, 149–178. Ithaca, N.Y.: DMLL Publications.
Trithart, M. L. 1977. *Relational grammar and Chichewa subjectivization rules*. Bloomington, Ind.: IULC.
Trubetzkoy, N. S. 1939. Le rapport entre le déterminé, le déterminant et le défini. In *Mélanges de linguistique offerts à Charles Bally*, 45–88. Geneva: Georg et Cie.

Tsai, W.-T. D. 1994. On economizing the theory of A-bar dependencies. Ph.D. dissertation, MIT.
Tsunoda, T. 1981. Split case-marking patterns in verb-types and tense/aspect/mood. *Linguistics* 19, 389–438.
Tsunoda, T. 1988. Antipassives in Warrungu and other Australian languages. In *Passive and voice*, ed. M. Shibatani, 595–649. Philadelphia: John Benjamins.
Uchibori, A. 1994. Case checking and quirky Case in the "dative subject construction". Ms., University of Connecticut.
Uchibori, A. 1996. Some asymmetries in the reconstruction effect on anaphora. In *Minimal working papers: UConn working papers in linguistics* 5, 81–115.
Ueda, M. 1990. Japanese phrase structure and parameter setting. Ph.D. dissertation, University of Massachusetts, Amherst.
Ueda, M. To appear. Notes on the derivative chain CH_{FF}. In *Studies in English Linguistics: For Akira Ota*. Tokyo: Taishukan.
Ura, H. 1993a. L-relatedness and its parametric variation. In *Papers on Case and agreement II: MIT working papers in linguistics* 19, 377–399. Cambridge, Mass.: MITWPL.
Ura, H. 1993b. On feature-checking for *wh*-traces. In *Papers on Case & agreement I: MIT working papers in linguistics* 18, 243–280. Cambridge, Mass.: MITWPL.
Ura, H. 1993c. Superraising and the feature-based X-bar theory. Ms., MIT.
Ura, H. 1994a. Hyper-raising and the theory of *pro*. In *Proceedings of SCIL 6: MIT working papers in linguistics* 23, 297–316. Cambridge, Mass.: MITWPL.
Ura, H. 1994b. On the economy condition on derivation: A preliminary sketch. In *Current topics in English and Japanese*, ed. Masaru Nakamura, 313–340. Tokyo: Hituzi Syobo.
Ura, H. 1994c. A parametric approach to the typological variation of the double object construction. Ms., MIT.
Ura, H. 1994d. A short note on Move-*F*. Ms., MIT.
Ura, H. 1994e. *Varieties of raising and the feature-based bare phrase structure theory.* MIT occasional papers in linguistics 7. Cambridge, Mass.: MITWPL.
Ura, H. 1995a. Acquisition of strong features in Child Japanese. Ms., MIT.
Ura, H. 1995b. Impersonal passive, anti-impersonal passive, and the theory of multiple feature-checking. Ms., MIT.
Ura, H. 1995c. Towards a "strictly derivational" economy condition. In *Papers on minimalist syntax: MIT working papers in linguistics* 27, 243–267. Cambridge, Mass.: MITWPL.
Ura, H. 1996a. Feature movement and minimality. Paper read at the 14th National Conference of the English Linguistic Society of Japan, Kwansei Gakuin University, Nishinomiya, Japan.
Ura, H. 1996b. Multiple feature-checking: A theory of grammatical function splitting. Ph.D. dissertation, MIT.
Ura, H. 1996c. On the structure of "double objects" and certain differences between British and American English. *Studies in English Literature* 72, 269–285.
Ura, H. 1997a. Conceptual/mathematical foundations of strictly local economy. Paper read at the 69th Annual Meeting of the English Literary Society of Japan, Miyagi Gakuin Women's College, Sendai, Japan.
Ura, H. 1997b. Procrastinate, Checking, and local economy. Ms., Osaka University.
Ura, H. 1997c. *Studies on raising*. Ms., Osaka University.
Ura, H. To appear a. Case. In *The handbook of syntactic theory*, ed. M. Baltin and C. Collins. Oxford: Basil Blackwell.
Ura, H. To appear b. Economy, equidistance, and the checking theory without Agr.

Ura, H. To appear c. Overt V-movement and acquisition of strong features in Child Japanese. In *A minimalist account of language acquisition: Functional categories and Case checking*, ed. U. Lakshmanan. Dordrecht: Kluwer.

Van Valin, R. 1977. Ergativity and the universality of subjects. In *Proceedings of CLS* 13, 689–705.

Van Valin, R. 1980. On the distribution of passive and antipassive constructions in universal grammar. *Lingua* 50, 303–327.

Van Valin, R. 1981. Grammatical relations in ergative languages. *Studies in Language* 5, 361–394.

Van Valin, R. 1991. Another look at Icelandic case marking and grammatical relations. *Natural Language & Linguistic Theory* 9, 145–194.

Verma, M., and K. P. Mohanan, 1990. Introduction to the experiencer subject construction, In *Experiencer subjects in South Asian languages*, ed. M. Verma and K. P. Mohanan, 1–11. Stanford, Calif.: CSLI.

Vikner, S. 1989. Object shift and double objects in Danish. *Working paper in Scandinavian syntax* 44, 141–155.

Vikner, S. 1994. Scrambling object shift and West Germanic scrambling. In *Studies on scrambling*, ed. N. Corver and H. van Riemsdijk, 487–517. Berlin: Mouton de Gruyter.

Vikner, S. 1995. *Verb movement and expletive subjects in the Germanic languages*. Oxford: Oxford University Press.

Vitale, A. 1981. *Swahili syntax*. Dordrecht: Foris.

Wasow, T. 1977. Transformations and the lexicon. In *Formal syntax*, ed. P. Culicover, 327–360. New York: Academic Press.

Watanabe, A. 1992. Wh-*in-situ, subjacency, and chain formation*. MIT occasional papers in linguistics 2, Cambridge, Mass.: MITWPL.

Watanabe, A. 1993. Agr-based Case theory and its interaction with the A-bar system. Ph.D. dissertation, MIT.

Watanabe, A. 1994a. A crosslinguistic perspective on Japanese nominative-genitive conversion and its implications for Japanese syntax. In *Current topics in English and Japanese*, ed. Masaru Nakamura, 341–369. Tokyo: Hituzi Syobo.

Watanabe, A. 1994b. Locative inversion: Where unaccusativity meets minimality. Ms., University of Tokyo.

Watanabe, A. 1995a. Conceptual basis of cyclicity. In *Papers on minimalist syntax: MIT working papers in linguistics* 27, 269–291. Cambridge, Mass.: MITWPL.

Watanabe, A. 1995b. Switch reference in control: Toward a minimalist theory of control.Ms., Kanda University of International Studies, Chiba, Japan.

Watanabe, A. 1996. *Case absorption and* wh-*agreement*. Dordrecht: Kluwer.

Watanabe, A. 1997. Absorption as feature checking. Ms., Kanda University of International Studies, Chiba, Japan.

Weber, D. J. 1989. *A grammar of Huallaga (Huánuco) Quechua*. Berkeley: University of California Press.

Wennevold Silva, E. 1989. *Ergativity and VSO word order: A configurational analysis*. University of Trondheim working papers in linguistics 10.

Wilder, C., and H.-M. Gärtner. 1996. Introduction. In *The role of economy principles in linguistic theory*, ed. C. Wilder et al., 1–35. Berlin: Akademie Verlag.

Wilkinson, E. 1983. Indirect object advancement in German. In *Proceedings of BLS* 9, 281–291.

Williams, E. 1980. Predication. *Linguistic Inquiry* 11, 208–238.

Williams, E. 1981. Argument structure and morphology. *The Linguistic Review* 1, 81–114.

Williams, E. 1984. Grammatical relations. *Linguistic Inquiry* 15, 639–673.

Williams, E. 1994. *Thematic structure in synatx.* Cambridge, Mass.: MIT Press.
Woodbury, A. 1977. Greenlandic Eskimo, ergativity, and relational grammar. In *Grammatical relations: Syntax and semantics*, vol. 8, ed. P. Cole and J. Sadock, 307–336. New York: Academic Press.
Woolford, E. 1991. Two subject positions in Lango. In *Proceedings of BLS 17: Special session on African language structures*, 231–243.
Woolford, E. 1993. Symmetric and asymmetric passives. *Natural Language & Linguistic Theory* 11, 679–728.
Wyngaerd, G. V. 1989. Object shift as an A-movement rule. In *Proceedings of SCIL 1: MIT working papers in linguistics* 11, 256–271. Cambridge, Mass.: MITWPL.
Yatsushiro, K. 1996. Case, scope, and feature movement. In *Proceedings of FAJL 2: MIT working papers in linguistics* 29, 319–335. Cambridge, Mass.: MITWPL.
Yip, M., J. Maling, and R. Jackendoff. 1987. Case in tiers. *Language* 63, 217–250.
Young, R., and W. Morgan. 1987. *The Navajo language: A grammar and colloquial dictionary.* Rev. ed. Albuquerque: University of New Mexico Press.
Zaenen, A., and J. Maling. 1982. Passive and oblique case. In *Papers in lexical-functional grammar*, ed. L. Levin et al., 159–191. Bloomington, Ind.: IULC.
Zaenen, A., and J. Maling. 1984. Unaccusative, passive, and quirky case. In *Proceedings of WCCFL* 3, 317–329.
Zaenen, A., J. Maling, and H. Thráinsson. 1985. Case and grammatical functions: The Icelandic passive. *Natural Language & Linguistic Theory* 3, 441–483.
Zubizarreta, M. L. 1987. *Levels of representation in the lexicon and in the syntax.* Dordrecht: Foris.
Zushi, M. 1995. Long distance dependencies. Ph.D. dissertation, McGill University.
Zwart, J.-W. 1996. "Shortest move" versus "fewest steps." In *Minimal ideas*, ed. W. Abraham et al., 305–327. Philadelphia: John Benjamins.

Index

A-bar movement 43, 73, 74, 76
A-movement 44, 73, 74, 78, 264
Abe, J. 257, 268
Absolutive 10, 222, 226, 227
Accusative/Accusativity 88, 96, 106, 134, 140, 161, 191, 202, 242, 251
   languages 10, 180, 185, 192, 197, 201, 202–204, 206, 217, 221, 223, 228
   object 114, 123–124, 145
   particle 174
   subject 153
Active (*see* Voice)
   morpheme 56
Adverb/Adverbial 65, 238–239, 245, 260–262, 274, 277
Åfarli, T. 94, 235
Agreement 24, 180
   head-head 239
   impersonal 117, 123, 128, 150
   long-distance 132
   multiple 81
   object (*see* Object)
   Spec-head 100, 191, 239, 268
   subject (*see* Subject)
   verb 181, 189, 193, 195, 211

AGR
   -less theory 25
   -projection 18
Algonquian 40
Anderson, S. 5, 191, 202
Andrews, A. 126, 128, 129, 136
Animacy 56, 60–61
Anti-passive 224–228
Aoun, J. 113, 178, 257
Apache 55
Apachean 40, 80, 92, 197
Arabic 36
Archi 182, 196, 210, 211
Arizona Tewa 63
Athabascan 63
Attract (Attract/Move) 19, 26, 35, 202
   definition of 31, 46, 48, 58, 143, 161–162, 164, 213, 269, 270
Avoid Redefinition Condition 89

Bailyn, J. 149
Baker, M. 4, 48, 50, 88, 94, 135, 199, 220, 225, 227, 242, 248, 285
Bamgbose, A. 74
Bantu 40, 55, 142, 143–144, 156, 282
Barss, A. 257
Basque 222

Bavin Woock, E. 71–83
Belletti, A. 11, 95, 104, 148, 151, 160
Bengali 94, 151
Besten, H. den 133, 137, 139
Bhat D. N. S. 126
Bhatt R. 151
Bhojpuri 193
Bidjara 188, 219
Binding 82
Bittner, M. 39, 76, 183, 186, 190, 199, 200, 203, 211, 215, 222
Bobaljik, J. 19, 25, 27, 51–52, 72, 137, 141, 169, 200, 202–205, 216, 222, 231–234, 237, 259, 281
Bok-Bennema, R. 199, 203
Bokamba, E. 41, 45
Borer, H. 4, 55, 81, 289
Bošković, Z. 23, 168
Bouchard, D. 149
Branigan, P. 33, 64, 65, 67, 255
Bresnan, J. 157–160, 162, 163–166, 170, 235
Brody, M. 15
Broekhuis, H. 139, 141
Bures, A. 230–232
Burushaski 189, 195, 218
Burzio, L. 94, 161, 168
Burzio's generalization 208, 225, 228

Calabrese, A. 152
Cardinaletti, A. 168
Carrier-Duncan, J. 104, 160
Carstens, V. 163–164
Case
  absorption 50
  Agr-based theory 97, 204, 232, 255, 277
  Agr-less theory 97, 180, 197, 202, 205, 234, 277, 283
  Filter 268
  government-based theory 198, 199
  inherent 104, 129
  morphological 24
  particle 174, 280
  structure-based theory 194, 197, 200
  structural 143
  three-layered theory 68
Chamorro 93, 225
Checking
  as a syntactic operation 35, 89, 122, 131, 217

configuration 89
domain 16
feature- 16
multiple 14, 64, 71, 74, 79, 87, 92, 94, 95, 104, 198, 207, 209, 235, 283
word-internal 50
Cheng, L. 23
Chepang 63
Chichewa 156–165
Chickasaw 93
Cho, E. 253
Choctaw 93
Chomsky, N. 3, 4, 5, 11–23, 25, 28, 30–35, 37, 45–47, 51, 53, 63, 66, 69, 76, 79, 89–90, 110, 117, 122, 123, 129–130, 140, 143, 156, 166–170, 180, 191, 199–202, 205–206, 208, 220, 230–234, 236, 238, 241, 246, 248, 255, 270, 283, 285
Chukchee 224
C-command 19
Clark, E. 171
Cleft 73, 158–159
Closeness 19, 48
Cole, P. 83–85, 88, 152, 153
Collins, C. 15–22, 24, 34–35, 46, 64–69, 74, 89, 123, 137, 142, 156, 171, 230, 231–232, 234, 236, 269
Complete Functional Complex 30
Computational system (C_{HL}) 15
Comrie, B. 10, 30, 70, 93, 187, 193
Control 7, 10, 13, 24, 55, 63, 68, 74, 76, 79, 81–82, 99, 105, 110, 119, 123–124, 150, 158, 164, 167–168, 173, 176, 185–186, 210, 215, 273, 276, 283
Coopmans, P. 170
Copula 33–34
Cotton, E. G. 97, 104
Cowper, E. 126, 128, 130
Croft, W. 3
Culicover, P. 170
Cyclicity 116
Czech 151
Czepluch, H. 244

Danish 137, 231–232, 234, 235–245
Dative 140
  subject construction 6–8, 25, 95–155
Davison, A. 151

DeLancy, S. 10, 187
Demotion 40, 45, 49, 55, 70, 76, 84, 85, 93, 159–160, 249
Déprez, V. 53, 72, 255
Derivation 15, 34
Desiderative
  complement 272–276
  suffix 154
Dikken, D. 137, 245
Direct (*see* Voice)
Dinka (Bor Dinka) 71, 72, 81
Dixon, R. M. W. 10, 30, 39, 183, 185, 187, 189, 190–191, 215, 222
Dutch 127, 139–141, 144–145, 152, 253
Dyirbal 10, 183–186, 215, 218, 224
Dzamba 41

Economy 18, 36
  condition 4, 15, 20, 26, 27, 68, 131, 141–142, 156, 209–210, 214
  derivational/local 34–35, 68
  global 35
English 33–34, 64–68, 73, 136, 167–168, 170–171, 184, 259
  American 232, 244–248
  British 232, 244–248
  Middle 146–149, 152
  Old 127, 146–149
  Present-day 147–149
Epistemic verb 116
Epstein, S. 14
Equidistance 31, 33, 45, 48, 68, 91, 138, 156
Ergative/Ergativity 9–10, 180–229
  languages 9, 180
  morphological 9
  shallow 208–212
  split- 9, 187–191, 195–196, 211, 218–219
  syntactic 9, 212–216
Ergative Hypothesis 198–199
Escalante, F. 71
Ewe 281
Existential 171, 173–178
Experiencer (EXP)
  inversion (*see* Inversion)
  verb 95
Expletive 53, 130, 167–168, 171, 242
  null 37

transitive 169
Extended Projection Principle (EPP) 88
Extraposition 65
Falk, C. 235
Falk, Y. N. 128
Faltz, L. 235, 249
Faroese 127, 237
Feature(s)
  [±construable] 38–39, 48, 49, 55, 62, 63, 76, 82
  formal 13, 16
  movement (at LF) 47, 48, 123, 209
  strong 17, 22
Ferguson, S. 111, 213
Foley, W. 160
Fox, D. 113
Frampton, J. 19
Franks, S. 150, 151
Free-rider 123
Freeze, R. 171
Freiden, R. 130
French 168
Fried, M. 151
Frisian 253
Fukui, N. 3, 4, 33–34, 55, 268–270
Fujita, N. 259–260
Fujita, K. 257–258
Full Interpretation 17, 23

Georgian 154–155, 187–188, 222
Gerdts, D. 98
German 36, 127, 133–134, 137, 138–139, 141, 145, 168, 252
Givón, T. 41, 235, 249
Goodall, G. 94
Government 191
Grammatical function 86
  changing 9, 43, 172
  splitting 4, 5, 6–8, 11–14, 24, 40, 63, 71, 76, 93, 95, 116, 117, 145, 172, 185, 196, 205
Grammatical relation 5, 6, 11, 192, 283
Greed 19
Greenberg, G. 150
Greenberg, J. 3
Grewendorf, G. 137

Grimshaw, J. 29, 104, 148, 160
Guéron, J. 33–34

Hale, K. 8, 18, 28, 29, 39, 40, 42, 55–56, 62, 76, 81, 166, 183, 186, 190, 195, 199, 208, 220, 222, 233, 284
Harada, S.-I. 100
Harley, H. 5, 10, 12, 126, 128, 130, 132, 284
Harris, A. 154
Head-movement 19, 31, 140, 247
Heavy NP Shift 267
Heath, J. 228
Hebrew (Modern) 36
Herschensohn, J. 168
Hermon, G. 153
Hestvik, A. 94
Hewitt, B. G. 154
Heycock, C. 34
Higginbotham, J. 23
Hindi 37, 151, 222, 268
Hoekstra, T. 139, 141, 170
Hoijer, H. 56, 58
Hoji, H. 256–257
Holmberg, A. 53, 130, 142, 220, 231, 234, 235–238, 269
Holmberg's generalization 255
Hoshi, H. 272
Huang, C.-T. J. 257

Icelandic 37, 51–54, 126–139, 141, 142–143, 169, 231, 237, 269, 281
Idiom(s) 199
Impersonal
 construction 118–120, 130, 146–149, 153, 167–168
 Parameter 36–38, 106, 223
 passive (*see* Passive)
Incorporation 248
Interpretable 17, 23
Intransitive 37
Inverse 9, 21, 42, 92, 143, 160
Inverse morpheme 56
Inversion
 experiencer 35, 139–141, 152
 locative 35, 156–179
 quotative 35, 64–68
 Subject-Object 40
Inukitut 227
Italian 151–152, 168

Jackendoff, R. 29, 126, 160
Jaeggli, O. 168
Jake, J. 83–85, 152, 153
Japanese 81, 82, 95–117, 127, 152–153, 171–179, 255–280
Javanese 93
Jayaseelan, K. A. 117
Jespersen, O. 244
Johns, A. 199, 203, 232
Johnson, D. 5, 235, 249–250
Johnson, K. 48, 50, 88, 94, 225, 227, 242
Jonas, D. 18, 25, 27, 51–54, 72, 128, 169, 220, 237, 281
Jones, D. 268
Jónsson, J. 130

Kabardian 218
Kachru, Y. 151
Kageyama, T. 98, 272–273
Kalaw Lagaw Ya 219
Kanerva, J. 157–158, 160, 162, 164, 170
Kannada 117, 125–126
Kashmir 151
Katada, F. 82
Kato, Y. 114
Kayne, R. 3, 4, 277
Keenan, E. 5, 235, 249
Keyser, J. 18, 28, 29, 166, 208, 220, 233
Khinalug 182, 193
Kibrik, A. E. 211
Kikuchi, A. 115
KiLega 41, 53
Kim, Y.-J. 98
Kimenyi, A. 41–42, 45, 49, 50
Kinyalolo, K. 41, 44, 47, 49, 50, 163–164
Kinyarwanda 41, 53, 158, 160, 165, 252
Kirundi 41, 51, 52
Kishimoto, H. 171
Kitahara, H. 16, 113, 177
Kitagawa, Y. 272
Klaiman, M. H. 8, 40, 42
Koizumi, M. 20, 23, 25, 27, 79, 97, 103, 105, 112–114, 174, 231–232, 245, 255, 259, 265–266, 281
Kondrashova, N. 149
Korean 81, 96, 99–102, 104–106, 112, 116, 152, 250, 251, 253, 268
Koster, J. 139
Koyukon 63
Kubo, M. 272

Kuno, S. 97, 171, 177
Kuroda, S.-Y. 97, 272, 276, 278

Laka, I. 222, 225, 228
Lango 71–83
Lasnik, H. 3, 14, 19, 81, 110, 230, 257
Last Resort Condition 16, 19, 31, 35, 46, 58, 143, 161–162, 164, 269–270
Law, P. 74
Lee, R. 33, 268
Lee, Y. S. 268
Lefebvre, C. 83, 85
Left-dislocation (*see* Topicalization)
Lehman, T. 7, 117–118
Levin, B. 149, 170, 180, 183, 186, 198, 203, 225, 228
Levin, L. 94, 128, 130, 139–140, 170
Li, A. 113, 178, 257
Likala 41
Lingala 41
Locative, inversion 35
Lyle, J. 219

Mahajan, A. 72, 151, 219, 228, 255, 268
Maki, H. 33, 39
Mande 281
Manning, C. 191
Malagasy 252
Malay 93
Malayalam 117
Maling, J. 126, 128, 130, 136
Manning, C. 10, 199, 202
Manzini, R. 280
Mapudungun 63
Marantz, A. 4, 11, 14, 24, 39, 154, 180, 183, 198–199, 203, 222, 239
Marathi 151
Martin, J. 30, 148
Martin, R. 110
Masullo, P. J. 152
May, R. 23
McCawley, J. 244
McClosky, J. 12
McDonough, J. 56
Mchombo, S. 159, 164
McGinnis, M. 50, 154–155
Merge 16, 19, 26, 234
Minimal Link Condition 19, 31, 35, 58, 162, 270
Minimal domain 19

Miyagawa, S. 255, 258–260, 268, 276, 278, 284
Mohanan, K. P. 117
Mohanan, T. 29, 151
Modifier 65
Morikawa, M. 97, 104
Moro, A. 33–34
Moshi, L. 235
Move 16, 26, 234
Mulder, R. 170
Müller, G. 133, 137
Murasugi, K. 200–204, 206, 216
Muysken, P. 11, 83, 85
Myers, S. 163–164

Nash, L. 219
Navajo 8–9, 55–64
Ndayiragije, J. 41, 44, 45, 49, 51–52, 55
Nemoto, N. 103, 255, 258, 267, 275
Nepali 94
Nez Perce 63
Nishigauchi, T. 272–273, 276
Nominative 7, 37, 40, 46, 49, 83, 85, 88, 90, 96, 106, 115, 132, 134
 object 97, 101, 103, 112, 114, 120, 123–124, 128, 131–132
 particle 174
 subject, 145
Noonan, M. 71–83
Northern Pomo 94
Northern Tiwa 63
Norwegian 137, 232, 234, 235–245, 255, 267, 270
Numeration 15, 16, 69

Object(s)
 agreement 158–159, 163
 deletion 228
 direct (DO) 30
 double 30, 230–254
 indirect (IO) 30
 long shift 72–83
 shift 53–54, 72, 137, 144, 237–239, 255–282
 syntactic 16
Objective 146
Obligatory Case Parameter 205
Oblique 146, 226
Obviation 86
O'Grady, W. 98, 99

Oehrle, R. 244
Ojbwe 63
Oka, T. 19, 33
Old Norse 127
Optimality Theory 22
Optionality 32–35, 45, 55, 56, 110, 255, 281
Oromo 253
Ostler, N. 160
Ouhalla, J. 77, 245

Palmer, F. R. 8, 10, 40, 41, 189
Parameter 14–15, 21, 37, 54, 55, 58, 63, 66, 121, 129, 143, 144, 147, 202, 206, 211, 215–218, 225, 226, 236, 244
    head- 268
Park, Y.-M. 105
Partee, B. 5
Participial 62
Passive 42–43, 50, 70, 83, 85, 133, 137–139, 141, 159, 164, 225, 227, 234–235, 240, 243–246, 248–253, 271, 272, 275–276
    adjectival 149
    anti-impersonal 71, 79–93
    impersonal 70, 93–94
    impersonal anti- 71
    morpheme 48, 72, 88, 135, 136, 226, 242
    syntactic 149
Perlmutter, D. 5, 37, 70, 76, 93, 94, 97, 99, 118, 151, 168
Pesetsky, D. 149
Phillips, C. 183
Phrase structure, "bare" 20, 238
Pied-piping 122–123, 210
Plains Cree 63
Platzack, C. 220, 231, 234, 235–238, 269
Polinsky, M. 158
Polish 151
Pollock, J.-Y. 34, 77, 245
Possessor-raising 103, 108, 277
Postal, P. 6, 37, 70, 93, 94, 149, 228, 251
Potential
    construction 153
    suffix 97, 105, 109–116
PP-approach 3, 11, 97, 180, 193, 284
Preslar, R. M. 150
Pro 205
    -drop 49, 55

Procrastinate 18, 19, 20, 22–23, 27, 32, 48, 52, 54, 58, 138, 142, 214, 217, 236–237, 240, 242–246, 248, 256, 270, 271, 275, 280
Projection Principle 11, 12
Promotion 48–49, 63, 70, 85, 86, 89, 93, 137, 244
Pronominal 220, 248
    copy 43
Proximation 86, 212
Psych-verb/predicate 103, 104, 106–108, 111, 122, 126, 128, 130, 139–140, 148

Quantifier, floating/floated 75, 78, 259–260, 263, 264–266, 276, 278
Quechua
    Cuzco 83
    Huallaga 83, 153
    Imbabura 83–93, 153–154
Quirky subject 95, 126–128
Quotative, inversion (*see* Inversion)

Raising 49
Rappaport, M. 149, 170
Reciprocal 258
Reinhart, T. 113
Relational Grammar 9, 51, 180
Relativization 43–44, 73, 158–159
Relation(s)
    (feature-)checking 13, 16
    multiple checking 22–24, 58, 109
    structural 11, 13
Representation 15
Rizzi, L. 11, 95, 104, 148, 151, 160, 248
Roberts, I. 48, 50, 88, 94, 225–227, 242
Rochemont, M. 170
Rothstein, S. 33–34
Rudin, C. 23
Russian 149–151

Sadakane, K. 174, 265–266
Safir, K. 37, 139
Saito, M. 104, 172, 257, 258–259, 267, 268–270, 278, 279
Samoan 222
Sanskrit 37, 94
Sapir, E. 56, 58
Sarma, V. 118, 268

Scandinavian 255
Schacter, P. 160
Schütze, C. 21, 128, 132
Scope 113, 178
Scrambling 172
    L(ong)- 268
    M(iddle)- 268, 279
    S(hort)- 255-256, 258-259, 263, 264, 267-271, 275, 280
Select 19
Serial verb 74
Shibatani, M. 97, 98, 100, 104, 171, 251
Siewierska A., 83
Sigurðsson, H. A. 126, 129, 130
Simpson, J. 128, 130, 195
Small clause 33
Smith, N. 128, 129
Sobin, N. 94
Spanish 151
Speas, M. 29, 104, 160
Spec(ifier) 22
    canonical/innermost 25, 28, 49, 82, 90
    definition of 20
    multiple 20, 22, 79, 214, 236, 284
    outer 25, 83, 90
Spell-Out 15, 17, 21, 22
Split VP Hypothesis 27
Sportiche, D. 78, 259
Sprouse, J. 130, 132
Sridhar, S. N. 117, 125, 126
Stative suffix 96
Stowell, T. 11, 33-34, 67
Structure
    D- 11
    S- 11
    Subject 5, 10, 12, 63, 75, 192
    agreement 13, 43-45, 48, 54, 55, 60, 63, 77, 86, 91, 102, 104, 117, 120, 121, 123, 128, 131, 140, 143, 146, 150, 153, 157, 164, 168, 169, 192, 283
    honorification 100-102, 104, 105, 116
    major 278-280
    multiple 81
    oriented reflexive/anaphor 7, 13, 24, 82, 92, 98, 101, 105, 118-120, 123, 127, 131, 150, 172, 176, 210, 283
Subjecthood 5, 40, 55, 63, 85, 117, 150, 158, 173, 176, 190, 215
Sugioka, Y. 97, 272, 276

Superiority 33
Swahili 41
Swedish 136, 231-232, 234, 235-245, 255, 267, 270
Switch reference 75-76, 79, 81-82, 86, 153

Tada, H. 32, 97, 103, 112-113, 256, 259, 264, 267, 268-269, 279
Takahashi, D. 19, 33, 115, 168
Takano, Y. 135, 255, 257, 258-259, 267, 268-270
Takezawa, K. 104, 115
Taraldsen, T. 128
Tamil 6-8, 117-125, 268
Tanoan 40
Tateishi, K. 278
Termination 25
Thematic Hierarchy 29, 104, 160, 165-166
Theta
    assignment 37
    -position 17, 37
    Position Checking Parameter 38, 206-208, 210, 215-221, 223, 227
    -role (θ-role) 5, 11, 28-30, 110, 160, 193, 198, 225, 228, 285
Thráinsson, H. 126, 128, 130, 136-137, 230, 231-232, 269
Tibeto-Burman 40, 63
Topicalization 43-45, 73, 84, 139-140
Toribio, J. 100
Tupí-Guaraní 63
Turkic 81
Turkish 36, 94
Tsai, W.-T. D. 33, 38

Ueda, M. 103, 213, 276, 278-279
Unaccusative 30, 37, 157, 207, 222
Unergative 37, 141, 148, 220-221, 223
Universal Grammar (UG) 4, 22, 192
Ura, H. 5, 6, 11, 12, 15-16, 19-22, 32, 33-34, 37, 46, 68, 79-83, 89, 90-94, 103, 104, 108-109, 111, 114, 142, 156, 179, 206, 213, 231-232, 236, 238, 253, 267, 277, 279
Uto-Aztecan 94
Uzbek 81

Van Valin, R. 126, 129, 130, 160
Veenstra, T. 74
Vikner, S. 53, 72, 142, 168, 220, 237, 242
Voice
  active 55
  alternation: active/inverse 9, 35, 40–68, 156, 165; active/passive 83
  direct 55
VP-shell
  Larsonian 230, 233–234
  three-layered 137, 256, 280
  two-layered 18, 28, 45, 110, 140, 220, 256

Walpiri 185–186, 195, 212, 218, 222
Wasow, T. 149
Watanabe, A. 16, 33, 39, 44, 50, 68, 81, 83, 86, 88–89, 93, 94, 103, 110, 113, 116, 135, 170, 209, 219, 225, 230, 232, 242, 255, 263, 269, 276–277
Welsh 94
West Greenlandic Inuit 190, 215, 218, 224

Wexler, K. 280
Wh-
  agreement 44
  feature 44
  fronting 23
  movement 33
  phrase(s) 33
Williams, E. 11, 239
Woolford, E. 71–74, 77, 79, 82
Wyngaerd, G. V. 72

X-bar Theory 11, 20, 79, 238

Yalarunnga 182
Yatsushiro, K. 177, 179
Yimas 182
Yindjibarndi 251
Yip, M. 126
Youn, C. 98

Zaenan, A. 126, 128, 130, 136
Zarma 27, 281
Zushi, M. 97
Zwart, J.-W. 33